A Concise History of the Caribbean

A Concise History of the Caribbean presents a general history of the Caribbean islands from the beginning of human settlement about seven thousand years ago to the present. It narrates processes of early human migration, the disastrous consequences of European colonization, the development of slavery and the slave trade, the extraordinary profits earned by the plantation economy, the great revolution in Haiti, movements toward political independence, the Cuban Revolution, and the diaspora of Caribbean people. Written in a lively and accessible style yet current with the most recent research, the book provides a compelling narrative of Caribbean history essential for students and visitors.

B. W. Higman is the William Keith Hancock Professor of History at the Australian National University and Professor Emeritus of the University of the West Indies. He is the author of ten books on Caribbean history, archaeology, and geography, including *Slave Population and Economy in Jamaica, 1807–1834* (1976, Cambridge; awarded the Bancroft Prize), *Plantation Jamaica 1750–1850: Capital and Control in a Colonial Economy* (2005), and *Jamaican Food: History, Biology, Culture* (2008).

Advance Praise for *A Concise History of the Caribbean*

"This riveting, highly informative, and concise account of the history of the Caribbean archipelago does not present the usual story in the usual way. There are several new thematic twists and turns based on recent scholarship, and all of them effectively illuminate this resilient maritime region of the world that continues to cope with daunting challenges. A first-rate interpretive overview that at present has no equal, by a master historian and insightful scholar."
– David Barry Gaspar, Duke University

"This is the best short general history available on the Caribbean, covering the area with magisterial authority as well as enviable comprehensiveness and competence. Higman demonstrates not only his unusual multidisciplinary command of the respective literatures but also his exceptional insightfulness about the entire Caribbean region. This permeates the entire work but nowhere is it more persuasively demonstrated than in the final chapter that utilizes canoes, caravels, and container ships to illustrate the significant turning points in Caribbean regional history."
– Franklin W. Knight, Johns Hopkins University

"An excellent comparative history by a leading historian of the Caribbean. Higman offers a perceptive analysis of West Indian people and their environment from ancient times to the present."
– Kenneth Morgan, Brunel University

"In this fast-paced, compact text, the prolific B. W. Higman chronicles familiar and new life-changing episodes in the history of those who settled voluntarily or involuntarily in the complex space we call the Caribbean. He confronts the brutality and savage genocide resulting from the activities of Europeans who came to the region for profit and play, but he is also at pains to highlight the resilience of their victims; their triumph over adversity and their insistence – be they from Salaloid or modern cultures – that living in freedom is the only way to be."
– Verene A. Shepherd, Professor of Social History and University Director, Institute of Gender and Development Studies, the University of the West Indies

CAMBRIDGE CONCISE HISTORIES

This is a new series of illustrated "concise histories" of selected individual countries, intended both as university and college textbooks and as general historical introductions for general readers, travelers, and members of the business community.

Other titles in the series:

A Concise History of Australia, 3rd Edition
STUART MACINTYRE

A Concise History of Austria
STEVEN BELLER

A Concise History of Bolivia, 2nd Edition
HERBERT KLEIN

A Concise History of Brazil
BORIS FAUSTO, TRANSLATED BY ARTHUR BRAKEL

A Concise History of Britain, 1707–1975
W. A. SPECK

A Concise History of Bulgaria, 2nd Edition
R. J. CRAMPTON

A Concise History of Finland
DAVID KIRBY

A Concise History of France, 2nd Edition
ROGER PRICE

A Concise History of Germany, 2nd Edition
MARY FULBROOK

A Concise History of Greece, 2nd Edition
RICHARD CLOGG

Series list continues following the Index.

A Concise History of
the Caribbean

B. W. HIGMAN

CAMBRIDGE
UNIVERSITY PRESS

CAMBRIDGE UNIVERSITY PRESS
Cambridge, New York, Melbourne, Madrid, Cape Town, Singapore,
São Paulo, Delhi, Dubai, Tokyo, Mexico City

Cambridge University Press
32 Avenue of the Americas, New York, NY 10013-2473, USA

www.cambridge.org
Information on this title: www.cambridge.org/9780521043489

First published 2011

Printed in the United States of America

A catalog record for this publication is available from the British Library.

Library of Congress Cataloging in Publication data
Higman, B. W., 1943–
A concise history of the Caribbean / B. W. Higman.
p. cm. – (Cambridge concise histories)
Includes bibliographical references and index.
ISBN 978-0-521-88854-7 (hardback) – ISBN 978-0-521-04348-9 (pbk.)
1. Caribbean Area – History. I. Title. II. Series.
F1621.H55 2010
972.9–dc22 2010041963

ISBN 978-0-521-88854-7 Hardback
ISBN 978-0-521-04348-9 Paperback

CONTENTS

LIST OF ILLUSTRATIONS

MAPS

PLATES

PREFACE

Any history leaves out much that might interest individual readers. The history of the Caribbean has its special difficulties, particularly because of the large number of states, polities, and islands in the region, all of them with their own individual as well as shared histories. I have simplified my task by dealing strictly with the islands and ignoring the surrounding rimland and the outliers – notably Belize, Guyana, Suriname and French Guyana, which are often included in general histories – except when these continental places connect directly with the experience of the islands. The definition of the extent of the rimland or hinterland, making up what has come to be known as the Caribbean Basin, is problematic. Including the peoples living in all these countries can greatly distort the demography, multiplying the population by as much as four times that of the islands. Another large region is sometimes defined as the Greater Caribbean or the extended Caribbean, stretching through the coastal and insular territories all the way from Virginia in the north to Bahia, the easternmost part of Brazil, in the south. These larger regional conceptions have validity for some periods and patterns of development but not for all. Confining the narrative to the islands sets limits but at the same time provides an ecological coherence that enables an attempt to write a systematic comparative history.

Seen in the context of this broader perspective, my own research projects over the years seem incredibly limited. I have therefore depended heavily for knowledge and insight on the labours of colleagues past and present and I thank them all for making it possible for me to construct my own interpretation and reading of their work. The book was written in the History Program of the Research School of Social Sciences, at the Australian National University. The maps were prepared by Kay Dancey.

Dates for years provided as BP are Before the Present; AD signifies the common modern calendar. Populations provided for the year 2010 are based on projections, the best estimates available at the beginning of that year.

A Concise History of the Caribbean

I

A History of Islands

The Caribbean is named for its sea but the islands define the region and make its history. As a marine environment, the Caribbean Sea is a creation of the land that encloses it, with an unbroken continental coastline to the south and west, and a permeable but continuous arc of islands facing the Atlantic Ocean. Without the islands there would be no sea. The water would be nothing more than another stretch in the fluid maritime history of the ocean. Equally significant, the islands of the Caribbean surround and demarcate the Sea rather than sitting in it. This geographical formation determined fundamental features in the development of the Caribbean and distinguished the experience of the region from that of other island histories around the world.

Islands can be scattered in many different kinds of patterns. Sometimes they stand alone, in splendid isolation, but often they occur in groups or clusters. The tropical Atlantic from the Caribbean to the coast of Africa is almost empty of islands. In this vast oceanic zone, islands are small, few in number, and extremely isolated. The islands of the Caribbean, by contrast, are numerous and vary greatly in size (Map 1.1). What determines the uniqueness of the Caribbean islands as a whole is the way they form an archipelago, spread through an extensive arc with large bodies of water to each side, and the way the archipelago floats free of the mainland. The Caribbean Sea, like the Atlantic, is largely empty of islands. The enclosing islands seem almost like a chain cast outwards by centrifugal force, straining to escape the pull of gravity.

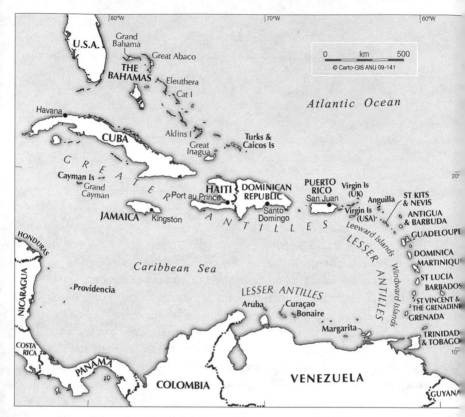

Map 1.1. The modern Caribbean.

The archipelago extends through 3,000 km, running east from Cuba to the Leeward Islands, then turning south to Trinidad, just 10 km from the mainland of South America. The surface area of the sea is eight times as extensive as the land component of the enclosing islands, making it the second largest in the world – exceeded only by the South China Sea – and slightly larger and significantly deeper than the Mediterranean. However, because none of the islands that make up the connected chain is visible from the mainland, the archipelago lacks anchors. It resembles the Indonesian archipelago more than the Greek, though the Indonesian has no single sea. Once started on the journey, however, whether beginning in Cuba or Grenada, it is possible to move from one Caribbean island to the next with the advantage of intervisibility almost without a break through the entire chain. At the same time, most of the larger islands are in sight of only two neighbours, one coming and one going, channelling movement along the chain.

The histories of the islands look both ways, towards the continental Americas on the one hand and across the Atlantic to Africa and Europe on the other. This does not mean they float in limbo, always searching somewhere else for meaning. Rather, the islands support unique creative cultures, reflecting their role as vital sites in the creation of the modern western world. In spite of this importance, the islands were challenging destinations for early people, requiring an initial leap into the unknown and possession of appropriate seagoing technology. When they finally did reach the islands, the first peoples brought with them ways of life constructed on continental lands that needed only minor modifications to make them viable in the tropical environments of the islands. What was different was the ready access they had to marine and littoral resources and the potential for development of insular identities.

Whereas the first human colonizers of the Caribbean were latecomers in the broad sweep of world history, the islands were prime sites in the fateful modern colonization that brought Europeans and Africans across the Atlantic to the Americas. It was on a Caribbean island that Columbus set foot on his first voyage of 1492 and it was in the islands that the Spanish built their first colonies. Rather than seeming a barrier, the sea now served as a conduit for European imperialism. Further, the easy accessibility of island shores, together with the islands' small size and long coastlines, made them ideal sites for economic exploitation. Mile for mile, it was cheaper to ship a barrel of rum or a bale of cotton across the seas than it was to haul it overland on a wagon.

This advantage remained true in the long term. It is now cheaper to move goods across the seas in container ships than to drive the same containers across country. On the other hand, the globalization of economic life that moved apace in the later twentieth century shifted the emphasis to bulk and large-scale production and, in this process, small islands, including those of the Caribbean, often lost out as producers and traders. The great advantages of accessibility associated with smallness and insularity mattered most in the context of the technologies of the seventeenth and eighteenth centuries and it was in those centuries, under those conditions, that the Caribbean was seen by Europeans as a prime site for exploitation.

The smallness and seaward accessibility of the islands meant also that competing colonizers could relatively easily attack and displace rival powers, resulting in changes in allegiance that affected culture and trade as well as governance. Thus, in the modern period, the significance of the insularity of the Caribbean stretched beyond the region and across the Atlantic. The low cost of transport by sea enabled the competitive shipping of tropical products to markets in Europe and North America and facilitated the forced movement of people, particularly through the Atlantic slave trade that brought millions from Africa to the Caribbean and created the foundations of a demographic pattern that differed significantly from that found on the continents to north and south.

Beneath the apparent symmetry of the island arc lies a more complex, slowly shifting foundation. The central building block, the Caribbean Plate, carries with it almost all of the islands, with the exception of Cuba and the Bahamas, which rest on the North American Plate, and Aruba, Curaçao, and Bonaire, which sit on the South American Plate. This geological structure came about through the long-term eastward movement of the Caribbean Plate from its origin as an oceanic plateau in the Pacific 90 million years ago, pushing its way through the North and South American Plates, resulting in considerable deformation along the edges. The Greater Antilles – Cuba, Jamaica, Hispaniola, and Puerto Rico – were formed in this process. Immediately south of Cuba, the Gonave microplate underlies parts of Jamaica and Hispaniola and its movement creates fault lines that contribute to the frequency of earthquakes in the zone. The Caribbean Plate continues to edge eastwards relative to the North American Plate at about 20 mm per year. On its eastern front, the Caribbean Plate collided head-on with the Atlantic Plate, creating the "ring of fire" that gave birth to the volcanic islands stretching from Grenada in the south to Saba in the north known as the Lesser Antilles. The collision of the plates also raised above sea level a number of islands composed of much older sedimentary rocks.

Thus, the main islands of the Caribbean can be said to belong to three distinct archipelagos: the Greater Antilles, the Lesser Antilles, and the Bahamas. The Greater and Lesser Antilles are separated by the Anegada Passage. The Virgin Islands and Vieques have an ambiguous position, being situated on the island shelf east of Puerto Rico and located west of the Anegada Trough but appearing in their surface morphology to belong to the Leeward Islands and hence the Lesser Antilles arc. In spite of the technical correctness of these definitions and distinctions, the notion of archipelagic coherence and unity of the whole of the Caribbean islands remains compelling.

These geophysical developments explain the contrasting shapes and sizes of the islands and island groups. In addition, by helping identify the periods during which the land was under water, they indicate the relative difficulty plants and animals faced in finding homes on the islands. Particularly in environments such as that of the low-lying Bahamas, changes in sea level were vital to determining the amount of exposed land surface. Jamaica, too, was mainly or entirely submerged during part of its history. Variations in sea level resulted from climate change as well as tectonic events. Particularly important in the very long term was the asteroid strike that hit the region about 65 million years ago, off the eastern tip of the Yucatan Peninsula, before the proto-Antilles had achieved their modern forms. It is probable that this strike and others like it, together with volcanism and climate change, ended the age of dinosaurs and made the world safe for mammals, clearing the way for the evolution of human beings. The tsunamis and hypercanes (gigantic hurricanes) that resulted from this event changed the Caribbean landscape.

Long-term variations in rainfall, over the period of human colonization, were also important in setting limits to the productivity of the environment. The earliest ventures into the Caribbean occurred during a relatively moist period of the middle Holocene that lasted from 8200 to 3000 BP (Before the Present). This was followed by a drier regime that, in turn, was replaced by wetter conditions in the late Holocene, beginning around AD 500 and continuing to AD 1100, when drier times returned once more. Over time, as human populations became more dense in the Caribbean, these changes were both influential and partially caused by human activity.

The geological and climate histories of the Caribbean had major consequences for the individual islands – indeed, their very existence. At the beginning of the twenty-first century, the number of Caribbean islands – land units permanently above sea level that individually occupy at least 1 km² – is about 3,700, of which only 1,600 have names. Almost all of the unnamed islands are tiny and uninhabited. Altogether, the islands contain 234,000 km², but they vary dramatically in size and topography and experience surprisingly different climate and weather patterns. The viable land space is concentrated in just a few. The Greater Antilles occupy 89 percent of the total land area, the Lesser Antilles 6 percent, and the Bahamas 5 percent. Of the four main islands that make up the Greater Antilles, Cuba alone, at 110,000 km², accounts for almost one half of all the land, followed by Hispaniola with 76,000, Jamaica 11,000, and Puerto Rico 9,000 km². Cuba stretches over 1,000 km. The highest mountain, Pico Duarte in Hispaniola, rises to 3,175 m. In spite of the contrast between the Greater and Lesser Antilles in terms of scale, and in spite of the differing landforms and geological origins of the elements, the islands are drawn together by the sea and by the linear pattern they form within that shared sea. Whereas the water creates the uniqueness of the islands and supports the perception of separate identities, it also connects and unifies.

A glance at the political map of the Americas, as it is at the beginning of the twenty-first century, shows clearly the consequences of these broad differences in geography and patterns of development. To the north of the Caribbean, the massive continent of North America is occupied by just two nation-states, Canada and the United States, and dominated by English-speaking peoples. South America, three-quarters the size of North America, is made up of 10 Spanish and Portuguese-speaking states, several of them large in population and area, and dominated by Brazil, together with three peri-Caribbean enclaves – Guyana, Suriname, and French Guiana – where the languages are versions of English, Dutch, and French. Stretching through Central and Middle America from Panama to Mexico are another seven Spanish-speaking states, most of them quite small, especially where the isthmus narrows, and the English-speaking enclave Belize.

Although the islands of the Caribbean have a land area less than 1 percent that of the Americas, they are home to 24 distinct polities, one more than the total on the continental landmass. The people speak four main European languages (but not including Portuguese) and a number of creoles. At the same time, the island polities have a total population of only 42 million, compared with the 900 million of the continental states of the Americas. The picture changes only somewhat if the balance is confined strictly to truly independent states. Of the 24 distinct polities in the Caribbean, only 13 are true sovereign states with separate membership in the United Nations. The others are represented by independent states located outside the region with which the islands are associated. By contrast, only one mainland territory – French Guiana – is not a member of the United Nations and has representation only through its parent state, France. Further, the islands have a more varied range of polities and political relationships, some of them defined as overseas territories of European nations and of the United States, others truly independent. Overall, the islands were slower than the nations of North and South America to establish their independence – only Haiti, the Dominican Republic, and Cuba were independent before 1900 – so that the experience of colonialism was much more extended. On a global scale, the Caribbean islands remained colonies much longer than the typical experience, almost all of them being colonies for more than 300 years and many closer to 500 years.

Both the priority and the longevity of the colonial experience in the islands of the Caribbean gave them a central role in the making of what has come to be known as Atlantic History and the Atlantic World and, more broadly, in the making of modern world history. They were the initial sites of contact between peoples previously separated by a vast ocean, and vital sites in the creation of new modes of economic organization, new languages, and new forms of social relations. In many ways, these developments are associated with the birth of the modern world and the concept of modernity, as well as the related and more recent concept of globalization.

It may seem strange to associate such concepts of modernity with the Caribbean, a region that now has a relatively low profile on the international scene and may be seen as a scattering of insignificant, small, and not particularly well-off mini-states, accidents of history and geography. Similarly, it may seem paradoxical that ideas of the modern and the global should be related to the Caribbean, a region that saw some of the harshest systems of exploitation and some of the most savage genocides. This is part of the point, however: "modern" often has meant brutality and the extraction of profit at any price; a world in which progress and human welfare could be swept aside for economic efficiency and selfish benefit. Equally important, the Caribbean witnessed wonderful examples of the resilience of the human spirit, in direct opposition to the harshness of the exploitative regimes put in place by imperialism and representing positive responses to the opportunities that even the most brutal systems permit the creative.

2

Ancient Archipelago

7200 BP – AD 1492

People came late to the Caribbean islands – late in terms of the broad sweep of human history and late in the peopling of the Americas. The islands of the Caribbean remained uninhabited longer than almost any other of the world's major resource-rich regions. Even when the process of colonization began, it proceeded in fits and starts and took thousands of years to complete. Strangely, some islands remained uninhabited long after their neighbours had been populated. Many still remain uninhabited because they are too small to support a population or lack the resources to be viable, or simply are too isolated to be attractive. Why were the islands colonized so late and why, once commenced, was the process so protracted and erratic? Looked at another way, the more difficult question may be why people chose to live on islands at all. Why leave behind the immense resources of the continents in order to live in small places surrounded by saltwater?

Migration into the Caribbean began about 7,000 years ago. The first people to live on a Caribbean island did not venture far from the South American mainland, however, going no farther than Trinidad. A separate initial movement occurred about a thousand years later, this time originating in Central America and establishing populations in Cuba and Hispaniola. Next, a second wave of migration from South America carried people through the island chain stretching north of Trinidad and these people eventually came to occupy Hispaniola and eastern Cuba as well. By about 3,000 years ago, most of the islands had established populations with societies well adapted to their environments. Even then, fertile territory remained uninhabited. Remarkably, Jamaica, third largest of all the Caribbean islands, was not colonized until about AD 600, more than 6,000 years after the first people entered the Caribbean and less than a thousand years before the arrival of people from the Old World far away across the Atlantic.

FIRST PEOPLES

The people who first colonized the Caribbean islands were part of the great migration that brought human beings from northern Asia across the Bering Sea land bridge to Alaska about 15,000 years before the present, near the end of the last Ice Age, when sea levels were 120 m lower than they are today (Map 2.1). It had taken a long time to get there. Modern humans, out of Africa, had begun spreading around the globe about 100,000 years ago. Once they reached the continental landmass of the Americas, however, they moved swiftly. The end of the glaciation meant a warmer and wetter world, and the migrant people gradually adapted to temperate and tropical environments, coming to depend on cultivated landscapes rather than the hunting of animals. The initial migration through the icy wastes cannot have been directed at the establishment of these agrarian societies, however, and it is probable that the movement had, as its original intent, the hunting of wild animals, including now-extinct megafauna such as the mammoth and the giant horse, that spread out over the newly exposed land surface in search of food.

Only as people moved into the temperate, subtropical, and tropical zones of the Americas did they have the opportunity to practice agriculture. Powerful states and remarkable civilizations emerged from this transition. One of the most important of these, the great rainforest civilization of the Maya, flourished on the lowlands of the Yucatan Peninsula, which faces both the Gulf of Mexico and the Caribbean Sea.

From the northeastern tip of Yucatan, the continental shelf thrusts out towards the western end of Cuba, 200 km away, seeming to create a first – submarine – link to the Caribbean archipelago. This was only one of the possible points of entry. Although the distance is greater, drifters and directed voyagers heading north from almost any point on the long coastline of South America that faces the

Map 2.1. The Americas.

Caribbean had good chances of making landfall in the Greater Antilles. In the north, a relatively short distance separates Cuba from Florida, with Havana little more than 150 km from Key West.

Each of these potential jumping-off points appears viable for migration from the mainland to the islands. All of them may have supported temporarily successful attempts. On the other hand, only the southern option began with islands in sight, and even to move on from Tobago to Grenada, a distance of 105 km, was sufficiently challenging. With the exception of the initial easy settlement of Trinidad, the original human voyagers typically paddled into the unknown, with few clues regarding what was over the horizon, however close they might be to dry land. Because they paddled, rather than using sails to harness the wind, they were not so likely to be blown off course or make chance discoveries of distant places. They might observe a concentration of clouds and guess that it was created by a far off island's atmosphere or they might follow the paths of birds on the assumption they were headed for land beyond the horizon. Whether driven by choice or carried along by currents, and whatever their starting point on the mainland's long coastline, the first voyagers had little to guide them.

As well as lacking knowledge of the geographical pattern of the islands, the first voyagers and settlers had no way of knowing what resources they might find. Early visits to the small islands fringing South and Central America would not have been encouraging given that most of these were dry and barren and, except for birds, lacked the rich biodiversity of the neighbouring mainland. Only Trinidad was different, being more a part of the Orinoco delta than an oceanic island and sharing much of the flora and fauna of the continent.

During the Last Glacial Maximum, which ended about 12,000 years ago, both Trinidad and Tobago were, in fact, part of the mainland. They rest on the continental shelf. The very first evidence of human presence in Trinidad, dated to 7200 BP, comes from a time when the island was probably still connected by an isthmus. It is no surprise that the earliest human colonization of the Caribbean islands began there and no surprise that this initial colonization was not quickly followed by progressive movement along the island chain.

Plants and animals faced most of the same challenges and hazards that confronted humans, and took advantage of the same opportunities in movement from mainland to island. Unless it arrived with the land, in geological time, everything had to find its way across the water or through the air. Caribbean plant life is remarkably diverse and the islands support many endemic species – those that are indigenous and unique. Indeed, the region is recognized as one of the world's leading hotspots for endemism. Reasons for this rich and unique plant life, formed over millions of years, can be found in the region's complex geological and environmental history and in its location between continental landmasses. Compared with its neighbours, the vegetation of the islands was most similar to that of Central America. Diversity was greatest in the larger islands and enhanced by differences in soil, elevation, temperature, and rainfall. In mountainous regions of Martinique, Puerto Rico, and Jamaica, for example, heavy and regular rain fell throughout the year, whereas other areas of the same islands had long dry periods and much less rainfall. The vegetation of the latter was marked by thornscrub and cactus; the former by montane rainforest. The character of the vegetation was also affected by differences in island size and isolation, but it is striking that the degree of diversity and uniqueness observed is not unlike that found on much more remote and isolated oceanic islands.

Animal life, before the coming of humans, also exhibited high levels of diversity and endemism. This was particularly true of the vertebrates, but in spite of this, compared with the nearby mainland, many major groups were missing. Thus, although the diversity and uniqueness of vertebrate species were impressive, they were confined to a small number of groups – particularly frogs, lizards, and rodents. Mammals and the larger animals that might be used for transport or food were rare, even in ancient times, particularly because of the lack of land bridges. Whereas the flying and swimming animals (birds, bats, and freshwater fish) that found their way to the islands had close ties to North and Central America (as did the plants), animals that lacked this facility of movement mostly had to cling to flotsam washed out from the rivers of South America. Reptiles, including crocodiles, were relatively successful. It was difficult for larger mammals to survive this transit by raft, though some sloths found saltwater dispersal no problem. In this "unbalanced" fauna, the lack of large mammals, including

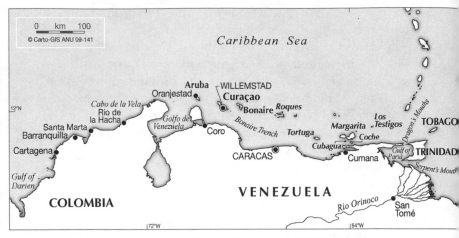

Map 2.2. Venezuela coast and Trinidad.

carnivores, opened niches for the animals that did reach the islands
and enabled the diversity of their varieties.

Navigators soon would have learned that the islands of the continuous archipelago are prime targets for hurricanes formed in the
western Atlantic. Even when the weather was calm, the North East
Trade Winds swept into the Caribbean from the Atlantic and, in all
seasons, blew towards the west. Seeing an island show itself above
the horizon was a good thing for voyagers; seeing a hurricane was
not. Whereas the coast of South America, all the way north to Honduras, was hardly ever struck by hurricanes, all of the islands to the
north were devastated with certain though unpredictable regularity.
Only the coast-hugging islands of Trinidad, Curaçao, Aruba, and
Bonaire were exceptions. The last three of these suffered tsunamis,
with significant consequences for their surrounding reefs and shore-
lines, but these events were rare compared to the frequency of hurricanes. Thus, whereas the people of Yucatan had direct experience
of hurricanes, those looking north from South America did not.

Voyagers paddling canoes were more concerned with currents
than with winds. After flowing across the Atlantic and along the
coast of South America, the South Equatorial Current becomes the
dominant Caribbean Current that enters the Sea through the southern islands, between Trinidad and St Lucia, then flows strongly
westward to the narrow gap between Cuba and Yucatan (Map 2.2).

There, it becomes the Yucatan Current before dividing to enter the Gulf of Mexico in one direction and, in the other, to turn east as the Florida Current, which ultimately contributes to the Gulf Stream. All of these streams play an important part in the circulation and renewal of the deep waters of the several basins that exist within the Caribbean, but it is the behaviour of the surface water that was most significant in determining the pattern of human voyaging and settlement. Although the Caribbean Current is complex and surface drifters are affected by its meanders and anticyclonic (clockwise) eddies, the westward flow is dominant. The important exception to this rule is that when the South Equatorial Current meets the water flowing out of the Orinoco in full flood it is deflected northward, creating favourable opportunities for migration along the chain.

The apparent lack of interest shown by the first inhabitants of Trinidad to move on northwards is symbolic of the autonomy of the archipelago and its location in the circulation of wind and water. In Trinidad, they were able to exploit familiar resources and feel themselves a natural extension of the mainland rather than living in an isolated, insular sort of place. Land animals were hunted but over time the people came to depend increasingly on marine resources. Shellfish and crabs were taken from freshwater swamps, mangroves, and streams, and fish from the seacoast. In this preceramic or Archaic Age, people used ground stone axes to hack out canoes. Spears for hunting and fishing had bone or flaked stone tips. Fishhooks and needles were made from bone or tooth fragments. Ground stone pestles and hammerstones served to pound vegetable materials into string used to make nets, baskets and hammocks, cloth and ornaments, toys and musical instruments. Similar activities focussed on the marine resources of the coastal zone are found in archaeological sites in Tobago.

Although people are known to have settled in Trinidad by 7200 BP, it took another 2,000 years to reach Tobago. It was from Tobago or perhaps points on the mainland that the true discovery of the islands of the eastern Caribbean began soon after 5000 BP, when people began to make their homes in Grenada, the island hidden beyond the horizon. Having crossed this challenging divide, the series of islands to the north showed themselves across the water and it was easy enough to progress rapidly along the chain. Voyagers

reached the Leeward Islands within as few as a hundred years and
continued as far as Puerto Rico. They also made the longer and
more hazardous voyage out into the Atlantic, to find the isolated
limestone island of Barbados, 160 km east of the main chain. However, although the Archaic migration through the Lesser Antilles
was relatively swift and extensive, the number of known archaeological sites is few. These hunter–fisher–gatherer people were highly
mobile, paddling their canoes from place to place, establishing temporary camps and then moving on again. They mainly depended
on fish, caught on the surrounding reefs using traps, and conch and
other shellfish. They carried with them, and renewed, ground and
flaked stone tools such as axes, mortars, and pestles.

In the meantime, before people began to make their way up the
eastern chain of islands, a separate migration began from Central
America. The initial leap across the Yucatan Channel to western
Cuba was accomplished by about 6000 BP. At this time, the people
of Yucatan had much in common with those who voyaged through
Trinidad. They were mobile hunter–gatherers, members of the preceramic Archaic Age, depending on stone tools and living in small
temporary camps. Agriculture came later to this mainland region
of tropical lowland rainforest, appearing no earlier than 3500 BP.
The first Maya communities began to emerge 500 years after this
but Maya civilization took another thousand years to reach its peak
around AD 600, only to collapse dramatically in the ninth century. The initial migration into the Caribbean from Central America happened long before these events. It was the work of Archaic
hunter–gatherers willing to take a chance or perhaps finding themselves swept up in circumstances they could not control. Lack of
agriculture, lack of pottery, and lack of knowledge have never been
enough to prevent human migration.

Once voyagers from Central America had taken their first brave
step across the water they moved rapidly through or, perhaps
more often, along the coasts of Cuba, Hispaniola, and Puerto
Rico, in much the same way colonization progressed in the eastern
Caribbean. Many scattered settlements were established, reaching
as far east as Maruca in southern Puerto Rico by 4900 BP. This
date coincides closely with that suggested for the arrival in the Leeward Islands of people from the south. It is possible that the people
whose migration had commenced in Central America also got to the

Plate 2.1. Stone axes, Boriken (a, b, c, d) and
Haiti/Quisqueya (e, f, g, h). *Source:* Jesse Walter Fewkes, The
Aborigines of Porto Rico and Neighboring Islands,
*Twenty-Fifth Annual Report of the Bureau of American
Ethnology to the Secretary of the Smithsonian Institution*
(Washington: Government Printing Office, 1907), Plate XIII.

Leeward Islands. Certainly, this was a zone of interaction between 5000 and 4000 BP, though beyond the sharing of materials and technologies it is difficult to reconstruct the nature of the exchange that took place between these highly mobile peoples of different language and culture. Some of the sites of this founding Caribbean encounter now lie below sea level.

In Cuba and Hispaniola, the Archaic phase of colonization, beginning circa 6000 BP, left few archaeological traces of permanent settlement. The reason for this appears to be that the people were organized into small bands dependent on hunting, gathering, and fishing. They pursued the limited species of mammals and other large fauna, exploiting them to extinction. The people lived along the coasts and moved their base camps frequently, following food resources where they were most plentiful. People began using fire to clear forest as early as 5400 BP in Hispaniola. Initially, at least, the intent of this burning was probably to facilitate the hunting of large mammals, but over time it became associated with the planting of fruit trees brought from Yucatan and the practice of incipient agriculture. The large animals went first, with only small-bodied species surviving until AD 1500. Land animals hunted in Cuba and Hispaniola in the first phase of human occupation included sloths weighing as much as 250 kg, large flightless owls, large insect-eaters, and rodents such as the hutia. The sloths were extinct as early as 4000 BP.

In the case of Puerto Rico, there is evidence of extensive anthropogenic forest burning as early as 5300 BP, suggesting this began soon after people reached the island. The hunting of large mammals and the reduction of their habitat led to extinctions. One large rodent of Puerto Rico, weighing up to 13 kg, was extinct by 3500 BP but other species survived to AD 1000. Although Puerto Rico is the only island of the Greater Antilles to have lost all of its pre-human land mammals, the process was extended over millennia rather than concentrated in the manner of the excesses that followed some human colonizations. In the long run, however, the land mammals of the Caribbean islands suffered the most extreme extinctions of any Holocene mammal fauna. These large mammals were not replaced by introductions from the continental mainland before 1492 and, in this long period, human beings lived in a world in which they faced no rivals and rarely risked injury from wild animals.

Marine mammals were also heavily exploited but they survived longer than their terrestrial counterparts and remained in abundance until 1492. Particularly vulnerable were the large, slow animals, such as monk seal, manatee, and turtle, found in estuaries and along the coasts. Turtles were easily killed when they came on land to lay eggs, during which time they were oblivious to all around them. The monk seal, weighing up to 200 kg, had no fear of humans and lacked escape responses. The even larger manatee, up to 500 kg, was alerted to the approach of predators by its acute hearing but defenceless when feeding in shallow bays and estuaries. These three animals were in abundance in the western Caribbean throughout this early period. Fishing and the collection of shellfish contributed little. With its strong focus on the meat of large animals, this was a diet unique in Caribbean history.

Along the coasts of early Cuba and Hispaniola, nothing more than a heavy wooden club was needed to kill turtle and seal. More refined were blades and microliths made of chipped or flaked stone, strongly suggesting a link with Yucatan. Later, sometime between 4000 and 3000 BP, the people became more sedentary and more numerous, and added to their tool kits ground stone and shell items, bowls, and ornaments. Over generations, they gained a better understanding of the character of the islands and what they had to offer on land and sea. Having depleted the stock, the people gradually shifted away from dietary dependence on large land animals and came to rely much more on the rich resources of the coastal environments, beginning to fish on the reefs and to collect shellfish. They introduced no animals from the mainland. The cultivation of crops was not central to their culture, but Archaic Age people did feed opportunistically on wild fruits, and seem also to have brought with them from Central America seeds of the sapodilla (sapote, naseberry) and avocado, and to have commenced the planting of these favoured trees. They also cultivated, or at least managed, plants such as the cycad zamia (used for its starch), West Indian cherry, and wild fig.

These and related changes led, in the long term, to a general neglect of stone tools, which proved less valuable in the island environments than they had been in mainland contexts. Emphasis shifted to things made from shell, wood, string, cotton, and clay. The use of clay is highly significant, given that Archaic Age peoples are broadly distinguished from those who came after them strictly in terms of whether or not they possessed and manufactured pottery. Recent archaeological research has overturned the notion that ceramic technologies were not introduced to the islands until the arrival of new waves of migrants from the South American mainland around 2500 BP. Pottery dating back at least 1,000 years before this date is now known from Cuba and Hispaniola, and perhaps Puerto Rico and the Lesser Antilles. This early pottery was typically coarse, with incised decoration, and apparently used most often for storing liquids or serving food, alongside natural vessels made from plants, such as gourds, rather than for cooking or other new functions. For these reasons, much of it was boat-shaped, though some of the vessels may have been used primarily to enhance the prestige of an emerging class of high-status individuals. Thus, it appears probable that ceramic technologies had an independent origin in the islands before the arrival of the later groups from South America, and that this earlier tradition fused with other pottery-making cultures in multiple variations. The belief that ceramic technologies become important only when people become sedentary and agricultural is not valid, for the Caribbean or any other ancient society. The permutations are much more varied.

Archaic Age colonization occurred also in Aruba, Curaçao, and Bonaire. However, although these islands might seem to possess much the same geographical advantage as Trinidad, lying close to the South American continent, their resource bases were less attractive and they were colonized later. The first people to live on Curaçao arrived only about 4500 BP and on Bonaire, 3500 BP. Aruba was not settled until about 2400 BP, by people from Curaçao rather than from the mainland. Aruba (and Margarita) are on the continental shelf, whereas Curaçao and Bonaire are separated from the mainland by the deep Bonaire Trench, from which cold nutrient-rich water wells up to support abundant marine life.

Like the other Archaic communities, the people of these southern islands lived in seminomadic bands, but a lack of land animals, apart from iguana, on these low-rainfall islands meant that they necessarily applied their technologies to extracting food resources from the coastal, reef, bay, and mangrove environments. Fish, conch and other molluscs, as well as sea turtle, monk seal, and oceanic birds were plentiful. However, over the roughly 4,000 years of settlement before the intrusion of Europeans, the southern islands were particularly affected by tsunamis. The most damaging of these occurred circa 4200, 3100, 1500, and 500 BP. The tsunami of 3100 BP had the greatest impact on the resources available to the hunter–gatherer–fisher people of the Archaic Age, causing large-scale destruction of reefs and mangrove stands.

To summarize, the initial colonization of the connected island chain began independently from both its western and southern extremes. These two migrations commenced about 2,000 years apart. The fact that the colonization of Trinidad got off to a rel-atively quick start gave no advantage to the southern route, how-ever, and the migration from Central America is regarded as the true beginning of Caribbean colonization. In each of the two migra-tions, once started along the continuous chain, the intervisibility of the islands enabled movement to proceed rapidly. Rather than fully settling one island before moving on to exploit the resources of the next, the early voyagers went ahead quickly exploring the new landscape, assessing its potential and settling in advance locations. This was possible because of the relative ease of moving from one island to the next and because the islands had no prior human pres-ence. Even when the two streams came to interact in the region of the Leeward Islands around 5000 BP, the highly mobile character of these small communities and the abundance of food resources minimized the chances of conflict and competition.

Much the same pattern of rapid initial settlement applied to the Americas at large, in which the first people to enter from the north journeyed rapidly through its continental length, but colo-nized tropical America more slowly and cautiously than the tem-perate environments. Such cautious behaviour in the tropics helps explain why the Caribbean islands took so long to be explored and colonized. It remains remarkable, however, that even the Greater Antilles were still not fully known at the end of the first migra-tion wave and that a second wave waited another 2,000 years to commence.

SECOND WAVE

A fresh wave of migration from the South American mainland began about 2500 BP, signalling the arrival of the Ceramic Age. These new peoples came from the tropical forests of the Orinoco and other river basins of lowland South America, where they had developed sedentary lifestyles, practiced agriculture, and made pottery. They travelled with this complete package of attributes, first to the islands of the eastern Caribbean and then into most areas of the Greater Antilles. There they came into contact with the nomadic hunter–gatherer–fisher Archaic Age peoples. The new peoples settled in permanent communities and their populations became dense on many islands. This migration has a central role in the history of the Caribbean before 1492. It demonstrates the importance of cultural diversity and its origin in the ways in which multiple migrant contingents interacted with different island environments, as well as the role of interaction within and among different island groups. Most importantly, it was fundamental to the emergence of complex societies. Because this migration was not matched by an equivalent movement from Central America, cultural patterns throughout the whole extent of the Caribbean archipelago came to have more in common with South America.

Rather than a progressive island-stepping process, the voyagers of the Ceramic Age migration seem to have started from a number of different points along the Venezuela–Guianas coastline and made a direct jump northward to Puerto Rico and the Leeward Islands (Map 2.3). Over time, they were joined by other voyagers from the continent, who intermingled with them and with the prior nomadic populations. A number of distinct cultures evolved from these processes, leaving their mark in the archaeological record.

The first of these cultures is termed Saladoid, so named because its distinctive ceramics resemble type examples found at Saladero in Venezuela. Saladoid culture prospered from about 2500 BP to 1400 BP. Its people spread through the Lesser Antilles and reached as far as the eastern end of Hispaniola, where the process of colonization came to a halt for several centuries. A coexistent Huecoid culture, centred in Puerto Rico, is also distinguished. After the Saladoid period, a new culture called Ostionoid flourished from about

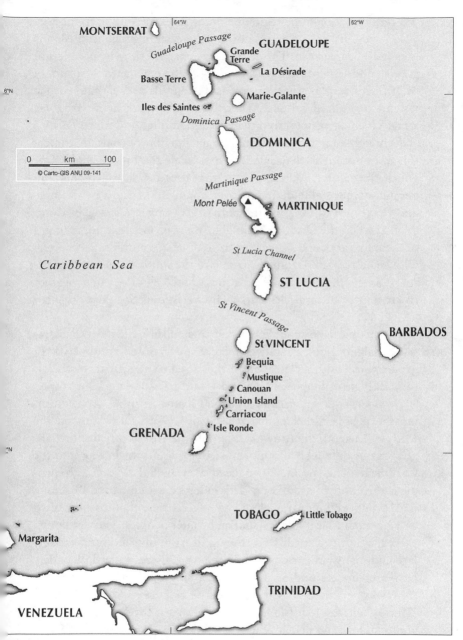

Map 2.3. The eastern Caribbean.

AD 600 to 1000, in the region from the Greater Antilles to the Virgin Islands. Its equivalent culture in the eastern Caribbean islands is called Troumassoid. This period was characterized by population growth and settlement spread, leading to the emergence of a variety of distinct complex societies. It was during this period that Jamaica was first colonized, around AD 600, and the islands of the Bahamas were settled by people from the Greater Antilles.

Although Saladoid culture is named for its Venezuelan source, this does not mean that Saladero represents the precise, single origin of the culture. Indeed, the migration of the so-called Saladoid people was probably quite complex, made up of multiple attempts and voyages of exploration rather than settlement followed by diffusion. Further, the Orinoco basin – the most probable regional origin of the migrant peoples – was fed from diverse cultural sources along its river systems and from Amazonia to the south. These diverse cultures, interacting in the lower reaches of the Orinoco, came together to create the cultural elements characteristic of Saladoid archaeological sites.

The people who made and lived this culture did not call themselves Saladoid but, in spite of their diversity – and the diversity of geographical and universal terms they used to identify themselves – they did speak languages derived from a single language family, Arawakan, and this became attached in the form *Arawak*, meaning the people rather than the language. With its origins on the Middle Amazon, the Arawakan family spawned many distinct languages but only a small number of these found their way into the Caribbean. The specific language spoken by Saladoid culture people is now known as Lokono. This emerged around 3000 BP, along with other evolving Arawakan languages – notably those identified as Taíno and Island-Carib – spoken by later peoples. Thus, although these languages were distinct, they split from one another relatively late and many similarities among them persisted. Indeed, they may be better understood as dialects of a single language. For example, the word canoe has been rendered as kanóa (Lokono), canoa (Taíno), and canáoa (Island-Carib). At a basic level, at least, people could understand one another.

These interpretations depend largely on archaeological, ethnohistorical, and linguistic data. Fresh perspectives have been supplied by recent analysis of ancient human physical and genetic data (mitochondrial DNA). The essence of these findings is that the Amerindian people of the Caribbean typically shared a common South American origin and were characterized by reduced genetic diversity. In turn, this points to a strong founder effect in the colonization of the islands, in which the earliest migrant groups had a proportionally large long-term influence. These findings match closely the knowledge gained from archaeology and linguistics. A more surprising finding is that the Cuban population contrasted with the rest, suggesting a separate origin (though not necessarily a Central American source). Accounts of remnant settlements of Archaic hunter–gatherer communities surviving in the western end of Cuba (people sometimes called Guanahatabeys or, less correctly, Ciboneys) might seem to explain this pattern, but these are poorly substantiated and could not, in any case, apply to the population of the island at large. Equivalent remnant groups are sometimes attributed to the western end of Hispaniola's southern peninsula.

What distinguishes Saladoid culture is its distinctive pottery, a vibrant style in which red clay is painted with white designs. Additional colour is used sometimes, as well as incised and modelled ornamentation. This style makes the vessels stand out, but their varied shapes and functions are more helpful in reconstructing the domestic economy and consumption patterns of the people who made and used them. Vessels in the complex include griddles, bowls, dishes, jars, pot stands, and incense burners, with refined features such as flat bases, rims, and handles. Not all vessels incorporated all of these refined features, of course, and ceramics of all kinds were used together with tools and utensils made from stone, string, straw, and wood. Together, they provided capacity for the preparation, cooking, and eating of food, as well as storage and transport. The great attraction of pottery was its use with heat, enabling varieties of cooking – such as boiling, steaming, stewing, and baking – that were hard to achieve with other materials (and without metal).

Early Saladoid voyagers reached Puerto Rico by 2100 BP, leaving evidence of settlement sites on scattered islands all the way from Trinidad. Radiocarbon dates for these sites, however, show that this was no regular wave moving steadily from south to north. Rather, the earliest settlements seem to have been made as far from South America as St Martin, Puerto Rico, and Martinique, suggesting an exploratory phase and possible repulsion on the part of the pre-existing Archaic peoples. A relatively tolerant mode of coexistence developed in which the early Saladoid settlers occupied niches less favoured by the fisher–hunter–gatherer communities. Thus, many of the first Saladoid settlement sites were made on relatively hilly or mountainous islands and located inland, hidden from the eyes of coast dwellers. These sites offer no archaeological evidence of armed conflict or defensive architecture. On the other hand, there is evidence of cultural interaction between the Archaic and Ceramic Age peoples, the two groups each transferring and adapting technologies from the other to make more efficient tools, using stone and clay.

Later Saladoid settlement sites, suggestive of a more permanent sedentary phase, occur on almost all of the islands of the eastern Caribbean, including Barbados, and reaching as far west as the eastern end of Hispaniola. In most places, these settlements were located alongside those of the nomadic hunter–gatherer–fisher first peoples, the two groups sharing a preference now for coastal and marine environments, and suggesting a more settled notion of coexistence. The new people constructed large buildings of poles and thatch, some of which were 20 m in diameter and big enough for several families. Such communal structures were intermixed with smaller buildings and mounded shell middens, often arranged around a central place that also included a designated burial area, at sites that had considerable continuity with occupation stretching over hundreds of years. The central place served as a focal point, as in South American practice, providing a site for ritual performance as the spatio-temporal focus of the symbolic circle of life that bound together cemetery and ceremony. Here can be seen, by about AD 600, the beginnings of social and political complexity, the emergence of elites rooted in kinship, and the forging of corporate institutions. The origins of these changes and their role in the creation of complex societies can be traced to the economic foundations of these communities and the notions they developed of the possibilities that existed for human manipulation of nature and at least a partial mastery of the hazards thrown up against them.

Saladoid economies depended, much more than any island culture that had gone before, on the exploitation of plants. Among these plants one stood supreme: *Manihot esculenta,* called cassava in Arawakan and sometimes known as yuca or manioc. It was, in many ways, revolutionary. Cassava is not indigenous to the Caribbean but rather a plant domesticated in Brazil about 4,000 years ago. It was introduced to the islands by Arawakan-speaking people from South America, along with the technologies appropriate to its cultivation, processing, and cooking. As the most important food plant introduced intentionally before 1492, cassava represented a new attitude to life in the islands. Rather than hunting and gathering whatever might be found on land and sea, the carrying of cassava to the Caribbean demonstrated an interest in settling with food sources that were already familiar and offered superior yields. Equally important, it represented a new attitude to the manipulation of the landscape, a willingness to transform natural land and water resources to extract a living. To this extent, the Saladoid people were similar to many migrating agricultural communities. Cassava also possessed specific qualities that made its cultivation and consumption seem to represent a mastery over nature and its hazards. It led the way in making demands on local forests, through the clearing of land for cultivation and the use of wood as fuel and building material. Not only did cassava play a large role in the food culture and food security of the people, it also facilitated sedentary settlement in many new ecological niches, underpinned greater population densities, and enabled the emergence of complex societies.

The central role of cassava requires explanation. It is the only staple crop, anywhere in the world, to be highly poisonous. The part of the plant eaten is its starchy roots or tubers and in the preferred variety of the species, known as bitter cassava, these contain toxic cyanide and must be processed carefully to be made safe for consumption. Both cultivation and processing made heavy demands on labour. The roots had to be peeled with a seashell, grated, and then placed in a woven container to squeeze out the poisonous juice using a weight. The juice might then be boiled to make a sauce capable of preserving both plant and animal foods, though the relative absence of land animals made this practice less common in the islands than it had been in South America. The pulp was dried and cooked on a buren or griddle (the ceramic remnants of which are common in Saladoid archaeological sites) and formed into large flat circular cakes. Pieces were broken off and eaten with a sauce. What cassava had to offer in the face of these hazards and this heavy labour was the ability to grow well on soils where other crops would fail, tolerate drought, give several high-yield crops from a single planting, and offer excellent storage qualities both in the ground and after processing. The dried cakes could be kept for two or three years and were an important voyaging food, light weight and long-lasting, enabling a canoe to be paddled the many days that the Saladoid people needed to reach the northern islands.

Cassava is a good source of carbohydrates and calories, with many advantages over its potential competitors, but it had first to win favour over several alternative candidates among the tubers. Most important of these was the sweet potato. Its chief disadvantages relative to cassava were that it was less tolerant of poor soil and water regimes and stored less well. Much the same applied to the tuber known in Arawakan as *yautía*, a variety of cocoyam or taro, brought from South America along with arrowroot and species of yam. The use of these in Saladoid times was limited.

Maize (corn) was not a major competitor. It takes more labour, yields less, is more demanding on soil nutrients, delivers fewer calories, and lacks the remarkable storage capacities of cassava. In any case, maize reached many of the islands relatively late. Archaeological evidence is limited largely to coastal sites in Hispaniola and St Thomas, and dated to the period after AD 1000. Maize was never a staple in the islands. It was cassava, above all, that led to the intensification of agriculture in the Late Ceramic (post-Saladoid) period, which began about AD 600. Cassava was then planted in formally prepared fields, made up of lines of circular mounds known as *conucos* in which the stem cuttings were set. In some cases, the land was terraced to make use of hillslopes. In ideal conditions, as found in much of Hispaniola, cassava delivered plentiful food, as abundant as that produced in the rice economies of southeast Asia or the yam belt of West Africa.

Other important elements of the plant-centred food of Saladoid people included leafy greens, peas, and beans. Fruit was abundant, including many that are now highly valued and continue to have an important place in Caribbean gardens and orchards. The names of these vary from place to place but some of the more common include those known in English as squash, peppers, pawpaw, guava, soursop, sweetsop, custard apple, sapodilla, mamey apple, star apple, cashew, guinep, pineapple, and passionfruit. Many of these fruits probably reached the islands much earlier, from Central America, and may have been introduced and consumed by Archaic Age migrants of the first wave. On the other hand, peanuts, a crop of the Amazon region, reached central Cuba during the Ceramic Age and were popular throughout the Greater Antilles, suggesting continuing long-distance relationships.

As the hunting of wild land animals ceased to be an option in the islands of the eastern Caribbean, reef-fishing and the catching of shellfish and crabs became increasingly important contributors to the diet. Although birds and the now-extinct rice-rat are common in Ceramic Age sites of the Lesser Antilles, opossum seems confined to Grenada. Agouti, a large rodent, was also common in the southern islands of the Lesser Antilles but this was a captive animal introduced to the islands by second-wave migrants. It proved difficult to maintain in captivity and probably contributed little to the diet. The introduced guinea pig was more successfully domesticated but apparently bred only in small numbers. Domestic dogs also were introduced but the evidence of burials suggests that they were not primarily regarded as a food resource. In the other direction, the hutía, a small rodent, was probably introduced to Puerto Rico from Hispaniola during the Ceramic Age, as a captive animal. It was native to both Hispaniola and Jamaica, where it is called coney, probably having made its way to these two islands on flotsam. It prospered in the absence of predators, or was managed, to enable extensive exploitation, particularly at inland sites lacking access to marine resources.

During the Ceramic Age, there was also change in the exploitation of fish resources, from large carnivorous species to smaller sizes, suggesting a degree of overfishing. Similarly, land crabs, which had been the primary source of protein in islands such as Puerto Rico, became smaller and less abundant. This developing shortage encouraged a shift to dependence on plants. Propagation and specialized orchard-horticulture were innovations of this period. Another response to such changes was migration to new islands and the abandonment of some of those already settled. This seems to have been the case in the isolated island of Barbados, where, in spite of an abundance of flying fish, food resources were constrained.

Indicative of the complexity and diversity of Saladoid culture is the separate identification within its sphere of the archaeological culture called Huecoid but also sometimes termed Huecan Saladoid, suggesting close parallels between the two styles. It is named for La Hueca, an archaeological site discovered in Puerto Rico in the 1970s, but the culture also is found in the neighbouring small islands of Vieques and St Martin. This culture is distinguished by its ceramics, which tend to be unpainted and thinner than typical of Saladoid vessels and, in some cases, are uniquely formed. In addition, it possessed striking and unusual carvings of birds, frogs, and bats made from stone and shell not found nearby. Thus, Huecoid culture may represent an isolationist enclave within the broader Saladoid presence or, more likely, evidence of peaceable cultural diversity. Towards the end of the Saladoid period, around AD 500, the islands of Curaçao and Bonaire were invaded by similar people with a Ceramic Age culture known as Dabajuroid. These people constructed dwellings and lived in permanent settlements close to their plantings of manioc, maize, and agave. Their way of life continued in this mode for the next thousand years.

Even later, but still essentially part of second-wave expansion, came the colonization of Jamaica and the Bahamas. The settlement of these islands, beginning only in the seventh century AD, occurred at the transition from Saladoid to Ostionoid, the latter culture flourishing in the Greater Antilles and representing a hybridization of Archaic and Saladoid ceramic styles. It seems improbable that the people of Cuba and Hispaniola lacked knowledge of the existence of Jamaica and the Bahamas, so it may be assumed that for a long time they made a conscious choice not to settle on them.

The many scattered limestone islands, cays, and banks of the Bahamas offered a limited range of resources, though not always very different from those found on islands to the east that had been settled much earlier (Map 2.4). Whereas today many of the islands, particularly in the southern zone, receive little rain and support only dry tropical forest, at the point of settlement around AD 700, the climate and soil of these small islands were much more attractive.

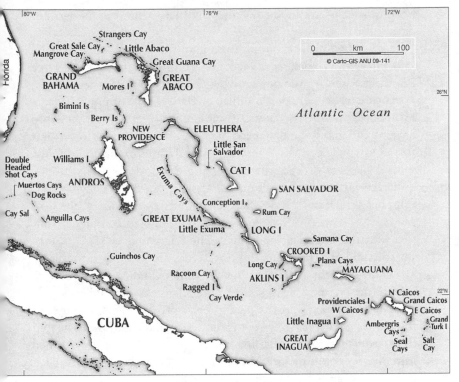

Map 2.4. The Bahamas.

The oldest sites contain ceramics with affinities to both Hispaniola and Cuba but the colonists soon began making distinctive Ostionoid-style pottery using the limited clay deposits of the
islands. Cassava was planted but may have been displaced as the
primary carbohydrate by zamia, which was used in other islands
to a lesser extent. Rather than dependence on horticultural practices developed in the Greater Antilles, the marine environment
of the Bahamas played a prominent role. Large mammals, such
as the monk seal, and turtles, were important at first but the few
larger land animals, such as the tortoise and iguana, were quickly
hunted to extinction. Reef fish became predominant, along with
conch and other shellfish. For fishing, large canoes were cut from
local trees and plant fibres were used to make nets and baskets. The
canoes also enabled the people of the Bahamas – the Lucayans – to

keep in touch with the people they had left behind in the Greater Antilles.

Jamaica had many environmental features in common with Cuba and Hispaniola, making it even harder to explain why this large island apparently was not settled until AD 600. The peopling of Jamaica can be seen as a product of the growth of population in Hispaniola, which also saw Ostionoid culture groups moving into eastern Cuba and the Bahamas, but this does little to help account for its long neglect. Distance was certainly important in the delay, with a passage of 140 km to Cuba and 180 km to Hispaniola, and even farther to the cultural hotspots in the zone bridging eastern Hispaniola and Puerto Rico. Once settled in Jamaica, the people hewed impressively large canoes that enabled continuing contact with the neighbouring islands. The relatively late settlement of Jamaica did give it an unusual character. The people who eventually came brought with them a refined understanding of appropriate agricultural systems, as well as plants such as cassava and mammals such as agouti and dog, that had already proved themselves useful. In spite of their relatively sophisticated baggage and tool kits and their sedentary habits, the first people to settle in Jamaica turned initially to exploit the island's large and defenceless animals, such as flightless birds, bats, sloths, monkeys and rodents. Many of these species became extinct. Ostionoid ceramics, known in Jamaica as Redware, were produced at sites scattered widely around the coast and occasionally inland.

After the Saladoid period, settlement moved inland and food production became more intensive in all of the Greater Antilles, including the late-settled Jamaica. Inevitably, a gap began to open between the lifestyles of the larger and the smaller islands, reflecting a divergence in resources. Less easily explained is the emergence in the Late Ceramic period of a dividing line, marked by the Anegada Trough (4500 m deep and 90 km wide), across which exchange and trade became rare or difficult. In terms of cultural development, however, both the Leeward Islands and the Virgin Islands came to have more in common with patterns associated with the Greater Antilles than with the southerly islands of the eastern chain. In this last "Windward" group, trade and social exchange with the South American mainland remained strong.

COMPLEX SOCIETIES

The complex societies that emerged in the Caribbean islands in the Late Ceramic period after about AD 600 incorporated elements of culture brought from the mainland in the succeeding waves of migration but equally represented original responses to the unique environments in which they evolved. Further, although these complex island societies shared many basic characteristics, they varied significantly in scale and structure. The large islands of the Greater Antilles had advantages in this development because of their land space, their substantial populations, and the way in which they provided sites for the interaction of at least two different peoples originating in separate mainland traditions. Even within the Greater Antilles, there were significant variations. The relatively late peopling of Jamaica inhibited its development. Cuba also lagged. The most completely developed of the complex societies were found in Hispaniola and Puerto Rico.

The people associated with these complex societies are known collectively as *Taíno*, a label derived from their language and meaning specifically "good" or "noble". Although the people used the word to identify themselves to the first European invaders of the region at the end of the fifteenth century – and this is how the terminology entered the historic record – there is little to suggest that the people thought of themselves as a language community that could be identified by the term Taíno. Rather, they thought of themselves as inhabitants of particular islands or groups of islands, for which they had names, or as members of specific polities. Some of the island-names have persisted to the present, as for example Cuba and Jamaica (Xamayca), while others are lost to the map, as in Boriken (Puerto Rico) (Map 2.5). The island known to the Spanish as Hispaniola (Little Spain) and now split between the nations of Haiti and the Dominican Republic was referred to alternatively by the Taíno as Haiti (Land of Mountains) and Quisqueya (Mother of All Lands).

Modern scholars have applied the term Taíno to the broad region stretching east from Cuba as far as the Leeward Islands, but not extending south from Guadeloupe. This broad sweep is further subdivided into Classic Taíno, occupying the region from the eastern tip of Cuba through most of Hispaniola and all of Puerto Rico; Western

Map 2.5. The Caribbean – Taíno names based on Jalil
Sued-Badillo (ed.), *General History of the Caribbean, Volume
I: Autochthonous Societies* (Paris: UNESCO
Publishing/London: Macmillan, 2003), Plate 8.

Taíno, taking in the central region of Cuba, as well as Jamaica
and the Bahamas; and Eastern Taíno, from the Virgin Islands to
Montserrat. The people of the Bahamas are sometimes distinguished
as Lucayan Taíno. Although language variety existed within these
zones, Taíno served as lingua franca that facilitated communication
and exchange. It was the intensification of such interaction, beginning around AD 600, that stimulated the emergence of the most
complex of these societies.

Political complexity had its origins in the emergence of social
stratification and simple chiefdoms. It indicated a transition from

essentially egalitarian to strongly stratified societies, from local-ized village communities to multivillage polities that spanned whole regions. Before AD 600, most Caribbean peoples lived in small clan-based communities or in villages rooted in kinship with pop-ulations in the hundreds. By the end of the period, on the eve of European invasion, the largest of the polities in the core of the Taíno culture each commanded tens of thousands of people in 100 or more associated nucleated settlements or villages. A single village might contain up to 1,000 houses and 5,000 people. In these highly stratified communities, large villages were governed by caciques or chiefs. Women could and did take the role. The realms over which they held sway were *cacicazgos* or chiefdoms. These realms should not, however, be thought of as equivalent to geographical terri-tories or small states with defined physical boundaries marked on the ground; they did possess strong spatial centres of ceremonial power but beyond these centres the authority of the cacique ebbed and flowed in both terrestrial and extraterrestrial dimensions. The caciques combined a number of roles – political, symbolic, and rit-ual – and mediated between the human and supernatural realms of existence. It was their duty to distribute tasks and resources, and to protect and direct their communities.

Beneath the caciques were lower social classes identified as the *nitaínos* (nobles or elite), *behiques* (shamans), and *naborías* (com-moners, servants). By 1492, there were, at least in Hispaniola and Puerto Rico, first and second order *cacicazgos* over which the most powerful of the caciques had paramountcy. The role of the *nitaínos* was to gather information for the *cacique* regarding their commu-nity and to execute orders. It was also their responsibility to orga-nize the labour of the *naborías* in all activities, including voyages and warfare. Typically, men hunted, fished, and cleared the land, whereas women were responsible for cultivation, harvesting, cook-ing, basketry, and cloth making. The *nitaíno* elite, including the caciques, were entitled to special foods, elaborate costumes, and ornament. These were the symbolic trappings of hierarchy.

Broadly, the principal features of complexity may be measured by the size and scope of a society, the number and differentiation of its component parts, the range of specialized social and political roles, and the variety of means by which these elements are coordinated as a functional unity. Thus, a complex society can be thought of as having much in common with a modern corporate enterprise or as the social equivalent of a biological superorganism. Whereas the "simple" Archaic hunter–gatherer societies counted a small number of occupational categories and social roles, often defined directly by age and gender, the complex societies of the Taíno possessed many more categories and associated political power with lineage groups who, in turn, attributed their authority to their connection with other worlds and supernatural beings. In the Taino political sphere, gender roles were relatively nonspecialized.

Underlying the notion of complexity is a recognition and performance of inequality which, particularly in its early stages, might be expressed in a single, starkly defined hierarchy represented by kinship. This was true of the complex societies of the Taíno Caribbean and it was this feature that made them essentially chiefdoms rather than states. In a state, not only is the scale of territory generally larger and its boundaries more permanently fixed, but power is delegated and the socially differentiated ruling class is professional and divorced from the narrow bonds of lineage. The differences among bands, tribes, chiefdoms, and states need not be drawn too precisely, however, and development is better understood as evolutionary. Thus, the complex societies of the Taíno can be seen to have their roots in Archaic as well as Ceramic formations, just as argued for ceramic technologies themselves. What was fundamental to Taíno complexity was the *cacique*, his or her kin, and the territorial *cacicazgo* or chiefdom over which he or she held sway.

What caused this shift from egalitarian to hierarchical social structure? And why did these complex societies flourish most fully in Hispaniola and Puerto Rico? These are difficult questions. Scale, both in territory and population, was a vital factor but unable to explain such developments alone. More obviously important was an increasing density of population. There is no doubt this density was greater in Hispaniola and Puerto Rico than in Cuba and Jamaica, but equally there seems no suggestion that the carrying capacity of the environments was stretched or overexploited in the period immediately before the emergence of complexity.

An alternative version of this argument is that, in order to ensure their sustainability, dense populations need management by a managerial hierarchy with authority for the allocation of scarce resources. Water is often central to this kind of argument, particularly the need for an authoritarian control of irrigation and drainage, but this has little merit in the case of the Taíno who depended on rainfed agriculture and seem to have made no substantial use of irrigation. More plausible is the notion that an emerging class, represented by the lineage of the *cacique*, sought to control the distribution of product, particularly in order to access an unearned share for itself, and worked to establish itself as the source of that product through intercession with the spirit world and its own (lineage) class of specialists in magic and ritual. By taking control of the rituals and ceremonies that came to be seen as essential to the reproduction and maintenance of resources and society, individuals were able to advance their claims to power and preference, for themselves as well as their immediate families and their lineages.

It also may be argued that population density created competition for resources at the margins and thus offered opportunities to the *cacique* to bestow his or her hegemony through the provision of protection. Certainly, the period witnessed small-scale movement into the territory of established peoples, a variety of invasion that required a conqueror. On the other hand, there is little evidence of significant conflict or local warfare at the fringes of the *cacicazgos*. The internal dynamics explain the emergence of complexity better than an argument based on external threats and conflict. These internal dynamics were not without their own varieties of conflict and contest, as rival groups of kin played out their ambitions in ceremonial space.

As in previous periods of Caribbean development, the emergence of complex societies was associated with changes in ceramic culture. Not surprisingly, the transformation of pottery – in form and decoration – occurred first in the central "classic" region of the Greater Antilles, whereas Saladoid patterns persisted much longer in the outlier zones and throughout most of the Lesser Antilles. Ostionoid redware became common in eastern Hispaniola, displacing polychrome patterns, suggesting interaction with Puerto Rico as well as internal evolution. The further articulation and refinement of these styles took place at specific sites, so that characteristic vessel shapes, colours, and moulded forms of ornamentation became associated with particular islands and regions.

Thus, within the Ostionoid tradition, it is possible to distinguish the "Ostionan Ostionoid" straight-sided redware of Jamaica from the "Meillacan" in-curved bowls with rough surfaces resembling woven baskets of the Dominican Republic, as well as the Chican Ostionoid unpainted, deeply incised vessels with their characteristic spouts and moulded effigies, which developed in the Dominican Republic then spread to Cuba, Puerto Rico, and the Virgin Islands. Some of these variations can be attributed to migration but the synthesis and elaboration of styles probably had more to do with the interaction of peoples, including the exchange of ideas and technologies between Archaic and Ostionoid peoples and, indeed, their long-term coexistence. It is wrong to think of the so-called Archaic peoples as somehow bound by tradition and relics of a more primitive age. It took a long time to happen but this flourishing of creative hybridization can be attributed to the activity of the Archaic peoples as much as to the invading Saladoid cultures. These processes took place throughout the Greater Antilles from Cuba to Puerto Rico.

The pattern of Taíno resource use and food production constituted a refinement and extension of that developed by Saladoid peoples, described earlier. Substantial population growth was made possible by a more efficient exploitation of food resources and by the spread of agriculture and settlement into new ecological zones. With the depletion of wild land animals and the limited range of settlement permitted by dependence on sea, stream, and wetland, the economy turned decisively toward agricultural production. Even more than on the American mainland, indigenous economic life in the islands came to be dominated by plants. It was the system of *conucos* that made possible increased and dependable food supply. Cassava remained the staple food, supplemented by maize. Fruit, collected from the wild and cultivated in orchard-gardens, was abundant. Sea fish remained important for people living along the coasts and others fished from inland ponds as well as mountain streams. The Taíno had no more experience of large land animals than their Saladoid precursors. Domesticated animals remained rare, unavailable for meat or for transport. On land, the movement of people and goods depended completely on human bearers.

On water, progress was limited to the speed of paddlers. Thus, although the sea may be seen as integrating the island chain into a viable route, along which people, ideas, and commodities could move and be exchanged with ease – so long as they were not bulky or heavy – it is important to observe that this was all it did. Because the Caribbean archipelago took the form of an extended tombolo, stretching out and enclosing the Caribbean Sea with a long arm that just happened to have watery gaps along the way, the sea did not beckon to the people. They did not become people of the sea, venturing out to trade or seek resources in the way that, for example, their contemporaries did in the Pacific Ocean. To do so required sails and knowledge. Oared-boats became too heavy once they had space for more than 200 rowers and were unable to carry substantial cargo. The people of the Caribbean lacked the necessary technologies, notably the sail and navigational tools essential to successful voyaging beyond the Sea. They were island people, most at home on land.

The development of Taíno resource use and food production technologies actively induced a movement of population inland, away from the coastal marine resources that had been so vital to earlier peoples. Interior river valleys were preferred but settlement spread almost everywhere in Hispaniola and Puerto Rico. These valleys were particularly fruitful and came to support dense agricultural populations. Only the steepest slopes, those that could not be terraced, and the wettest of the poorly drained lowlands remained unoccupied. In Hispaniola, settlement was most intense and population most dense in regions such as the basin of Maguana, the northern coastal plain of Marien, and the elevated limestone zone of Higüey. The spread of population and agriculture went together with extensive forest clearance and the overexploitation of natural resources. The increased moisture regime of the late Holocene, together with the clearance of steep slopes, also led to the extension of coastlines and increased turbidity. The resulting development of mangrove reduced the availability of resources in coastal zones, notably by choking with clay and silt the many mollusc and other species that formerly thrived in these situations.

Although the landscape of Hispaniola and Puerto Rico was transformed by the emergence of complex societies and the intensification of agricultural systems, the pattern of settlement was not marked by substantial urban development. As in many ancient cultures, the production of food was not separated from other livelihood activities or from governance. To this extent, the pattern of settlement and population distribution resembled more a federation of large-scale village communities of relatively equal weight than a hierarchy of settlements differing in scale, function, and power. In many ways, the sites resembled the communities described earlier as representative of the later Saladoid period, with houses and middens arranged around a central open area, though on a larger scale. The houses were not arranged according to a geometric street plan. The most significant change after about AD 600 was the relocation of the community's cemetery from this central area to be scattered among the circling houses and mounded middens and the redevelopment of the central open area as a dedicated ceremonial space. The relocation of burial indicated a shift away from group identification with the dead towards a more individualistic attitude. Communal communing with the ancestral spirits gave way to a situation in which individual kinship networks took precedence. This shift towards individualism and lineage organization may be seen as a precondition for the emergence of hierarchy within the village polity.

Other changes in the landscape that reflected the emergence of complex societies included the building of permanent extensive open plazas. These were designed to become central elements in the ceremonial spaces located at the centre of a *cacicazgo*. The *cacique* built his or her dwelling nearby. In the largest of the settlements, such as that of Tibes on the southern side of Puerto Rico, there were multiple ceremonial plazas, generally rectangular in shape and paved or cobbled, and dated to around AD 800. These plazas overlay earlier burial grounds. In some cases, the plazas were merely outlined with stone, aligned perhaps to the stars and planets, and bounded by tall standing stones with incised figures of animals or human heads. When Tibes went into decline around AD 1200, it was replaced by the even larger site of Caguana, which maintained its ascendancy for the next 200 years or so and developed a uniquely rich iconography. These were the largest of the centres in Puerto Rico. They were not associated with substantial sedentary populations.

Ceremonial centres were fewer in Hispaniola and it was rare for any one settlement to have more than a single plaza. Some of them had cobbled pavements and standing stones, however, and the impressive plazas and stone causeways at Chacuey and Corral de los Indios are, by far, the most extensive of all the ceremonial centres. Cuba, too, has only a small number of ceremonial plazas but the ones known to exist, in the eastern end of the island, were on a scale equal to that in Hispaniola. One plaza has been identified in the southern Bahamas but none has yet been found in Jamaica. Everywhere they existed, the construction of these ceremonial sites represented a very considerable investment of labour time, though none of the Caribbean complexes came near to rivalling the massive pyramids and sophisticated urban settlements of the Aztecs and Mayas. Rather, the pattern in the Taíno core of the Greater Antilles suggests that the hierarchy of settlement pattern that might have been established by a system of scaled urban centres found expression instead in a hierarchy of ceremonial sites, with significance measured in terms other than their resident population numbers or economic roles.

Whatever the spiritual or ritual significance of the ceremonial plazas of the Taínos, the best known activity associated with them was the ball game. It was played only in the core zones of Taíno culture in the Greater Antilles. In the ceremonial plazas, the outlined spaces marked playing fields. The game was played between two teams, each of twenty or thirty people, sometimes men and sometimes women. They lined up at the ends of the enclosure and one player threw a rubber ball to the competing team who then attempted to get the ball back to the other end without it touching the ground. They did this by bouncing the ball off prescribed parts of the body, using shoulders, buttocks, knees, and closed fists. As well as exciting entertainment, the ball game may have served to stage competitions between the different chiefdoms or *cacicazgos*, and the plazas similarly performed double duty as meeting grounds for trade and perhaps intermarriage ceremonies.

The most fully developed forms of ritual performance were associated with the most substantial polities. These were confined to Hispaniola, where, by the fifteenth century, the island was dominated by at least five impressively extensive *caciazgos* or coalitions of towns (Map 2.6). The largest was Magua, ruled by the cacique Guarionex in 1492, and the others, Xaraguá, Maguana, Marien,

Map 2.6. Hispaniola.

and Higüey. The distribution of known ceremonial plazas did not match this pattern directly, in the sense that there was not one substantial ceremonial space at the centre of each of these territories that might have been associated with a single political and spiritual lineage. Rather, the largest plazas were concentrated near the centre of the island, towards the west, and smaller ceremonial spaces were scattered more broadly.

Something similar was true of Puerto Rico, where at least five major *cacicazgos* were identified in 1492, and some accounts claimed the entire island fell under one or perhaps two paramount caciques, Agüeybaná I and Guaybanex. In Hispaniola, the paramount chieftess Anacaona of Xaraguá was said to have as many as 300 subordinate caciques. Elsewhere, the concentration of power and ritual performance was less obvious, suggesting a less hierarchically organized system. In eastern Cuba, where the existence of large plazas may be interpreted as evidence of active competition among lineages seeking to build up a following rather than indicating the possession of extensive authority by any one individual, the process of political development was still working itself out.

SPIRIT WORLDS

Over time, the significance of the ceremonial plazas changed in response to growing competition among the elite lineages and chiefdoms. After about AD 1200, the *nitaínos* found it increasingly necessary to maintain their status and power through the performance of their genealogy, to demonstrate the superior character of their lineage's connection with those who had gone before. To achieve this, it was necessary to establish links between the world of the living and the world of the dead, and to connect with the supernatural beings who occupied the spirit world. Ritual objects known as *cemís* or *zemis*, moulded from natural materials or pottery, were used to enable this link, and it was the cult of the *cemís* that formed the most distinctive element of Taíno religious cosmology.

The ceremonial plazas, previously used largely for the physically competitive ball game, became sacred sites. The ornamented standing stones that marked the boundaries of the plazas became more closely associated with the *cemís* and the plazas became sites for the performance of song and dance known as the *areyto*. Such performances provided connections with the spirit world and appear to have been the most significant of all the ceremonies performed at the central plazas of Tibes and Caguana in Puerto Rico, for example, in which the standing stones carved with effigies played an important role. Hundreds of people performed together, moving in unison. Drumming, oral performance and the use of hallucinogenic drugs, particularly by the elites, facilitated altered states of consciousness and enabled an easy communication between the living and the dead. The *areyto* was not merely entertainment or even spiritual performance but often a praise song, a central element in the glorification of the *cacique* and his or her kin, living and dead, and intended to reinforce their power and position. In this way, the ceremonial plazas shifted from being communal centres of connection and enjoyment to sites designed to celebrate and confirm the power of the chief and his chiefdom – *cacique* and *cacicazgo* – both internally and externally.

Connection with the spirit world was placed in the hands of shamans or "medicinemen", known as *behiques*, *bohíte*, or *buhuittihu*, who were members of the elites specialized in rituals of divination. The *behiques* bridged the gap between the natural world and the world of spirits, bringing together magic and religion in curing rituals. In these rituals, the *behique* might suck on various parts of the sick person's body, then spit out some object indicating that he had got rid of the cause of the illness. Curing rituals were often conducted with the help of tobacco and hallucinogenic substances. The evening primrose, a mild narcotic, occurs in archaeological sites associated with ceremonial centres, particularly in Puerto Rico, and the psychoactive properties of its seeds may have been used for ritual or medicinal purposes. The plant was originally introduced from Cuba, where it survives in pockets. The earliest indications of tobacco, an introduced plant, are found in sites in the Dominican Republic around AD 1000.

The *behiques* were custodians of cosmological knowledge and interpreters of *cemís*. Represented in physical form as effigies or "idols", the *cemís* were used by *behiques* and caciques to confer on themselves the authority to perform religious and magical acts and to give commands. Some of these *cemís* were in the form of animals, such as frogs and turtles, or human beings, and so large they could not be carried. These massive *cemís* sometimes served as boundary-marking standing stones, as already observed. Similarly fixed in place were pictographs, incised and coloured on the walls of caves and other landscape sites. The important site of Caguana in Puerto Rico was located within the limestone belt where karst topography created many caves and sinkholes. These caves provided surfaces for pictographs and represented the transition from the surface of the earth to an underworld of mystery. They were the home of bats, thought to be the souls of nonliving beings who roamed the frightening forests by night. The central plaza of Caguana was framed by limestone slabs quarried from the karst, whereas the monolithic boulders that marked the boundaries were brought from nearby streams, matching the symbolic landscape of the surrounding tower karst. In these ways, the "natural" landscape and the ritual symbolism of standing stones and *cemís* became one and the same, uniting past and present, real and imagined worlds.

Smaller idols or amulets, made of hard stone (such as alabaster), coral, shell, bone, wood, or pottery, were portable and worn on the body. Many of these represented features of the human body, from ears to genitals, and naturalistic or abstracted animals, such as birds. Hybridization and grafting of human and other animal elements suggest both an important role for animals in Taíno ritual and myth, and the notion that, in the spirit world at least, they might become one, as represented, for example, in bat–men, owl–bats, bird–men, or men–birds, including birds with human hands at the ends of their wings. Not all of the plastic art of the Taínos should be understood as possessing spiritual significance. Probably much of it was designed simply as human adornment and decoration, such as necklaces of carved beads and pendants, and bracelets, made typically of shell, stone, bone, or wood, but occasionally of gold. They also practiced body piercing, for ear plugs, lip plugs, and nose ornaments. Other craft works, such as the special carved stools or *duhos*, had both practical and ritual functions.

Although Taíno spiritual performance had its ceremonial spaces, its ritual objects, and its specialist practitioners, none of these elements constituted the foundations of an institutional religion. The intellectual world of the Taínos was one that did not make

Plate 2.2. River pictographs, Boriken, representing the human face (k, m, n, p, s), head (q), head and body (r, t), moon (l), and water (o). *Source:* Jesse Walter Fewkes, The Aborigines of Porto Rico and Neighboring Islands, *Twenty-Fifth Annual Report of the Bureau of American Ethnology to the Secretary of the Smithsonian Institution* (Washington: Government Printing Office, 1907), Plate LX, Part 2.

distinctions between knowledge of religion and science or between theology and philosophy. Rather, religion was at the very core of the Taíno universe. Its system of beliefs, symbols, and rites worked together to make sense of the world and to attempt to take some control within nature. The foundation of this way of thinking about the world was rooted in the notion of a compact between humankind and the rest of nature, in which human experience provides a model for understanding everything else. This understanding involves an animation of the natural world, so that even the earth – its rocks and stones, its geology – can be assimilated to the human life cycle and understood in terms of human emotions.

Nature was not simply anthropomorphized. Rather, a reciprocal relationship was established in which it was required that human beings respect all elements of the enveloping world in order to be respected in turn. This respect had to be shown not merely to the visible universe – the plants and animals, the rocks and the water – but also to the invisible beings who might be just as influential and might, indeed, represent the alter egos of those once living but now passed to the other side. Within this system of belief, the *cemís* played a vital role, particularly in ensuring fertility – both human childbearing and the fruitfulness of the fields – and also in healing and in funeral rites – the beginning and ending of life, and its regeneration.

DISRUPTION

The long-term trend in which human settlement spread steadily throughout the islands, and societies and polities became increasingly complex, did not always run smoothly. Indeed, the very processes that created increasingly dense populations and increasingly hierarchical social structures contributed to competition for resources and territory at the interface of cultural difference. Notably, the process of settlement was disturbed around AD 1200 in the region of the northern islands of the Lesser Antilles chain, where the Taíno extended their influence into the zone of smaller islands that had not shared in the drive towards complexity. As a result, local populations were reduced and some islands abandoned.

This disruption has often been seen as the outcome of the aggressive northward movement of a third wave of migrant peoples originating in mainland South America. The people belonging to this supposed migrant group have long been known as Caribs, Caribes, or Caraïbes. Although Carib is a Taíno word meaning island or islanders (specifically peoples from distant lands), it came into currency in early European discourse as a useful term to construct a world made up of contrary elements: "Indian" versus Carib or Arawak versus Carib. Whereas the Indians/Arawaks were seen as peace-loving sedentary people living in harmony with their environment, the Caribs were considered wild marauding cannibals. This simple dichotomy and its supposed cause, the invasive migration of a Carib cultural group, no longer are accepted. They do not fit the archaeological record – as indicated, for example, by the absence of a distinct style of ceramics that can be associated with these people – and earlier linguistic arguments appear equally flawed.

The people who made up the supposed third migration wave were thought to speak Cariban, another language derived from the Arawakan language family with its roots in South America. However, the language now known as Island-Carib evolved from a mixing of grammars and lexicons, no doubt reflecting a mixing of the peoples themselves in the islands and resulting in a long-term decline in the proportion of Carib forms and an increase in elements familiar to Lokono and the now-extinct Taíno languages. As with the so-called Arawaks and Taínos, the Cariban-speaking people who settled in the eastern islands did not refer to themselves as Caribs. Rather, they called themselves Kalinago or Kalipuna, yet another term derived from the language of a people (and first recorded in the seventeenth century), or used local names that attached them to particular islands or island groups. Most of these island names have not survived – as for example, Carucairi/Guacana (now Guadeloupe), Guaticabon (Dominica), Iguanacaera/Matinino (Martinique), Guanarao (St. Lucia), Yarumai Yaramaqui (St. Vincent), and Camajuya (Grenada). However, in spite of the more limited geographical spread of the Cariban speakers and their relatively late arrival in the region, it was these people whose generalized name was given to the sea: the *Caribb*ean. Both the people and their language are now known as Island-Carib or, more correctly, Kalinago.

Rather than experiencing a distinct third migration wave, it appears more probable that in the fourteenth and fifteenth centuries, the Windward Islands were marked simply by an intensification of the same variety of contact with the mainland as had been going on for many centuries. It was this long process of interaction, exchange, and persistent migration, spread over many generations, that resulted in the emergence of a distinctive cultural synthesis in the Windward Islands. Compared with the Taíno zone, the eastern islands depended on a food production complex more closely assimilated to that of mainland tropical South America, with a larger role for cassava and fish. The people were more mobile, living in small settlements, with a strong preference for the fertile coastal plains and valleys. Their society was less hierarchical than that of the Taíno. It was this distinctive pattern of life that made the people seem deserving of their own label – hence Carib – and that equally led to their being mistaken for a distinct migrant contingent.

Guadeloupe marked the effective northern limit of "Carib" culture, where it looked across the waters to Montserrat and the other islands belonging to the Eastern Taíno that represented the outer limit of that culture (Map 2.7). Whereas earlier connective networks and movements had extended their reach all the way from the South American mainland into the Leeward Islands and even Puerto Rico, and there had been signs of Taíno exchange from Puerto Rico back to the Leewards, the period after about AD 1300 was marked by disruption. Several of the islands, from Saba to Nevis and perhaps more generally, were temporarily abandoned.

Although this apparent depopulation and the retreat of settlement cannot be fully explained, it appears to represent the existence of a zone of intense conflict. This was what made these previously attractive islands seem unsafe and, no doubt, it was this perception that contributed to the first Europeans reading the situation in the way they did: as the outcome of an aggressive northward migration of bloodthirsty peoples. However interpreted, this disruption of the established pattern of life was nothing compared to the disaster that was to be the immediate consequence of the European invasion about to descend on the Caribbean.

By the fifteenth century, in the years immediately before the dramatic disruption caused by the European invasion, all of the major islands were peopled. Empty places were uncommon. Abandonment

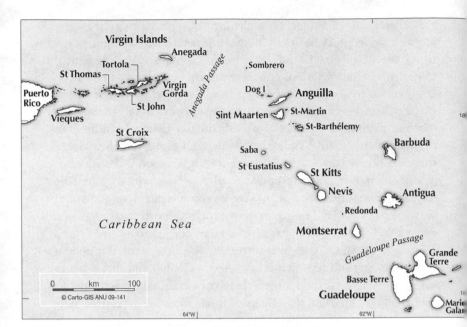

Map 2.7. The Leeward Islands.

was unusual. Many islands and large regions were densely populated, supported by the productive (and spiritual) relationship they
had established with the environment. Estimating the actual number
of people living in the Caribbean in the fifteenth century, however, is
a difficult task. There is no doubt that the greatest number, perhaps
one half of the total, lived in Hispaniola, where Taíno complex societies had reached their Caribbean maximum and the population was
both densely settled and geographically widespread. Estimates for
the island go as high as eight million but a number between one and
two million appears more probable. In Puerto Rico, the numbers fall
somewhere between 250,000 and 500,000. Where Taíno cultural
and political development was less, the populations were significantly smaller. The population of Cuba was perhaps 100,000 to
150,000. Jamaica's population was probably fewer than 100,000,
with settlement sites largely confined to a narrow coastal zone.
The Bahamas held perhaps 40,000. Putting together what has been
argued for all the islands, an estimate of two million for the total
Caribbean population in 1492 appears conservative.

The dense populations of the Caribbean were made possible by an efficient adaptation to available resources and environmental conditions, together with the introduction of plants and technologies tested and known from the South American mainland. External shocks to this well-tuned system more often were the product of the forces of nature than of hostile invasion. Volcanic eruptions, earthquakes, and tsunamis could be devastating but, as noted in the case of the southern Caribbean at least, tsunamis were rare and widely spaced, occurring at intervals of about 1,000 years. No planning or social memory could be of much help in avoiding or preparing for such overwhelming events. Their consequences were often revolutionary, however – for example, encouraging the adoption of agriculture when coastal marine resources were destroyed.

Less destructive but much more regular and frequent were the hurricanes that wheeled across the Atlantic. Funnelled towards the Caribbean, the islands seemed almost to have been placed where they were as targets. The disruption to island societies caused by hurricanes was typically relatively minor, the kind of temporary difficulty that could be planned for by producing food with good growth and storage qualities and accepting the necessity of constant rebuilding. On the other hand, intense hurricanes were much less common but also more disruptive, their frequency varying over the long term, in response to changes in the status of El Niño/Southern Oscillation and the West African monsoon. Extreme hurricane events were relatively frequent before 3600 BP, and this was followed by a quieter period until 2500 BP, then an intense period to 1000 BP, and a particularly quiet period to AD 1700. The quiet of this last long period was, however, interrupted by the tsunamis of 1498 and 1530, which struck the islands along the Venezuelan coast and left sedimentary evidence in the Greater Antilles. The tsunami of 1498 occurred shortly before the third voyage of Columbus across the Atlantic. In spite of the terrifying, immense scouring force of hurricane and tsunami, it was this seemingly puny human intervention that was to prove most catastrophic.

3

Columbian Cataclysm

1492–1630

Unlike the original peopling of the Caribbean islands, which came late in the human settlement of the Americas, it was in these islands that the secondary – Columbian – colonization of the continents had its beginning. This was not the only significant difference between the two colonizations. The secondary phase, which reached the islands in 1492 with Columbus did not have roots in the tropical rimland, as did the first colonization, but rather had its origins far away across the Atlantic, in Europe. It brought in its wake peoples, plants, animals, and technologies not only from Europe but from across the globe – particularly Africa, but also from the world beyond the Atlantic, from Asia and the Pacific. Further, whereas the first colonization peopled the islands, the initial impact of the secondary wave was characterized not by an augmentation of island populations but their destruction.

When Europeans first voyaged to the Caribbean, the Taíno population they encountered was relatively homogeneous and derived from a limited continental source. In the islands, the founder effect was so powerful that genetic diversity was being reduced rather than expanded. The first colonizers of the Caribbean brought with them few animals, but over time reduced the species diversity of the islands through extinctions. They carried with them a wider variety of plants and some of these, notably cassava, were fundamental to the food supply of a growing population, but at the same time the spread of agriculture was accompanied by the burning of forest. In these ways, the Taínos changed the landscape of the islands but did no more than shift the balance towards a biodiversity more representative of the surrounding tropical mainland cultures from whence came their technologies, languages, and social patterns. The people adapted to island environments and created their own political and symbolic systems, but even the most original of these features was homologous with patterns found in their larger – essentially South American – world. Indeed, it was possible for individuals not only to move relatively freely within the larger regional communities of the islands but also to return to the mainland.

The secondary, European, colonization was unlike the primary peopling of the Caribbean in a variety of ways. In the first place, the new colonization, almost everywhere, was invasive. People already occupied the islands and there were few places that could be regarded as terra incognita or terra nullius. Only by pushing aside, removing, enslaving, or killing those people could European colonization make space to succeed.

Secondly, the systems of plant and animal use introduced after 1492 fundamentally altered the biodiversity of the islands, most obviously through the introduction of large domesticated mammals and the broad-acre planting of grasses, trees, and other plants, many of them having their origins far away. In order to achieve these results, the forest was burned on a scale far greater than anything accomplished by the Taíno and their forefathers.

Thirdly, the newcomers brought and imposed new ways of claiming rights to land and labour, and new systems of government. The essence of this transformation was the establishment of capitalism as the primary means of articulating an economy, the export of wealth to Europe as a driving objective, and metropolitan imperial rule as the primary political form. Ultimate authority, backed by military might, was located outside the region. Social inequality was taken to a height far beyond anything achieved in the hierarchical complex societies that had gone before.

Fourthly, all of these fundamental social, political, and environmental changes depended on a new cosmology – new ideas about what it is to be human. At the core of this new cosmology was the belief that human beings could think of themselves as beyond and outside nature because of their special situation in a great chain of being that placed them between the brutes and the angels. This was a model that distinguished believers from unbelievers and under-pinned ideas of social hierarchy. In the Caribbean, it confronted the animism of the Amerindians and the connections they made between natural and supernatural worlds. They were cast as hea-thens and pagans, people lacking true religion. Most of these new cosmological elements came from the other side of the Atlantic, nur-tured in the religious tradition of Christianity, and only gradually found nourishment in Caribbean soil.

Finally, rather than a population in which genetic diversity was reduced, the bringing together of peoples from Europe, Africa, and Asia, together with the native peoples of the Americas, resulted in a significant increase in diversity of heritage. The consequence was the emergence of peoples, languages, and cultures that were identified as characteristically hybrid or creole, rooted in the Caribbean but created from elements that were universal rather than localized.

The consequences of these differences between the primary and secondary colonizations of the Caribbean were momentous. Rather than being at the tail end of a long, drawn-out process of world migration, as was the first settlement, the Caribbean islands played a leading role in the second great redistribution of the world's people. Rather than being simply at the receiving end of cultural transmis-sion, this time the islands were at the centre of things and formed the furnace in which new cultures and new peoples were forged – precursors of modernity and globalization.

Some elements of the European colonization of the Caribbean took generations to find their full expression but many of the most fundamental appeared early in the encounter. The first 30 years, from 1492 into the 1520s, were formative. Within that short period, structures were developed that were to direct the process of colonization within the Caribbean and throughout the Americas at large. The sequence of events that occurred in the islands was repeated elsewhere, alarmingly often. The Caribbean formed the mortar in which the elements were crushed and pounded, with the complex societies of the Taínos at the very centre. In order to under-stand these patterns and to explain the models and templates that emerged, it is necessary to consider this initial period of encounter in detail. It was a chaotic, disastrous time, with a variety of potential outcomes.

FIRST ENCOUNTERS

Whereas the chronology of the first colonization of the Caribbean remains clouded in uncertainty, the modern European colonization can be located with precision. On 3 August 1492, the experienced Genoese sea captain, Christopher Columbus, set sail to cross the Atlantic from Palos, a small port in the Bay of Cadiz on the southern coast of Spain (Map 3.1). He sailed in a round-hulled *nao* named the *Santa María*, with a crew of 40 men, and accompanied by two caravels, the *Pinta* with 26 and the *Niña* with 24 men. This tiny squadron sailed first for the Canary Islands off the coast of Africa, where they made repairs and replenished their provisions before leaving again on 6 September. It was hurricane season but Columbus was lucky with the weather. After sailing another 5 weeks and travelling 6,000 km, they sighted Caribbean land that now is part of the Bahamas and, on 12 October, set foot on the island known by its Taíno inhabitants as Guanahaní. Columbus planted the Spanish flag, claimed the island, and, in honour of the Catholic saviour Jesus Christ, named it San Salvador. From this initial encounter, he moved on to the territory of the Classic Taíno, sailing along the north coast of Cuba's eastern end and the north coast of Quisqueya/Haiti which he named Española (Hispaniola). Turning north, he sailed to the latitude of Lisbon before heading due east and eventually arrived back at Palos on 15 March 1493.

The relative certainty and precision possible in dating and locating these events should not conceal the fact that Columbus was quite wrong about where he had reached and what he had learned. He sailed on the basis of cosmological theory, with no knowledge that the Americas existed, let alone the Caribbean islands. Certainly, he knew that the earth was a sphere, but sailing into the unknown, across the open ocean and far from land, was frightening enough to make some of the men he attempted to recruit refuse to sail with him. What Columbus lacked – as did everyone else – was a reliable world map.

The best globe he had told him that sailing due west would take him to the East, to the coast of mainland Asia, with its rich spice markets and stores of gold that had become essential to the functioning of the monetary system; and that along the way he

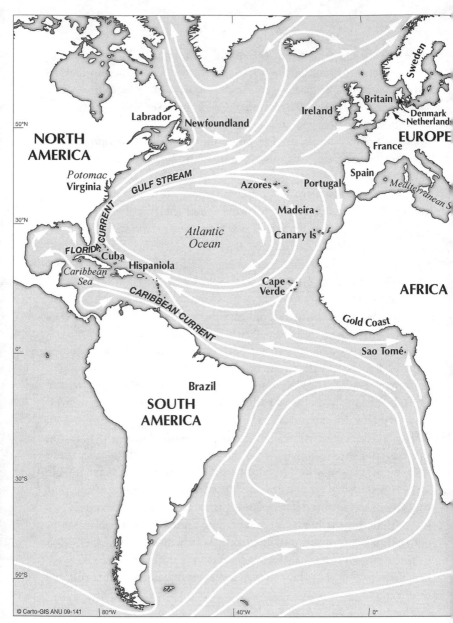

Map 3.1. The Atlantic.

would pass various islands, including the fabled Cipangu (Japan). However, the globe also told him that the earth is smaller than it is. The consequence was that although Columbus navigated his proposed route with precision, he calculated he had already gone beyond Cipangu when, by chance, he came upon Guanahaní. He did not find the Orient he had expected to encounter but tried hard to convince himself and others that he had, in fact, done so, creating the incredibly persistent application of *Indies* to the Caribbean islands (the West Indies as distinguished from the East Indies) and *Indians* to the aboriginal people of the Americas.

In spite of his failures and the continuing confusion he created, Columbus did demonstrate successfully that he possessed the technologies and skill needed to sail a great distance across the open sea and to keep his ships pointed in the direction he intended to travel. Long distance voyaging depended on light sailing ships that used the wind to move them along rather than demanding large crews of hungry and thirsty rowers in heavy wooden ships that could not face the waves and winds of the open sea. The Chinese had mastered these technologies by about 1400 and journeyed as far as Africa but depended on square-rigged sails. They also had invented gunpowder – by 1040 – and cast the first true guns, before the end of the thirteenth century. The first functional long-distance, armed sailing ships of the Atlantic world – small, light, manoeuvrable caravels, with three masts, combining square with triangular lateen sails – were those developed by Europeans in the fifteenth century. Fitted with cannon that fired iron balls, shot out by the explosive force of gunpowder, these fighting ships were highly effective at sea. Dragged on land, their guns were a match for most defensive earthworks and stone walls. The Europeans added two other Chinese inventions – the compass and the rudder – that vastly improved navigational potential.

Once invented, these ships quickly began venturing aggressively beyond their natural horizons in all directions, far beyond the clues offered by flights of birds or cloud formations, though these and floating masses of weed were always good signs that land might not be far away when crossing the open ocean. The first Portuguese voyagers clung to coastlines, however, reaching Senegal in 1444 and Angola in 1486. Vasco da Gama did not round the Cape of Good

Hope and cross the Indian Ocean until 1497. Columbus' crossing of the Atlantic in 1492 stands out.

The first voyage of Columbus across the Atlantic was not merely a technical victory and a cosmological failure. It must be seen also as part of a larger mission, born from a spiritual world that contrasted strongly with the religious understanding practiced by the Taínos. Certainly, commercial objectives were to the fore, making the voyage part of the long running European extension of trade on land and sea, but Columbus, along with many European Christians, also saw it as the global extension of a militant religion. It was of a piece with the Crusades, represented in the fifteenth century by the expulsion of the Muslims and the Jews from the Spanish kingdoms, but matched in the East by the fall of Constantinople to the Ottoman Turks in 1453 and the end of the Byzantine Empire. This last event was aligned with an alternative chronology, that of the eastern Christian faith, which held that secular, earthly time would come to an end with the close of the seventh millennium AM (*anno mundi*, counting from creation), or precisely AD (*anno domini*) 1 September 1492. By these computations, Columbus sailed into the unknown a month before doomsday and reached Guanahaní after the end of the world. The world did not end for Columbus but without doubt he brought doomsday to the Taínos.

Columbus expected to find in Asia not only fabulous wealth and exotic commodities wanted by European consumers but also a mass of people eager to become Christian. Bringing true religion to the heathen was not so much a desire as a duty. His voyage was not a private venture but rather a project of his patrons King Ferdinand and Queen Isabela, whose union had brought together the kingdoms of Aragón and Castile, which accounted for most of the territory of modern Spain. Known as the Catholic Monarchs, Ferdinand and Isabela were responsible for the final reconquest of the kingdom of Granada, accepting in 1492 the surrender of the last Muslim ruler and expelling those Jews who refused to become Christians. Making the world Roman Catholic, not merely Christian, became a global mission.

Whereas Columbus had a clear enough idea of his mission, the Taínos were taken by surprise. However wrong he was, Columbus had set out to find a way to people and places already known to Europeans, and he did his best to believe he had been successful;

that he had found the people he wanted to find. His sailors knew the landscapes of their home places and something of the lands and waters between, giving them a variety of ways of understanding what they encountered in the Caribbean. The ships in which they sailed were filled with familiar things that represented the world they had left behind. For the Taínos, on the other hand, the ships of Columbus were symbolic containers, packed tight with alien peoples and alien technologies that could not easily be unpacked to create an image of the world from whence these strangers had come.

What the people on both sides of this encounter shared was the knowledge that the world contained more diverse varieties of humankind than previously thought and (in spite of Columbus' public denial) therefore more places, perhaps even continents, than thought imaginable. The only viable alternative explanation seemed to be that the Europeans belonged to the world of spirits rather than being accommodated within any theory of migration history or, viewed from the other side, that the people of Guanahaní were not part of the creation revealed in the sacred text of Genesis. Looked at from any angle, the world suddenly became more complicated.

It was just as well the people of Guanahaní could not understand the ritual performed on their beach, in which Columbus claimed the land and changed its name to that of the holy saviour of Christendom. None of it could have made much sense to them in the context of their own established political and spiritual order. The commodities offered by Columbus, such as glass beads, small bells, and items of clothing, were easier to comprehend and appreciate, and the commercial imperative that drove Columbus helped elicit gifts in return. The people of Guanahaní, who probably did not regard such exchange as the foundations of commerce, brought gifts such as parrots, balls of cotton thread, and arrows. Little of this impressed Columbus, hopeful as he still was of tapping into the cornucopia of spices and precious metals of the great mart of Asia.

Columbus did note that the people lacked tools made of iron, not so much because he sought to trade in such heavy objects but rather because it implied that they had no weapons of which to be fearful – no guns, no swords, no crossbows – but possessed only tools made of shell, bone, stone, and wood. He was impressed by the scale of the dugout canoes of the islanders, the larger of which could carry as many people as his own caravels. Not much else struck Columbus as substantial; the people going "naked", he said, indicated a low level of material culture and civilization. He did see them as potentially well fitted for labour. He had no compunction in taking on board seven men of Guanahaní, intending to carry them to Spain to be taught Spanish so they could serve as interpreters on later voyages, and to be converted. Columbus also saw these men as providing proof of his success in finding exotic lands.

After just two days at Guanahaní, Columbus sailed towards another island, directed towards it by the people as the largest of the many they could name. Here, two of the men taken on board escaped. Clearly, they had no desire to sail into the unknown world of Columbus and been forced on board. In Cuba, Columbus took women as well as men, hoping this would prove more successful. He then sailed east towards Quisqueya/Haiti. There, near the modern town of Cap Haitien, Columbus' flagship the *Santa María* ran aground on a sandbar and broke up. The territorial cacique Guacanagarí of Marien province helped save the ship's cargo and offered every kind of assistance. While there, Columbus accumulated more gold than he had been able to get anywhere else.

The loss of the *Santa María* meant, however, that some of the crew had to be left behind when Columbus sailed for Europe on 3 January 1493. Some of them made places for the Taínos Columbus was determined to exhibit. The crew left behind – 39 of them – were to live in Guacanagarí's town, which Columbus named La Navidad, and trade peaceably, seeking more gold and searching for its source. They were also to build a fort for protection, suggesting a more uneasy relationship than Columbus was willing to admit. Although unintended and unplanned, Columbus quickly imagined this tiny colony as part of a grander scheme, as the potential centre of a flourishing commerce with the Great Khan, and painted himself as its founder. Even the wreck of the *Santa María* seemed to him a sign of God's plan. Once Columbus had left the island, however, everything fell apart.

EARLY MODELS OF COLONIZATION

Paradoxically, in view of Columbus' mission to bring Christ to the world, no priests sailed with his first fleet. On his return to Spain in 1493, nevertheless, Columbus declared the people he had found to be good candidates for conversion, peaceful and strong, and inhabiting a paradise not unlike the Garden of Eden. He had with him the surviving "Indians" brought from Guanahaní and other islands, as well as some of the green parrots he had been given, as proof of his successes and evidence of the peoples' need for Christ. Priests were included on his second voyage of 1493 to 1496. This time, he had a much larger fleet, some 17 ships, and he navigated a more southerly route, expecting to find more islands along the way. This new route enabled him to take advantage of the northeastern trade winds, which carried him across the Atlantic on a line from the Canary Islands to the Dominica Passage, between Guadeloupe and Dominica, before travelling along the leeward (western) sides of the islands to the north. This proved a more efficient route than that of Columbus' first voyage and it was followed by many later voyagers from Europe. His entry to the Caribbean through this particular space gave birth to the division of the islands between the Leewards, north of the Dominica Passage, and the Windwards to the south.

On his return to La Navidad, towards the end of November 1493, Columbus found both the fort and Guacanagarí's town burned to the ground. All of the European men were dead. According to Guacanagarí, some had died of disease while others were killed in fights after they seized gold and other goods, and took women into their camp. The others died when a rival cacique, Caonabó, attacked them. Guacanagarí claimed to have attempted to defend the Europeans. Columbus was not convinced by this account but for the next year maintained a fragile peace, contrary to the advice of many in his party. He had already observed pillage, rape, and murder among some of his own as they passed through the Leeward Islands, and had gained a strong sense of the difference between idealized peaceful "Indians" (meaning the Taíno) and warlike, cannibal "Caribs" (the Kalinago). The notion that the Caribbean would continue as some sort of paradise was quickly abandoned as harsh realities and imagined horrors mingled and transformed. Constructing a picture of an Amerindian world that divided the societies between extremes of good and bad behaviour neatly fitted a Christian model of the moral universe and cleared the ground for the justification of European retaliation and forced conversion. A relationship founded on trust and mutual respect was not a possibility.

Columbus' instructions required him to establish a trading-post colony as a royal monopoly. No private trade was allowed and the settlers were paid wages. Columbus himself was declared admiral and entitled to a commission of one tenth of all profits. These arrangements fitted well enough with Columbus' original conception of settlement as limited to the establishment of fortified trading posts designed to tap into existing centres of trade. This was the most he might expect of his hoped-for journey to the coastal ports of Asia and it was a model already applied by the Portuguese on the coast of Africa, where Columbus had, himself, visited. This pattern of peripheral, niche settlement was abandoned only when Columbus found the potential for trade quite different from his expectations, even if he really was on the fringes of Asia as he supposed.

Columbus moved quickly to conceive of a process of island colonization, similar to that practiced by the Portuguese in the Canary Islands, which involved the settlement of European colonists and the introduction of plants and animals that could make such new-found islands profitable commercial enterprises. Existing resources also might be harvested. As well as never giving up hopes of finding gold mines, on his first voyage, Columbus saw groves of pine trees in Cuba that were suited for masts and planking for ships, located close to a place where water could be harnessed to power a sawmill. He also came quickly to the notion that, rather than trading with them, the Taínos of Quisqueya/Haiti were well suited to being put to work for Spanish Catholic colonists. He saw the Taíno as physically strong but timid and easily ordered about. In all of this, Columbus drew directly from the model of colonization he had observed in the Atlantic islands.

Leaving behind the horror of La Navidad, at the end of 1493, Columbus sailed east along the north coast of Hispaniola and found a suitable location for the new settlement he was to build, La Isabela. Laid out to match the coastal geographical features of the site, there were both public buildings – including customhouse and storehouse, magazine for munitions, and church – and thatched houses, together with a plaza and cemetery, all surrounded by a wall made of packed earth rather than stone. But sickness spread quickly among the people, who faced hunger and fatigue. Above all, the settlers failed to adjust to the material and social realities of life in Hispaniola.

Columbus came to believe that successful settlement would require the importation of food for the sick as well as the healthy and, for the longer term, the introduction of a wide variety of plants and domesticated animals. He also came to accept that the fabled gold mines were, indeed, no more than fables, though large nuggets brought from the interior of Hispaniola were sufficient to keep the dream alive. He looked beyond Hispaniola, sailing in April 1494 to resume his exploration of Cuba and, directed by the people inhabiting that island's southern coast, came to Jamaica. He encountered hostile Taínos but found no gold. Overall, it became clear to Columbus that the proposed trading-post model was unlikely to bring great wealth to his royal patrons or himself.

With little moral difficulty, and following the pattern already well-known from the Canary Islands, Columbus adopted the view that in the short term, at least, the only way to extract a certain profit was to enslave and export people, specifically those he labelled (reformed) cannibals. In proof of the viability of this scheme, he sent a small fleet back to Spain in early 1494 under the command of Antonio de Torres to report on the progress of the expedition and replenish supplies and to carry twenty or more people who were to be sold on arrival in Seville. There, Ferdinand and Isabela began to doubt Columbus' skills as a director of colonization and showed no enthusiasm for the enslavement of their new subjects, whatever their moral state. The Taínos, observing the hostile behaviour of the Europeans, feared for the future.

In spite of these misgivings, Columbus pushed ahead with his plan and rapidly took on the role of conqueror while still publicly proclaiming his belief that he had reached the edge of Asia and was on the verge of establishing the great trading hub that would enrich his patrons through commerce. The tipping point came in 1495, when Columbus sent out armed parties, mounted on horses and accompanied by fighting dogs, with the direction that when they encountered hostility they were to take captives, with the belief that such prisoners were casualties of a "just war" and qualified for enslavement. The consequence was that about 1,600 people were made captive across Hispaniola. Of these, some 550 were shipped to Spain and 650 allocated to settlers. When the rest were released, they fled as far as possible from La Isabela in fear of recapture.

Living in close proximity to the Spanish invaders was increasingly seen as not merely unattractive but outright hazardous, even deadly. The population of Hispaniola had already begun to shrink as a consequence of disease and the depredations of the Europeans and their livestock.

As well as bringing priests to the islands, the second voyage of Columbus sought to provide for the cultivation of many plants central to Spanish foodways: wheat, grapevines, chickpeas, melons, olives, stone fruits, onions, and lettuce, for example. Some of the temperate zone plants grew poorly in the tropical environment. Wheat was everywhere a failure within the tropics, and the grapevines and stone fruit trees struggled to survive, whereas the citrus flourished and hybridized to produce varieties and juice sweeter by far than their heritage stock. Sugar cane cuttings loaded in the Canary Islands on the second voyage were to prove transformative in both the short and the long run. An equally heavy and more immediate impact on the land was made by the hooves of large mammals – notably horses, cattle, goats, sheep, and pigs, all relatively high feeders and active dispersers of the seeds of citrus and other fruits.

Of these mammals, only sheep proved unsuccessful in the long term. The pigs and cattle, on the other hand, multiplied rapidly and quickly became feral, roving the islands and trampling the carefully gardened landscape of Taíno cultivation. As early as 1507, the stock of cattle, pigs, and horses was so well established that breeding animals no longer needed to be imported, and feral pigs were so common that licenses were issued for hunting them. For purposes other than providing food, fighting dogs were sent to terrorize the people of the islands and cats to catch rats. The rats, mice, and vermin that found their way to the islands were unintended introductions, coming concealed among the cargo. The swine and horses communicated the first strains of influenza that laid low the early European colonists, already afflicted by dysentery and other stomach complaints.

Relations between the Taínos and the Spanish went from bad to worse, with a pitched battle in the densely populated and richly resourced interior valley of Maguá or La Vega Real, in March 1495, a battle won by Columbus' men. The Taínos had no answer to the guns, armoured cavalry, and fighting dogs of the Spanish. Many of the leaders were taken and burned alive. Guarionex, generally considered the most powerful of the caciques in the Vega Real, was captured. He attempted for an extended period to mediate between the two sides and to satisfy Spanish demands for gold, labour, and food supplies, but later died when placed on a ship bound for Spain that sank in a hurricane off Hispaniola.

To encourage his troops, Columbus established a general system of forced labour in Hispaniola, assigning Taínos to work for the settlers, and constructed a system of forts across the island to protect their ventures. The settler population itself was depleted by death and disease and by escape back to Spain. In addition to the labour requirements, Columbus instituted a tribute system that demanded payment by the Taíno communities in gold, cotton, or spices. Columbus' claim that the island was some sort of paradise was in ruins. So was his claim that the islands would bring great wealth to his patrons. At the same time, the complex societies of the Taínos were approaching a point of collapse.

Leaving his brother Bartolomé in charge of Hispaniola, Columbus returned to Cadiz on 11 June 1496. His authority was under a shadow but he managed to retain the patronage of Ferdinand and Isabela, principally because of the competition they saw arising in their rival, Portugal. Columbus did not return to Hispaniola for another two and a half years. During his absence, Bartolomé captured two of the island's caciques and shipped more people to Europe to be sold as slaves.

Columbus' dream that Hispaniola would prove a great source of gold was not fulfilled. Gold there was, but the Taínos were content to collect nuggets they found in riverbeds and did not mine it. In 1496, a new source of gold was found in the San Cristóbal mountains, in the south of the island. The following year, gold miners skilled in placer techniques were sent from Spain, as well as farmers and vegetable gardeners, and bundles of tools – from hoes, spades, pickaxes, and sledgehammers, to crowbars and millstones. To exploit the new gold mines, a route marked by forts was made across the island, from La Isabela to a newly established port, Santo Domingo. With its superior harbour and fertile agricultural lands, Santo Domingo quickly grew to replace La Isabela, though initially having little more to offer in terms of its architectural mass. Santo Domingo led the way in establishing the rectangular street grid that would provide the model for urban form throughout the Americas. In both of these towns, the first buildings were mainly constructed of wood and thatch, the materials favoured by the Taínos.

In 1497, the *repartimiento* was introduced as a system for the distribution of land. Derived from practice developed as a means of resettling lands taken back from the Muslims in Castile and applied in the colonization of the Canary Islands, the granting of land to independent settlers marked a significant deviation from the original trading-post model. These settlers were required to establish themselves as residents on their grants and to farm or ranch the land for at least 4 years. At the same time, it remained the intention of Ferdinand and Isabela that the number of Spanish settlers in Hispaniola should be kept small – fewer than 1,000 – and that they be salaried, with only a limited amount of open commerce permitted.

In his third voyage, commenced on 30 May 1498, Columbus navigated his most southerly route, to enter the Caribbean through the narrow passage between Trinidad and the South American mainland. Columbus had insufficient information to recognize that he was, in fact, for the first time, in touch with the continent, and in crossing the mouth of the Orinoco he thought only that he must be on the edge of the earthly paradise of holy scripture. The glimpses of continental land he had were interpreted as evidence of even more islands. Cuba remained the best candidate for continental status, still purportedly thought to belong to Asia. When Columbus got to Hispaniola, he found turmoil and strife. In his absence, there had been mutinies, a failure of the tribute system, and continuing hostility to enslavement. The building of the new settlement at Santo Domingo was well underway. Drastic measures taken to clean up this mess led to the execution of rebels among the settlers and, in turn, the arrest of Columbus in October 1500 and his being sent home in chains.

Stripped of his governorship of Hispaniola, Columbus was replaced by Nicolás de Ovando, who sailed with a large fleet in February 1502. The Spanish population of Hispaniola was greatly boosted but still numbered fewer than 3,000. Many of these people died within months of their arrival. Although not permitted to accompany the fleet, Columbus soon after was able to undertake a fourth and final voyage. This time, he entered the Caribbean between St Lucia and Martinique and, against orders, sailed direct from there to Hispaniola. The most important result of this fourth voyage was Columbus' investigation of the isthmus beginning in the north at Honduras, where he encountered large trading canoes, probably coming from Yucatan. He did not attempt to locate their origin and continued south to Panama. He then sailed north to Cuba but was stranded in Jamaica for 8 months – from June 1503 until March 1504. There, some of his crew mutinied and plundered local villages. When the Taínos began to demand more and more for the food desperately needed by the marooned Europeans, Columbus claimed to have put them in awe of his powers – and his ability to intercede with the Christian god – by correctly predicting a lunar eclipse. Although this might seem merely an opportunistic exploitation of scientific knowledge, it fitted neatly with Columbus' vision of himself as Christ's messenger. Eventually rescued, Columbus returned to Spain, where he died 1506, claiming to the last that he had come close to finding a western, Atlantic route to Asia.

The four voyages of Columbus have a central place in Caribbean history but are equally momentous in the context of world history. These voyages provided the stage for the first continuing encounters between the people of the connected continental landmass of Europe, Asia, and Africa, and the people of earth's only other supercontinent, the Americas. Five hundred years earlier, the Vikings of Scandinavia had found their way along the islands of the far north Atlantic to the fringe of North America but, by the time of Columbus, these ephemeral contacts were remembered only in myth and saga. Further, although it is true that the peoples of the Americas were children of ancient migrations from Asia, and that all human beings have their roots in even more ancient migrations from an original home in Africa, it is just as true that the societies – and the natural environments – of these two great units developed independently and uniquely. This is why the process of exchange that followed Columbus was so fundamental to the shaping of the modern world.

It is equally significant, for the world as well as the Caribbean, that Columbus found his way first to the islands, which might look easy to miss, rather than hitting the massive target offered by the coastline of the continents that stretches almost from pole to pole. Had Columbus been driven off his initial projected course by contrary winds or currents, he could have found himself on the banks of the Potomac or at Yucatan or Brazil. By the time of Columbus' death in 1506, Europeans had, indeed, found their way north to Labrador and Newfoundland and south to Brazil. However, the encounters between Amerindians and Europeans that occurred in the Caribbean came first and established patterns that proved both enduring and disastrous. What came much closer to happening in 1492 was a landfall on the Florida coast, somewhere south of Daytona Beach – the point Columbus would have reached if he had held to his course due west from the Canary Islands. He maintained this line steadily until he was in the longitude of Puerto Rico but then veered south, seduced by false sightings of land and flights of birds, and drawn towards the sun and the wonders of that unknown otherworld – the tropics. Had Columbus landed at any of these plausible alternatives, the Caribbean may have remained relatively neglected much longer. The reality was fateful for the island populations.

Columbus returned again and again to the islands, partly because he could be certain of what he would find and had no way of knowing what he was missing to the north and the south, but also because he was directed to do so. As early as 1479, Spanish and Portuguese monarchs had negotiated an agreement that the Portuguese should have a claim to lands found south of the Canary Islands. In 1493, Ferdinand and Isabela sought authorization from the pope, as head of the Catholic Church, in granting Castile sovereignty over all lands found in the region explored by Columbus. The following year, Portugal and Castile signed the Treaty of Tordesillas, which gave Portugal rights to the east and Castile to the west of an agreed line running through the Atlantic from north to south. This was an abstract division but the outcome, from an arrogant European geopolitical point of view, was that Portugal had claim not only to Africa and the route to India but also to Brazil, whereas the kingdom of Castile could consider itself the rightful imperial power for almost the entire Americas. Although the treaty did not confine Columbus' future designs on the islands, his preoccupation persisted.

Not only was the Caribbean the testing ground for models of tropical colonization, the islands served also as a staging post for the Spanish-American empire. Hispaniola, the island first invaded and colonized, was the origin of most new ventures into the other islands and the mainland. Puerto Rico came first, in 1508, and was quickly followed by Jamaica (1509) and Cuba (1511). The occupation of these islands typically followed fierce but short-lived resistance from the Taínos. Particularly in the case of Puerto Rico, chroniclers commonly attributed the strong resistance met by the Spanish to *caribes* from the eastern islands. Increasingly, the Spanish came to identify and define as *caribes* all those groups who opposed their advance and to equate this resistance with wildness and the eating of human flesh.

Only after the colonization of these islands did Spain move on to the mainland: Florida, Mexico, Panama, Cartagena, and, in the 1530s, Peru. Spanish colonization radiated through the western Caribbean and through the isthmus, moving north and south and, in consequence, focussed initially on the Pacific coast. Only later did the Spanish begin to show interest in the Atlantic shores of the Americas and, as a result, these vast regions had a very different colonial experience.

Even after the Spanish had established themselves firmly as conquerors on the mainland, they exhibited no real interest in attempting to invade and colonize the Lesser Antilles. Puerto Rico came to represent an eastern frontier, beyond which the Spanish chose not to venture. No doubt this failure or neglect had something to do with the picture that had been built up of the *caribe* as savage and cannibal, but the task of annihilating the people of the eastern Caribbean must have seemed no greater challenge than doing so on the mainland. It is likely the resources of these islands were regarded by the Spanish as simply not worth the trouble when compared with the riches that beckoned to the west. The consequence of this neglect was that the eastern islands became refuges for any Amerindians who could find their way there. The survival chances of these populations remained relatively good through the sixteenth century.

It was in the complex societies of the Taínos of the Greater Antilles that the immediate impact of European invasion and colonization was felt most heavily. Because island populations are especially vulnerable to introduced hazards – notably epidemic disease – the immediate consequences of the encounter were particularly dire. All of this gives immense weight to the character of the first encounters between Columbus and the Taínos on the shores of the Caribbean islands.

TAÍNO RESPONSE

Why did the Taínos not kill the Europeans when they first set foot on Caribbean sand? With knowledge of the outcome of their encounter, this can been seen as a rational and, indeed, moral action. It was the response the Skraelings showed the Vikings and, in fact, the Taínos were not slow to kill the men of La Navidad when they transgressed the rules of exchange. Their very first response, however, without the benefit of hindsight, was one of pure wonder and amazement. The Europeans and their ships were impossible to place in the continuum of life and death, natural and supernatural. Their numbers were few and their presence brief, almost dreamlike. Simple incomprehension played its part. At first, it was not obvious that the actions of the Europeans were hostile or exploitative or that they came with evil intent. There were good reasons for the Taínos to interpret the behaviour of the Europeans in this benign way and Columbus himself did not know exactly where he was or what he was doing there. In the context of honest courtesy and unalloyed wonderment, it is easy enough to see why the Taínos did not seize the initial advantage to defeat the invaders. In any case, for such a response to have been successful, a carefully planned attack would have been essential. A spontaneous rush at the Europeans would simply have encouraged Columbus to use his superior firepower even more quickly than he did. It was an unequal match.

However, the Taínos did not accept their fate as inevitable. As soon as they had the opportunity, one way or another, they killed the Europeans left by Columbus at La Navidad. Nor was the building of its replacement, La Isabela, tolerated passively. In much the same way as had occurred before, parties sent out from the new settlement to seek gold helped themselves to much more and, in retaliation, were ambushed and killed. As well as such individual reaction, the caciques of Hispaniola, by the end of 1494, had joined in an alliance to resist the colonists. They were led by Caonabó, the supposed destroyer of La Navidad, though Guacanagarí strategically distanced himself from this coalition. When Columbus ordered forts be built beyond La Isabela, the men posted were sometimes massacred in large numbers. His response was to make a show of force in a punitive expedition, mounted in early 1495. The Taínos were not afraid to engage the Europeans in pitched battle, but they did not prevail and the outcome was the first open enslavement of the native peoples.

When, soon after, Caonabó was captured and sent to La Isabela in chains, the coalition of caciques prepared a major assault on the settlement. However, joining with Guacanagarí and his allies, Columbus managed to thwart this attack and the slaughter and enslavement that ensued effectively put an end to the capacity of the Taínos to attempt any further action on such a scale. The remaining caciques were either killed or unable to respond aggressively. On top of this defeat, the years 1495 and 1496 were marked by famine, perhaps caused in part by the Taínos destroying their crops in order to thwart the Spanish or, alternatively, resulting from the inherent vulnerability of the conuco system of agriculture. Increased labour demands, disease, and disruption all contributed to a rapid depletion of the population.

Central to the extraction of labour was the *encomienda*, a Spanish-American institution linked from the beginning with the *repartimiento*, in which grants of land were associated with rights to the labour and allegiance of groups of people and their caciques. The supposed benefit for the people was their introduction to the Christian religion and, even less obviously, the refinements of European civilization. Unlike the *encomienda* of medieval Spain, which saw the assignment of Moorish villages to members of the military orders, the New World version carried with it no allocation of land or rents but was simply the assignment of people to an individual *encomendero* for the purposes of compulsory labour.

The Taíno found it difficult to comprehend the Christianity that Columbus hoped would bring salvation, not so much because the behaviour of the Christian Spanish seemed to contradict the notion of a gracious God, but more directly because its separation of humankind, nature, and the spirit world challenged the fundamentals of their cosmology. On the other hand, the Taínos had no difficulty in accommodating at least some of the elements of Catholic ritual and worship. They saw the idols and icons of the church as no different in quality to the *cemís* they had long venerated and accepted them into the pantheon as potentially valuable channels to the gods of nature. Thus, for example, the Taínos thought it appropriate to bury Christian statues in their cassava fields and to urinate on such icons, just as they had done with their *cemís* in order to ensure fertility.

In spite of the swiftness of the Spanish impact, at the end of the fifteenth century, only some regions of Hispaniola were under Spanish government and the *repartimiento*. Several of the caciques retained authority in their realms but they were not allowed to live in peace for long. In 1501, in response to the enslavement of the Taínos under Columbus, Ferdinand and Isabela renewed their directive that the people should be regarded as crown vassals rather than slaves, thus providing a legal basis for an *encomienda* system controlled by officials. The intention was to put authority in the hands of government, a useful tool in controlling the settler–colonists and giving favours to persons of high rank. At the same time, the crown sought to locate the Taínos in towns close to gold mines and to promote conversion. When the Taínos resisted these measures and fled to mountain refuges, the crown attempted a stronger version of compulsion in which their labour was to be extracted through control imposed by the caciques. The hierarchical society assisted in the implementation of this system, given that the existing class of *naborías* had learned that they owed labour to the caciques. Pressure was also applied to the caciques to accept Spanish rule but most resisted.

A brutal military campaign carried out in 1503 and 1504 wiped out many villages and caciques – including the *cacica* Anacaona – and their subordinate allies were brutally murdered, often by means of duplicity and deception. It was this campaign that effectively destroyed the polities of the Taínos and placed all the people who could be rounded up under assignment to individual European settlers and forced to build towns. The crown's intention was to establish civilization through urban life – in 15 prescribed towns, ruled by their own *cabildos* or town councils – rather than permitting scattered, ungovernable settlement, but the outcome was a distinctive island lifestyle, quite different from that attempted at La Isabela.

By 1508, only those Taínos who had fled to the hills and maintained a rearguard resistance remained outside the sphere of Spanish control. The complex societies constructed by the Taínos had been destroyed, their system of government demolished. They lost their claim to the land. Those who still lived were effectively the property of individual Spanish colonists, and the numbers of the Taíno diminished catastrophically, as the settlers competed aggressively for the dwindling supply of labour that was the sole basis of their relative prosperity. It was a race to the bottom.

Gold mining peaked around 1508 and gave way to ranching and agriculture, including sugar. The demand for labour in Hispaniola, together with the rapid shrinking of the Taíno population, helped impel the Spanish to begin their expansion into other Caribbean islands. This process was encouraged by the permission granted by the crown in 1509 for the enslavement and forced movement of the people of the Bahamas – the Lucayans – to other islands, notably Hispaniola. Raids were also made on Florida and the coast of Yucatan in order to replace the population of Cuba when it, too, suffered demographic collapse. The result was the rapid depopulation of the Bahamas, within a decade of the beginning of the plan. Barbados and several other islands were depopulated in the same manner. Raids extended as far south as Trinidad. On the other hand, by 1515, the Spanish population of the 15 towns established in Hispaniola in 1505 had grown to about 5,000, with a proportion of women and children. As the Spanish population grew and became more productive, trade expanded and the crown was able to extract an income from duties on imports, with tithes and taxes on gold dwindling.

Some of the most successful survivors of the encounter were those Taínos who were able to maintain an existence in the mountain refuges of Hispaniola. There they were joined by native people from other Caribbean islands who had been enslaved and imported and by enslaved Africans. Known as cimarrones – the original Maroons – these fugitives attacked Spanish settlements. The most successful of these bands were led by the caciques Enriquillo, who had been educated by friars, and Tamayo. Together, they opposed the Spanish in a war centred in the Barauco Mountains, in the south, from 1519 to 1533. As was to prove the case many times over, the guerrilla tactics of the cimarrones proved effective and, in 1533, the Spanish signed a treaty with Enriquillo, by which he agreed to cease hostilities in return for freedom and a grant of land.

In spite of the demographic crisis, archaeological evidence suggests that some social groups among the Taíno lived through the first decades of contact without making major concessions in their way of life or household organization. Those best equipped to resist changes to their social practice were women and elite men. The success of these people reflects, on the one hand, the hierarchical character of Taíno society and, on the other, the relative lack of specialization in gender roles. Inequalities in wealth and living conditions persisted among the Taíno after contact. The ones to suffer most directly were men who did not belong to the elite, largely because the commitment of labour through the *encomienda* was their particular burden. The caciques organized these labour drafts. Women and elite men (and probably their kin) were spared the heaviest of these demands and thus had the capacity to continue living much as they had before, in the same kinds of houses and eating the same kinds of food. Indeed, it seems that because of the lack of strongly defined gender roles, women may have taken up the slack and performed tasks previously associated with men, such as making tools from stone, bone, and shell; hunting; and fishing.

Ritual performance, strongly associated with the elite – both men and women – also continued well into the sixteenth century. Further, it appears from the archaeological record that, among the households that survived relatively intact, there was active rejection of, or lack of interest in, the adoption of European material culture. The European colonial households of early Hispaniola, however, showed a readiness to incorporate the new culture they found on the island, particularly in the female domain of pottery making and food preparation.

Alongside active, aggressive resistance, and more passive forms of resistance to adaptation, there is also evidence of integration in the relations of Taíno and European in sixteenth-century Hispaniola. The towns that developed across the island after 1505 were laid out according to the rectilinear plan favoured by the Spanish and built of brick and stone rather than the traditional straw, thatch, and mud, but at the same time they also incorporated many features associated with the Taínos. Contrasted with the earliest settlements, such as La Isabela, which had been overwhelmingly dominated by men, these new towns had substantial proportions of women and children, and a good number of these were Taíno. As a result, methods of food preparation showed a mixing of cultures and ingredients. Whereas the meat of mammals entered the diet, so did the meat of turtle and manatee, along with cassava and corn. Europeans quickly came to appreciate the pleasures of the hammock and of tobacco smoking.

In addition to these exchanges of material culture, and in spite of the brutality displayed by the Spanish towards the Taínos, intermarriage occurred and proved a vital means of accommodation. Even before being formally sanctioned by church and state in 1514, such marriages were common. It was, however, a one-sided relationship. European men married Taíno cacicas, nitaínos, and other elite women, seeking by this means to validate their claims to land, labour, and tribute. The lack of European women who might have married caciques in the earliest stages of the encounter might seem sufficient explanation of this imbalance, but even when white women were more plentiful, the pattern remained the same. Outside marriage, many Spanish men lived informally with Taíno women. The children born of these relationships quickly formed a substantial mestizo population. Raised by their mothers, these children learned what they could of Taíno culture and language. This new generation played a central role in the emerging creole community and the interaction between their parents provided a model for the society of Spanish-America that affected many aspects of social development. New people and new communities were born.

As early as the middle of the sixteenth century, the social and material patterns of life typical of households and communities in the Caribbean matched neither those established in the complex societies of the Taínos nor those of peninsular Spain. Increasingly, too, the culture came to incorporate elements from Africa. This was not an outcome intended by Spain, but almost any strong concept of intention or planning had necessarily been surrendered along with Columbus' failure to find his way to the hinterland of the commercial mart of Asia. With the fulcrum of the Spanish imperial project relocated to the mainland, Hispaniola and the Greater Antilles generally entered a period in which a new variety of relative isolation enabled the development of a unique species of creole society and a unique understanding of identities.

All of these forms of resistance, adaptation, and accommodation occurred within the context of a demographic crisis. The choices made by the Taíno must be seen in the light of this disaster, as attempts to survive somehow or other in the midst of a holocaust. As well as the open slaughter, the extreme labour demands, and the destruction of food resources, the peoples of the Caribbean suffered heavily when first exposed to diseases endemic in Europe and Africa but unknown in the Americas. The most deadly was smallpox, but influenza, measles, malaria, yellow fever, typhus, and the bubonic plague also took a heavy toll. The isolation and inevitable lack of immunity that characterized the Caribbean populations made them particularly vulnerable.

The decline of Hispaniola's population was catastrophic. The greatest part of this decline occurred within the first few years of the encounter with Europeans, with the years 1496 and 1497 probably the worst. In this short period, the population of Hispaniola was almost halved each year. The rate of decline then slowed but the result was equally catastrophic. In 1508, only 60,000 Taíno were counted in Hispaniola; in 1514, some 30,000; and in 1518, just 11,000 survived. Not all of these people had been born in the island; perhaps one-third had been brought there as slaves from other islands and even the mainland. The same was true in Puerto Rico and Cuba. Protests led by religious leaders, beginning in 1512, resulted in reform of the labour demands and helped slow the decline, but came too late to prevent the downward spiral. In 1518 and 1519, epidemics of smallpox and other diseases killed large numbers in Hispaniola. By 1570, only a few hundred Taínos remained in the island. Whatever the true number of people at the beginning of 1492, the speed and depth of the population collapse was probably greater in Hispaniola than anywhere else. Whatever the intentions of the Europeans – whether or not they consciously set out to annihilate the population of Hispaniola – genocide was the outcome.

The pattern established in Hispaniola was repeated in the other Taíno populations of the Greater Antilles. In Jamaica, no attempt was made to convert the people. They were simply put to work to produce food supplies and weave hammocks and cloth for the Spanish. The depopulation of the island proceeded rapidly and was nearly complete as early as 1520. Here and elsewhere the depopulation was almost absolute, the new immigrant people taking a very long time to make up the deficit.

The decimation of the original population of Hispaniola as well as its neighbours, together with the slow and unsteady growth of the Spanish settler community, was quickly followed by the inauguration of trade in enslaved Africans across the Atlantic. The enthusiasm shown for this long-distance trade in people may seem at first an improbable response on the part of the Europeans. Why did it appear profitable to engage in such a long-distance and intricate enterprise? Why was it not more attractive to the Spanish colonists to seek more people on the American mainland or, alternatively, to force migration from Europe? Why were extreme forms of forced labour seen as such a necessity by the European invaders?

Enslaved Africans were part of the colonization of Hispaniola from its early stages. The first arrived around 1500, sent by Ferdinand to work on the construction of forts and others soon came as miners. All of these African men came on ships from Spain. In spite of the pleas of Bartolomé de las Casas, who renounced his *encomienda* in 1514 in order to defend the Taínos from maltreatment, that the fate of the Africans should not be the same, numbers increased steadily as the demographic collapse of the native population continued unabated. Down to 1550, more Spanish and Portuguese migrants crossed the Atlantic than Africans but the balance then shifted. By the middle of the sixteenth century, the population of enslaved Africans in Hispaniola was perhaps 30,000. Rather than saving the Taínos from decimation, the Africans became simply a replacement population and their numbers did no more than replenish a small proportion of those who had lived in the islands before 1492.

Whereas the enslavement of the Taínos was opposed because, in legal theory, they were subjects of the Christian state of Castile, the enslavement of Africans was justified on the grounds that papal pronouncements had denied Spain territory in Africa and the state therefore had no obligations to the people of that continent. This relationship applied to many other peoples, of course, including most of Europe. In the early modern period, the justification of enslaving Africans but not Greeks, for example, had something to do with the fact that the Africans were not Christians but rather heathens, infidels, and Muslims. However, difference of belief was not sufficient in itself to justify enslavement in the European mind, and the Spanish actively sought to convert enslaved Africans once they were in the Caribbean, without any thought that conversion required liberation.

Beyond these perceived differences of religion and citizenship lay hierarchical notions of human diversity, which, in the European mind, placed Africans lower in the so-called great chain of being that stretched from the inanimate to the angels, with human beings somewhere in the middle of the continuum. There was not in this period a well-defined concept of "race" – this did not emerge until the eighteenth century – but Europeans did relate assessments of the humanity of different peoples to perceptions of physical features. Increasingly, the people considered by Europeans as eligible for enslavement – perhaps even deserving of it – were defined as "outsiders" not simply in terms of their statehood or religion but in terms of their physical characteristics.

The European discovery of the Taínos had disturbed some of these ideas, because it became necessary to try to explain why these people had been allowed by God to live so long without knowledge of his truths. They were pagans rather than infidels because they had never had the opportunity to accept or reject the true faith, and therefore were not theologically candidates for condemnation to slavery. The question was more difficult when related to Africans, some of whom, in ancient times, had the potential for such knowledge and had, indeed, in some cases embraced Christianity.

An alternative interpretation was that Africans were black because God had made them that way in order to announce their moral failure and their inferiority. These were ideas that helped Europeans live comfortably with the notion that whereas slavery had largely disappeared from Europe, the institution might still have a place in Africa and the Americas, and that the enslavement of Africans did not transgress religious and moral norms.

Running parallel to these ideas and their development were the more concrete matters of epidemiology and economics. The Taínos were well adjusted to the disease environment in which they lived and, as long as they remained isolated from the diseases of other peoples, they could flourish and live healthy lives. The arrival of Europeans and their commensal animals – including a host of carriers of disease – shifted this balance dramatically and, together with the brutal treatment received from the Spanish, led to their demographic collapse. When taken to Europe, the Taínos did little better. The Europeans, too, in coming to the Caribbean, entered a strange disease environment, a tropical world with its own range of deadly vectors, such as the mosquito. Africans had a different experience, encountering in the Caribbean an environment more similar to that of their homelands. Thus, there quickly emerged in the European mind the stereotype of the black African as an effective survivor in the Caribbean and a strong worker.

These perceptions of health and strength were underpinned by the rapid development of the trade in enslaved people from the forts of European merchants established along the coast of West Africa. Initially, this trade in enslaved people was merely a minor part of a trade in commodities such as gold, pepper, and gum arabic, and this is why the enslaved people were sent north to Spain before being shipped to the Caribbean. The slave trade across the Atlantic, direct from Africa to the Americas, was inaugurated in 1518, when the first shipment of enslaved people reached Hispaniola. In the sixteenth century, there were also attempts by some African rulers to stop the trade or limit the flow of people from the interior to the forts. However, although the surge in demand for enslaved labourers came only after the wide-scale establishment of plantation systems in the Americas, the sixteenth-century beginnings set the pattern that was to persist for another 300 years. Cassava and maize travelled in the opposite direction, transferred to West Africa, where they quickly regained their status as voyaging foods. This time, they served the cause of the trade in people, joining African yams in providing food for the middle passage.

Being a trade, the forced migration of Africans was governed above all by cost and price. It depended on the supply of people to the trading forts in Africa and this flow, in turn, was determined by internal politics and patterns of local warfare that affected the numbers delivered and their price. The existence of the trade was influential, however, in encouraging the hierarchical development of West African societies and in separating subordinate "slave" statuses from systems of kinship and household economy. The development of the slave trade depended also on the integration of shipping into the larger pattern of European trade with the Caribbean and mainland America, and the existence of a merchant class in the islands. Above all, the trade in African people across the Atlantic depended on the presence of a class of proprietors with potentially profitable enterprises that were sufficiently productive to enable paying the price of buying people.

The sixteenth-century Caribbean possessed some of these characteristics but, particularly after about 1520 when the Taíno population had been drastically reduced and the golden riches of the mainland frontier beckoned, demand remained limited or suppressed and the islands came to be seen as something of an economic backwater. In addition to this limitation of demand, the supply of enslaved people from Africa to the Spanish empire faced political difficulties. Because the Spanish had no significant bases or forts on the coast of Africa in consequence of the Treaty of Tordesillas of 1494, they depended on other states to supply them with enslaved labourers. This was achieved through a series of contracts known as the *asiento de negroes* that, beginning in 1518, permitted private individuals to bring fixed numbers of enslaved people direct from Africa in return for payment of a substantial fee into the royal treasury. The asiento system was intended to circumvent smuggling into the Spanish colonies but, in practice, it often had the opposite effect, providing a conduit for illicit commodities carried on the same ships.

A SECOND SIXTEENTH CENTURY

Chronologies of Caribbean history often refer to a "long sixteenth century", stretching all the way from 1492 to 1650. European history can be attributed a similar experience, with 1492 marking not only the commencement of the Columbian exchange but also the reconquest of Spain and the expulsion of the Muslims and the Jews, or an even longer sixteenth century, spanning the years from 1450 to 1650 (with 1453 marking the fall of Constantinople). Alternatively, a "second sixteenth century" stretching from 1550 to 1650 can be conceived for European history, a period that saw the twilight of the Mediterranean and the shift of capitalist accumulation and economic power to northwestern Europe, as well as the division of Europe between Catholic and Protestant.

The notion of a second sixteenth century also makes good sense for the Caribbean, but with its beginning dated to 1530 and its end 1630. This century comprehends the period in which the islands remained relatively and often increasingly depopulated, in which the demographic balance shifted from Amerindian peoples to people of European and African descent, together with their mestizo and mulatto offspring, and in which the Spanish claimed title to all Caribbean land but did little to develop or exploit the potential resources. The enslavement of Taínos was officially banned in 1530, though people designated "Caribs" could still be enslaved and imported into the Greater Antilles. The end of this period was signalled by the bankruptcy of the Castilian throne in 1627, and its loss of control of the Hapsburg empire. Although Western Europe looked towards the Atlantic, attention was divided between a growing interest in the Americas and a concurrent concern for maritime ventures to the east. The islands of the Caribbean had no prominent role. Thus, the hundred years from 1530 to 1630 represented a hiatus, falling between the dramatic encounters and devastation of the period 1492 to 1530 and the intense competition for Caribbean territory and the radical transformation of economy and society that marked the period 1630 to 1680. In this second sixteenth century, the islands experienced a growing integration into the developing world system and, at the same time, a new kind of isolation, in which the currents and eddies of change washed around them while the real centre of action was known to have moved to new frontiers.

Whereas Santo Domingo served for a generation as the centre of administration for the whole of Spanish America and as its maritime gateway, the second sixteenth century belonged to Havana. For a brief period, Cuba and Hispaniola together were the vital logistical staging posts in Spain's expansion into the mainland, but although Santo Domingo became the seat of the audiencia of Santo Domingo in 1529, the city rapidly fell behind as a navigational and commercial centre. By the 1530s, the Greater Antilles already seemed to lack a purpose within the grander scheme of empire. The Spanish population of the islands, which had gradually built up at the same time as the indigenous population declined, moved on as each new continental frontier opened up, leaving in its wake a second depopulation. The principal exception was Havana, which grew rapidly in population and strategic importance well into the seventeenth century.

Founded in 1519, Havana was provided with a special opportunity by the shifting fulcrum of the Spanish empire and its emerging network of communications and trade. This new role derived directly from the geographical advantages of the port, placed as it was at the starting point for silver fleets returning to Spain from Mexico, which increasingly sailed through the Straits of Florida, riding the Gulf Stream. Havana serviced their needs for fresh water and food and came to be an important maritime centre. The strategic role of Havana made Cuba important in the Spanish imperial project. The island had little else to offer. Gold production had shrunk to almost nothing by the end of the 1530s, having peaked as early as 1519. Between 1520 and 1540, roughly 80 percent of the Spanish population left Cuba for more golden pastures. With its population mainly gone and no viable export commodity on the horizon, Cuba seemed faced with abandonment or territorial surrender. It could produce food and livestock but had no hope of competing with the fertile fields of Mexico and the isthmus. In order to hold on to Cuba, the *encomienda* system was permitted to continue until 1553, beyond its scheduled abolition in the islands. Rights to labour were made hereditary and, acknowledging realities of *criollo* culture, were allowed to include illegitimate heirs. Much of the labour performed in agriculture, construction, and manufacturing was shouldered by the remnants of the Taínos well into the sixteenth century, though the balance shifted definitively to enslaved Africans by its end.

The growth of Havana and its transient maritime market created a thriving agricultural hinterland surrounding the port city. Essentially, this was a provisioning system rather than an economy in which shipping was drawn to the port in order to carry away its valuable commodities, but it had many ramifications and many possibilities for the encouragement of further growth. Small-scale sugar mills needed pottery moulds to cure their sugar, resulting in the establishment of specialized potteries on the fringes of Havana, whereas others made tiles and bricks for the building trades. Foundries were also vital. In addition to the assault on the surrounding forest that followed the spread of agriculture, the hinterland's timber resources were exposed to the demands of construction and shipbuilding. Before 1519, in the period during which the focus of Spanish exploration and colonization was fixed firmly on the islands, local shipbuilding quickly emerged in response to demand for vessels to engage in trade within the Caribbean, as well as raiding the islands and mainland for people who might be enslaved and brought to the Greater Antilles. By the beginning of the seventeenth century, Havana was by far the largest shipbuilder in the Caribbean and among the most important in the Atlantic world. One of its great selling points was the high quality of the hardwoods available in Cuba's forests.

Although Havana's commerce was heavily oriented to the ocean routes that linked mainland America with Spain, the port also had significant intercolonial trade within the Caribbean. It distributed cloth, wine, oils, and spices, but more importantly received provisions such as cassava bread, salt meat, and corn meal from Jamaica. The concentration of wealth and shipping that resulted soon came to make Havana an attractive target for marauders, and this in turn led to substantial capital investment in fortifications and shipyards, paid for from the imperial purse, and attempts to build up the population – both slave and free. The governor lived there from 1553, rather than in Santiago, the island's capital. By the beginning of the seventeenth century, Havana was almost impregnable.

It took many years for Havana to assert its demographic dominance, however, and, as late as the 1570s, it placed second to the inland, southern town of Bayamo, which benefited by its location in the fertile valley of the Cauto River. Bayamo had both easy access to the sea and a naturally defended site that was to prove an ideal setting for contraband trade with European venturers other than Spanish traders. The separate, illegal economy of the eastern end of the island developed so strongly that in 1607, a second governor was appointed, based in Santiago, and this town then flourished on royal resources and came to displace Bayamo. Only after 1570 did Havana experience really rapid growth. For a time, its population grew more rapidly than that of any other city in the Americas and by 1620 it had danced up the scale to become the ninth largest city in the Spanish-American realm. Havana, with a population of more than 12,000, at that time was by far the largest city in the Caribbean.

Enslaved Africans became a large proportion of the population of Cuba, making up almost one half of the total by 1620. The forced migration from Africa was facilitated by the union of the crowns of Spain and Portugal in 1580, which also enabled a rapid growth in the Portuguese – and hence the Jewish – population of Cuba. As well as the enslaved people who were brought direct from Africa, others were traded from neighbouring islands. For all of these enslaved people, whatever their origins, exposure to Christianity and the Catholic church was common. Baptism was relatively usual, as were Catholic death rituals, and marriage, a church ceremony, was available to enslaved Christian people. However, although these ceremonies and celebrations were intended to accommodate both free and enslaved Africans in the social functions of Christianity, the opportunities created by church-directed religious fraternities and brotherhoods served equally to maintain the cultural memory of their particular nations within Africa.

In view of the great – and seemingly unfulfilled – demand for enslaved people, the rate of manumission in sixteenth-century Cuba was remarkably high. In this legal practice, a person might be freed by their owner or by payment of an agreed amount. Some enslaved people accumulated enough to purchase their own freedom and that of their families, while others were manumitted by their owners without the requirement of payment. In Cuba, *criollos*, in particular, had a good chance of gaining their freedom and often at an early age. This apparent tolerance developed in parallel with a persistent attempt on the part of the ruling white elite to establish a rigid hierarchy founded in colour gradations. These patterns were not confined to Havana but had their most precise expression there.

For Cuba at large, the consequence of Havana's growth was a shift of population and capital away from the island's southern coast and away from rural activities. Apart from their illegal activities, the smaller coastal towns engaged in trade with Havana, sending there local products such as provisions, animals, hides, and tallow, and high-value woods such as ebony. Most of these commodities were produced by the numerous *hatos* or cattle ranches sprinkled across the island. These units operated flexibly, in response to the feral qualities of the livestock herds and the lack of secure tenure. In Cuba, livestock grants made to grantees in the sixteenth century were often circular, with vaguely defined unfenced boundaries that did not pack together tightly. The notion of space entailed was, in fact, not unlike that attributed to the caciques, whose realms had clear spatial centres of power but lacked fixed/defined boundaries marked on the ground.

Hispaniola's second sixteenth century was rather different from that of Cuba. Lacking the advantages of geographical location possessed by Havana, as early as the 1510s, Hispaniola found itself isolated from the centre of imperial commerce. However, Hispaniola had yielded much more gold than Cuba and this provided capital for investment in local enterprise. The model of the Canary Islands remained important, as it had been for Columbus, and resulted in the establishment of a sugar industry, the first in the Caribbean, long before it came to Cuba. Combining local capital and the skills of men brought from the Canary Islands, a mill was built in southern Hispaniola as early as 1516. The industry was encouraged by privileges and immunities given by the crown to the sugar makers in 1529 and 1534. By then there were more than 30 mills working, scattered around the island but generally in the vicinity of ports, notably Santo Domingo. The sugar mills became the major source of demand for the labour of enslaved Africans and they emerged as the earliest examples of plantation slavery in the Caribbean. Some employed hundreds of enslaved people. Sugar production and the number of enslaved Africans increased steadily and, in tandem, reached their maximums in the third quarter of the sixteenth century. Production peaked in 1570 and then declined dramatically, because competition from Brazil depressed prices in the European market and because planters realized greater profits from ginger (a more convenient commodity in contraband trades) and switched their fields to this crop.

The failure of sugar in Hispaniola saw the island return to its cattle economy. This was not a market for meat or draft animals, but one based on the export of hides. The island had a ranched herd of more than 400,000 in the middle of the sixteenth century, as well as large numbers of feral cattle. In the 1580s, about 50,000 hides were exported each year. Otherwise, there was little to ship apart from small amounts of cotton and ginger. For the local population, however, meat became extraordinarily cheap, establishing a long-standing high level of consumption within the island. This was completely different from the balance in the Taíno's diet but, on the other hand, the plant foods of the Taínos – the cassava, vegetables, and luscious fruits of the island – were readily embraced by the Europeans. The lack of enthusiasm for maize persisted for a long time. The abundance of food resources in Hispaniola, however, was simply the other side of the demographic coin. The population was at its lowest point in the late sixteenth century, totalling only 20,000 in the 1580s. Enslaved African people were a large majority, with the Taínos reduced to fewer than 1,000 and the free settler population – whites, mestizos, and mulattos – not much more than double that number. No wonder these few ate well. Bleached bones covered the land.

Puerto Rico and Jamaica had second sixteenth centuries parallel to the experience of Hispaniola. After early experiments with sugar in Jamaica, the island was effectively depopulated, the people replaced by feral herds of cattle and pigs. Jamaica was a productive contributor of provisions but supported only a tiny population, with adult Spanish said to number a mere 500 in 1611. Puerto Rico suffered the same depopulation (starting in 1530 with fewer than 2,000 Amerindians, the majority of them enslaved), tried sugar with success and exported substantial quantities of hides and some

ginger, but by the late sixteenth century became an almost forg
ten element in the Spanish empire, supporting only a few thousan.
people. The Bahamas lay decimated, almost completely empty o.
people. Throughout the Greater Antilles, by the end of the sixteenth century, the complex societies of the Taínos ceased to have
an effective presence in the landscape and had not been replaced
by any substantial new cultures. It was within this landscape that
Havana stood out. It had no real rivals.

In the eastern Caribbean – the Lesser Antilles – the situation was
somewhat different. These islands had been largely neglected by
the Spanish, except for the raids that carried people away to die
elsewhere, and it may be that the spread of disease was muted. The
Spanish had a firm foothold in few of these places. The villages of the
Kalinago were small relative to those of the Taínos, more widely
scattered and more independent, giving them some advantage in
the face of epidemic disease. Partly because of the less devastating
impact of disease and slaughter, and partly because of the flight
of people from the islands most vulnerable to raids, the mountainous, thickly forested islands stretching from Grenada north to
Guadeloupe maintained relatively dense populations into the seventeenth century. The isolation of these islands and their compara-
tively strong demographic survival had interesting, sometimes paradoxical, consequences.

Whereas the Taínos of Hispaniola showed little interest in adopting the plants and animals or the tools and techniques of the Spanish,
the Kalinago picked and chose whatever seemed functional. They
were quick to see the advantages of iron axes for felling trees and
hatchets for hacking out the trunks to fashion large canoes, and
equally quick to add sails to them. These large, fast vessels gave the
Kalinago an advantage in carrying out their own raiding and trading. Iron fishhooks, knives, cooking pots, griddles, and weapons
also proved attractive. Sugar cane and pigeon peas, pigs, and chickens all entered the Kalinago economy, though cassava, the supreme
voyaging food, retained its central role. Compared with the relative gender equality of the Taínos, the Kalinago lived in male,
warrior-dominated societies. They took prisoners – Spanish, Taíno,
and African, particularly women and children – and learned from
them, soon developing a dialect. The mingling of genetic heritage

d the foundation for the "Black Carib" communities that became ominent later in the seventeenth century and helped ensure the survival of the people in the long term. The Kalinago stoutly resisted Christianity.

Although outside the sphere of the Kalinago, the island of Trinidad had a similar sixteenth century. Its people suffered by disease and by raids from the north, carried out by both Spanish and Kalinago, but remained numerous down to the end of the century, when they numbered perhaps 20,000. This was a population reduced by roughly one half over the century – a demographic disaster that appears less catastrophic than it might have been only because the experience elsewhere was so much worse. Many people escaped these ravages by retreating into the thickly forested uplands and the interior. Much more than in the Greater Antilles, the people of Trinidad were able to preserve their agricultural systems, partly because they persistently killed the horses and cattle placed on the island by the Spanish down to the 1570s and the land was free of feral herds. Trinidad was not effectively colonized by the Spanish until 1592, when it was conceived as a base for expeditions to El Dorado, the fabled place of riches. The population declined more rapidly in consequence.

A voracious consumer of people in the sixteenth century was pearl fishing. Although not thought of as possible sites for El Dorado, islands off the mainland shore of South America, notably Cubagua and Margarita, were found to have rich pearl beds. Enslaved men were forced by the Spanish to dive for the pearls, in a cruel business that consumed the lives of the divers and quickly exhausted the resource. As many as 40,000 Amerindians were brought to these two islands, some from nearby Trinidad and others from as far away as the Bahamas. Increasingly, over time, they were replaced by enslaved Africans.

The impact of plant and animal introductions, as well as new peoples and new technologies, was not evenly spread throughout the Caribbean. Down to the beginning of the seventeenth century, a sharp line continued to divide the Greater from the Lesser Antilles, the latter touched relatively lightly by the Spanish invasion. Indeed, it can be argued that the stark distinction made by the Spanish between peoples defined and identified as "Indians" and those painted as *caribes* underpinned the long-standing division between

CANAV·POVR·PECHER·LES·PERLES

Plate 3.1. Pearl fishing, Margarita, circa 1570. *Source:* Drake manuscript, Pierpont Morgan Library, folio 57. Reproduced with the permission of the Pierpont Morgan Library, New York.

Greater and Lesser, Leeward and Windward. The division itself can be interpreted as the product of European perceptions, rooted not so much in the realities of Amerindian polities as in the strategic exigencies of empire and invasion. The consequence was that the Lesser Antilles overall were allowed to continue their existence relatively undisturbed and to provide homes for Amerindians seeking refuge and African *cimarrones*, as well.

CONFLICT AND COMPETITION

Although the audiencia of Santo Domingo formally retained authority for the government of all the islands in the Caribbean, as promulgated by the Spanish crown, by the last three decades of the sixteenth century its capacity to assert its authority had become severely attenuated. The more distant elements of the insular empire became largely a law to themselves, and the *cabildos* of the larger cities, notably Havana, exercised an informal independence in many respects. Injustice and corruption often held sway, as, for example, under the governors of Jamaica, because the costs of maintaining a tighter rein on such small, scattered communities were simply too great and insufficiently vital to the larger scheme of empire. In some cases, the Spanish crown and the Council of the Indies attempted to deal directly with the provincial governors, avoiding the trouble of going through the hierarchy at Santo Domingo. Even within Hispaniola, the government in Santo Domingo had difficulty imposing law and order throughout the island.

With a small and thinly spread population, and the feeble state of economic development, the islands, together with much of the Caribbean rimland, became ungovernable. As well as being beyond the arm of effective imperial authority, the scattered settlements were off the closely regulated Atlantic trade routes of the Spanish and lacked access to the market for enslaved people brought from Africa. Settlers felt neglected, if not forgotten. They also felt undefended, unable to resist incursions by marauders, and often equally willing to join with such invasive forces simply to minimize damage to what they possessed. The weakness of the forces of law and order and the demand for people and commodities, together with the perception of the potential wealth that might be derived by exploiting the region's rich resources, combined to create the framework for anarchy. Smuggling and piracy obviously were attractive. Even the appointed representatives of government had temptation dangled before them in bribes and favours, rewards for turning a blind eye.

The other ingredient that stirred competition for Caribbean territory and trading rights in this period was the growing maritime power of several states in northwest Europe – notably the Dutch, the French, and the English. The rapid spread of trade routes and the beginnings of European colonization and settlement in many places around the globe kindled a desire in the northern European states for a share of the riches of the Americas. Spain possessed a natural advantage in voyaging to the Caribbean simply because its more southerly location made it the ideal place in the system of Atlantic winds and currents from which to set out and similarly the easiest place to which to return. The northwestern European states lacked this advantage but, in the long run, the navigational difference was overcome by economic and ideological shifts.

By the end of the sixteenth century, the lines drawn in 1493 and 1494 by the authority of the pope and the Spanish and the Portuguese no longer appeared compelling, especially for the Protestant states that had lived through the Reformation of the 1520s and '30s. Military conflict on land and sea within the European sphere spilled over into Spanish fears for the security of their tenure in the Americas. The English defeat of the Armada in 1588 simply confirmed the onset of Spain's decline as a dominant force. By 1596, France, England, and the Netherlands had joined in alliance against Spain, and the Spanish were quickly forced to make peace with each of these states, though without accepting that they had been defeated and remaining determined to use diplomacy to restore their monopoly in the Caribbean. Spain's rivals were equally unwilling to surrender their claims.

Within the Caribbean, large-scale warfare between Spain and other states seemed relatively improbable, and did not occur, but the potential for the loss of territory through conquest was real enough, and went together with the pernicious threat posed by alien raiders and traders, with their love of robbery and ransom. The attractive possibilities offered by islands for small-scale assault launched from seacraft became apparent to privateers and pirates, who posed a problem not only for the Spanish but also the other contending European states.

The penetration of other European rivals into the Spanish Caribbean sphere was led by the ventures of private individuals. Some acted strictly on their own authority, flouting the wishes of their governments, whereas others had tacit support from their rulers. The process was made up of many daring and dramatic episodes. The French came first, trading fine textiles for hides, in an exchange that seemed almost normal. But the French also collaborated with Dutch and English smugglers and corsairs in a wide range of illegal ventures. The Dutch came on the scene relatively late, in the 1590s, looking for salt and any kind of contraband trade they could find. For the English, the first significant venture was that of John Hawkins who, in the 1560s, undertook voyages to Africa and the Caribbean in order to enter the trade in enslaved people. The hostilities roused by these ventures were sufficient to convince English traders that the Caribbean was not a viable market for trading expeditions, and down to 1600, the English presence in the Caribbean was led by roving raiders, pirates, and privateers, often acting in diverse groups that included *cimarrones*. The only solution in many places was to accept that trade could not be controlled and that contraband was the best exchange that could be made under such chaotic circumstances.

By the end of the sixteenth century, the attacks of raiders and marauders had the effect of even further depopulating the substantial sections of the islands that lay beyond the defensive reach of governments. In Hispaniola, the whole of the north and west of the island, beyond the reach of Santo Domingo, was effectively evacuated, and much the same happened in the south and east of Cuba, beyond Havana. Puerto Rico and Jamaica were raked for whatever they might yield. San Juan was fortified and Santo Domingo regularly blockaded to keep raiders at bay, but this did not prevent the capture and sacking of these cities by the English. The Spanish sent galleys to attempt to ward off attack but their range and capacity were limited.

Almost all of this raiding and illegal trading activity was confined to narrow coastlines and poorly defended port towns, the raiders moving swiftly from place to place by sea and rarely venturing far inland. In the fertile interior valleys, untouched by these maritime marauders, the destruction of the Taíno population and their system of agriculture enabled the resurgence of the forest. Given the chance, the forest can regain impenetrable thickness within a decade, in a mix of trees large and small, capped by epiphytes and festooned with vines. Only where feral cattle maintained large herds did savannas survive as open grasslands surrounded by rings of high forest. Most of the montane forest remained intact. However, the invaders who approached by the sea were not confronted by these formidable walls of wood.

Although the vulnerability of the Spanish settlements and of the Spanish military force had been laid bare by the 1590s, the opportunities for gain by plunder were, in turn, directly reduced by the plunderers themselves. Large-scale evacuation of territory and retreat into scattered refuges was a rational means of defence for the Spanish colonists, but it left little in warehouses, stores, and ships that might profit a raider. The early sugar boom was long forgotten, the pearl fisheries unproductive, and even the trade in hides much reduced. Where tobacco might seem to offer a window of prosperity, its planting was banned by royal decree, because it (together with hides) was a favoured commodity in illegal trade. In this drastically unpeopled, poverty-stricken landscape, what was left was the land itself, with its well-watered tropical soils and fertile fields. Spain's European rivals began to see the possibilities in a different light and to think of the Caribbean as a potentially profitable place for investment and colonization in which the state could play a leading role. However, it was not the depopulated zones of the larger islands that proved the first sites of this new colonization. Rather, Spain's rivals began their colonization of the Caribbean by picking off loose outer islands in the eastern Caribbean, where the Spanish had not settled but Amerindian populations remained relatively dense, with the exception of those such as Barbados and Antigua, which had been thoroughly depopulated.

At the beginning of the seventeenth century, the Spanish claimed title to all of the islands and understood the importance of holding them as part of their American empire. It was in this context that, when attacked, the Spanish saw reasons for defending the most strategic elements of its Caribbean realm while easily surrendering those parts that seemed unprofitable or too costly to defend. The French, Dutch, and English similarly understood their objectives within broad imperial frames, in which Caribbean colonies represented an important part but always as elements in larger projects. All of these nations had ambitions to take land on the North American seaboard and to create opportunities for trade as well as the settlement of their own peoples. Indeed, the English colony at Jamestown, Virginia, founded in 1607, preceded the Caribbean ventures. They also looked south to the coast of Africa but, in this period, almost always only for trade – in people as well as commodities – rather than colonization. There, the Dutch, English, and

French were content to establish themselves in fortified niches scattered along the Atlantic margin, as for example Cape Coast Castle on the Gold Coast.

The Europeans who saw the Americas as their New World, at the beginning of the seventeenth century, represented a limited number of states. Even in the longer term, the only European states to succeed in taking land and establishing colonies in the Americas all came from the region on the Atlantic fringe of Western Europe stretching from Spain in the south to Denmark in the north. All of these had sea-going traditions and coastlines with many potential sites for port cities, but the same could be said of the Mediterranean and the Baltic, from whence only Sweden was later to gain a toehold in the Caribbean. Although Columbus was Genoese, from the Ligurian Sea, he sought sponsorship for his voyages not from Italians but from Spaniards. The other ancient Mediterranean colonizers, the Greeks, were engrossed by the Ottoman Empire, which had grand ambitions but never extended its reach into the Atlantic. In contrast to these places and to all of central and eastern Europe, the states of the western fringe of Europe had, by the beginning of the seventeenth century, developed vibrant capitalist economies, derived from their participation in the commercial prosperity of the sixteenth century. Governments offered protection through the regulation of trade and, with growing technological efficiency, naval firepower. The aristocracies faded while entrepreneurial gentry classes looked for ventures in which to invest. The Dutch Republic emerged as the commercial and financial capital of the region and, down to 1740, dominated the world of shipping and trade.

Whereas they represented only the narrow, Atlantic-facing region of Europe, these few states saw the whole sweep of the American landmass and its islands as offering potential sites for settlement. Their map of the Americas was still far from complete, still surrounded by mysteries. Fundamental as well as subtle distinctions between places in terms of their climate, soil, and resources, and an understanding of what they might be capable of producing and by what methods, remained to be established. The emergence of specialized zones of production and distinct patterns of social formation was preceded by a period of trial and error.

It took even longer to create what seemed coherent integrated imperial systems that took advantage of diversified environmental conditions and trading possibilities. In the initial, experimental period, the English, French, and Dutch took territory from the Spanish and the Amerindians in an opportunistic fashion, seeking to catch their opponents unawares and attack them at their weakest sites. At first the Spanish conceded territory without putting up a fight. This was the case in some of the smaller islands of the eastern Caribbean, where the Spanish had never established substantial settlements or fortifications. These islands were not regarded as having substantial resources worth defending and the already stretched Spanish navy and army were unable to deploy forces. They were not on the routes used by the Spanish fleet and therefore their loss seemed to pose no threat to the major settled Spanish colonies in the longer term, though, in 1606, the Spanish did propose fortifying Guadeloupe or some nearby island. Spanish naval strength declined steadily, to reach a low point around 1616, and the stray outer islands of the Lesser Antilles were exposed to the persistent invasions of the corsairs. The Amerindian populations of these islands were small and ultimately unable to defend their lands from the guns and diseases of the Europeans.

Several minor and accidental camps and nascent settlements survived temporarily in scattered and isolated places, but the first long-lasting colonization by Europeans other than the Spanish occurred when the English colonized St Kitts in 1624. There, the settlers proceeded to plant tobacco, for which there was a rapidly expanding and lucrative market – a market encouraged by the official Spanish prohibition of the crop's planting. A party of French settlers arrived the following year and, in 1627, agreed with the English to divide the island. The English and French by this time had jointly massacred or driven off the majority of the Kalinago in an act of genocide. Another tobacco-growing settlement was established by the English soon after, in 1627, on the uninhabited island of Barbados. Nevis was settled from St Kitts in 1628 but these two islands had to be recolonized after the settlers were briefly dislodged by the Spanish in 1629. Additional English settlements were made in 1632 on Antigua and Montserrat. In 1635, the French established themselves in Guadeloupe and Martinique, where they traded with the Carib peoples while gradually taking more and more territory.

The early government of these new European colonies was generally left to the private adventurers and proprietary corporations that had founded them, acting under royal protection but given a free hand. Thus, the French legitimized the initial colonization of St Kitts by setting up a semipublic chartered company, the Compagnie de Saint-Christophe, encouraged by Cardinal Richelieu, who, in 1624, became chief minister to Louis XIII, king of France from 1610 to 1643. At the same time, the first English settlers on St Kitts in 1624 acted without authority from the crown but merely represented a syndicate of London merchants. Their leader, Thomas Warner, moved quickly to legitimize his position and in 1625 gained from Charles I a commission as Lieutenant Governor of St Kitts, Nevis, Barbados, Montserrat, and any other of the islands in the eastern region not claimed by another European power. However, Warner lacked the aristocratic status required of a proprietor and letters patent over the whole of the islands as far south as Grenada were, instead, granted in 1627 to the first Earl of Carlisle. Under the terms of the patent, Carlisle was effectively granted unlimited powers to make laws, tax, make appointments to public offices, and administer justice. He was permitted to exercise his authority through deputies. Carlisle chose to be an absentee from his government and appointed governors to each of the English islands. The distance of the colonies from the metropolis and the slowness of communication meant that these governors had extensive powers in practice. However, the great transformation that was soon to take place in the islands was not so much a product of decisions made by governors or governments as it was the outcome of choices made by individual capitalist colonists about how – for their own direct benefit – they might most profitably exploit the resources of the islands and the labour power of other people.

4

Plantation Peoples

1630–1770

By the beginning of the seventeenth century, European colonization had reduced the Caribbean islands to a blank canvas. In truth it was not so much a blank canvas as one that had been thickly painted by a series of hands, scoured and scraped, then smeared with a rough bloody cloth, and cleaned again of yet another attempted landscape. The people and the civilizations that had flourished in the Greater Antilles before Columbus had been virtually obliterated. They had not been replaced by any new substantial population or any new form of civilization. Even regions the Spanish had attempted to populate were being evacuated. The land that had been brought to a high state of cultivation by the Taínos was being reconquered by rainforest. Exotic trees made themselves at home in the woodland. Large feral animals introduced by the Spanish crashed through the undergrowth of this landscape, otherwise silent but for the night sounds of crickets and frogs, the occasional noisy cascade or crack of thunder. Only in the smaller islands of the eastern Caribbean, which the Spanish had touched less heavily, did the indigenous people survive in significant numbers.

Although new European peoples had begun to show an interest in exploiting the opportunities offered by the disorganized state of Spain's Caribbean empire and although some of these same nations had encouraged attempts at settlement in the 1620s, there were few clues to the revolutionary transformation that was about to occur. The new, tentative colonizers had only poorly developed under-standings of the rich resources of the islands and at first they dabbed and dabbled, trying one thing after another. Quite quickly, however, they turned to sugar-growing and sugar-making. The outcome was the "sugar revolution". Its ramifications were far-reaching and long-lasting. Once inscribed on the surface of the islands, sugar created a landscape that proved highly durable and a system of exploitation of land and people that was capable of withstanding social and political shocks. It was in this process and in this period that the modern Caribbean was born. Where the sugar revolution was worked out most completely, the landscape was dominated by sugar cane, a vast expanse of giant grass, homogenous in texture and colour. This smooth, undulating surface was interrupted only by the occasional rainforest-remnant copse or rugged hill, but dotted with clumps of factory buildings, their chimneys standing out prominently above the sea of cane.

THE SUGAR REVOLUTION

The sugar revolution brought with it a series of interrelated transformations that had fundamental implications for all aspects of the economy, society, and government of the islands. These changes were not unique to sugar or to the Caribbean, but the attribution of such transformative power to a single agricultural commodity is unusual in economic and social history, and it was in the Caribbean that the revolution found its fullest expression as a coherent whole. The status of the sugar revolution as a revolution recognizes the determining role of sugar – the physical and mechanical characteristics of the sugar cane and the related processing requirements for making crystallized sugar – in the economic, social, and political transformations that were its consequences. The most important features of the sugar revolution were a shift from diversified agriculture to monoculture, from small to large scale farming units, from low to high value output, from sparse to dense settlement patterns, and from free labour to slavery. On the stage of world history, extending beyond the Caribbean, more elaborate claims have been made for the sugar revolution. It has been made responsible for a massive increase in the Atlantic trade in goods and enslaved people, new patterns of nutrition, enlarged European interest in tropical colonies, and the provision of capital vital to the industrial revolution.

The sugar revolution did not commence in every island at the same time. Indeed, some islands entered their sugar revolutions only after 1770. Few escaped it entirely, however, and even where sugar did not become a dominant crop, the ramifications of the revolution reverberated. The most striking feature of the geographical pattern of transformation was that it commenced in the smaller islands of the eastern Caribbean, on the fringes of Spanish influence, and took a relatively long time to spread through the Greater Antilles. There were several reasons for this pattern but one of the more important was that islands and particularly small islands had advantages of accessibility in this stage of development that larger islands and landlocked regions lacked. It was in this period of Caribbean history that the small island was the vital focus of activity, not only in the process of economic and social transformation but also in the struggle over territory that proved so persistent in the seventeenth and eighteenth centuries.

There was nothing inevitable about the sugar revolution and nothing inevitable about its Caribbean genesis. Although there was little chance of the islands reverting permanently to forest or of Amerindian peoples being able to reestablish their hegemony in the islands, beyond these alternatives, many others can be easily conceived – because they proved to be the outcome in other places and at other times – none of which required growing sugar, plantation agriculture, or slavery. Further, growing sugar did not, in itself, entail the plantation or slavery. It was the emergence of the plantation as the dominant mode of enterprise that determined the structure and contents of the landscape and the character of daily life. The sugar plantation not only covered a relatively large area of agricultural land, it also required a large work force committed to labour exclusively for the plantation, a substantial factory complex, and a hierarchical system of management. Together, these factors created a land unit that resembled a small region or domain, with the equivalent of a village at its centre, and a population and architectural mass to match. It was a realm unto itself, a microcosm, yet linked vitally to distant worlds. The plantation proved itself resilient, persisting and even flourishing after the abolition of slavery and proving itself capable of maintaining its presence in the absence of sugar. It permeated Caribbean life and landscape.

The shift to sugar was not a matter of innovation. Sugar can be extracted from a variety of plants and produced by a variety of agrarian systems. Choosing among these sources and systems can have momentous consequences. For the Caribbean, the great transformation of economy and society that occurred throughout many of the islands in the seventeenth and eighteenth centuries can be traced directly to the choice of sugar cane as the source and the plantation as the production system. The fundamentals of sugar cane cultivation and appropriate processing technologies had been known for many centuries. What was revolutionary about the sugar revolution had more to do with the scale of production and the articulation of the elements in an extensive monoculture. These elements came from far away and took a long time to reach the Caribbean but it was there that they came together to create the great transformation of life and labour. The sugar cane itself had its origins in New Guinea and gradually spread, with human assistance, through southeast Asia, then gained significance in China and India. In these settings, processing technologies remained simple and cultivation was typically on a small scale, for local consumption. It was when sugar moved into the Middle East and the Mediterranean, in about 900, as part of Arab economic transformation, that market-oriented plantation-scale production began to emerge. With these ancient and medieval roots, sugar cultivation and processing moved into the Atlantic islands of Madeira, the Azores, Cape Verde, and São Tomé, in association with the beginning of Portuguese expansion into Africa in the fifteenth century. The colonization, deforestation, and agricultural development of these islands were dramatic but sugar was based on small-scale units and made only limited use of enslaved labour. After Columbus, the complex spread to Portuguese Brazil, where the export orientation established on the Atlantic islands was maintained and the large-scale plantations began to emerge as the fundamental units of enterprise. The Caribbean inherited these models and technologies.

The key element of the sugar complex lay in its combination of agricultural and industrial practices and processes. Whereas the physical characteristics of the plant were essential, the outcomes for agrarian systems were always negotiable. Sugar cane is a tall grass, with a tough outer skin and a spongy core. The core is made up of cellulose and contains, within its cells, a vast store of sucrose, pure sugar. Although the cane can be stripped of its tough skin and chewed or pressed for its juice, concentrated sugar in a dry crystallized form is preferred as a commodity because it has good storage properties and can be consumed in small amounts added to other foods. These properties provided the foundations for long-distance trade. In the seventeenth century, sugar commanded high prices throughout Europe because there were few alternative sources of sweetness. To maintain this market, the sugar supplied had to be of good quality, the crystals uniform and dry rather than clumped up in sticky globs. Demand also developed for white rather than dark sugars, the former regarded as superior for its purity though less nutritious.

In determining whether, and how, to produce sugar, these technical requirements were vital. Harvested cane is bulky and subject to rapid deterioration. If the juice is not extracted within a few days, the sugar is lost. This means that the extraction of the juice must always occur close to the site of cultivation. In the early seventeenth century, when transport technologies were limited largely to carts pulled by cattle over rutted and muddy tracks, the rate of deterioration combined with transit challenges limited the distance over which canes might be hauled. Industrial-scale processing required, first, a mill to extract the juice by crushing the canes between cylindrical rollers. In the seventeenth century, these mills typically consisted of two or three rollers placed vertically side by side and turned by cattle or mules attached to long poles. More efficient mills, powered by water wheels or windmills, were unusual. The animal mills often struggled to crush more than half the juice from the canes. Once extracted, the juice was boiled in a series of large copper pans until it began to crystallize. This sticky mass was then ladled into barrels and left to drain. The molasses that seeped out might then be boiled again to attempt to crystallize more sugar or, alternatively, used in the distillation of rum. The products that emerged from these processes were raw sugar (muscovado), molasses, and rum.

At the beginning of the seventeenth century, the scale of a sugar-producing enterprise was determined, above all, by the need to process cut canes soon after harvest, the high cost of moving canes over land, and the capacity to crush and crystallize. The result was interdependence between field and factory. This balance could be achieved by a variety of agrarian systems and, indeed, this variety can be observed in other places and other times. One solution was to place cane production in the hands of farmers who supplied their crop to an independent factory for processing. In this system, the factory could be owned by an independent capitalist or by the cane farmers as a group. The farmers could operate on a small or a large scale. Elements of this system of small-scale cane cultivation combined with independent mills existed in the seventeenth century but did not survive. They failed partly because the transportation factor meant there was a low upper limit to the viable size of farms and because small farmers could not easily be tied to a single mill. Sugar factories had such limited supply regions that potential entrepreneurs were unwilling to invest their capital without control of the surrounding cane fields.

Sugar remained a scarce commodity – a luxury – for most of the period from 1600 to 1770. This is why prices were so high and why great fortunes could be made from what might seem paltry quantities of product and small pieces of land. At the beginning of the seventeenth century, the sole exporter of sugar in the Atlantic and, indeed, the world, was Brazil. The Atlantic islands no longer contributed; their mills and cane fields were abandoned, while the great producers of sugar for domestic markets, India and China, exported only trivial quantities. Even in the longer-settled islands of the Greater Antilles, agriculture generally was limited to the production of food crops for local consumption on small-scale farms. The Spanish showed no interest in attempting to revive sugar production in the now-depopulated islands of Hispaniola, Cuba, and Jamaica. Still dazzled by the prospects of precious metals and dreams of imperial greatness on a continental scale, they saw their main chance on the mainland.

Initially, down to the 1630s, the new European colonial enterprises of the French, Dutch, and English were equally uncertain of their direction. In many cases, these Caribbean ventures were not distinguished from colonies established in the northern, temperate zones of North America. Particularly for the English, the idea of religious mission and exile, as crystallized among the Puritans, applied equally in hot and cold places. However, early experimentation with crops led to a focus on tobacco, indigo, and cotton, all of them potential plantation crops. Tobacco enjoyed a brief boom but had environmental troubles. Particularly important in encouraging renewed enthusiasm for the plantation was the colony established in 1630 on the tiny volcanic island of Providence (now Providencia, part of Colombia), off the coast of Nicaragua. There, English settlers sought to build a Puritan colony along the lines of their contemporaries in New England, but quickly turned to intensive slavery and tobacco growing before moving on to privateering and piracy. They did consider sugar but the fabric of the colony had fallen apart by 1641 and Providence soon disappeared from imperial memory.

The sugar revolution came first to some of the smaller islands of the eastern Caribbean. Most accounts find it first in Barbados, beginning in the 1640s, then Guadeloupe in the 1650s, Martinique in the 1660s, and St Kitts, Nevis, Antigua, and Montserrat in the 1670s. The speed of the revolution – the number of years required to bring it to completion – depended on the size and internal diversity of each island but few achieved closure in less than a decade. Other colonies entered the revolutionary process more slowly and much later. The success of the revolution, however, was by no means a foregone conclusion; it might have evaporated as easily as the tobacco boom. Its long-term survival and prosperity depended on high prices and their protection through mercantilist preference.

Why did the sugar revolution occur in the colonies of the French and the English rather than in those of the Spanish? In part, the failure of the Spanish to develop major sugar plantation economies before 1770 had to do with their continuing focus on the mainland. The empire was already stretched in its ability to protect and govern its vast domain. Simply holding on to Cuba, Santo Domingo, and Puerto Rico while the rest of the islands fell into the hands of other European imperial powers seemed an achievement in itself. The essentially defensive attitude of the Spanish made them see the maintenance of barriers against trade and traders as necessary to

avoid further surrender of territory, but doing so inhibited investment, commerce, and access to the Atlantic slave trade.

As early as 1650 Barbados could export 7,000 tons of sugar, joining Brazil with 30,000 tons. By 1700, the islands of the English –
Barbados, Jamaica, Antigua, Nevis, and Montserrat – produced
about 25,000 tons of sugar, more than Brazil's 22,000 tons at
that time. St Kitts, a pioneer in the sugar revolution, had temporarily dropped out as a result of devastating French raids. The
French islands produced just 9,000 tons and the only other significant exporter was Dutch Guiana (Surinam), with about 4,000
tons. Thus, in 1700, there were only ten substantial exporters globally, all of them Atlantic colonies. Together, they exported 60,000
tons of sugar, more than half of it coming from the islands of the
Caribbean.

No new substantial exporters joined these ten colonies up to
1750, but by 1770, there were twenty. In 1750, exports totalled
about 150,000 tons, more than double the amount fifty years
before, and by 1770, they exceeded 200,000 tons. In 1750, the
Caribbean islands contributed more than 70 percent of the total;
in 1770, almost 90 percent. With the exception of St Domingue
and Jamaica, the major producers were all small islands located in
the eastern Caribbean. The world's greatest exporters in 1770 were
St Domingue (60,000 tons) and Jamaica (36,000 tons), together
accounting for roughly half of the Caribbean output.

The increase in world sugar exports between 1650 and 1770, and
the increasingly dominant role of the Caribbean islands in the trade,
reflected the expansion of cane growing into new regions rather
than improvements in productivity. Down to 1770, innovations in
cultivation and milling technologies were few. A superior method of
planting and manuring was diffused from Barbados to other islands,
along with improved boiling techniques and the use of bagasse as
fuel. The use of aqueducts to power mills, rather than depending on
animals, also increased productivity. However, it was the opening
of new lands and the destruction of rainforest that mattered most
in boosting output.

With the exception of the French colonies, mercantilist regulation generally confined planters to the production of raw (muscovado) sugar. Differential duties ensured that value-adding occurred at

refineries located in metropolitan countries, where the dark brown molasses was removed to create a pure white sugar. An intermediate grade was made, however, by placing the raw sugar in pottery cones to drain the molasses, then sealing the top with a layer of damp clay, the water from which percolated through the cone and whitened the sugar. When the sugar loaves were removed from the cones, they contained a gradation of qualities, top to bottom, ranging from white to brown. This process was labour-intensive but also created a local demand for ceramic cones, which formed the foundation of a colonial pottery industry. Prices varied with the qualities and colours of the sugars.

The sugar revolution brought great wealth to planters and the most successful of them came to own multiple estates. These sometimes were located close to one another but, more often, they were scattered across large regions or even in separate islands, as far apart as Barbados and Jamaica. This necessitated more complex systems of management to ensure the planter received his due share of the profit and that the plantation continued to be operated as efficiently as possible. Agents were contracted to manage these multiple plantations in addition to those of absentee-proprietors. Because the only means of communication was by letter and replies to questions or directives took about six months, many decisions had to be delegated to overseers, agents, attorneys, and local merchants. Every single plantation had its own resident manager, often called an overseer, but he might, in turn, be responsible to an agent or attorney who reported to the owner and might have charge of a series of plantations belonging to several different planters. The overseer was typically a free white unmarried man, with a practical knowledge of agriculture, eager to become an owner himself. The agents were sometimes derived from among the overseers but often came from the urban merchant class, with a superior knowledge of shipping and trade.

As well as being an agricultural and managerial revolution, the sugar revolution brought with it an ecological transformation. The rainforest – dense and diverse – was cleared and often burned, the trees replaced by sugar cane planted across the landscape in regimented land units. Secure land tenure was essential to the system to avoid disputes over the ownership of growing canes, and the land was surveyed precisely with straight line boundaries where the topography allowed. The plots of canes were laid out in neat geometrical figures, squares and rectangles, wherever possible. Fences and boundary walls became common, though, generally, the objective was to contain livestock within fences or pens, to prevent them trampling field crops, rather than attempting to build barriers around the perimeters of the cropped areas. Where the revolution was less complete, the landscapes were more varied and more likely to be interrupted by extensive forests and alternative agriculture. These differences in the impact of sugar down to 1770 demonstrated the revolution's uneven chronology as well as the significant role of variations in topography, soil, and climate. Local environmental factors interacted in complex ways with differences among the European empires, their systems of regulation, and their mercantilist policies, as displayed most obviously in the colonial landscapes of the Spanish compared with those constructed by the English and French.

Barbados, the purported home of the sugar revolution, was denuded of almost all its native vegetation as early as 1665. Sugar plantations were tightly packed across the island. With the forest gone, the timber needed by the plantations to fire their factory furnaces, to build, and to make barrels, all had to be imported. Cattle and horses, essential for hauling carts and turning some mills, had to be given pasturage. The cost of doing so encouraged many of the planters of Barbados to construct windmills, taking advantage of the reliable sea breezes. Space was at a premium and the cultivation of food for local consumption was largely achieved by intercropping.

Guadeloupe, the first of the French colonies to make the shift to a sugar monoculture, had features similar to Barbados but took a good deal longer to clear its forest. Where islands contained a relatively large proportion of steep, elevated land, as in St Kitts and Nevis, for example, the pattern varied yet again, with sugar cultivation concentrated along the flatter coastal zone. Within this ring, moving inland and upland, were further zones of pasturage for livestock, food crop cultivation, and finally, towards the peaks, woodland. In these islands, the internal diversity of the plantation system was contained within the individual plantation, each unit having its share of the different land types and taking its slice of the pie. Here, the island formed a microcosm of the pattern within the typical sugar plantation of the period, in which the mill and factory were placed as close as possible to the centre of the property, and surrounded by roughly concentric rings of cane fields, pasture, and woodland.

Even in the islands in which the sugar revolution was most complete, internal regional variation was common. In the same way that transportation costs contributed to determining which of the islands would be first developed in sugar and contributed to setting the optimum size of plantation units, they also impacted the potential for complementary local industries producing inputs for the plantation sector. Such subsidiary enterprises were least developed wherever a high proportion of an island's surface was flat or gently sloping, with good soil, reliable rainfall, and easy access to shipping. Islands of this type tended to be small and homogenous, and among the first to experience the sugar revolution.

Large islands and colonies offered more opportunities for diversity of land use and variation of labour organization. Jamaica offers a clear example of what was possible in this period. Although sugar plantations were numerous and spread widely across the island, there remained many regions of relatively poor soil and rainfall that were marginal for sugar production but well-suited for raising livestock. Thus, Jamaica developed a strong pastoral sector that supplied most of the demand from the plantations for animals used in haulage and powering mills. These livestock-producing properties, known as pens, were, themselves, large in terms of their area, stocking, and labour force, and often grouped together in extensive regions. Jamaica also retained extensive forest cover, some of which was exploited for the plantations' demand for timber. Other properties specialized in the production of food crops for local consumption, selling corn and plantains to the sugar estates. Jamaica was different from the sugar monocultures of the eastern Caribbean in finding space for the continuing production of crops other than sugar. Before 1770, the most important of these were cotton, pimento (allspice), ginger, indigo, and the dyewoods logwood and fustic. Some of these commodities were produced on specialized plantations, which, in turn, exchanged goods with the sugar estates and pens. In other cases, the plantations and pens produced such secondary export goods in niches within their own boundaries.

Another striking feature of the plantation landscape during slavery was the development of a system by which the enslaved were made largely responsible for producing their own food. This system, commonly referred to as the provision ground system, was particularly associated with Jamaica but existed in other Caribbean colonies where the conditions were appropriate. Unlike the case of Barbados, where the planters tightly controlled the production and distribution of food, the provision ground system was designed to reduce the planter's costs of supervising labour and to minimize expenditure on the purchase of local or imported foodstuffs. Under the system, the planter allocated a defined area of land to be used by the enslaved people to cultivate particularly staple carbohydrate crops such as the tubers (yams, cocoyams, and cassava) and the plantain, its green fruit eaten roasted or boiled. These grounds were typically located on steeper lands within a sugar plantation and were intercropped rather than cultivated as a monoculture in the fashion of the cane fields. Shade trees were often used to protect the lower levels of the cultivation, so that the canopy might blend into nearby forest. The products of the provision grounds were largely consumed by the people who produced them but a proportion might also be sold in public markets. Where the provision ground system operated, the enslaved received from the planter only rations of salted or pickled fish, imported from North America, as did those in the colonies where food came in rations from the master's store.

Unlike Jamaica, the planters of Barbados did not allocate provision grounds but chose instead to allocate plantation land to growing yams, plantains, pigeon peas, and Guinea corn (sorghum), the last of these commonly fed to cattle as well as enslaved people but rarely eaten by whites. During "crop" (harvest season), enslaved people could chew on sugar cane, and they also received allowances of molasses and rum. Some of the food consumed by the enslaved people of Barbados, however, was imported – notably salt fish – in order to maximize the land planted in cane and hence the profit to the planter.

The great wealth delivered to individual capitalists by the sugar revolution was built both on the management of elaborate industrial and agricultural processes and on the brutal exploitation of working people. Although the plantation complexes may appear insignificant in the shadow of the massive mills of later periods, down to 1770, and the beginnings of the industrial revolution in Europe, the sugar factories and plantations of the Caribbean, in fact, were some of the largest private enterprises operating anywhere in the world in terms of their capitalization, output, and labour force.

Technological change between 1600 and 1770 improved some efficiencies, particularly through the adoption of the horizontal mill, but, overall, the system changed little. Thus, the upper limit on factory capacity and field cultivation remained critical throughout the period and growth in sugar production depended on the proliferation of plantations rather than the expansion of the boundaries of individual properties. Rather than expanding, a planter with money to invest established a new, separate plantation with its own complete internal farming system. In consequence, although the peak in Caribbean sugar production did not come until much later, by 1770, the number of individual plantations came near to a maximum. Caribbean land thus acquired value not only for the individual capitalist entrepreneur but also for imperial states. Possessing a piece of it seemed worth fighting for, and worth defending.

WAR AND PEACE

By 1770, every piece of Caribbean land was the colonial possession of some European state. This no longer was a theoretical possession such as the sweeping claims of the Spanish in the sixteenth century but an effective occupation. It was a relatively brief period of absolute dominance, not to last beyond the end of the eighteenth century. In 1770, the development of each of the colonies was controlled from a metropolitan, European centre, with only limited powers placed in the hands of the colonists. The only breaches in the system were internal and limited, as in the isolated partial autonomy of Maroon groups throughout the Greater Antilles. Looking at the Caribbean from a broader perspective, the year 1770 marked not only a peak in the imperial domination of the islands but also a high point in the European control of land and peoples throughout the

Americas. This broader regional domination was also to disappear by the end of the eighteenth century.

Another unique feature of the period from 1630 to 1770 is the intensity of European conflict over Caribbean territory. A good number of the islands changed hands more than once and the sea between them was the scene of major naval battles. Although this conflict was not finally concluded until the beginning of the nineteenth century, the major struggles were over by 1770 and thereafter the pattern of European possession changed very little. The reason for this focus can be found in the great wealth that could be obtained from sugar. Caribbean land had a relative value it would not achieve again. It was also the great period of the island, in which a small place easily accessible by sea had attractions, that would not be repeated once continents could be crossed by railroads and oceans by steamships.

Only in rare cases did a small island remain the long-term property of a single European state outside the Spanish system. This was the case in Barbados, a colony of the English from 1627 to 1964. On the other hand, St Kitts, the first island colonized by the English, attracted rival French settlers almost immediately after the arrival of the English in 1624, and the Spanish briefly regained control in 1629. The initial colonizations of the English and French in the 1620s and 1630s, in the Leeward Islands, Martinique, and Guadeloupe, were also marked by conflict with the Kalinago. In Guadeloupe, the French were at war with the Kalinago until the early 1640s, when an uneasy peace was brokered and most of the Kalinago agreed to move to Grande-Terre, the windward part of the island, or to Dominica. The Kalinago launched guerrilla attacks. None of these island colonies was ever regained by Spain and they remained in the hands of the French or the English until the twentieth century. It was these islands that provided the sites for the sugar revolution.

A second phase of conquest involved military conflict between Spain and the English. This campaign began in 1654 when Oliver Cromwell launched his "Western Design" with the intention of making inroads into the highly valued Spanish territories of the Greater Antilles. Although his plan to take Santo Domingo failed, Cromwell's forces did manage to conquer the weakly defended and barely populated island of Jamaica in 1655. Skirmishes continued for some time but the Spanish proved unequal to the task of reclaiming their territory and English possession was formally recognized in the 1670 Treaty of Madrid. The English took no further territory down to the middle of the eighteenth century but focussed on developing and defending the sugar economy of the islands already in its hands.

The French established small informal settlements on the western coast of the island of Hispaniola beginning in the 1670s and these gradually coalesced to form the colony of St Domingue. The sparse Spanish population of Hispaniola was concentrated in the eastern end of the island and was barely capable of defending itself let alone repossessing the lands occupied by the French in the distant west. The two groups quickly came to a pragmatic agreement to leave unsettled the central cordillera that came eventually to mark the mountainous border between the modern states of Haiti and the Dominican Republic. When Spain formally ceded this territory at the Treaty of Ryswick in 1697, the French too stopped looking for fresh sugar land. No further attempts were made by the Europeans to replace the Spanish in their major territories.

Whereas conflict between the Spanish and other European states was all about territory, competition between the English, French, and Dutch became more a matter of jealousy and trade. Territory changed hands but only on a temporary basis. In the later seventeenth century, the focus was on the Dutch and the way in which they used their colonies at Curaçao, St Eustatius, Saba, and St Martin (shared with France) to trade, often in contravention of the rules of mercantilism set down by the sugar-producing French and English. Thus the so-called Second Dutch War, stretching from 1665 to 1667, and the Third Dutch War of 1672 to 1678 saw many sea battles and attacks on shipping. There were also occasional land battles, including attacks on the shared islands of St Kitts and St Martin, and the prosperous ports of the Dutch. The typical pattern was a raid on a section of an island, the destruction of crops or warehouses, and the taking of enslaved people. These small-scale skirmishes were confined largely to the Leeward Islands in the later seventeenth century, and many of them were planned and prosecuted by colonists rather than being part of metropolitan imperial policy. In the western Caribbean, ventures of this sort more often were associated with a resurgence of buccaneering but raiding came to be regarded as detrimental to the long-term development of trade in a settled plantation economy. In Jamaica, one of the major bases of buccaneering enterprises, the end of such activity was marked dramatically by the earthquake of 1692, which destroyed the pirate port of Port Royal.

By the end of the seventeenth century, the pattern of territorial possession contrasted strongly with that at its beginning. The changes that occurred were not initiated by the sugar revolution but it was sugar and slavery, and the trades they generated, that drove rivalry in the period after 1650 and determined the character of conflict. Amerindian peoples had lost effective control almost everywhere, though Caribs remained dominant and relatively unmolested in a few islands, notably St Vincent and, to a lesser extent, Dominica, where the French held a loose authority. They struggled hard against colonization in Grenada and Tobago. The grand claims of the Spanish were much reduced but they did still control the largest area of Caribbean land, in Cuba, the eastern end of Hispaniola, and Puerto Rico.

The territories of the French and English were less extensive and more dispersed but highly profitable. The French had effective control of Martinique, Guadeloupe, St Croix, Grenada, and Tobago. They shared some islands: Hispaniola with the Spanish, St Martin with the Dutch, and St Lucia with the English. In the west, the English held Jamaica, the Cayman Islands (ceded in 1670 together with Jamaica), and the sparsely settled Bahamas (1648). In the east, they had Barbados and the Leewards settlements of St Kitts (the French section of the island having been wrested from them in 1691), Nevis, Anguilla (settled 1650), Montserrat, Antigua, Barbuda (1685), and the eastern group of the Virgin Islands (1672), where the English drove out Dutch buccaneers. The Dutch had Curaçao, Aruba, and Bonaire off the coast of South America and, in the Leewards, St Eustatius, Saba, and St Martin (shared with France). St Thomas was Danish but almost completely dependent on the Dutch for its capital development. In 1733, St Croix was sold by the French to the Danish, who sought to redevelop the island as a sugar colony and had already occupied St John with similar intentions.

The pattern of conflict continued much the same throughout the first half of the eighteenth century. Disrupting trade and weakening the capacity of competitors to produce sugar remained central. Raids continued. Most important were battles with the Spanish that had to do with trade rather than territory. The Spanish took a narrowly defensive approach to strategy, installing massive fortifications to protect their chief port settlements and establishing permanent battalions at Havana in 1719, Santiago de Cuba in 1735, Santo Domingo in 1738, and San Juan in 1741. Beyond the walls of these fortified refuges, the relative weakness of the Spanish was not confined to their capacity to defend their possessions but extended also to their ability to provide resources to their colonists through trade. They reluctantly granted the *asiento* to Britain in 1713 but the contract failed to operate efficiently because it was substantially subverted by the smuggling of enslaved people and manufactured items, particularly in the zone between Jamaica, Hispaniola, and Cuba.

It was in this context that the so-called War of Jenkins' Ear occurred, precipitated in 1739 when a Spanish coast guard officer searching for contraband took his sword and sliced an ear off a British sea captain, Jenkins. Reprisals escalated and attacks on Spanish territory in Cuba and on the Isthmus led to the British capture of ships and cargoes from the Spanish convoy to great value, seriously affecting Spanish commerce. This Anglo–Spanish conflict developed into the War of the Austrian Succession and hostilities with France. Although this war saw battles between the French and the British in the Leeward Islands, it became essentially a European war. No Caribbean territory changed hands under the Treaty of Aix-la-Chapelle, concluded in 1748, that brought the war to an end.

The Treaty of Aix-la-Chapelle did, however, open an important alternative path for the development of the eastern Caribbean. Under the terms of the treaty, Dominica, St Lucia, St Vincent, and Tobago were declared "neutral" and reserved for the Carib peoples, who remained relatively numerous in these islands. The intention was that this agreement continue "forever" and that all informal settlements made by Europeans on these islands should be dismantled. This plan arose more from a desire for the long-term security of the already colonized islands than from a late-discovered enthusiasm for the protection of indigenous peoples and cultures. Whatever its origins, the plan seemed doomed to failure in face of the history of the region and indeed it was breached almost immediately with French incursions into Dominica, which lies between Martinique and Guadeloupe. The British also abandoned their side of the deal, though without taking immediate action in seeking settlements. The peace and neutrality of the islands was short-lived.

The final grand naval conflict that resulted in a significant fresh shuffling of European possession in the Caribbean was the Seven Years War of 1756 to 1763. This was a global conflict, extending from Asia to the Americas. The central combatants were the French and the British, though the French fought in alliance with the Spanish in the later stages of the conflict. The Dutch had become less significant as a force in both Europe and the Caribbean. The outcome was victory for the British, who then commenced a long-lasting naval supremacy and added substantially to their dominance of the eastern Caribbean. The Treaty of Paris that concluded the Seven Years War saw a general reshuffling of European possession. In the Caribbean, the British secured three of the neutral islands – Dominica, St Vincent and Tobago – and Grenada, which came to be known as the "ceded islands". Elsewhere, the British gained Canada, Florida, and Senegal. The French regained Martinique, Guadeloupe, and St Lucia. Spain recovered Havana, which had been occupied by the British in 1762, in exchange for Florida. Thus, the Spanish yielded no Caribbean territory but, by 1770, the only Spanish colony to survive in the eastern Caribbean was Trinidad and even it was soon to be dominated by French settlers before finally becoming British at the end of the eighteenth century. The big gainers in 1763 were the British and the metropolitan sugar interest, with the addition of substantial potential plantation land that might be gradually brought to production, though the opportunity to monopolize the market by securing Cuba, Martinique, and Guadeloupe was not taken. The indigenous peoples saw any last hopes of maintaining an independent existence, even within a few individual islands free of plantation colonies, slip away.

Although the seventeenth and eighteenth centuries seem dominated by these naval battles between European states anxious to secure for themselves a greater share of the profits produced by Caribbean colonies, some of the colonies were, at the same time, at war within themselves. In several of the islands, bands of enslaved Africans managed to escape the oppressions of sugar and slavery and establish themselves in semipermanent secluded settlements. In Cuba and Puerto Rico, these settlements were known as *palenques*, fortified sites protected by palisades or fences, hidden from sight. Often, they were merely temporary encampments, however, and the people survived by adopting a transient approach, ready to move whenever threatened by military force.

Topographic conditions were more propitious in some locations and occasionally enabled *marrons* to engage effectively in full-scale war. In Jamaica, Maroons took refuge in the rugged mountains and forests, establishing themselves in physical and psychological niches that offered defensible refuges. The nature of the environment made such action difficult in many places, such as the relatively flat and open small islands of the eastern Caribbean that were fully developed as sugar plantation landscapes. On the other hand, the forested limestone landscape of the Cockpit Country of western Jamaica was ideal for guerrilla warfare and the mountain ridges in the eastern end of the island were equally attractive as sites for secluded settlements. The enslaved people who took refuge in this way were regarded as a threat to the stability of the slave society and the British army, as well as local planter militias and mercenaries, applied much effort to destroying their bases.

In spite of their superior firepower, the British lost the battle. Their tactics were inappropriate to the field of conflict and no match for the strategies deployed by the Maroon bands, commanded by the obeah woman Nanny in the east and the bush-fighter Kojo in the west, in making themselves almost invisible within the woods. The First Maroon War was eventually concluded with a treaty, agreed in 1739, by which the Maroons of Jamaica secured their freedom. They also gained the right to occupy specified lands unmolested in two settlements, one in the east and one in the west, each with its own internal polity, on condition that they ceased further incursions on the plantations and refused to admit to their populations enslaved people who attempted to join them in the future. Indeed, so long as the system of slavery persisted, the viability of these separate, secluded communities depended on keeping them small and on accepting an ambivalent role in ensuring the security of the plantations.

In St Domingue, the rugged mountains and forests offered numerous sites, the best known being Maniel, close to the border with Santo Domingo, that the French struggled unsuccessfully to eradicate. A treaty was signed with the people of Maniel in 1785, granting them independence and land.

In addition to these sometimes successful struggles to attain an independence within the structure of slave society, there were also attempts to destroy the plantation and slavery as an institution. None of the large-scale efforts were successful before 1770 but they played a central role in forming the character of the societies. Warfare, local and international, was central to government.

GOVERNMENT

The government of the Caribbean colonies down to 1770 was dominated by metropolitan control. All the European states that held colonies – even the Dutch Republic – were, themselves, monarchies of one sort or another, with limited forms of representative government. In the islands, government almost everywhere was in the hands of wealthy adult men, most of them white and slave owners. Even among this select group, exclusions occurred on the basis of religion. The only significant exceptions to these broad rules occurred among the small communities of the Maroons, where black men and women could have a political role, though treaty arrangements often led to a whittling away of the authority of the leaders or "captains". Broadly, variations in the structure of government reflected differences among the particular European states, their systems of government, and their attitudes to colonization.

Spanish colonization continued to be closely regulated by the state. Only after the humiliation of the Spanish army in the siege of Havana in 1762 did reform emerge as an objective, in the early years of the reign of the enlightened monarch Charles III (1759–1788). A fundamental change involved increasing the proportion of local men in the Spanish-dominated military, a move formerly feared as a potential threat to royal political control, and making the demographically pragmatic decision to arm free black (*moreno*) and coloured (*pardo*) battalions of militia. In 1769, the Cuban militia were granted special privileges in both civil and criminal law, making them immune to ordinary justice but subject to their superior officers. These changes were progressive in the sense that they extended a variety of equality to free men, but at the same time conservative in the way in which they strengthened the system of military government and the role of the captains general.

Military government played a smaller role in the colonies established by the English, French, and Dutch. Initially, individual private adventurers and chartered companies played a significant role. In return for lucrative monopolies, these companies undertook tasks normally expected of the state but rarely received capital from the crown.

In 1635, the French set up the Compagnie des Isles de l'Amérique, managed by a group of trusted officials, purportedly to bring Christianity to the islands of the eastern Caribbean. In theory, the charter granted by the crown entitled the Compagnie to assert sovereignty, appoint lieutenant generals or governors, rule in matters of justice, and control the movement of people. In practice, the Compagnie ran its own system of justice and attempted to appoint sovereign councils in the islands to support it. The crown had little capacity to impose its authority, particularly because commerce and finance had fallen largely into the hands of Dutch traders. When the Compagnie was wound up in 1650, Martinique, Guadeloupe, the French section of St Kitts, and other pieces of territory did not revert to the crown but were sold to individual proprietors.

Proprietary government continued in the French colonies until 1664, when Louis XIV set up a new Compagnie des Indes occidentales françaises. By this time, with minimal direction or assistance from the state, the settlers had succeeded in the process of taking land and life, fighting or finding accommodation with the Caribs, finding a viable staple crop, and finding and forcing labour, thus establishing the fundamentals of a plantation economy based on sugar and slavery. Their success in setting up this sordid system of exploitation once again drew the attention of the crown, seeing the colonies as potential sources of tax revenue and envious of the commanding place in trade held by the Dutch. Royal authority was gradually imposed on the French colonies, in a tendency towards absolutism that paralleled events in France over the following hundred years. Acceptance of this new relationship between colony and crown depended heavily on protections granted to plantation produce under mercantilist legislation, which made up for the loss of market advantages that had been appreciated in the period of Dutch dominance, and was encouraged by the patriotism roused through service in warfare under the banner of the king.

Efforts to assert greater control included the appointment of the first French royal intendant, Jean-Baptiste Patoulet, in 1679, to head a revived system of sovereign councils to oversee colonial administration and justice, though denying them the right to apply military justice to civil matters (in contrast to tendencies in the Spanish colonies). By the end of the seventeenth century, the Caribbean colonies of France had been loosely integrated within a centralized system of imperial government that persisted down to 1770 and the revolution. It was a system in which the crown and the metropolitan state ruled over its colonial offspring, seeking to balance the interests of contested claims, but determined ultimately to always apply its power and authority to ensuring the security and profitability of the system of sugar plantation slavery within its empire.

Although the pattern of colonization was relatively similar for France and Britain, the systems of government of these two European states showed greater difference, reflecting contrasting internal, metropolitan political histories. Rather than marking the beginning of a long growth in the power of the monarchy, the seventeenth century was, for the British, a period of turmoil. Scotland remained separate from England, with its own kings and queens. Ireland was a prime site of colonization. Struggles between Catholic and Protestant, church and state, born in the Reformation, persisted. These conflicts infected English colonization of the Caribbean, as seen in St Kitts.

The early English governors might have attempted to act as petty tyrants but they chose instead to appoint councils of men from among the settlers. These councils continued throughout the centuries of colonialism but their unlimited powers, exercised arbitrarily in conjunction with their patron, the governor, began to be pared back with the establishment of representative assemblies. The first of these assemblies was set up in Barbados in 1639. They soon gained the right to initiate legislation and from then on the political histories of the individual islands diverged from their initial uniformity. The centralization and unification fundamental to the French and the Spanish systems of imperial government were much less evident in the case of the English. In every English colony, the character of popular representation was much the same, the elected members of the assemblies chosen from a tiny, narrow class. Candidates had to be wealthy free white Protestant adult males. In the long term, down to 1770, most of these men were planters and slave owners, and they served their own interests. Even this limited form of representative government contained the conditions for internal conflict and, particularly in Barbados, quickly came to reflect the metropolitan struggle between crown and parliament. However, the Civil War in England that commenced in 1642 saw the colonial assemblies extending their powers significantly and the emergence of a virtual self-government in Barbados.

When Jamaica was conquered by the English in 1655, its initial military government was swiftly brought into line with the pattern of governor–council–assembly that applied elsewhere and the island's colonists became some of the most vocal advocates of their constitutional liberties within the context of an emerging plantation economy based on slavery. At a more local level, the island colonies were generally divided into administrative units known as parishes, each with its Church of England and priest. The parishes elected vestries to deal with public works and justice, requiring the planters to employ their enslaved people in making and repairing public (parochial) roads, for example. The system of colonial government continued little changed, though down to 1770 there was constant conflict between governor and appointed council and the elected assembly. Generally, the assemblies won the day. They effectively bridled the prerogative of royal governors, who were forced to accept legislation in order to ensure revenue. It was the great wealth of the sugar planters, extracted through plantation slavery, that made them targets for taxation and at the same time gave them the capacity to obtain what they wanted through the assemblies. They arrogated power by restricting the suffrage, excluding even wealthy men who happened to be Jews or Roman Catholics.

A problem of government largely confined to the British colonies was absenteeism. Not only the proprietary patentees but also many holders of patent offices chose not to reside in the islands. Their duties were carried out by local deputies. More importantly, the growth of absenteeism among the planter class that paralleled the profitability of sugar production, particularly after 1740, substantially reduced the pool of potential candidates qualified for election to the assemblies and appointment to councils. Whether this affected the quality of government in the colonies is a matter of debate but it went together with the capacity of absentee planters and merchants to form a powerful lobby in the British parliament. The influence of this lobby group was seen in the maintenance of mercantilist policies that gave overwhelming tariff preferences to British planters in the British market, underwriting profits through price protection for sugar and other plantation staples. Absenteeism also reduced the ability of the colonial populations to recruit to the local militias, but, again, this was balanced by the increasingly powerful protection offered by the British army and navy, which defended the colonies from attack by other European states and contributed to the relative internal stability of the slave societies. The political strength of the British planter class in island government was matched by the growing political and military strength of the British state.

In the Dutch colonies, government was in the hands of the West-Indische Compagnie (WIC), founded soon after the United Provinces resumed war with Spain in 1621. The WIC followed the model refined by the more powerful joint-stock Verenigde Oost-indische Compagnie (the VOC or Dutch East India Company), established in 1602. The VOC brought commercial success to its merchant members by avoiding competition with one another and gaining an advantage in the market through collective purchasing and selling. The VOC's board of directors (the Heren XVII or Gentlemen Seventeen) swore allegiance to the States General of Holland but had authority to make treaties, build forts, and raise armies. The WIC was governed by the Heren XIX. In theory, this board was responsible for economic strategy but, because the Atlantic was more accessible than the eastern trades and more diverse in the commodities offered, the region naturally opened up to smaller investment ventures and it proved much harder to monopolize trade.

At first, the States General saw the WIC as primarily a military agency and its main purpose as winning back territory from the Catholics and more particularly the Spaniards. It did not prove the great financial success hoped for and was replaced in 1674 by a new WIC, governed by the Heren X, more firmly directed at participation in the trades in sugar and people in Africa and the Caribbean. Together, however, the VOC and the WIC helped enable the Dutch Republic to dominate world trade from the end of the sixteenth century to the early eighteenth century. At their peak, the Dutch held roughly one half of all the world's seagoing ships, a remarkable achievement for what was the smallest of all the European colonizing states. The Dutch seemed to be everywhere, trading in everything. In their Caribbean island colonies, however, the monopoly of the WIC was gradually diminished. Local merchants and shippers were largely in charge of the organization of trade and commerce. Particularly during the seventeenth century, this often involved trade with neighbouring colonies in the hands of other European states rather than a bilateral trade with Holland. This made monitoring the collection of tax much more difficult, because commerce was more diffuse and often crossed legal and political lines, mixing plunder with prudence.

For these same reasons, the Dutch had a less rigid notion of the advantages of mercantilist policies and a more flexible approach to the sources of profit. Because, at least in the islands, the Dutch generally kept at arm's length from the direct ownership and management of plantations and enslaved workers, there was no substantial planter class to balance the merchants or to seek representation in colonial polities. The colonies of the Dutch were exceptions to the general rules that guided economic, social, and political development down to 1770, hard to fit into the broad pattern of Caribbean life though vital to its creation. The Dutch, as traders, however, did play a disproportionate role in the Atlantic slave trade and thus contributed to the system of forced labour that underpinned the plantation economies of the Caribbean.

SLAVERY AND THE PEOPLE TRADE

The system of plantation agriculture at the centre of the sugar revolution came quickly to an almost exclusive dependence on a single form of labour and a particular group of people – enslaved Africans and their Caribbean-born children. There was nothing inevitable about this outcome. Other systems of labour organization might have been chosen and, indeed, a variety of options were tried before slavery became the dominant form. It is as necessary to explain this outcome as it is to explain the dominance of sugar.

In the early seventeenth century, slavery existed alongside free wage labour and indentured labour. By 1770, indentured workers were uncommon almost everywhere in the Caribbean, their places filled by enslaved people. Free wage labourers dwindled and, in the sugar plantation sector, became concentrated in specialist occupations. Wherever sugar dominated, small-scale peasant agriculture was similarly reduced to a tiny group of free self-employed farmers. Only in the towns did free labour continue to flourish alongside slave labour. The first of the systems to perish, in these conditions, was indentured labour.

Down to 1770, almost all of the people who entered indentures were white Europeans. Under indenture, they were subject to formal contracts that required them to labour for a particular proprietor for a fixed term. The length of the indenture was typically seven years. While under indenture, the proprietor was required only to provide the basics of food, clothing, and shelter. Indentured workers could be put to whatever tasks a proprietor chose and worked for whatever days and hours the proprietor demanded. The indenture itself was a tradeable instrument, meaning that one proprietor could sell to another the remaining time of an indentured worker, without regard to the wishes of the worker. The indentured person had no right to seek transfer to a new proprietor. When the term was concluded, the person released from indenture might receive cash or commodities or, if any was available, a grant of land.

Some indentured people agreed to their contracts willingly. They did so because the system provided them with the prospect of landownership, something they could not otherwise contemplate. The heaviness of the labour they had to perform and the harshness of the regime were understood less concretely. Typically, those who engaged voluntarily lacked the capital and knowledge to make more informed assessments of the risks and benefits, and many of them entered their contracts before sugar became established. They expected something less oppressive, an easy entry to the possibilities opened up by imperial ventures. Many of the indentured workers of this period, however, were involuntary labourers, kidnapped or tricked on to ships. These people had much the same contractual rights and disadvantages as the volunteers but less enthusiasm for the tropical colonial project.

Several reasons account for the decline of indenture. Once sugar emerged as the dominant crop and the harshness of its labour regime became known, voluntary European indentures were harder to find. The mortality rate was high for both the voluntary and the involuntary. Many did not survive long enough to complete their terms. Alternative forms of colonial settlement opened up in the Americas that were more attractive to those wishing to become small farmers. The rapid expansion of sugar, however, created a voracious demand for labour that the poorly organized indenture system was simply unable to supply.

The sugar planters of the Caribbean were happy enough to use indentured labour initially, as they experimented with cropping techniques, manufacturing processes, and styles of labour management, but they came to regard the labour of enslaved black African people as superior. The moral status of the institution of slavery was rarely questioned by Europeans before 1770 and it existed already within Caribbean society from the time of Columbus. Amerindians remained among the enslaved into the eighteenth century. For the sugar planters, enslaved people were more valuable than indentured because their labour was purchased for life rather than for a limited period of years and the children of enslaved women were declared slaves at birth. The slave was defined in law as property rather than owing a limited term of labour-time. Caribbean sugar planters also saw black Africans as better fitted for the tropical climate, more resistant to disease, and stronger than Europeans. The slave trade from Africa was organized with brutal efficiency, often through companies established and regulated by the state, and seemed capable of supplying almost unlimited numbers of people.

In order to meet the demand for labour in the Caribbean, an alternative might have been to enslave European people rather than contracting them to indentures. This possibility faced legal and moral objections. Although European nations had accepted slavery as a legal status – for European people, in Europe – down to the Middle Ages, by the seventeenth century this no longer was the case. Should this rule also apply to all the peoples of the New World? The Spanish had already resolved the question, but the new European states had to face it as well. Often, as in the case of the English, the answer appeared without philosophical or moral justifications. The building up of legislation to control the practice of slavery and the daily lives of the enslaved indicated acceptance of the institution rather than announcing its inauguration. Formal declarations of the legitimacy of the enslavement of Africans for use in the colonies were rare, though Louis XIII of France did make such a proclamation in 1638 in spite of some supposed misgivings.

Only in the eighteenth century were questions asked about the status of persons held as slaves in the New World colonies once they set foot on European soil. Ideas of political liberty incorporated the idea of the individual's right to freedom from slavery, within Europe, at the same time as the institution of slavery was being dramatically extended in Europe's colonies. The moral paradoxes beneath these ideas remained effectively hidden down to 1770. Europeans, whether in Europe or in the Caribbean, were not bothered by demands to construct philosophical or religious justifications for slavery. Nor was there any concern about the moral status of involuntary indenture. If it had seemed more profitable, indenture rather than enslavement might have emerged as a dominant form of forced labour in the Caribbean. Allowed the choice, however, slavery seemed to offer many benefits to the planter class, while the free people who did not belong to that class raised few objections and sought only to see where they could find their own advantage and entry to the system that delivered such wealth to the few.

Slave owners rarely doubted that slavery was the most profitable system of labour available to them. They were concerned only to extract the maximum from the people they owned by organizing and managing their labour as efficiently as possible. Particularly because the enslaved person represented capital – a value that could be realized through sale – it was equally in the interest of slave owners to be concerned about the health and longevity of the people they owned, but the frightening mortality of the Caribbean and the unpredictability of death made this concern seem less compelling than the daily extraction of hard labour. To attempt to ensure the maximization of productivity, sugar planters began with a notion of optimum plantation size, measured in area, labour, and output. Although the scale of operations increased considerably over the period, even in 1770, it was hard to find anywhere a sugar plantation with a single factory complex that had more than five hundred enslaved people or less than one hundred. Whatever the total, some fixed principles applied to the allocation of people to tasks, determined by the characteristics of the people themselves and the technological demands of the sugar-producing process.

Enslaved children were expected to perform work once they turned four or five years of age. There was no clear final age for labour. Only those severely diseased or physically unable to work were released from the requirement. The greatest demand for labour was in the cane field. The heaviest labour, with the highest mortality rate, occurred during the establishment of these fields, when the forest was cut down and burned and the soil dug for the first time. All of these tasks were performed with hand tools: axe, hoe, and cutlass. The sugar planters hardly ever used ploughs pulled by cattle in this period. Generally, the soil was stiff and heavy. The strongest of the slaves, women as well as men, were grouped into gangs to dig the broad square holes into which canes were planted. Each gang was composed of about twenty people and supervised directly by a driver – generally an older enslaved man – whose task was to ensure the holes were dug and laid out according to specifications and that the labourers kept to their work throughout the day. The driver did not himself dig but carried a whip or switch that he used to lash those who fell behind or performed inferior work. The people in these gangs also did the heavy labour of cutting canes in crop time.

Separate gangs, each with its own driver, performed the lighter tasks of manuring, weeding, and trashing (removing dead leaves from the growing canes). The children were also organized into gangs, with older women as drivers, to do weeding work and collect grass to feed penned livestock.

Particularly in the period to 1770, gang labour generally meant working from dawn to dusk, with breaks for meals. The planters had specific expectations about how much ground could be dug or cropped in a day but they rarely measured daily performance or attempted to quantify individual contributions. Occasionally, they kept records of the yield obtained from particular fields, but these numbers were seen to reflect soil and rainfall rather than differences in labour inputs. The task system, by which a gang was set a fixed task for the day and could stop work once it was complete, was an uncommon practice in sugar before 1770. On the other hand, sugar planters sometimes did employ jobbing gangs to perform heavier tasks such as cane hole digging, and this work was paid by area. These jobbing gangs might be drawn from neighbouring plantations or be owned by individuals who did not have plantations of their own.

A significant proportion of the enslaved people on a sugar plantation did not work regularly in gang labour. Some of these were carters and wagoners, responsible for moving cut canes from the field to the mill or transporting barrels of sugar from the plantation to the wharf. Where the plantation contained forest, woodcutters were sent to collect timber for building and for the factory's furnaces. Where a plantation was located close to sea or stream, fishermen might be employed to catch fish for the planter's table. Watchmen were scattered about the plantation, living in small huts. All of these slaves necessarily lived relatively independent lives, spending much of their time unsupervised and out of sight. Almost all of them were men. Other enslaved men worked at the centre of activity, as coopers producing barrels or blacksmiths making items needed in the factory. There were also masons and carpenters, employed in building. At the beginning of the sugar revolution, most skilled workers were free or indentured white men. By 1770, in the sugar colonies, most of the masons, carpenters, coppersmiths, coopers, and the like were enslaved men. The hours of work of all the people engaged in such jobs was easily monitored by the white supervisors on a plantation, and their output typically came in measurable units. A fisherman who caught no fish could be punished for his failure, whipped alongside the field labourers.

During crop season, the daily rhythm altered. Whereas cane cutting was confined to the hours of daylight, the mills and the boilers were run as continuously as possible, all day and all night, and cooled down only on Sundays. Gang labourers who worked cutting cane during the day, women as well as men, were required in addition to work through all or part of the night in the factory. They fed canes into the rollers of the mills and carted away the crushed stalks to trash houses where they were dried to be used later as fuel. They ladled boiling juice and filled barrels with raw crystallizing sugar, rolling them into place in the curing house. They carried molasses to the distillery and produced rum. Specialist "sugar boilers" made the decisions about when to strike the sugar, when to commence the cooling down that resulted in crystallization. As with other skilled occupations, enslaved people soon came to understand this art and science better than their white supervisors, and their judgment came to be relied on.

There was one more significant group of enslaved workers – the domestics or "house slaves" who spent their time in the houses of the planters, tending to their daily needs. Cooks and washerwomen were the most specialized of these but other women and children were employed in cleaning and miscellaneous household chores. This was the only area in which women tended to outnumber men among the enslaved. Often, domestics were chosen from among the "coloured" people, those whose fathers were white. The choice represented a grudging recognition of parenthood and a desire to treat these enslaved people favourably but also reflected the view that coloured people were less well equipped than blacks to withstand the rigors of field labour in the tropics. The hours and days of work of the domestics were long throughout the year but the heaviness and the hazards of the tasks were lighter. Much the same idea led to a predominance of coloured men among the skilled workers on plantations.

Where crops other than sugar were grown, the pattern of work varied with the pattern of production. Cotton, indigo, pimento, coffee, and corn, for example, made lighter demands on labour during cultivation and processing. Whereas the crop season often extended through six months on sugar plantations, the harvest was typically much shorter for the other export crops. Some tasks, such as cutting dyewoods, were not seasonal at all.

There was a similar lack of seasonality in the work of enslaved people in towns. The shipping of sugar did have some concentration, with an incentive to see it on board before August, when the hurricane season commenced, but before 1770, much of the sugar was shipped from minor ports – one of the advantages of plantations on small islands with a high ratio of coastline to area, and of small ships with shallow draughts – so there was less focus on the towns. Enslaved people in towns most often were employed in moving goods around, providing personal service, and small scale manufacturing. Some of them worked in gangs, but the opportunities for independent, unsupervised work were generally greater than on rural properties. The outcome was a more flexible system of slavery. The reason for this was that many of the slave owners located in towns held few slaves and it was not efficient for them to constantly monitor small contracts. For example, a woman sent out to sell goods on behalf of her owner had to find her customers and bargain for the best prices or an enslaved man employed as a porter might do a series of jobs in a day. It was not profitable to have to refer every time to the owner in order to agree on each contract, sale, and price. Thus, there emerged a system of "self-hire" in which the enslaved person was required to pay a set sum to the owner at the end of each month, the enslaved person being free to make whatever contracts he or she could from day to day. In some cases, the person had to pay their own way, finding their own shelter and food. In other cases, the slave owner paid "board wages" in cash, expecting the enslaved person to make his or her own living arrangements even when performing daily labour under the owner's direct supervision.

Because most of the towns of the Caribbean before 1770 were coastal ports, they were at the centre of external trade. Plantations did occasionally operate their own shipping points or wharves where vessels came directly to anchor, but most of the ships that crossed the ocean spent at least some time in a larger port and all of these had urban populations. It was to the towns that slave ships came from Africa, the people being either sold on board or displayed and purchased on shore. The occasional slave trading voyage originated from a Caribbean port, organized by local merchants, but the vast majority of the Atlantic slave trade was directed from Europe. As noticed in the previous chapter, the Spanish depended totally on the asiento and other states to supply enslaved people to their colonies. Thus, the three major European states involved in this trade were England, France, and Holland. All of these set up monopoly companies and only gradually replaced them with a "free trade" – a term used without irony – that allowed individuals and groups of merchants to participate independently, though generally on payment of a commission. The French permitted such free participation from 1672, the English from 1689, and the Dutch from 1730.

Trade, particularly the trade in people, sometimes provided the foundation for an entire colony's economy. Thus, Curaçao, an arid island off the coast of Venezuela, was taken by the Dutch in 1634 and quickly developed into a collecting station for enslaved people taken from foreign ships. From the 1650s, Curaçao became a major centre for the Atlantic trade, supplying enslaved people to the Spanish territories either by smuggling or through the asiento system, reinstated by the Spanish government in 1662. In the eighteenth century, however, the Dutch lost control of the asiento and the inhabitants of Curaçao were forced to pay more attention to the production of salt, lumber, and minor agricultural products such as ginger, indigo, and cotton. Dutch ships employed in the Atlantic slave trade attempted to obtain return cargoes, on their voyages back to Holland, but they were often paid in Spanish silver and could not always find bulky goods of value to fill the remaining space. Wood products were important in the early eighteenth century but the supply dried up as the forests were depleted. Sugar produced in the Dutch plantations on the mainland soon became the primary commodity carried but some ships were forced to take on ballast, even sand.

St Eustatius, in the Leeward Islands, was initially intended as a plantation colony when taken by the Dutch in 1635, producing tobacco then sugar, but failed because it suffered frequent droughts.

Amerindians were taken from the Guianas to work the plantations but by the middle of the seventeenth century they had been replaced by enslaved Africans brought from Curaçao. For a brief period, in the 1720s, St Eustatius became a significant centre for the Dutch slave trade, seen as the northern counterpart of Curaçao. It supplied enslaved people to the French colonies of Martinique and Guadeloupe and also to some of the English islands. St Eustatius lost most of its market after 1730, however, when English slave traders dominated and the island then played only a marginal role in Dutch commerce down to 1770. As with Curaçao, return cargoes from St Eustatius included significant quantities of sugar, and the success of St Eustatius as a commercial centre was based more on this commodity than its trade in enslaved people.

POPULATION

One of the most striking features of Caribbean history in the seventeenth and eighteenth centuries is the extent to which the sugar plantation system consumed people. Not only did the population depend on forced migration into the region to enable absolute growth, it needed a constant inflow even to maintain existing numbers. The enslaved population was one in which deaths typically outnumbered births. In the face of this failure of natural increase, the rapid growth that was achieved is remarkable. The eighteenth century was the peak period of migration into the Caribbean. Equally striking is the way in which the sugar revolution switched the balance of the population from white to black, from Europe to Africa.

   The population of the Caribbean grew from about 100,000 in 1600 to 1.4 million in 1770. The rate of growth was slow at first, but increased rapidly with the beginning of the sugar revolution. In 1750, before the Seven Years War shifted the balance in favour of the British, the colonies of the French were the most populous (about 360,000 people), followed by those of the British (310,000), the Spanish (286,000), the Dutch (26,000) and the Danish (17,000). Almost 70 percent of the people lived on "sugar islands", colonies dominated by sugar, and enslaved people made up 67 percent of the total. Thus, there was a strong relationship between the dominance of sugar and the presence of slavery, even though many enslaved people did not actually live on sugar plantations but found themselves employed in other types of enterprise, both rural and urban.

Wherever sugar and slavery expanded, so did population. The two largest sugar colonies in 1750, St Domingue (182,000) and Jamaica (142,000), were significantly more densely populated than the largest island, Cuba (170,000), where sugar remained to be developed as a dominant plantation crop. The sugar revolution, from very early in its history, was celebrated as the site of some of the world's most densely populated countries. Pride of place went to Barbados with 183 persons per km² in 1750, followed closely by St Kitts (140), Antigua (125), and Montserrat (122). After these came Nevis (73), Martinique (73), and Guadeloupe (32). All of these were small islands of the eastern Caribbean, with their size as well as their seaward accessibility enabling rapid saturation. Even the sugar colonies of the Greater Antilles failed to come close to these high densities, though Jamaica (12) and St Domingue (7) were more thickly peopled than Cuba (2), Santo Domingo (2), and Puerto Rico (5). Jamaica and St Domingue had dense regional populations, where sugar filled coastal plains and interior valleys, but the diversity of the topography meant that the challenge of filling the land was much greater.

The Greater Antilles held a smaller proportion of the total Caribbean population in the eighteenth century than in any other century – about 40 percent. This distribution represented a significant imbalance between land and people, with greatly augmented populations in the sugar islands and dramatically depleted populations elsewhere. Because the land space of the Greater Antilles was so overwhelming, the outcome was that in spite of the rapid growth of population between 1630 and 1770, and in spite of the localized high densities, the total population of the Caribbean at the end of the period was well below that supported by the agricultural systems that had flourished before Columbus. The gardens of the Taíno had fed their cultivators. The plantations of the Europeans produced vast quantities of food but the calories were exported, not consumed by the producers.

The great increase in population in the sugar colonies depended almost entirely on the forced migration of enslaved people from Africa. In this migration, which stretched over four centuries, the eighteenth was, by far, the most important. This was the century in which the Caribbean sugar colonies reached their peak and it was the demand from these plantations that constituted the major driver. Of the perhaps 12 million enslaved African people forced on to ships bound for the Americas in the entirety of the Atlantic slave trade, only 10 million survived the atrocious conditions of the "middle passage" and reached the Americas alive. Over the centuries, the totals increased from fewer than 400,000 shipped in the period before 1600; to 1.9 million in the seventeenth century; rising to a peak of 6 million in the eighteenth century; and, in the period of abolitions, 3.3 million in the nineteenth century.

Together with Brazil, the greatest consumers of enslaved people in the Americas were the Caribbean sugar colonies. In the long eighteenth century (1701–1810) some 60 percent of all the enslaved people landed in the Americas were taken to the Caribbean colonies. Brazil took about 30 percent and North America just 6 percent. Within the Caribbean, the British colonies received about 23 percent of the total, the French 22 percent, the Dutch (including Suriname) 8 percent, the Spanish colonies 6 percent, and the Danish less than 1 percent. The dominance of the Atlantic slave trade by British and French ships was even greater than these proportions. Of the individual colonies, the largest numbers arrived in St Domingue (790,000) and Jamaica (660,000), followed by Martinique, Guadeloupe, and Barbados. In the period between 1630 and 1770, Barbados received about 360,000 enslaved people and in 1770 had a population of just 70,000. In the Spanish-American colonies and North America, in contrast, small contingents of enslaved people formed the foundation of vastly larger populations through natural increase. The numbers show starkly the way the Caribbean sugar plantation colonies gobbled up enslaved people, and were never satisfied.

The enslaved people taken to the Americas in the eighteenth century had homes in Africa stretching around the coast from Senegal to Mozambique. At the beginning of the century, more than half of the enslaved were from the region between the Gold Coast and the Bight of Benin (roughly, modern Ghana to western Nigeria) but at its end, these regions had been displaced by the Bight of Benin and Central Africa (eastern Nigeria to Angola). The general tendency was for the slave trade to move southwards. Throughout the eighteenth century, however, people were taken from many different cultures and language groups and typically found themselves surrounded by other Africans whose situation was the same but whose languages and customs they did not necessarily share.

Whatever the cultural and geographical origins of the enslaved Africans brought to the Caribbean, the destination of the majority was a sugar colony and a plantation. It was the sugar planters who had the capital to buy people and it was the sugar planters who had the best expectations of extracting substantial profits from the labour of the people they bought. The outcome was a deadly combination. Almost everywhere, sugar was associated with high death rates. To some extent, this heavy mortality had to do with the fact that plantations were located in unhealthy regions, exposed to malaria and yellow fever. These were the great killers of Europeans in the Caribbean. Africans had developed long-term immunities to these mosquito-borne diseases but, in turn, were less well equipped to resist smallpox, influenza, and cholera. The medical attention given to enslaved people before 1770 was limited and cures and preventive measures poorly understood. Whether enslaved or free, most people were better off without the heroic medicine of the European tradition and better off outside its hospitals. Africans brought with them an appreciation of herbal remedies and added newfound plants from the West Indian pharmacopeia, and the women and men who possessed this knowledge were more likely to be of help than the planters' doctors, a fact occasionally acknowledged by the whites. They knew also how to procure abortions.

More important in the high death rates experienced by the enslaved on sugar plantations was the work regime, which pushed the body to its limits and exacted extreme hours of labour. The brutality of the system stretched throughout the life of the sugar plantation slave, symbolized in the role of the whip but not confined to it. Housing and sanitation were poor. Levels of nutrition were also relatively poor on sugar plantations. This was true whether the people received rations or were forced to depend on the produce of their own provision grounds. The clearest proof of the effects of this combination of inadequate nutrition together with poor living conditions can be found in the fact that in the harshest versions of the sugar complex, particularly in the early stages of establishment, enslaved children were shorter than their parents. This reduction in height occurred only in the sugar regions and contrasted strongly with the experience of other crops and regions, where children were typically taller than their parents. These factors contributed also to high rates of infant mortality and a reduction of fertility. Broadly, the more intense the sugar regime and the higher the productivity of the slaves, the higher their mortality and the greater the necessity of the slave trade simply to maintain numbers.

The heavy mortality and strong demand for enslaved labour that persisted from 1650 to 1770 meant that the populations of the sugar colonies always contained large proportions of African-born people. The creole or Caribbean-born component grew much more rapidly in the colonies where sugar did not dominate. These differences had important consequences for the structure of the populations, affecting the proportions of males to females and young to old. In the sugar colonies, the preference of the Atlantic slave trade for young adult males resulted in a distorted pattern whereas a more "normal" distribution emerged in the colonies that did not focus on sugar and its corollary slavery. The potential for family formation also was somewhat better where generations of creoles were more numerous but the stability of any kind of family unit was always threatened by death and the separation of people through sale.

Creole people were subjected to classification by colour. The systems and terms differed among the colonies but there was always a graduated identification of types of people between the black and the white. These terms and gradations were important because they were used to allocate people to occupations, as noted earlier, but even more so because they were used in a highly specific and rigid manner to determine the legal status of individuals. The basic rule was that if a person's mother was enslaved then that person would also be enslaved. The exception occurred when the child's father was white and the enslaved mother had a sufficient number of generations of white male ancestors. In this case, the child would be free and recognized in law as having full civil rights. In the sugar colonies, this happened only rarely before 1770. In the other colonies, particularly those of the Spanish, access to freedom and legal equality was generally easier through processes of manumission, partly because the demand for enslaved labour was less and partly because of differences in the laws.

In the Spanish colonies, beginning in 1712, the practice of *coartación* was recognized in law. This allowed setting a fixed price for which an enslaved person could purchase their freedom through payment by instalments. It became customary to allow those under the scheme to change their masters in order to improve their ability to pay off the required sum. The money required could be accumulated by the enslaved person or by a third party. Slave owners, particularly in the Spanish colonies where the demand for labour in sugar was insignificant, frequently manumitted their own children by enslaved women. Other slaves, not kin of the master, might be freed in recognition of their long service or as a reward for some special action, such as warning of a threat to the life of the slave owner or his family. Occasionally, enslaved people were freed by governments for special services of this sort and, occasionally, these individuals might be granted the rights of whites whatever their place in the hierarchy of colour. In all aspects of the process of manumission, differences among the various types of colonies were strong, resulting in the striking contrast, noticed already, between Puerto Rico, where "free people of colour" made up one half of the population in the middle of the eighteenth century, and the founding British sugar colony of Barbados, where they were barely one third of 1 percent.

For most people, migration to the Caribbean before 1770 meant they would die there. The occasional enslaved African found a way to escape and travel the Atlantic, and perhaps even return home. A larger number of enslaved people found themselves in Europe, taken there by their owners. In the period before 1770, as noted earlier, setting foot on the free soil of liberty-loving Europe did not expunge the colonial slave status of these people. Some spent many years in Europe and some blended into growing black communities in London and other big cities, but most were sent back to the Caribbean and the plantations.

In contrast, for many sugar planters, the true proof of their success was measured by their capacity to leave the islands and return to live in splendour in Europe. This created generations of plantation owners who were born in Europe and inherited estates, often never even visiting them. Later, there also emerged a class of investors, most of them metropolitan merchants, who purchased plantations or foreclosed on the properties of indebted clients without any intention of visiting them. Both of these types of absentee ownership were relatively rare before 1750. In the first hundred years of the sugar revolution, the most common pattern was for individuals to travel to the islands, purchase land or receive it as a grant from government, and then rule over the development of a plantation and act as its immediate and resident manager. It was common for this to continue for two or three generations. Only when a planter felt his plantation was firmly established and flourishing could he consider leaving it in the hands of managers.

Absenteeism began to become common by the middle of the eighteenth century, at least for the most profitable of the sugar colonies. As their wealth increased and their personal empires became larger and more dispersed, many chose to live in Europe. The planters of this period preferred European residence because they retained kinship and patriotic links with their home countries, they regarded the Caribbean environment as unhealthy, and they wished to flaunt their wealth – strut their stuff – on a larger stage. However, leaving the plantations behind meant putting strangers in charge of their fortunes. Over time, the owners had less and less understanding of what their properties looked like and how they were being run. A growing proportion of the absentee proprietors were, in fact, born in Europe and never travelled to the Caribbean even for a cursory visit. They simply enjoyed the profits transferred to their accounts. This was particularly the case among the British. In some colonies, such as Jamaica, by 1770, there were more absentee-owned properties than plantations on which planters lived.

The primary cause of these high rates of absenteeism was found in the great wealth of these planters. The incomes they earned from sugar and slavery were extraordinarily high by comparison with enterprise in North America or metropolitan Europe, particularly before 1700. Not every colony offered the same opportunities for exploitation, however, and some fell behind. Barbados, the pioneer, generated great wealth for its planters in the first decades of the sugar revolution but then ran out of space for expansion. The island retained its resident planter class much more successfully than Jamaica in the eighteenth century, partly because the plantations of Barbados were relatively small and individually unproductive at that time, yielding fortunes less capable of supporting an absentee in style.

SLAVE SOCIETY OR CREOLE SOCIETY?

What kinds of places were the Caribbean islands in 1770? All of them could be seen as offshoots or subalterns of particular European states and these relationships offered a primary mode of identification. Elements of culture made such European colonial identities visible and audible – through language and dress, storytelling and books, architecture and foodways, music and dance – but often these were no more than clues to something much more diverse and hybrid. Even those born in the islands found it difficult to know what to make of the societies they inhabited. The immobility typically imposed on enslaved people made them inhabitants of small worlds and even the many who endured the middle passage typically inhabited just two small worlds with a nightmare in between. For many, both enslaved and free, there was an intense desire to escape, to live somewhere else with a different status. Escape was not so easily achieved, however, and, as perhaps for most people in most periods of human history, it was necessary to make choices about daily life that spilled over from merely coping into creativity.

Two key ideas have been used to characterize the Caribbean world of the later eighteenth century. These models can be seen either as competing or complementary, but they do broadly offer distinct images of the structure and dynamics underlying social development. The first – slave society – has a long history and a wider use in world history. The term has been applied not only to the Caribbean but also to ancient Greece and Rome, Brazil, and the South in the antebellum United States. Its emphasis is on power relations and the "merely coping" view of behaviour. The second model – creole society – is more recent and more commonly has been applied exclusively to the Caribbean. It has more of an eye for creativity.

The slave society concept has often been used to distinguish between the numerous communities in which slaves are present but relatively peripheral and the rare communities in which slavery is so pervasive an influence that it permeates life totally. This is a distinction between slave-owning societies or "societies with slaves" and "genuine" slave societies. In the common former type, slavery may exist alongside other forms of bondage, whereas in a genuine slave society, such alternatives are uncommon. The character of slavery was transformed wherever slaves came to have an essential role in the economy and this process, in turn, transformed the entire society. In true slave societies, enslaved workers dominate large-scale production and generate a major share of revenue, and are held in mass by an exclusive exploiting class. In order to qualify as a true slave society, enslaved people must make up at least one third of the population and must maintain their demographic weight over a long period of time.

By these definitions, most of the people of the Caribbean lived in slave societies by the beginning of the eighteenth century. By 1750, as many as two thirds of the region's people were enslaved. White people accounted for less than one quarter of the whole and so-called free people of colour less than one tenth. Important exceptions to this general pattern were Cuba, where whites were two thirds of the population and free people of colour were almost as numerous as enslaved people. In Puerto Rico, the difference was even greater, with free coloured people making up one half of the whole. These were colonies in which the sugar revolution was yet to occur. The only other colonies with more whites than slaves around 1750 were Spanish Santo Domingo, the Bahamas, and the tiny islands of St Bartholomew and Saba. In the developed plantation colonies, enslaved people made up about 90 percent. All of these were overqualified for the "slave society" label. They fitted the model fully and inevitably had many features in common, in spite of the apparent geographical and political fragmentation of the region. These common features can be traced directly to the association of sugar and slavery.

An alternative way of describing the situation is to say that in this period the people of the Caribbean lived in plural societies, in which the social structure consisted of segments defined by ethnicity and culture, and sharply distinguished from one another in terms of status and legal and political rights. In this model, the highest ranks were occupied by whites who held to a Europe-oriented culture, whereas the lowest ranks were made up of enslaved field labourers who looked to Africa for their cultural roots. What enabled such a divided society to function in the face of these stark inequalities was brute force and notions of subordination. Although the plural society model shares much with the slave society idea, a plural society could exist without slavery and is not defined by a particular institution of subordination.

Whereas the plural and slave society concepts see the Caribbean in the later eighteenth century as a poorly integrated community of plantation microcosms held together by power relations, the creole society model places emphasis on complex and subtle cultural interactions between peoples and the creativity that existed within and in spite of the brutality and exploitation of plantation slavery. Thus, the idea of creole society necessarily applies always to an entire society, working together somehow as a whole, rather than seeing the society of the enslaved or the whites as separate and closed to influence. The idea derives directly from the contemporary Spanish term *criollo*, meaning both born in or native to a place but not indigenous. In English, *creole* came to be applied to any person or animal born in the Caribbean of imported or immigrant ancestry. The creole was therefore a new being, growing up in an environment other than its ancient "natural" setting and interacting with hitherto unknown social groups. The process of cultural development for these peoples therefore was one of *creolization*, marked by the creation of new languages (creoles) and mores, which were neither inferior to their ancestral roots nor lacking in authenticity.

In the period to 1770, the Caribbean was no more than a partial creole society. New contingents of peoples from varied cultural regions and language groups flooded in from Africa and Europe, contributing strong elements of cultural continuity that existed alongside the new creole forms that sprouted up. It was impossible for a unified creole culture to emerge, even within a single island colony, and, often, the varieties of creolization that were possible contributed to the persistence of segmentation rather than enabling a synthetic outcome. Tension and conflict were generally more apparent than any tendencies towards blending and hybridization. These tendencies and these tensions remained vital to processes of Caribbean social development after 1770 and continued even beyond the period of slavery.

5

Rebels and Revolutionaries

1770–1870

Enslaved people never accepted their lot. They found themselves trapped, often for generations, unable to see a way out but given half a chance, they grasped the opportunity to escape and live in freedom. For numerous reasons, the decades after 1770 offered many more opportunities than had come before. Wherever they could, enslaved people seized these opportunities – to rebel and revolt – and to a striking degree they proved successful. These were the decades labelled by modern historians the "age of democratic revolution", associated at first with the period 1760–1800 but later broadened to encompass the hundred years 1750–1850 and simplified to an "age of revolution". The key events of the period initially were identified as the American Revolution and the French Revolution but the revolution in St Domingue demands an equal place in this narrative. Similarly, the struggle for political liberty in Spanish America and the struggle for the abolition of slavery constitute vital elements of the age of revolution.

The resistance and rebellion of enslaved people in the Caribbean now was embedded in a broader struggle that saw white people in conflict with their rulers both in the metropolis and the colonies. Arguments about the rights of man to liberty and equality – keystones of the French and American revolutions – could not be confined easily to a select group of free white men. The consequence was a broader debate about the right to resist tyrants – is it just to spill the blood of oppressors and how high should the price of freedom be set?

RESISTANCE AND REBELLION IN SLAVE SOCIETIES

For enslaved people, unwillingness to bow to authority or be cowed by coercion took many forms. Some committed suicide rather than live in slavery. Individual enslaved workers on sugar plantations found numerous less self-destructive ways of fighting back: temporary or long-term escape (*marronage*), sabotage, destruction of property, arson, and the murder of their masters. Groups of enslaved people acting together could achieve more but attempting concerted resistance made it harder to keep secrets from the slave owners. As was the case before 1770, the most successful forms of resistance were the permanent escape of individuals, generally overseas as "maritime maroons" or simply disappearing among the crowds of a large town or, on the other hand, by the establishment of autonomous communities in special geographic niches such as the Cockpit Country in Jamaica and the *palenques* of Puerto Rico.

Few new autonomous communities of successful Maroons were established after 1770. In Jamaica, the Second Maroon War of 1795 was fought in order to maintain settlements already established rather than to extend or multiply them. This hard-fought conflict involved only one community, the Maroons of Trelawny Town, and was apparently provoked by the British governor of Jamaica, who sided with other Maroons. The struggle was prolonged because the Trelawny Town Maroons chose to burn their settlement to the ground and retreat into the Cockpit Country where they could fight on their own terms and tactics. They were defeated only through the deceit of the governor, who negotiated a peace promising not to deport the rebels, but then broke his word and sent almost all the people of Trelawny Town – about 600 of them – to Halifax, Nova Scotia.

A different variety of resistance, but with a similar outcome, was the defence of territory in St Vincent by the so-called Black Caribs, who fought two bitter wars against the invasion of their land by British planters in the 1770s and 1790s. These people descended from a group of Africans whose slave ship was wrecked on the nearby island of Bequia in the late seventeenth century and the generations of children they had with Amerindians and other escaped Africans in St Vincent. The Black Caribs eventually lost the battle and, in 1797, some 5,000 of them were transported by the British to an island off the coast of Honduras where they flourished as the "Garifuna".

Where individual or group resistance was found out, enslaved persons faced a typically arbitrary and often brutal code of retribution. On the plantations themselves, whipping was common, the lash wielded by the hand of the driver, but various aggravated atrocities such as the rubbing of salt, lime, and pepper into open wounds were regularly practiced. Being shackled or chained to heavy iron weights made escape physically impossible or at least excruciatingly painful. Being placed in bilboes or stocks was even more immobilizing. Individual slave owners and their employees were often barbaric in their treatment of enslaved people, adding excruciating pain to social indignity. The most severe whippings resulted in death or physical disability. Some were forced to swallow piss and shit, others had limbs or genitals chopped off, or were buried alive up to the neck. The desire to instil fear in order to extract the maximum amount of labour and profit slid easily into unrestrained brutality and sadism.

Sent to court, generally without any real opportunity to defend themselves, enslaved people could be sentenced to death, transportation, imprisonment, or hard labour on public works. Death sentences might be carried out by the relatively humane method of hanging with a noose, or by the more drawn out means of hanging from a rope tied by the wrists or being placed in a metal cage and left to rot. Carrying out these sentences in public was designed to drive terror into the hearts of the enslaved. In towns, the heads of executed slaves were stuck on metal spikes to continue the terror.

All of these forms of resistance and marronage – and all of these forms of vicious retribution – had existed among the enslaved people of the Caribbean before 1770. What was different about the last three decades of the eighteenth century was that the resistance and rebellion of the enslaved occurred within the context of a larger framework of recalcitrance the free, white people of the colonies displayed towards their imperial governors. The origins of this recalcitrance were generally external to the Caribbean colonies but the attitudes of free people to revolt were well known and expressed publicly, often within the hearing of enslaved people. Slave owners typically believed that the enslaved were either incapable of understanding or simply uninterested in their philosophical and political debates about the nature of liberty and the right to resist tyrants. They were wrong about this. The revolutionary ferment of the Atlantic world naturally spilled over into the ideas and objectives of enslaved rebels, with both minor and major consequences.

When the thirteen British colonies of mainland North America declared their independence of Great Britain in 1776, it seemed possible at first that the colonial settler governments of the British colonies in the Caribbean might follow suit. The assemblies, with their limited form of representative government, had long protested the inequities of the system under which they were subservient to King and Parliament. They had attempted to resist the imposition of new forms of taxation under the Stamp Act of 1765. Up to this point, they stood beside their fellow colonists in North America. As British settler colonists, they had a good deal in common culturally, and they actively engaged in trade. The Caribbean offered a major market for North American commodities such as rice, flour, provisions, fish, lumber and dry goods, for which the islands exchanged sugar, rum, and molasses. This was a profitable trade. Its disruption during the American War of Independence (1775–1783) had a significant impact on the colonies. But it was far less vital than the trade between the British Caribbean colonies and Great Britain, which took the larger part of the plantations' product into a protected market and paid premium prices.

The planter governments of the Caribbean did not seek to fight for their political independence. The principal reason for this difference between the islands and the mainland was the contrast in social structure and demographic balance. Whereas the colonists of North America lived with enslaved people, they did not feel vulnerable to large-scale attack from those people. The white settlers of the Caribbean, living in populations where they were outnumbered by the enslaved in a ratio of roughly one to ten, had no faith in their ability to ensure their own security. They lived in fear. With good reason, the whites believed their viability as a community depended on the presence of the British army on land and the navy at sea. To attempt independence seemed far too risky a business, however much the colonists might proclaim their rights to political liberty. The island colonies remained loyal to George III and took in similarly minded refugees from the mainland.

Something similar occurred in the Spanish colonies. On the Caribbean rimland, the Spanish colonies of Venezuela, Colombia, and Panama – which formed the Viceroyalty of New Granada, established in 1718 – gained independence from Spain in 1819 and, with Ecuador, became constituted as Greater Colombia. Rumblings of discontent with Spanish rule had first boiled up in revolt in Venezuela in 1795. In Mexico, a short war led to independence in 1821. The Spanish island colonies did not immediately join the mainland's liberation struggle, though Cuba expressed dissatisfaction with Spanish rule in the late 1830s and the Dominican Republic was independent by 1844. The chaos that accompanied the Latin American wars of independence gave a vital boost to the economic development of Cuba, particularly its emerging sugar sector, and at the same time gave the colony a larger role in a much-reduced Spanish empire. Rather than encouraging or enabling movement towards independence, the new importance of Cuba to Spain helped tighten the imperial grip and made its relinquishment difficult to contemplate.

A stronger immediate impact was felt in the French colonies of the Caribbean from the Revolution that began in France in 1789, with its call for liberty, equality, and fraternity. Unlike the American Revolution and the movement to independence in Spanish America, this was not a revolution in some outpost of the colonial empire but rather a rebellion of the metropolis that struck at the heart of the French monarchy and empire. Because of the nature of the relationship between colony and metropolis, it inevitably drew in the colonists. In many respects, the colonial version of the revolution paralleled the phases of the metropolitan revolt, including its radicalization and progression to authoritarian, imperial government. In France, the calling of delegates to the National Assembly was intended to give a voice to the voiceless but in the Caribbean colonies – Guadeloupe, Martinique, and St Domingue – the white elite arrogated these rights to representation. They were already in conflict with the French government over their entitlement to commercial autonomy, particularly because they sought to engage in trade with the United States, and had opposed metropolitan attempts to have the colonists pay the costs of defence.

Although the whites at first saw the Revolution as a chance to advocate autonomy, they quickly came to fear its potential consequences. Thus, they sought to suppress news of events in France and of documents such as the Declaration of the Rights of Man. These fears and this news did, however, become well-known to the enslaved in the colonies, and rebellion began in Martinique and Guadeloupe as early as April 1790. As was often the case in such rumour-filled events, the enslaved came to believe that the King had proclaimed the end of slavery and that the people were held unjustly by their masters, or understood that the National Assembly had abolished whipping and reduced the days of plantation labour.

When the white French colonists of Martinique, Guadeloupe, and St Domingue argued that they alone were entitled to claim seats in the National Assembly, this was protested by the free coloured. They had a limited victory when, in 1791, the National Assembly declared that the colonial legislatures should extend suffrage to all taxpaying adult males with free parents, but this was annulled a few months later. In 1794, the revolutionary government in France abolished slavery in all of its colonies, without compensation, something the slave owners had not included in their understanding of the scope of liberty and equality. Although this decision was made within the context of the metropolitan revolution's radical program of wealth redistribution and social transformation, it also represented a response to the struggles of the enslaved people of the French colonies for their own freedom, their own liberty and equality. Nowhere was this objective expressed more strongly or achieved so successfully as in St Domingue.

REVOLUTION IN ST DOMINGUE

The revolution in St Domingue was the most successful rebellion of enslaved people in world history. It saw the end of slavery, the establishment of the first black state in the Americas, and the expulsion of a major European imperial power. These events were dramatic in themselves but made even more striking by the fact that they occurred, not in an isolated, barely profitable colony, but happened in one of the most valuable. Indeed, in the 1780s, the French could rightly claim St Domingue as the richest colony not just in the Caribbean but in the world. St Domingue produced almost one half of world sugar exports and an even larger proportion of the world's coffee. Other important exports were cotton, indigo, and cacao. All of these crops, with the exception of capital-intensive sugar, could be produced efficiently on small plantations, and the large population of poorer whites and free coloured people increasingly sought to live on their own properties and make the colony their home. Strong versions of local identity emerged, in opposition to the habit of absenteeism, and in the late 1760s, there were small rebellions of creole whites and free coloured in support of self-rule and commercial freedom. Many major French ports depended on trade with St Domingue and the related Atlantic slave trade, while the port cities of St Domingue were equally prosperous and supported large white and free coloured populations. Enlightenment arts and sciences prospered in the midst of one of the world's greatest slave societies.

By 1789, the population of St Domingue was about 520,000. The white population and the free coloured and free black population were roughly equal in numbers, each group accounting for about 5 percent of the population, but the other 90 percent of the people were enslaved. St Domingue had by far the largest slave population in the Caribbean. Because it had grown very rapidly in the eighteenth century – increasing three times between 1750 and 1789 – as many as two thirds of the people were Africa-born, the largest contingents coming from Central Africa. They worked in many occupations and an unusually high proportion were owned by free coloured and free black people, generally on small rural holdings or in the towns, but the common situation of those employed on sugar plantations was as harsh as elsewhere. Surprisingly, rebellions had been rare in St Domingue throughout the eighteenth century, though the unsuccessful Makandal conspiracy of 1757 had sought to achieve not only the complete destruction of the white master class but also political independence. Marronage was made relatively easy by the survival of forest in the interior.

The free coloured people of St Domingue had, thirty years before 1789, commenced a struggle for equal rights, but faced newly raised barriers that made their legal status worse than in most other slave societies of the Americas. They were then denied entry to certain occupations, such as that of surgeon or midwife, and inhibited by sumptuary laws that defined the hairstyles and dress they might wear and the kinds of furniture they might have in their houses. Not only were the civil rights of the free coloured and free black people of St Domingue limited, but even what they had were being eroded away. The consequence was that the white colonists and the free coloured and free black people of St Domingue entered a period of conflict but without any of these free people seeking to include the enslaved in their struggle.

The enslaved people of St Domingue commenced their own struggle against slavery and their masters in August 1791. Unlike many earlier conspiracies, which had been betrayed, this time, the well-organized plan, developed over several weeks, was successfully kept secret until the last minute. The revolt spread swiftly along the northern plain. Many sugar and coffee plantations were burned, many French people killed, and many more forced to flee. With skilled leadership, the enslaved became an efficient fighting force, organized into highly mobile bands and employing guerrilla tactics wherever possible, in the manner of the Maroons. They fought in sites where cliffs and gorges made ambush easy, setting booby traps along the way. Whenever it seemed to offer an advantage, the rebels retreated into the hills and regrouped their forces for counterattacks, while returning to burn and ravage plantations.

Propertied free coloured men often fought alongside the whites, particularly after the grant of full civil rights in April 1792. The conflict became increasingly complex when governors representing revolutionary republican France were sent to St Domingue, with mixed messages on the attitude of the metropolis towards slavery. By the middle of 1793, Cap Français, the major port city on the north coast, lay in ruins. Thousands of whites fled the colony for the United States, Jamaica, and other nearby slave societies.

While declaring allegiance to France and a willingness to fight for the nation, the enslaved people of St Domingue made it clear they wished slavery to end, not only for fighting men but for all people, male and female, young and old. By August 1793, the institution had been officially abolished by the French revolutionary government's representatives in most regions. However, the people were required to remain on their former plantations and work for wages, with the capacity to determine work schedules and other aspects of management. In the south of the colony, freedom was to be granted to slave soldiers only if they took the side of France, while the rest of the people were to return to the plantations. These pragmatic declarations made in St Domingue were eventually ratified by the Convention, in Paris, in February 1794. At the same time, the protestations of allegiance to France were diminished when some of the armies of the enslaved joined forces with Spanish troops from Santo Domingo – the eastern section of Hispaniola – in a project to take St Domingue from the French. The British had also joined the battle and they, too, like the French and the Spanish, attempted to gain the support of the rebel armies, particularly in the south, though all the while hoping to make St Domingue – the great rival of Jamaica – a British colony. It was hard to know who to trust.

From this apparent chaos emerged the best known leader of the St Domingue revolution, Toussaint Louverture. He was sceptical of the opportunistic declarations of the revolutionary representatives. A creole, born on a sugar plantation in 1743, Toussaint had worked his way up through the ranks of the rebel forces and found ready agreement among his fellow troops that the only realistic approach was to ignore the conditional proclamations of liberty and the solicitations of the Spanish and the British. To ensure final victory, Toussaint sought rather to expand the revolt. He rapidly increased the size of his army and joined battle with the free coloured forces as well as the French. By the beginning of 1794, only a handful of urban zones remained in French hands. However, the British occupied about one third of St Domingue and continued to pour in troops down to 1798. Initially regarded as liberators, the unfair behaviour of the British against the free coloured people led them to join forces with the slave contingents. Forced to fight the British as well as the Spanish on separate fronts, Toussaint eventually had to make an alliance with republican France in the middle of 1794. His army of 20,000 wore down the British troops, large numbers of whom died of disease, particularly yellow fever and malaria. When Spain ceded Santo Domingo to France in 1795, Toussaint became governor of the enlarged colony.

By 1796, some things seemed more certain. French elites were no longer powerful in St Domingue. Thousands of whites had been killed. Thousands of blacks had died, killed in battle with one side or the other, while thousands of enslaved people had been forced to migrate with their owners. The idea that those who remained should be once more enslaved or forced to bow to some form of white overlordship was impossible to accept. In the north, blacks were in control. In the south, the free coloured held sway, with the British in charge of the region's west. The old plantation system was in tatters, with production reduced to one quarter of what it had been five years before. Free coloured men were given lands in the south formerly held by whites, while blacks were forced to remain on the properties as workers. Although some of the formerly enslaved people feared that Toussaint wished to restore slavery, his plan was, rather, to restore the plantation system, and for this purpose he welcomed returning planters and sought to install a labour regime that was harsh but something less than slavery.

With the French, the British, and the Spanish finally out of the way, the potential for conflict between former allies became hard to ignore. War between the south, led by André Rigaud, and the north, commanded by Toussaint's fellow officer Jean-Jacques Dessalines, ended in victory for the northern army. Rigaud went into exile and many of his officers were shot. This left Toussaint the effective ruler of St Domingue and, ignoring France, he took sole responsibility for making treaties with the United States and Britain. In 1801, he proposed a constitution, based on the model of revolutionary France, which abolished slavery, installed equality, made commerce free, and established the Roman Catholic church as guardian of the one public religion. St Domingue was to be a colony of France but self-governing.

Toussaint then overreached himself by invading and annexing Santo Domingo, the former Spanish part of Hispaniola but now a French colony, a bold act that enraged Napoleon. Sending a large military force to St Domingue in 1802, Napoleon demanded the restoration of slavery in Santo Domingo, as the Spanish aristocracy desired, as well as advocating the maintenance of the newly established system of forced labour in the west. Napoleon's men succeeded better than expected and a vacillating Toussaint was deported to France, where he died in 1803. However, the people of St Domingue soon came to realize that Napoleon's desire to restore plantation slavery was no mere threat. They learned that slavery had, in fact, been reestablished in the other French colonies and that the equal rights granted the people of colour had been taken away. Refusing to accept this as the fate of St Domingue, cohorts of rebels emerged all through the north, using guerrilla tactics to mount a broad attack. The French responded with general slaughter, killing tens of thousands of black and coloured people between late 1802 and early 1803. The rebel leaders, Dessalines and Henri Christophe, responded in kind. By the end of 1803, the French had been defeated in both the north and the south. The French army, reduced in numbers by perhaps 50,000, finally left the colony. The rebel armies were victorious. Many of the remaining white people were executed and the French were warned not to return.

Haiti, the black republic, declared its independence on the first day of 1804. In taking the ancient Taíno name of Haiti, the new state declared its indigeneity and its historicity, and perhaps also pointed to a manifest destiny that would see Haiti expand to occupy the entire island. Hearing that the French had made Napoleon their Emperor, Dessalines took the same title for himself and behaved in the same absolutist manner. Within two years he was dead, executed and humiliated by his own troops. In 1809, the French lost control of Santo Domingo and it became again a colony of Spain; slavery was restored but the plantation system languished. Eventually, the French abandoned their dream of once more imposing slavery on their formerly great plantation colony and even surrendered their hopes of making Haiti a French colony. In 1825, the independence of the Haitian republic was recognized by France and also by Great Britain. The United States delayed recognition until 1862, when it was advocated by Abraham Lincoln in the midst of the Civil War and linked with schemes for the resettlement or "colonization" of U.S. blacks in Haiti and elsewhere. The French recognition of independence came at a high price, granted only on condition that the Haitians pay an indemnity – 150 million francs – to cover the costs of the war. It was a heavy burden, though only ever paid in part.

Plate 5.1. St Domingue executions, 1803. *Source:* Marcus
Rainsford, *An Historical Account of the Black Empire of
Hayti* (London: James Cundee, 1805), opp. 337.

The success of the Haitian revolution is remarkable. The enslaved
people achieved what the Taínos had been unable to do 300 years
before, principally because the enslaved had access to weapons and
horses, creating a more level battlefield. The enslaved people of
St Domingue also achieved what their fellow slaves in the other
French colonies of Martinique and Guadeloupe failed to secure.
The comparison is important because, although both sets of colonies

shared the seemingly favourable context of metropolitan revolution with its cry for liberty and equality, only the enslaved people of St Domingue were able to make their own successful revolution. Their relative advantages were rooted in scale and topography, the broad and varied landforms of western Hispaniola and its long coastline creating ideal conditions for guerrilla warfare, together with the unusual feature of a long inland boundary. The people of St Domingue also benefited by the divisions and chaos resulting from the British and Spanish interventions. Further, to defeat the armies of the French and the British required not only quality military leadership, but also the resilience to carry the fight to the bitter end and a willingness to match atrocity with atrocity, massacre with massacre.

The outcome of the struggle remained uncertain to the end. The rebels declared their goal as "liberty or death" but it was the complementary motto "death to all whites" that drove them to victory. However bloody, it was this determination that ultimately ensured victory and established the great fear that inhibited attempts to restore slavery. The insurgent mass of enslaved people, unwilling to admit compromise, saw more clearly than did their leaders the necessity of continuing the war and completing the destruction. Their achievement was unique but it created a context in which the abolition of slavery elsewhere in the Caribbean seemed more certain, because the revolution invoked fear as well as hope. It also meant that, for much longer, the nation of Haiti would be forced to live as an outcast.

OTHER ABOLITIONS

The case of St Domingue was unusual in that the end of slavery as an institution preceded and effected the end of the Atlantic slave trade to that colony. Elsewhere in the Caribbean and throughout the Americas generally, the abolition of the Atlantic trade in people came first and often there was an extended period between this abolition and the abolition of slavery as a legal institution. The reason for the separation of the two abolitions and for the interval between them was essentially that it was easier to prohibit the trade than the institution because the owners of enslaved people in the

Americas claimed these people as their property and might therefore make claims for compensation on their release from bondage. It was also argued that ending the Atlantic trade in people would force slave owners to improve living and working conditions and so enable the emergence of a naturally reproducing population that had no need to depend on the slave trade for replenishment.

White political movements advocating the end of the Atlantic slave trade were typically located in Europe and rarely had supporters in the Caribbean colonies. The struggle of the enslaved people living in the colonies was naturally directed at slavery, the institution that ruled their existence. With the exception of Spain, abolitionist movements became active in most of the European imperial states from about 1770, and legislation was proposed in the following decades. None of these attempts to end the Atlantic slave trade was successful before the revolution in St Domingue, as vested interests were strong enough to prevent the passing of laws. After 1789, the situation became more complicated. Although the actions of the French revolutionary governments were contradictory, the success of the revolution of the enslaved in St Domingue made the end of slavery and the slave trade appear more probable and, indeed, imminent at the same time they increased the fears of the slave owners. On the other hand, the great reduction in French colonial production of sugar and coffee that followed the revolution created immediate market opportunities for other producers, notably the British colonies and, in the longer term, Cuba. This unanticipated competitive advantage made abolition harder for the slave-owning classes to contemplate.

The Danish colonies stopped receiving enslaved people from Africa in 1803, the British in 1808, and the Dutch in 1818. A variety of factors converged to bring about the end of the Atlantic slave trade. The British took a leading role in the movement, in spite of the fact that they were then heavily involved in the trade in people and in plantation slavery. The ending of slavery may be interpreted as an example of creative destruction, which enabled the British to move forward in their Industrial Revolution as advocates and beneficiaries of free trade and free labour principles. At the same time, emerging ideas about natural rights and political liberty, associated with Enlightenment reason and radical Christianity, merged with changing popular opinion and activism. These ideas came together in 1787 with the establishment of the Society for the Abolition of the Slave Trade, supported by the mass petitioning of Parliament and the introduction of legislation, which seemed to have a good chance of success as early as 1792 but was not carried until 1807.

In the colonies of the British, the Dutch, and the Danes, the abolition of the Atlantic slave trade was effective, with only a relatively small number of enslaved people brought to them by nationals, against the laws of their imperial states. A large trade in people did continue, however, carried out by Spain, France, Portugal, Brazil, and the United States. The French abandoned the Atlantic slave trade temporarily during the Napoleonic wars but resumed when peace returned. Enslaved people were brought to the French colonies in the Caribbean until the 1830s and to Cuba into the 1850s. Spain did not sign a treaty with Britain to end the trade until 1867. These differences had something to do with variations in the economic status of the islands – particularly the flourishing sugar industry of Cuba – but also reflected the naval and political effectiveness of the British in seeking to end the Atlantic slave trade, in practice as well as principle, and their ability to apply diplomatic weight to the Danish and Dutch. The British navy applied a good deal of pressure, capturing large numbers of ships, but the illegal slave traders responded by using faster sailing ships and turning to steam to attempt to escape their pursuers. The Spanish Caribbean colonies, where the Atlantic slave trade had had its beginnings more than 350 years before, clung to the slave trade longer than any other Spanish-American territory. In spite of this longevity, Cuba received only 700,000 slaves over the entire period of the Atlantic slave trade, legal and illegal, a number significantly less than its smaller neighbours St Domingue and Jamaica.

An alternative response to the abolition of the Atlantic slave trade was to move people from place to place within the Caribbean. This applied more often to Caribbean-born enslaved people than to the Africa-born, resulting in a double displacement. This internal trade, however, was limited because few populations within the Caribbean achieved natural increases and because trade between the different imperial groups often was prohibited. The most common of these internal movements was of people from colonies that did not produce sugar but experienced substantial population growth – for example, the Bahamas – to newly established sugar colonies. There also was some movement from the older, less profitable sugar colonies to the newer territories, where greater profits could be extracted, independent of any differences in population performance.

Although the abolition of the institution of slavery was more often linked to events within the Caribbean colonies than was the case in the abolition of the Atlantic slave trade, the abolitions of slavery tended similarly to be applied across imperial groupings. The period between the abolition of the Atlantic trade and slavery itself was typically extended over several decades, and the two abolitions did not follow in sequence. Slavery was formally abolished in the British colonies in 1834 but effectively only in 1838, thirty years after the abolition of British participation in the Atlantic slave trade. The Swedish abolished slave trading across the Atlantic after the Napoleonic wars, and abolished slavery in its one Caribbean colony – the island of St Barthelémy, with just 600 slaves – in 1847. The Danish slave trade had been suspended earlier, in 1803, but slavery continued in the Danish colonies until 1848. The French abolished slavery definitively the same year, though having prematurely abolished it in 1794 only to reinstate it in 1802. The Dutch did not abolish slavery until 1863, some 45 years after ending their participation in the slave trade. Events in the Spanish colonies were less closely coordinated, reflecting their more varied political histories, with slavery not abolished until 1873 in Puerto Rico and 1886 in Cuba. Then, the only remaining slave state in the Americas was Brazil, and it held out just two more years. Slavery, as a legally constituted institution authorized by the state, persisted longer in Cuba than in other place in the Americas.

The causes of the abolition of slavery paralleled the causes of the abolition of the Atlantic slave trade but responded more often to rebellion and unrest within the enslaved populations of the colonies. In the British case, the great rebellion of Christmas 1831 in Jamaica was influential. On the other hand, the notorious 1844 revolt against slavery in Cuba, known as La Escalera, had much less immediate impact. In general, the European states other than the British worked closely with the colonial slave-owning classes to determine the timing of abolition and were much less influenced by antislavery associations. Hence, the long gaps between the ending of the slave trade and the ending of slavery in Dutch and Spanish colonies. The Spanish, in particular, favoured a painfully drawn out process of gradualism. Issued by the Spanish government in the course of the war of independence in Cuba, the Moret Law of 1870 freed new-born children of slave mothers and aged enslaved people in an effort to counter the actions of rebels in the east of the island who offered freedom to enslaved people willing to join their cause. Paralleling the French case, abolition in Puerto Rico was linked to metropolitan revolution, the declaration of freedom in 1873 an act of the Spanish First Republic.

Once one territory had been freed of slavery, the knowledge quickly spread and the precedents became more varied than the example set by the people of Haiti. In some places, knowledge of the end of slavery in neighbouring territories created opportunities for immediate physical escape that went far beyond the chances offered by marronage. For example, in 1840, an enslaved person on the Danish island of St John might reasonably risk rowing a boat across the water to the nearby British colony of Tortola. The enslaved people living in the Dutch sector of St Maarten successfully negotiated their freedom in 1848 by threatening to move to the French part of the island, where abolition had been declared.

The formal abolition of slavery was typically followed by a period of fettered freedom. In the British colonies, a period of Apprentice-ship lasted from 1834 to 1838, with the stated intention of intro-ducing the formerly enslaved to the new system in which they would have to bargain for wages, pay rent for house and land, and cover medical expenses. The people learned little and, indeed, had little to learn. Apprenticeship had more to teach the planter class. The system was designed to assist the planters to make the transition to free labour by tying the supposedly freed people to the plantations for the duration and requiring them to work a minimum number of hours without payment, receiving wages only for hours worked above that minimum. Thus the Apprenticeship was, in effect, a form of compensation to the planters and an opportunity to attempt to establish a new relationship that might keep the formerly enslaved people living and working on the plantations on which they had been slaves.

In the British colonies, the Apprenticeship went together with the payment of compensation. This was not money paid to the formerly enslaved for the exploitation they had endured under slavery and, in the British debates over abolition, the possibility that the money should go to the injured party was hardly ever raised. Rather, the compensation was money paid to the slave owners for being deprived of their private property – the control they had had over the bodies of the enslaved. The enslaved people were individually valued and compensation paid to their former owners, the amounts varying according to the relative productivity and profitability of the colonies. The total amount allocated by the British government was £20 million, a substantial sum, but much of it was used to pay off existing debt and went directly into the pockets of metropolitan merchants rather than contributing to the West Indian economy. The money was paid only in order to secure the cooperation of the slave-owning colonists, whose representative governments were largely responsible for passing the legislation. Thus, whereas the abolition of the Atlantic slave trade was achieved by legislation passed in the British Parliament, the abolition of slavery was ultimately the subject of legislation by the individual colonies. Compensation was also made to former slave owners in the Dutch colonies, but elsewhere nothing was paid, either to the owners or the enslaved.

DEMOGRAPHIC CHANGE

The hundred years between 1770 and 1870 saw a great revolution in the numbers and character of the Caribbean population. The total increased almost four times, from about 1.4 to 5.1 million. Although the rate of growth was no more rapid than it had been in the earlier part of the eighteenth century, the numbers and the density of population became much greater. The earlier maximum achieved by the Taínos in 1490 – about 2 million – was surpassed for the first time around 1840. Again, although the rate of growth changed little over the period from 1770 to 1870, the composition of the population changed dramatically, as did the sources of growth.

Down to 1790, the increase in the total population paralleled very closely the growth of the slave population and depended on the Atlantic slave trade. After 1790, the slave population declined as steeply as it had previously grown, but the total population forged ahead just as before. The revolution in St Domingue marked the watershed.

In 1770, the typical colonial population in the Caribbean was made up of a large proportion of enslaved people and a large proportion of recent immigrants, most of them brought to the islands against their will. Overall, enslaved people accounted for more than 60 percent of the total in 1770. By 1870, only Cuba and Puerto Rico had slaves and enslaved people made up fewer than 3 percent of the regional population. Immigrants, both Africans and Europeans, became relatively rare. The majority of the people were second-generation natives, born in the islands of creole parents. Migration between islands and out of the region was uncommon around 1870. In these ways, whereas 1790 was the high point of slavery, 1870 marked the high point of localized, native-born populations in the history of the modern Caribbean.

In spite of these large-scale broad tendencies, the trajectory of population change was, by no means, uniform throughout the region or throughout the period. Initially, the populations of the slave societies founded on sugar grew rapidly. In St Domingue, by 1790, the population had achieved a density roughly equivalent to that among the Taínos, based on a different, though equally intensive, agrarian system. The numbers of enslaved people living in the Caribbean peaked at 1.1 million in 1790, immediately before the revolution in St Domingue. They accounted for 70 percent of the total regional population. The enslaved of St Domingue numbered about 465,000, so the ending of slavery in that colony had a dramatic impact on the Caribbean at large. Elsewhere the numbers continued to grow until the abolition of the Atlantic slave trade. When the British trade ended in 1808, the British colonies in the Caribbean reached their peak enslaved population of about 750,000. Jamaica, St Domingue's strongest rival, held 370,000 slaves. The rest of the enslaved people were distributed widely through the British, French, Dutch, and Danish colonies, but the Spanish took a long time to surpass these competitors. Cuba's slave population numbered only 30,000 in 1760 but grew rapidly and reached 370,000 by 1860.

Demographic change played an important part in the ending of slavery, typically as a consequence of the abolition of the Atlantic slave trade. In a few marginal regions of the Caribbean, outside the sphere of the sugar plantation, the enslaved population grew rapidly and the density of people suggested that wage labour could be obtained cheaply. Within the plantation zones, on the other hand, the equally rapid decline in the populations meant that the labour force began to fall short of the numbers demanded by the planter class and pushed up the cost of purchasing people. Generally, the production of sugar went together with the heaviest demands on labour, the heaviest mortality, and the lowest levels of fertility and reproduction. Creoles, young people, and people of colour all became more common among the enslaved. The population became less fitted to the ideal labour force of the planters. At the same time, the expectations of the enslaved people themselves, even within the limits imposed by the system of slavery, became harder to achieve and more likely to engender rebellion. Manumission and natural growth in the free coloured populations similarly shifted expectations and created a landless labour force that could be employed relatively cheaply on plantations.

In 1770, the white sector of the Caribbean population accounted for about one quarter of the total. Of the larger island populations, whites dominated only in Cuba, where they made up almost two thirds of the people in the last years before sugar and slavery changed the complexion of the landscape. Overall, free people of colour were only about 10 percent of the population in 1770, but they had already come to outnumber both whites and enslaved people in Puerto Rico and Santo Domingo.

In Cuba, the growth of the slave population after 1770 was sufficiently strong to outstrip the free coloured sector, resulting in an "Africanization" scare that contributed to the final acceptance of abolition by the white population. In spite of this perception, the slaves of Cuba never became a majority. In fact, Cuba was unusual in the way the development of sugar went together with a large white population that grew rapidly between about 1840 and 1860 to become a majority of about 70 percent of the total population.

Although Cuba's white population was largely creole, it did contain a significant and influential minority of Spanish-born people, the *peninsulares*. This pattern contrasted strongly with that in the British and French colonies during slavery, where the enslaved typically made up more than 80 percent. By the time of the abolition of slavery, free coloured people outnumbered whites in Martinique and Guadeloupe, as they did in almost all of the British colonies. After the abolition of slavery, the white population diminished in many places. Often, white people had found migration to the Caribbean a more attractive idea while they could profit by the labour of enslaved people and achieve social status. Without slavery the islands lacked this allure.

The revolution in St Domingue was costly in human life. Death and emigration and the associated ending of immigration of all sorts resulted in the loss of about 300,000 people. In 1804, the population of Haiti was reduced to about 400,000 but it recovered quickly, to reach 1.2 million in 1870. However weak the republic appeared in the international economy, population growth was rapid for these free people. By comparison, the populations of Martinique and Guadeloupe, where slavery persisted, increased by only about 10 percent between 1790 and 1830, then growing more rapidly after the abolition of slavery. Everywhere, the abolition of slavery enabled the development of more healthy family and household arrangements, without the threat of arbitrary separation and movement, the burden of individual immobility, the constant threat of rape by white men, and the harsh living conditions associated with sugar production under slavery. Freedom offered hope and the potential for domestic and community social development. In some places, especially the larger islands, freedom might also mean the possibility of an independent existence, and there the population flourished.

In terms of the geographical distribution of population, the period from 1770 to 1870 witnessed a drift away from the smaller to the larger islands. This shift reflected changes in the viability of sugar technologies and transport, and the simple saturation of many of the smaller islands, which lost their initial advantages of accessibility and soil. In 1770, the most populous colony was the rapidly growing St Domingue (350,000), followed by the other major sugar colony, Jamaica (200,000), and the sparsely settled Cuba (170,000). None of the other colonies had populations of more than 100,000, though the prime sugar producers Barbados, Martinique, and Guadeloupe came closest and were densely settled. The other large colonies, Puerto Rico and Santo Domingo, had not yet emerged as rivals.

By 1870, the balance had shifted significantly. The smaller of the islands often had little room for further growth as long as they remained dependent on agriculture, so the most dramatic increases occurred in the larger territories. Cuba had the most people, with 1.4 million, closely followed by Haiti (1.2 million), then Puerto Rico (700,000), Jamaica (500,000), the Dominican Republic (290,000), Guadeloupe, Barbados, Martinique, and the rapidly expanding sugar island, Trinidad (110,000). The outcome was that, whereas in 1770, the four islands of the Greater Antilles together contained only about 56 percent of the Caribbean population, by 1870, they contained 80 percent. Size began to matter more than islandness. After lagging behind Hispaniola through all of history, Cuba, the largest of the islands, finally came close to catching up.

The rise of Cuba was founded on the continuation of slavery and the Atlantic slave trade but, as already observed, this forced migration was paralleled by a substantial immigration of white people, most of them from Spain. Throughout the Caribbean, migration into the region from 1770 to 1870 was dominated by these two major sources. Before 1800, a small flow of indentured white men, often with skills or crafts, continued to arrive. Most of these men came with the intention of settling in the Caribbean colonies, hoping to work their way up to wealth. Following the American Revolution, small numbers of white Loyalists came to settle in the British colonies and some of them brought enslaved people with them. The Loyalists had their greatest impact in the Bahamas, where their arrival after 1783 tripled the population and they introduced the plantation and cotton, which had a brief period of prosperity. In 1806, a contingent of Chinese was brought to Trinidad – the first to the Americas – but they proved reluctant field labourers in the context of slave society and most quickly turned to trade.

After the abolition of the Atlantic slave trade, there was a small immigration of "voluntary" African labourers, particularly to the French and British islands. There was a significant flow into the French colonies as late as the 1850s, fed by the rationalization that people purchased as slaves in Africa could be liberated once on the high seas, then delivered to the West Indies as workers under contract.

People were not free to move to wherever the demand for labour was greatest and the wages best. Even internal migration was closely monitored. In Martinique and Guadeloupe, a domestic passport was introduced two years after the abolition of slavery, intended to control the movement of working people and prevent them from abandoning the plantations. This passport was to be shown even when moving from commune to commune within the islands. In addition to the passport, a pass system was introduced in 1852 designed not merely to control movement but to ensure contractual labour. Every person working for a wage or holding a contract for a term less than a year was required to have a pass. The objective was to attach workers to plantations on long-term contracts. Those who had neither pass nor contract were treated as vagabonds. Response to this system, however, was uniformly hostile and gangs collectively refused to accept passes. Violence persisted between workers and police, and the potential plantation labour force was reduced, leading to calls for indentured immigration.

Indentured servitude had a second life after the abolition of slavery. Rather than white Europeans, this new movement drew migrants from the poorer districts of India and China. These indentured migrants were generally expected to work on plantations, cultivating and processing the same crops that had previously been produced by enslaved people. Unlike the first wave of indentured migrants, the Asian recruits frequently exercised their rights to take up return passages to their home countries. They did not come to settle permanently but agreed to work for a fixed period, typically five years, over which they hoped to accumulate earnings that, on repatriation, would seem substantial. They could not bargain for wages but were required to work for a specific plantation and allowed only limited geographical mobility. Like most temporary migrants, however, many accommodated themselves to life in the Caribbean and established households. Some chose not to return home. The cost of indentured migration fell on the planters or the colonial governments, so only those with vibrant sugar plantation economies took large numbers. Trinidad was the most important receiver of

Indians, taking about 40,000 by 1870, followed by Guadeloupe and
Jamaica. Cuba dominated the larger movement from China, some
125,000 arriving there between 1848 and 1874. This second wave
of indenture, like the first, was composed largely of adult males and
rarely included family groups.

LABOUR AND LAND

The changing geographical distribution of the population was associated in seemingly contradictory ways with changes in patterns
of settlement, land tenure, and resource exploitation. As before,
there were strong differences among islands, regions, and different
colonial groupings. On the one hand, places formerly occupied by
plantations were transformed into peasant economies and on the
other, sparsely settled areas came to be packed with plantations.
Again, some places continued relatively unchanged, their landscapes
of plantations and smaller landholdings looking much the same in
1870 as they had 100 years before.

Underlying these contrasting patterns of land and labour exploitation were differences in the density of population and the ratio of
people to (potential) agricultural land. Although the explanation
does not work equally well in every case, it seems broadly true
that a low ratio of people to land was conducive to the development of coercive systems of labour relations, wherever individual
entrepreneurs sought to exploit people in this way and the state was
willing to condone such systems. This was the situation throughout
the period of slavery in the Caribbean, when the principal land tak-
ers and labour exploiters were the sugar planters and their allies. On
the other hand, where populations were dense, the need for coercion was less and entrepreneurs were able to employ free labour at
low wages and monopolize the land. Under these conditions, the
abolition of slavery seemed easy to accept, especially when slave
owners were paid compensation.

The labour–land ratio can also be used as an explanation of the
contrasting patterns of change observed after the abolition of slavery. Where population was dense and the people could be discour-
aged or prevented from migrating, planters could employ labour
cheaply and, for several decades at least, the plantation systems

might continue to flourish much as before. This was the case in Barbados down to the 1860s, when even the planters finally realized that the island was overpopulated and emigration might ease the drain on the public revenue. Where the population was sparse, the survival of plantation agriculture depended heavily on continued forced migration or indentured labour inputs. Where these two patterns were found intermixed within a single island or large region – in other words, where densely populated plantation districts were located close to thinly peopled but potentially productive areas – the outcome was likely to be varied. Here, in this third situation, abandoned plantations were to be found next to thriving peasant agriculture as well as marginally efficient plantations. Finally, where a viable planter class no longer existed or had been eradicated, as in Haiti, a relatively dense population might be able to establish a completely new system of resource use. The case of Haiti shows clearly that the land–labour ratio is not sufficient in itself to predict the outcome of abolition. The pattern depended also on the existence and status of potential classes of people with capitalist intent, anxious selfishly to garner to themselves the fruits of land and labour.

The large islands of the Greater Antilles, home to an increasing majority of the Caribbean people, illustrate starkly most of these variations. Sugar and the plantation continued to occupy an important place in the landscape at the end of the period, but in new regions and in new forms. Broadly, sugar found fertile soil where slavery and the slave trade continued longest – in Cuba and Puerto Rico – and retreated most dramatically where the early ending of slavery – notably in Haiti and Jamaica – was associated with alternative forms of subsistence. This pattern of expansion was not simply indicative of a moving frontier, in which the plantation occupied virgin soil, exploited it remorselessly, then moved on, leaving behind landscapes and soils ravaged by sugar growing. In fact, sugar cane is relatively protective of soils and its matted root system resists erosion. Where it became naturalized, as in the pioneer Barbados for example, sugar cane remained dominant for centuries. The abandonment of sugar, as occurred on a massive scale in St Domingue/Haiti and on a more selective basis in Jamaica, had little to do with the advance of a frontier but rather reflected both revolutionary political events and the marginal qualities of the topographic niches into which sugar was sometimes pushed. In some environmentally marginal places, such as the British Virgin Islands, exports effectively ended by 1850.

At the close of the eighteenth century, St Domingue and Jamaica were not only the largest sugar producers in the Caribbean but also the world's largest exporters. However, they were neither monocultural nor homogeneous in their land types. Thousands of plantations, large and small, dotted the plains and hillsides of St Domingue, producing independently or in combination with sugar, crops such as coffee, cocoa, cotton, and indigo. Sugar production peaked in 1791 in St Domingue, when the colony exported almost 80,000 tons. St Domingue also was the world's leading exporter of coffee. Jamaica possessed a similarly varied topography, with small interior valleys that created niches for sugar plantations, many of which were on the margins of profitability and were the first to be abandoned when conditions deteriorated, even before the abolition of slavery. Benefiting by the revolution in St Domingue, where output slipped as low as 10,000 tons by 1800, Jamaica became the world's largest exporter, shipping more than 100,000 tons of sugar in 1804, the product of about 700 plantations. A few years later, Jamaica was the world's largest exporter of coffee, much of the crop grown on new mountain lands (Blue Mountain coffee) with advice from emigré planters who had fled the revolution in St Domingue. In addition to its plantation sector, Jamaica also developed a profitable livestock industry on lands not suited to sugar. During slavery, this industry was not directed at producing meat but rather at the supply of working animals – particularly cattle, mules, and horses – required to power the mills and pull the carts and wagons on the sugar estates, and to get the produce to the wharves.

In Haiti, the early years of the republic saw a struggle over the role of the plantation economy and the distribution of rights to land. A gap opened between theory and practice in the northern and southern regions, grounded in the early history of the revolution. In the north, down to 1820, state ownership of land was advocated by the region's leaders, from Toussaint to Christophe. Under Dessalines, all those who were not soldiers or practitioners of crafts in towns had to perform agricultural labour. White people – foreigners – were denied ownership, but plantations with serf-like labourers were given to the elite on five-year leases, on condition that they paid a tax equal to 25 percent of the annual crop. In the south, under Alexandre Pétion, state ownership of land was quickly ended and land was distributed in smallholdings primarily as a means of paying the army and perhaps also in order to lure settlers from the north. By 1808, the minimum holding size in the south had been reduced to 30 acres and the following year, every soldier was granted 15 acres freehold. Compulsory labour was ended and systems of *métayage* or crop-sharing were encouraged.

United under Jean-Pierre Boyer in 1820, both north and south of Haiti saw a continuing struggle between competing models of land tenure and labour organization. The Code Rurale introduced in 1826 attempted to attach people to the land in order to provide labour for estates, but the reality was that the example already set in the grant of smallholdings proved much more appealing to the people. Farming on a small scale was widespread by the 1840s, and the price of land became relatively cheap as units of fewer than 15 acres were allowed to enter the market. As many as one third of the population became squatters and as much as one half of the crop was produced by share-farmers. For the remainder of the nineteenth century, fragmentation proceeded apace with the breaking up of the old plantation units into holdings occupied by family households.

For the mass of the people of Haiti, the central objective of the revolution, after sovereignty and the end of the hated slave system, was the capacity to occupy their own piece of land and to be free to practice an economy of individual, household self-sufficiency. Although this objective was suppressed during the long years of conflict and was initially inhibited by the different expectations of the revolution's leadership, the goal was eventually achieved in the universality of small-scale peasant proprietorship and community structure that was firmly established by 1870. This was a pattern of economic and social self-determination that cared little about the role of the state in a wider, modernizing world, but matched the isolated, outcast status of the nation. Whatever the aims of the leadership, most of the people did not hanker after citizenship in a modern state, but found satisfaction in their direct attachment to place and earth.

Although Jamaica did not follow Haiti into independence in this period, the abolition of slavery had comparable consequences for patterns of land tenure and labour organization. Sugar exports declined absolutely and were halved between 1838 and 1870. Further, exports declined as a proportion of gross domestic product, falling dramatically from about 50 percent in the final years of slavery to just 20 percent in the 1850s. The economy turned in on itself. The highly concentrated pattern of land settlement associated with the plantation system under slavery largely disappeared and, in many regions of the island, was quickly replaced by dispersed smallholder settlement, with a higher overall population density but a less nucleated network of communities. Under slavery, the areas dominated by sugar were divided into large land units blanketed by cane, with village communities huddled close to the mill and great house, often near the centre of the landholding and invisible to travellers passing by along the country roads. There were few interior settlements as large as these plantation villages and few coastal ports with populations as large.

After the effective abolition of slavery in Jamaica in 1838, the planters often attempted to coerce the people formerly owned by them as slaves to remain on the plantations and continue living in the same village settlements, but now being paid low wages and charged rent for occupation of their houses and grounds. Initially, many of the newly free people did remain on the plantations, close to their relatives and acquaintances and enjoying the fruits of their gardens. Others, however, left the plantations as quickly as they could, finding niches in the surrounding rugged wooded landscape where they could squat on land and establish provision grounds or purchase lots from planters who decided to sell. These people were soon joined by others who were ejected by the planters for failure to pay rents or perform labour on their plantations, and those who refused to accept the coercive tactics of their former masters. The price of land fell steeply wherever sugar was abandoned. Many settled in "free villages" founded by churches, most of them located in isolated sites and designed to engender wholesome Christian communities living together in small settlements, going out each day to farm the surrounding plots. As well as the niches surrounding and contained within the old plantation lands, large regions of Jamaica remained unsettled in 1838 and these soon came to be some of the most densely populated districts of the island, producing largely for an internal provision market as well as supplying new export crops such as ginger, pimento, cocoa, and logwood.

By 1870, the number of sugar plantations in Jamaica had been reduced to just 300, from a peak of about 1,000 in 1770. As many as 70,000 people owned freeholds of 50 acres or less by 1870, up from about 2,000 in 1838. This new class of black smallholders depended on the produce of their gardens and grounds for subsistence and laboured for wages on the surviving plantations only in extremis. Thus, in Jamaica as well as Haiti, the abolition of slavery was followed quickly by a genuine redistribution of wealth, principally in the form of land. Income was redistributed less positively and improvement in the standard of living was less consistent, but the psychic value of landownership, and even the possibility of landownership, outweighed these losses. Most of this transformation was completed within a decade of abolition.

The experience of Cuba and Puerto Rico, where slavery continued beyond 1870, was dramatically different to that of Haiti and Jamaica in this period. However, the consequences of the delayed sugar revolution in Cuba and Puerto Rico were inevitably similar to those of the French and English colonies 200 years before: a concentration of wealth in the hands of creole whites, increased foreign investment, and a reduction in the role of smallholders. In Cuba, much of the capital required came from local sources, particularly the merchants of Havana, at least down to about 1840 when U.S. traders became important suppliers of credit, especially for the purchase of slaves and machinery. Local initiative was demonstrated in the activities of the Havana Economic Society, founded in 1791 to advocate radical change in land tenure as well as discuss more philosophically science and the arts, commerce and industry, agriculture and education. In the absence of substantial absentee proprietorship, much of the profit remained in the island to be ploughed back into new ventures, which enabled the planters to avoid having to obtain credit at very high rates of interest. Sugar production increased massively, from 10,000 tons in 1770 to 100,000 tons around 1830 and 726,000 tons in 1870, when Cuba accounted for about 40 percent of world exports. By 1870, there were about

1,200 mills in Cuba, each producing an annual average of 600 tons of sugar.

The development of the industry in Cuba was stimulated by the British introduction of large numbers of slaves during the Seven Years War, the removal of all restrictions on the slave trade into the island from 1789, the removal of duties, and the influx of emigrés, particularly into eastern Cuba, following the revolution in St Domingue. Previously opposed by the Spanish navy, from 1815, a royal decree allowed private property owners to clear trees on their land, opening up vast expanses of fertile soil and bottomless supplies of building materials and firewood for the sugar mills. Cuba also became the world's largest copper miner, supplying the British industrial market, but this did not last beyond 1870 and no local processing industries resulted from the activity.

Puerto Rican sugar output was much smaller than that of Cuba, beginning at barely 1,000 tons in 1770 and remaining trivial until the 1820s. The industry was hampered until 1815, when a prohibition on foreigners and non-Catholics was lifted and sugar lands were made available on attractive terms. Planters were then attracted to Puerto Rico, particularly from the Danish colonies, and these planters forced their enslaved people to move with them to the fresh fields. Puerto Rico's sugar plantations were concentrated in a small zone in the south of the island but achieved an export of 105,000 tons by 1870.

Examples of growth in the sugar industry after the 1830s were relatively rare outside Cuba and Puerto Rico. For most of the nineteenth century, Hispaniola produced only trivial amounts of sugar for export. Significant development began in the Dominican Republic only around 1870, when Cuban migrants commenced the revival of the sugar industry. However, rapid expansion occurred in Trinidad, where sugar production increased fourfold after 1838 to reach 50,000 tons by 1870, making it the third largest exporter in the Caribbean. Trinidad's success depended on the exploitation of fertile soils and combined modern technologies with heavy use of indentured Indian workers. The same was true of the French colonies of Martinique and Guadeloupe – particularly the latter, where the survival of the plantations was grounded in the indenture system. In St Croix, sugar peaked around 1820. The eruption of

Mount Soufrière in St Vincent in 1812 damaged plantations but only in localized zones and with little impact on longer term development of sugar production.

Patterns of land and labour were quite varied elsewhere. In the smaller islands of the eastern Caribbean, the land had long been covered almost perfectly from shore to shore with sugar plantations, and this landscape remained little disturbed down to 1870. In Barbados, sugar production increased steadily, helped by minor innovations in field and mill, rising from less than 10,000 tons in 1770 to a temporary peak of 50,000 tons by 1868, almost double the output achieved by Jamaica. As in Jamaica, the planters of Barbados, after 1838, had often pushed the people out of the plantation village settlements but the island presented few opportunities for the purchase of small lots or for squatting, and the outcome was the development of a unique form of light housing modules – known as chattel houses – that could be moved from place to place when a household changed employer or found a tiny spot on the roadside where they could locate. Much the same happened in the sugar-producing British colonies in the Leeward Islands, where output stagnated or declined absolutely down to 1870, but the topographically varied British Windward Islands, from Grenada north to Dominica, offered opportunities more similar to the conditions found in Jamaica, and there the peasantry flourished relatively undisturbed.

Sugar plantations got much bigger between 1770 and 1870, increasing massively both the area planted in cane and the capacity of their mills. These changes in scale demanded more labour but also went together with new systems of cane supply and delivery. In Cuba, the plantations came to be known as *centrales*, dominated by massive modern steam-powered mills and related innovations, the first of these built in 1831. Railroads with steam trains were soon added, both to bring cane speedily from more distant locations and to transport goods to and from the coastal ports. These new technologies dramatically increased the scale of the plantations and the quantity of their output, but they could be built successfully only where there were extensive relatively flat expanses of fertile soil.

Most of the new technologies in the sugar industry were designed to increase the efficiency of processing and transportation operations. Most of them consisted of machines, fabricated from iron or, beginning in the 1850s, steel. Most were powered by steam, the first experiments beginning in Jamaica in 1770. On the other hand, innovations in cultivation and harvesting were relatively insignificant, though in the few places where it happened, the application of fertilizers – notably guano in this period – and the breeding of superior varieties of cane, did improve yields. The outcome was a vastly increased appetite for cane to be fed to the mills and, hence, a substantially expanded cane field. The work of cultivation, weeding, and harvest remained almost entirely in the hands of field workers wielding hoes and cane knives. Ploughs were introduced in some places but remained crude until the 1850s, when the newly invented steel mouldboard was introduced. Mechanized tillage, first advocated for sugar in the 1840s, was little used outside Cuba before 1870. The earliest versions, in which the plough was pulled across the field by a cable attached to a fixed steam engine, were uncommon and clumsy. Rather than the new technologies reducing the demand for labour in the sugar industry, the innovations increased it. The close balance between mill capacity, cane field, and labour that had been at the core of plantation management down to the 1830s was threatened by these developments.

One solution to the emerging imbalance between mill and field was to separate the two operations. If cane growers were not also obliged to have their own mills, they no longer needed to proportion their cane field to the capacity of a processing plant. A "central" mill could be owned either by an individual large planter or an independent miller who might not even cultivate cane. This separation, which began to be discussed seriously in the British and French Caribbean colonies after the abolition of slavery, enabled a completely new dynamic, in which large plantations and smallholdings could coexist. In Cuba, as well as cultivating their own cane fields, the *centrales* often drew cane from *colonos* or smallholders who cultivated and cut the crop but lacked the capital or scope to own mills of their own. In some cases, these independent cane growers owned the land they farmed; in others, they leased land from the mill owner and were tied to the price structure of the miller through binding contracts.

In the Windward Islands, a system of share-cropping or *métayage* emerged, in which a similar relationship between farmer and miller enabled the smallholder to participate in the sugar economy and the miller to take advantage of the farmer's need. An opposite tendency was the introduction of small-scale mills, powered by a mule, which the peasant producer could use to make cruder types of wet sugar for the local market, of a quality closer to that of the seventeenth century than to the relatively dry and more refined sugars that could be produced by the large modern mills with their vacuum pans and centrifuges.

Salt – sugar's opposite – continued to be important for some marginal economies. In Anguilla, it was the island's only significant export by the 1830s, and when prolonged drought caused the failure of the crops, the inhabitants faced starvation. Salt was equally important to the Bahamas in the last years of slavery. The separation of the Turks and Caicos Islands from the Bahamas in 1848 removed a major source from the public revenue, derived from the salt tax, and new salt pans were opened, flourishing down to the end of the American Civil War, when the market slumped.

Although the stock of turtles was greatly diminished, the trade continued much as before, dominating the economy of the Cayman Islands. The green turtle became scarce in those waters by the 1790s, so fishermen moved on to the banks south of Cuba until this area, in turn, was depleted by the 1830s, when they moved again, this time to the cays off Nicaragua. Other forms of fishing were typically small-scale and directed at local, fresh fish markets. A local whaling industry did emerge in the 1820s, however, exploiting the seas from Trinidad to St Vincent. Most of the whale oil was sold in the islands. Sponge-fishing developed in the Bahamas after the 1840s, taking advantage of the shallows of the Bahamas Banks, where it was possible to collect the sponges from small boats rather than using the complicated trawls and diving equipment required in the Mediterranean and other parts of the world. This activity dominated the export economy of the Bahamas well into the twentieth century.

TRADING PLACES

Although the period following the abolition of slavery saw some movement of people into urban settlements, the tendency was not marked. Relatively few people could see gain in trading places and wherever they could, they chose to become smallholders, masters and mistresses of their domestic domains, in charge of their own lives so far as they were allowed. The urban lifestyle was not particularly attractive and perhaps even unhealthy. Almost all of the Caribbean's towns were essentially commercial centres. They offered few opportunities for employment in manufacturing or secondary services. Throughout the Caribbean, most people continued to live rural, agricultural lives, whether they lived on plantations or on their own small holdings. Down to 1870, the inward-looking, internalized tendency in Caribbean economic and social life helped emphasize this rurality and domesticity.

In spite of these inclinations, the towns remained the interface with the world outside. They continued to be the sites of the major internal markets, both for trade in food and for the exchange of local and imported processed and manufactured goods. In islands dominated by peasantries, the weekly trip to town to sell and to acquire was an important part of social life that enabled physically scattered households to meet people from other communities and districts and to have some exposure to the larger world of ideas and commodities. In islands of this sort, many new small towns emerged in the interior districts, where none had existed during slavery, thus redistributing the functions performed by the larger port towns and cities. Improved road networks and the establishment of internal railroad passenger services, beginning in Cuba and Jamaica in the 1840s, helped ensure the viability of these new towns. Outside of the surviving sugar plantation colonies dependent on indentured and enslaved workers, few people lived in plantation villages.

Few were forced to rely on the plantation or company store for provisions that tied them to labour through debt. In the Bahamas, however, the "truck system" was applied in the sponge-fishing industry, where most of the boats were owned by merchants or poorer whites in the out-islands who took one third of the catch and tied the black crews to them through advances, generally made in kind rather than cash.

For the peasantry, sources of credit were always limited before 1870. Many depended on their own African-derived informal rotating credit systems, in which a respected individual known as the "banker" collected standard amounts of cash, called "hands", from a group of participants. Each week or month one of these was given the full amount collected, the participants being given the total sum in turn until each member had received the benefit. These systems depended on trust and did not deliver an initial advance to every contributor, but they required no payment of interest and saved the peasant from interview by a commercial banker in a town office or falling into the hands of an extortionate village money-lender.

There were no banks anywhere in the Caribbean before 1830 and indeed there were no commercial banks in Spain either, only a royal bank. The first was the Colonial Bank of the West Indies, established by British royal charter in 1836, which quickly extended its operations to Cuba and North America. It was allowed to issue notes. In Cuba, local capitalists founded the Savings and Loans Banks of Havana in 1842, and the Bank of Spain was established by 1850, but these were concerned almost exclusively with the needs of the merchant class. Elsewhere, most of the banks at first were interested only in providing capital to the mercantile and plantation sectors, and even in this were reluctant and limited lenders. Savings banks began to gain importance only in the middle of the nineteenth century. Insurance companies also were founded in the Caribbean in this period but, once again, played only a small role in providing credit. Banks became increasingly important after the abolition of slavery, particularly because the new need to pay wages depended on a monetization of the economy. They were also important in managing the finances of an expanded pubic sector, in which policing, hospitals, and education were shifted from the planter to the state.

Although many of the island economies came to have a strong domestic orientation by 1870, almost all of them conducted trade in money terms. Barter persisted, among the planters as well as the peasantry, but even this style of exchange was typically transacted, notionally at least, in money terms. During slavery, the people who sold in the local public markets often came to hold a large proportion of the coin that circulated within the islands, particularly the smaller denominations. Before 1800, the Caribbean was dominated by Spanish coin from the Mexican mint, entering the French and British colonies through contraband and free-port trade. This flow resulted in a shortage of coin in the Spanish colonies and after

1800 an additional drain occurred towards the United States. By the 1840s, the shortage was so great that counters made of tin, wood, or even cardboard circulated as small change in the Spanish colonies, and the currency was not put on a firmer footing until 1870. In the British colonies, the need for cash to pay wages after abolition resulted in the importation of British silver coin. From 1839, the use of colonial "creole" currencies (valued at a fixed rate against British money) was abolished and all money was assimilated to British sterling. In this way, the imperial powers sought to impose their metropolitan monetary systems on the colonies, cutting across flourishing creole economies.

External trade continued to be channelled chiefly through the imperial systems to which the colonies belonged. Although the British moved steadily away from the old protectionist policies of mercantilism during this period, free trade policies were not always beneficial to the Caribbean colonies and, in any event, the growing British dominance of world manufacturing and trade limited the possibilities of establishing new markets and sources. Local, colonial manufacturing was not encouraged, and the islands continued to be seen almost exclusively as producers of exotic tropical food crops. Spanish commerce remained tightly controlled throughout the nineteenth century, though beginning in the 1820s, steps were taken to reduce prohibitive customs tariffs and permit trade with foreign ships, in an attempt to undercut contraband. The reality was quite different. By 1870, Spain took only 3 percent of Cuba's exports, the bulk of the sugar – now accounting for 90 percent of total value – going to the United States and Britain. This shift indicated a growing dependence on American credit and capital as well as integration into a new wholesaling network. Even the British colonies in the Caribbean saw their trade shift away from Britain to the United States and to Canada. The shift would have been even greater by 1870 if the United States had removed the protection given its own sugar producers.

During slavery, local markets were dominated by food products, most of it locally produced. As noted for the period before 1770, items such as flour, rice, saltfish, and pickled meat were imported in large quantities but mainly distributed on the plantations. Only a small proportion of these imported foods entered the public markets, where they often were exchanged for local goods. The abolition of slavery changed this pattern significantly because food, cloth, and tools no longer were distributed by planters to employees, and the people were now able to make their own choices more easily. They purchased from scattered small retailers who, in turn, depended on an emerging class of centralized wholesalers. Imports and inbound shipping increased strongly after the abolition of slavery as a result of this new pattern of demand, whereas the value of exports often declined. In Jamaica, for example, salted codfish was much preferred to pickled herrings, so the pattern of imports changed rapidly to match this demand. Wherever the peasantry grew strongly, locally grown food was prominent in the markets.

Although the range of animals used in the food systems of the Caribbean was essentially fixed long before 1770, the last decades of the eighteenth century did see the introduction of a number of important food plants. Indeed, this may be seen as the last great period of plant introductions. After 1800, hardly any new plants of importance were brought to the Caribbean. The process of naturalization proceeded rapidly, so that by 1870, most of the plants in the Caribbean landscape seemed to belong to the islands as part of a creole vegetated landscape. Examples of the important plants that reached the Caribbean between 1770 and 1800 include the mango, breadfruit, jackfruit, ackee, cinnamon, strawberry, and turmeric. Ganja, *Cannabis sativa*, was a latecomer, reaching the Caribbean from India by about 1850.

Trade in imported manufactured commodities between the 1830s and 1870 was heavily influenced by the industrial dominance of Great Britain. In the Caribbean, this dominance helped build the concept of a "British world" of goods, not only in the British but also in the French, Dutch, and Spanish colonies. Thus, for example, much of the modern machinery and railroad rolling stock in Cuba and Puerto Rico was British made.

Where the rainforest remained sufficient, the houses of both rich and poor used its timbers in construction. The forest was much more likely to disappear under the axe in clearing land for planting sugar cane or building railroads. Often, the felled forest was simply burned rather than being used for building or furniture-making. In colonies where the rainforest had much earlier been removed or reduced to a remnant, as in Barbados, for example, houses built after 1770 typically depended on imported lumber, boards, and posts, most of it coming from the pine forests of North America. Boards were favoured for the chattel houses of Barbados, because they needed to be light and flexible for easy mobility, and cheap.

Although some poor people lived in houses of rough-hewn rock, generally, stone was the fabric of the planter class. Most of it was hewn from local quarries or, in rubble-wall construction using limestone, collected from the building site itself or nearby sources, and mortared together. Bricks, on the other hand, sometimes were imported and sometimes baked locally. Window casements and window glass, the preserve of the rich during slavery, were always imported. Occasionally, a completely prefabricated public building of cast iron might be imported, as in the naval hospital constructed in Port Royal, Jamaica, in 1811, but generally, whatever the scale of the residence, local craftsmen were responsible for the design and building of Caribbean houses. They introduced some unique features, such as the piazza and the cooler window, but often followed the fashions of Europe. The Georgian great house architecture of the British colonies contrasted with the Baroque elements of Spanish-American places, with their enclosed courtyards and tiled roofs. For plantation workers, the period after 1830 was marked by the decline of relatively independent construction styles and village layouts, and the growing dominance – for indentured workers as well as the enslaved – of regimented layouts and multi-unit barracks.

Although goods of European manufacture came to dominate in the local shops, stores, and public markets of the Caribbean, some local crafts continued to flourish in spite of the competition. Handmade ceramics – bowls, water jars, and cooking pots – sat in the markets alongside imported cast iron pots and cheap chinaware. In some places, notably Haiti, the local products competed strongly. Glass bottles were recycled, the empties lined up in local markets for sale. Haitian tinsmiths and coppersmiths set up shop in the markets too, repairing vessels that had sprung leaks or lost their handles. Elsewhere, particularly in the trade-centred commercial colonies of the Dutch and the Danish, the local product had much less chance of competing with imports. The houses of the poor were typically furnished with a mixture of local and imported goods, handmade beds and benches decked with traded linens and glassware. The rich had a larger proportion of imported things but still held on to appropriate creole technologies. Some of these ancient methods – for example, the preparation of bitter cassava – were inherited from the Taínos and remained unchallenged by industrial alternatives. Rich people also could afford furniture made from the best of the local timbers, such as mahogany and cedar, and these luxurious inlaid items coexisted comfortably among things made of North American and European woods.

Clothing, on the other hand, was, for all classes in all colonies, principally made from imported cloth, using imported needles, thread, thimbles, and scissors. Although some of the islands exported raw cotton, none of them produced textiles. In the eighteenth century, much of the imported cloth came from India, and played a part in the transaction of the slave trade in Africa. Some came from European states that did not participate in the colonization of the Caribbean, such as the cheap, prickly, flax oznaburgh that was woven in the German town of the same name. After about 1800, the great industrial growth of textile-making in Britain and France replaced much of this material, and cheap cotton prints came to rule the market. Down to 1870, the local seamstress and tailor did most of the sewing, taking to the Singer machine soon after its invention in 1851. Readymade clothes and shoes remained uncommon. The same was true for rich and poor, though the rich were the first to consider looking for garments in shops.

During slavery, the clothing of the workers was typically rough and ready, sometimes reduced to rags. Some worked semi-naked, even in households. In the midst of such deprivation and poverty, however, opportunities for a superior display and for festivities were eagerly grasped. Such opportunities were generally associated with seasonal festivals, most of them declared and celebrated by the slave-owning classes. These events were permitted as rare "holidays" within the normally unremitting timetable of plantation life and work. The end of the sugar harvest was recognized in "crop-over" festivities, encouraged by the planters, while the commencement of the new yam crop was the justification for a "yam festival" as practiced in West Africa. These were rural events, played out on the plantations by localized communities, and focussed more on food than fashion.

The more important festivities, and the major opportunities for wearing clothing that was out of the ordinary, were the holy days determined by the Christian calendar, notably Christmas and Easter. These celebrations were performed on the streets of the major towns, loosely associated with the rituals of the church. Christmas was the most important day for the Protestant colonies, notably the British, and the holidays were allowed to spill over for several days. Costumes and masks made from imported and local materials were used to transform the bodies and identities of the enslaved and the free coloured. The characters portrayed sometimes were derived from European models – as Jack-in-the-Green, for example – but often derived from unique or overlapping African precedents – notably, the several variants of Junkanu. The details of the social structure of the slave societies were played out, as in the Set Girls of Jamaica, who dressed uniformly and fashionably, and organized themselves according to their gradations of colour, dancing on the streets of Kingston and Spanish Town.

In the Catholic colonies – both Spanish and French – the best known public festivity during slavery was the Carnival that marked the end of the period leading up to the beginning of Lent – Ash Wednesday – and the season of self-denial that continued until Easter Sunday. As well as representing the opposite of abstention, Carnival permitted role reversals that were often played out through costume and mask. A man could dress, and dance, as a woman. White people could dress like slaves, lit by flambeau to the cane field. The poor could appear rich for a day or two, the rich could pretend poverty. Black, enslaved men could dress as whites, poking fun at their statuses and roles in society. All of this was done with great care through costume and make-up, permitted temporarily as a kind of safety-valve, but played out for the entertainment of onlookers on the streets of the major towns.

As revolution and rebellion spread through the Americas, colonial governments became increasingly nervous about such festivities, fearing they might prove cover for attacks on the system. In general, the governors concluded that attempts to suppress these holidays were more likely to create trouble than permitting them to continue. They called up the military just in case, but generally remained tolerant. Only in one major case, the so-called Christmas rebellion of 1831 in Jamaica, was the opportunity exploited successfully by the enslaved. However, that was an essentially rural rebellion, breaking out well beyond the streets of the port towns where the displays of finery – and the trading of social place – had their centre.

SOCIETY

The abolition of slavery fundamentally altered the legal and social relations of the peoples of the Caribbean but it did not, everywhere, transform the social structure built on slavery. Only in Haiti was change truly revolutionary. Elsewhere, the people formerly enslaved, and their children and grandchildren, remained at the bottom of the heap and, well beyond 1870, were forced to struggle up through the rankings as best they could. The principal reason behind this pattern of continuity and persistence was the fact that, with the exception of Haiti and in spite of the importance of rebellion and resistance in ending slavery throughout the region, the legislated abolitions of slavery came from the hands of the slave owners and the imperial governments. The aims and expectations of the imperial governments changed with abolition, often resulting in a mission to mould the peoples of the Caribbean in the shape of their imperial masters. However, this new view of the importance of the colonies did not go together with an interest in encouraging the transformation of social structure or gender relations. Where white men, particularly white men born in Europe, had been at the top of the pyramid as exploiters and wealth-seekers, so they sought to remain dominant in societies that perhaps were less rewarding to capitalist investment but offered opportunities for the maintenance of status and rank derived from the public performance of social control through a model rooted in class as well as race and ethnicity.

In addition to the fundamental contrast between Haiti and the rest of the Caribbean, other significant differences marked the hundred years to 1870. At the beginning of the period, in 1770, all of the societies of the region could be designated slave societies, as discussed in the previous chapter. The revolution in St Domingue saw the first emergence of free communities, but in all the other colonies, slavery persisted for more than half the period, with the next abolition occurring in the British colonies in 1838, followed by the French and the Danes in 1848 and the Dutch in 1863. In all of these colonial systems, the period of freedom, down to 1870, was brief but long enough to offer strong indications of where development was headed. Cuba and Puerto Rico remained slave societies throughout the entire period. Thus, although all of the Caribbean colonies were grounded in the experience of slave society, the period between 1838 and 1870 was unique in holding, contemporaneously, both free societies and slave societies.

The slave societies of the Caribbean changed little in their structure and functioning after 1770. In most places, including Cuba, the more important changes were essentially demographic. The growth of the creole and coloured components of the enslaved populations shifted expectations of mobility within the highly constrained ranks of plantation communities, but the inability of the system of labour management to meet these hopes meant that having a white father or being born in the islands rather than Africa ceased to ensure easy access to manumission or elevation within the hierarchy of occupation and status. The growing numbers of the free coloured and free black populations also placed pressure on their ability to obtain special privileges, and although they became significant owners of enslaved people, this indicator of wealth did not guarantee civil or political rights. The erosion of the existing rights of the free coloured and free black people of St Domingue, through the imposition of new limits on occupational choice and conspicuous consumption, played an important part in fuelling their enthusiasm for revolution. In other colonies, the free coloured generally obtained civil and political rights ahead of the abolition of slavery but often only just before. The degree to which free coloured and free black people were accepted into the higher ranks of society was not simply a matter of their legal status or wealth, but depended also on personal presentation as judged by speech, dress, manners, education, and appearance.

Whatever else they lacked, during the period of slavery, white men believed that their whiteness gave them an unchallengeable claim to superiority. Particularly in the colonies in which whites formed a small minority, the poorest white male vagrant liked to think that he could front up to any planter's door and receive basic hospitality. The same white male might similarly expect redress under the law if any black or coloured person should insult or injure him in any way. A perceived egalitarian reciprocity within the white male community had its limits, however. White men born in Europe typically thought themselves superior to white creoles. Jewish men were not accepted as equals either, though, by the beginning of the nineteenth century, many of them had lived for generations in the islands and possessed great wealth derived from their enterprise in trade and plantations and they owned many slaves. In Jamaica, for example, Jews were free to worship openly and to build synagogues but were not granted full civil and political rights until 1831. Roman Catholics also suffered discrimination, achieving their political "emancipation" only a few years before the abolition of slavery. Such discrimination became difficult to maintain, however, when the British conquered colonies formerly claimed by Spain and France and found it unfruitful to attempt to apply the same intolerance to the many Catholic settlers.

With the exception of Haiti, a simple pyramidal model of social structure applied as well after the abolition of slavery as it had before. This pyramid represented demographic weight closely correlated with colour and ethnicity. The great mass of people at the base were almost all black, of African birth or ancestry. The narrow apex of the pyramid was occupied by the elite, exclusively white, of European birth or ancestry. Between the top and the bottom were the people of colour. During slavery, slave status cut across the coloured and black levels, with most of the people enslaved but some free. The introduction of new ethnic components – Indians, Chinese, Portuguese, Germans – had relatively little impact on the basic pattern. The new peoples were slotted into the old pyramid, with their own narrow layers in more nuanced variations of the model.

The idea of Caribbean society as a pyramid suggests a certain solidity and stability, the whole dependent on the components knowing their place and keeping it. The image appears to work fairly well for the Caribbean generally between 1770 and 1870, in spite of revolutionary rumblings. What held it together? Was it simply the weight of the building blocks or were the elements kept in place by some sort of cultural mortar? As discussed in the previous chapter, the "creole society" model would argue that there was a pervasive unity – a kind of mortar – that ran throughout the societies, as evidenced in shared creole languages and speech, shared material cultures, shared responses to an environment that they gradually naturalized as their own, and shared patterns of family and household organization.

These relationships were disturbed somewhat when colonies changed hands, as was relatively common in the late eighteenth century. For example, the British capture of Trinidad from the Spanish in 1797 spread a layer of British imperial power and culture over an existing Catholic, French, and Spanish ruling population, creating cross-cutting levels of national identity and language. Such differences were important but they were accommodated easily enough within a hierarchy that gave priority to colour. Similarly, the new cultural components introduced after abolition were simply absorbed, the new peoples creolized in much the same way as those who had come before. In the plural society model, discussed in chapter 4, it is the weight of state power that holds the pyramid together, regardless of any cultural mortar. In this plural model, the new components were more disruptive, more likely to create conflict with the preexisting peoples, and more determined to maintain their own separate ways. In the case of Trinidad, Indians formed one quarter of the population by 1870 but remained largely outside creole society and were still seen as sojourners rather than a permanent part of the population.

Although the heavy hand of state power often was applied to the maintenance of the social order in the period after slavery, the slow-growing but inexorable process of grassroots cultural change proved victorious in the long term. In the short period between the ending of slavery and 1870, however, the process was barely beginning and it was in this vital window that the imperial states commenced their attempts to mould the colonial populations in their own image. Whereas the states had had little interest in education or in policing, for example, during the period of slavery, these tools of social control quickly emerged as vitally important after abolition.

Schooling had been a largely informal matter during slavery, children taught by their parents and picking up knowledge where they could. Few slave owners showed any interest in instructing enslaved people beyond what they needed for their daily tasks. Just a few enslaved people were employed in occupations that required literacy, such as printers' typesetters. However, the ability to read and write did become more common after 1770 and proved particularly useful in communication between rebel leaders. This was true of Sam Sharpe of Jamaica, leader of the rebellion of 1831, for example. In the case of St Domingue, Toussaint was highly literate but Dessalines and Christophe were effectively illiterate. Some enslaved people arrived in the Caribbean with knowledge of Arabic, a language unknown to most Europeans, and were able to use it in secret communication. In the British and Danish colonies, the final years of slavery saw a growing interest in the education of enslaved children, generally as part of Christian missionary activity.

At abolition, the vast majority of the people could not read or write. Many planters argued that education should be restricted to the teaching of practical agricultural knowledge, attitudes of civil obedience, and acceptance of a social order in which black people were destined to perform manual labour on plantations. The churches and the imperial governments, on the other hand, argued for the establishment of schools that would impart the basic elements of reading, writing, and arithmetic, and produce good colonial citizens, loyal to imperial monarchies and republics, happy to accept their lot. The British wished to produce West Indians who could think of themselves as colonial Britons, loyal to Queen and country. The French wanted to produce a French version of the same thing. They did not want to rule over Caribbean people who sought to find their identity in Africa or even in their own islands. European, particularly British, education had a strong cachet in the early nineteenth century and, as a result, was embraced enthusiastically as a potential means of freedom from plantation labour. It was sought after even by leaders of the Haitian revolution. On the other hand, the early decades of the Haitian republic saw very low levels of school attendance; those who had already achieved the goal of possessing their own piece of land and making their own life had little time for schools.

Essential to the post-slavery educational project was teaching in the language of the imperial state and teaching from its books. The speaking of creole was frowned on, but this common language had become so deeply rooted throughout the societies that it was impossible to suppress. The result was a practical bilingualism, in which Caribbean people became fluent both in their domestic creoles and in the languages of their European masters. This also contributed to a permanent unintelligibility between peoples of neighbouring islands. The speaking of Spanish, English, French, and Dutch, together with their related creoles, set communities apart and grounded their imperial identities. It was here that the fragmented colonialism of the Caribbean, voiced as linguistic regions such as the English-speaking Caribbean and Francophone Caribbean, for example, had its most systematic grounding.

The inculcation of national cultural traditions occurred in almost all of the schools established after slavery, whether founded by churches, missionary societies, or the state. Initially, Catholic and Protestant denominational schools sometimes taught more particularly and more divisively. In multicultural Trinidad, for example, the different schools established during Apprenticeship taught separately in French and, occasionally, Spanish, as well as in English. All of these schools taught religion of one persuasion or another. For the British, the subsidization of Catholic instruction was unattractive, and this led to a strong push for secular schooling in Trinidad. This was, indeed, attempted between 1849 and 1867 in a system of secular government schools funded from local government rates. Religion was completely excluded from the curriculum and all classes were taught in English. Secondary schools or colleges, from the 1830s, were also a mix of church and state in Trinidad, but this level of education was provided almost exclusively for the upper levels of society.

The struggle between church and state, played out in the educational systems of some of the colonies, existed alongside struggles between established religion and traditional African belief systems, and struggles between traditional Christian and populist churches.

In St Domingue, Vodun (voodou) was actively practiced in secret by enslaved people, keeping alive religious beliefs brought from Africa. It was an active ingredient in carrying out the revolution, though the leaders of Haiti initially disparaged these practices and promoted Christianity, particularly the religion of the Catholic church. On the other hand, the church in Santo Domingo was deprived of property during the Haitian occupation.

Competition between European and North American versions of revivalist Christianity reached the Caribbean in the wake of the American Revolution. The first Baptists to come to Jamaica were black men, who established churches in the 1780s which became known as Native Baptist, and later came into conflict with the European Baptist branch. The Baptists became associated with rebellion, notably the so-called Baptist War of 1831 in western Jamaica, and contributed to the Great Revival of 1860. From these influences came Zion Revival and its relatives, which introduced African cosmologies and rituals that were frowned on by mainstream Christian denominations.

The performance of religion connected with other areas of expressive culture, such as music and dance. It was the fear of governments that the abolition of slavery would see not only the choice of leisure over labour but also a preference for (African) bacchanalia over decorous demonstrations of pleasure. Celebrations of the abolition of slavery itself raised these questions, added to the extended periods of leisure traditionally associated with Christmas, Carnival, and crop-over.

Similar concerns were expressed about sport. In the Bahamas, the first notice of the game of cricket occurred in the bill abolishing slavery, which included a clause that specifically prohibited playing the game on the public parade ground or streets of Nassau. This suggests that it was a popular activity among the urban poor but later matches in the Bahamas were played often by whites for white spectators, pitching locals against British regiments. Cricket was then still a common sport in the United States, where it was soon displaced by baseball. Although cricket was played in some of the British Caribbean colonies, such as Barbados, in the late eighteenth century, it was only after 1870 that it came to be seen as good way to teach discipline and learn respect for rules, as well as inculcating notions of manliness and masculinity. Women rarely engaged in sport in this period, whatever their class or colour.

GOVERNMENT OR POLITICS?

In the slave societies of the Caribbean, the central objective of colonial government was the maintenance of an oppressive system of law and order designed to deliver great profit to the slave-owning planter class. Colonial governors and governments were ultimately responsible to their imperial masters, whose objectives were to defend their territorial claims to islands supremely suited to the production of exotic tropical commodities and to benefit from trade in these commodities not only directly by collecting considerable revenue but also indirectly through the encouragement given to home industries and shipping. Governments saw their responsibility as limited to ensuring the security of these elements of political economy. They had little interest in the social or moral progress of the colonial community at large and even less interest in direct intervention in the lives of enslaved people. Only in the final decades of slavery and the slave trade did imperial governments begin to apply pressure to encourage the "amelioration" of the conditions of life of the enslaved people.

The abolition of the Atlantic slave trade and of slavery itself fundamentally changed the role of government. In the first place, with the exception of Haiti, the abolitions had their origins in legislation passed by the imperial governments, thus placing on them a responsibility to take an interest in the consequences. Secondly, the abolition of slavery changed the structure of society and, at least potentially, moved from slave owner to government any supposed responsibility for investment in human resource development and the security of the community – education, policing, justice, and health. The extent to which governments were willing and able to enter these fields depended on the structure of political power. As before, the colonies differed significantly in their political organization between 1770 and 1870, and these differences proved crucial to the pattern of social transformation. Although the European imperial states had much in common, belonging to one rather than another could make a significant difference in the experience of the colonial population. The timing of abolition was just the beginning.

Before the abolition of slavery, the European imperial states continued to compete enthusiastically for Caribbean territory, just as white European people had shown enthusiasm for migration to these societies. There were great gains to be made by individuals as well as states. The decades following abolition witnessed a rapid cooling in this enthusiasm, as individual white people and European states predicted a great decline in the profits that might be made under the new system. The European desire to migrate and colonize did not wane but it shifted away from the Caribbean towards the temperate continental lands of North and South America, and a new frontier in the East – India, Australia, and the Pacific – where so-called settler colonies might be developed that seemed more like the temperate European communities the migrants had left behind than the enervating tropical islands with their overwhelmingly African populations. The Caribbean ceased to be a centre of naval warfare between European states.

European enthusiasm for Caribbean land dissipated well before the coming of abolition, effectively ending in 1815 with the conclusion of the Napoleonic wars. Territories did change hands between 1770 and 1815, as the outcome of naval warfare and treaty-making, but without the frenzy of the Seven Years War. Hardly noticed by anyone, Sweden obtained the island of St Barthélémy from France in 1774, returning it in 1877. Grenada was captured by the French from the British in 1779, but became firmly British after its recapture in 1796. At the Peace of Versailles, agreed by Britain, France, Spain, and the United States in 1783, Britain recognized the independence of the United States and recovered its West Indian possessions, while France got back St Lucia and Tobago.

The immense enthusiasm exhibited by France and Britain and, to a lesser extent, Spain, to hold or acquire the colony of St Domingue in the midst of its revolution was part of a wider continuing competition among European states for Caribbean land. St Domingue was the biggest prize, by far, throughout the Caribbean but the profitability of sugar and coffee planting based on the exploitation of enslaved workers remained highly attractive to European states before and after 1791. In 1793, the British captured Martinique,

Guadeloupe, and St Lucia, but retained only St Lucia. In 1797, the British took Trinidad, and held it formally from 1801. St Lucia and Tobago, having changed hands several times during the war with Napoleon, became definitively British in 1803. In 1815, the British purchased former Dutch colonies on the mainland of South America to create British Guiana.

After 1815, the islands ceased to have the same lustre and allure for European states and the political geography of the region entered a long period of relative stability. The major exception was the internal conflict within Hispaniola. Haiti occupied Santo Domingo from 1822 to 1844, subjecting the people of the former Spanish colony to government by French and Creole-speaking black and mulatto men, and applying the unknown Napoleonic Code of laws. Slavery was abolished once more and many planters lost their properties. A powerful nationalist secret society emerged, however, and, with other elements, seized power. The true independence of the nation was dated from that day – 27 February 1844 – when it became known as the Dominican Republic.

The internal political forms of Haiti and the Dominican Republic contrasted strongly. In Haiti, the death of Dessalines in 1806 was followed by a continuing separation between the south, ruled by the "mulatto" Pétion as president, and the north and west, ruled by the black Christophe. These two states within a state lived in conflict until 1820, Christophe seeking a complete break from France whereas Pétion remained enamoured with French culture. In both of the states, the political tendency was autocratic rather than democratic. The political objective of the revolution was sovereignty – and the ability to live without slavery – and had no place for any form of democracy, let alone gender equality, for example. Christophe even had himself crowned king, and surrounded himself with a court made up of dukes, counts, princes, and chevaliers.

The Haitian occupation had long-lasting implications for the government and politics of the Dominican Republic. Although the short-lived initial independence from Spain, first won in 1821, was regained in 1844, the Dominican Republic's most influential leaders kept looking over their shoulders, fearing the threat of invasion and blackness. Limited invasions were, in fact, launched in 1849, 1850, and 1855, during the rule of the Haitian dictator Faustin Soulouque (emperor Faustin I), but these incursions merely pushed further east the border along the central plateau.

The Dominican Republic's first president, Pedro Santana, immediately exiled the liberal leaders of the nationalist revolt and hoped for some form of protectorate status or even outright annexation by the United States or a European state. His political rival, Buenaventura Báez, took much the same stance. They struggled down to 1861, when Santana succeeded in briefly making the Dominican Republic a colony of Spain. They found little interest among the other European powers but some United States strategists of the 1860s did consider annexation as a means of establishing a Caribbean naval base. Under the new Spanish colonial regime, Santana served as Captain General, until his death in 1864, but Spanish officials replaced Dominicans in the bureaucracy, the church, and the army. When the Spanish forces left in 1865, the republic was at a low ebb, with little productive activity or commerce. Báez, who replaced Santana as president, continued to look beyond the seas for salvation. Political chaos persisted.

Puerto Rico, formerly a colony, became a province of Spain in 1869. Thus, by 1870, only Haiti and the Dominican Republic, the joint occupants of Hispaniola, had shaken off their European imperial overlords, though in different ways and with different consequences. Government continued in the French, Dutch, and Danish colonies much as before 1770. Within the British colonial system, an influential new form of government – crown colony – emerged even before the abolition of the Atlantic slave trade. Established first in Trinidad following the British occupation in 1797 and, in modified form, in St Lucia after 1803, the crown colony system was designed to put control firmly in the hands of governors and the newly emerged Colonial Office in London. Rather than an Assembly made up of rich white men elected by their equals, the governor of a crown colony needed only the support of a Council, the members of which he nominated and most of whom were officials appointed ex officio. The governor, in turn, was under the thumb of the Colonial Office.

The original justification for this new mode of government was that it was needed to protect the interests of the large free coloured and French Catholic populations of Trinidad and St Lucia, but it proved useful when troubles emerged in the colonies that retained the old representative system. Essentially unchanged at the abolition of slavery, the Assemblies and Councils were expected to accommodate the newly free people without regard to colour or ethnicity, but retained the traditional restrictions on participation based on gender, age, and wealth. Where the planter class remained firmly in control of the land and the development of peasant populations proved slow and difficult, as was the case in Barbados, the system remained stable, at least down to 1870, and white planters, merchants, and professionals held on to their power. Elsewhere, the old representative system came under great pressure and, in fear of riot and rebellion, was replaced by crown colony in most British Caribbean territories. Crown colony was imposed on Jamaica following the Morant Bay rebellion of 1865 in which the peasantry protested violently over issues of wages and rents, access to land and the administration of justice. Although the rebellion was brutally suppressed, a fearful Assembly readily acceded to their own dissolution and the establishment of crown colony. Over the next ten years, with the exception of Barbados and the Bahamas, the other British colonies made the same change.

Even before the general shift to crown colony government, the role of the public sector expanded substantially following the abolition of slavery. Throughout the British West Indies, central government now had responsibility for health, education, and policing, on top of its traditional tasks of administration, maintaining law and order, and contributing to defence, but still leaving to local (parochial) government matters such as road maintenance and poor relief. The free system created a demand for courts, police, workhouses, treadmills, and gaols. In spite of these increased demands, those governments that did not have crown colony status frequently chose to limit expenditure when revenue came under pressure. In Jamaica, for example, public spending grew by 50 percent between 1830 and 1870, the rate of growth being rapid down to 1850 then falling away. The concept of deficit-budgeting was unheard of before 1870.

Abolition transformed the revenue base of the public sector. In the British colonies during slavery, revenue was raised largely through taxes paid by the free, slave-owning population. After abolition, the

Plate 5.2. Courthouse, Spanish Town, Jamaica, built 1819.
Photo: B. W. Higman, 1967.

burden shifted towards the population at large and indirect taxes collected at a high rate on the imported goods that were articles of common consumption – such as flour, rice, saltfish and pickled beef – whereas items required only by large planters – such as steam engines and machinery – were exempt. An unintended consequence of this inequitable system of taxation was that it encouraged the production and consumption of domestic, creole foods, thus strengthening the peasant sector and reducing the necessity of plantation labour for wages to pay for imported goods. These taxes were increased in several of the British colonies, particularly in the 1860s, causing resentment among those denied the franchise, but they were rarely sufficient to force the smallholder or the fisherman back to the cane field.

Grounds for resentment were equally strong where public taxes were used to finance the immigration of indentured workers. The purpose of these schemes, at least in part, was to create competition for employment, induce a return to plantation labour, and perhaps even reduce wages. The planters of Trinidad looked to Britain for loans to pay for these schemes and did receive aid down to 1860, after which the colony was required to find the majority of its finance. Indentured immigration was costly, taking about one third of Trinidad's budget in the 1860s. The system worked in much the same way in the French colonies, except that there, the public revenue was sourced more fairly, from export duties on sugar and land taxes that fell on the planter.

Taxation was also heavy in Haiti. In the north down to 1820, a tax of 25 percent imposed on domestic production was the major source of revenue, whereas trade was not taxed, which encouraged a prosperous commerce and made the system relatively equitable. Pétion, on the other hand, did not impose direct taxes but charged a heavy tax on external trade, thus making coffee production less profitable. Boyer followed Pétion's approach, so that Haiti, like the British colonies, became heavily dependent on tariffs for its public revenue.

The sugar revolution in Cuba transformed public revenue. Whereas before 1790, Cuba had been a drain on the imperial purse, it then became a great contributor. In all of the Spanish colonies, the collection of taxes was centralized under the crown and directed, above all, at customs duties because of the ease of collection, and, following the opening of the private market in land, derived from new forms of sales tax. All classes felt the weight of these taxes and in 1865 a delegation was sent from Cuba to Madrid to advocate the reduction of customs duties and the introduction of property or income taxes. Although some of the British Caribbean colonies also proposed income taxes, these schemes had been rejected and, indeed, income taxes remained rare throughout the world. The Cuban request of 1865 was ignored and in 1867 the Spanish government imposed a new tax of 6 to 12 percent on real estate, income, and all types of business, while leaving the customs duties intact.

The new tax of 1867 had major political consequences, sparking the Ten Years War, which lasted from 1868 to 1878. Rather like the Morant Bay uprising, the war in Cuba had its roots in an outlying province of the island and in the resentment that came from what seemed inequitable and burdensome taxation combined with the perception of political marginalization. The tax created particular resentment in the eastern provinces of Cuba, outside the major sugar region. Whereas the rich planters of the western end of the island favoured the maintenance of the metropolitan connection, the insurgency in the east brought together a ragged coalition that included advocates of independence and abolition along with small-holders and even those who saw economic advantage in annexation to the United States. The war dragged on because of the temporary effectiveness of guerrilla tactics adopted by the rebels in their battle with the Spanish army and its allies. Yet these tactics proved more an irritant than a fatal blow. Although the Ten Years War heralded the long-delayed end of slavery and nurtured nationalism, it did not make Cuba independent.

6

Democrats and Dictators

1870–1945

If the middle decades of the nineteenth century saw the Caribbean becoming relatively sufficient unto itself – turning away from traditional genetic and trade links that had tied the region to an Atlantic world but more specifically Africa and Europe – the decades after 1870 were marked by the growth of a much more clearly defined North American orientation. This new connection had three main sources. In the first place, the United States replaced the European nations as the hegemonic imperial power in the region. Secondly, the Caribbean developed increasingly strong economic links with the United States and, to a lesser extent, Canada in terms of trade, capital flows, and investment. Thirdly, it was in the period after 1870 that Caribbean people began, for the first time, to migrate out of the region in large numbers. Most common among the destinations of these new emigrants was the United States and its outliers. This newfound orientation towards North America laid the foundations for longer-term challenges to understandings of identity, nationality, and allegiance.

Looking northwards, rather than south towards the continental mainland or east to Africa and Europe, had precedents. North America had had close links with some of the Caribbean colonies – notably those of the English and the French – down to the Seven Years War and the American Revolution. These connections waned after 1783 and, in any case, had never weighed more heavily than the links the Caribbean had across the Atlantic with Africa and Europe. The shifting of the balance after 1870 created new opportunities and new challenges, many of them arising from developments that had their origins outside the Caribbean. Within the region, dictators prospered in the absence of continuing strong imperial government, whereas foreign states – often vociferous advocates of democracy at home – became the new imperialists. Hegemony took on multiple, intertwined personalities.

IMPERIALISM REMADE

The stability that had emerged in the pattern of imperial possession within the Caribbean after 1815 was disrupted dramatically in the late nineteenth and early twentieth centuries. This disruption did not spring from the old rivalries between western European states. Indeed, the declining enthusiasm the European states showed towards their Caribbean colonies persisted even in the face of potential threats and interventions. The new imperialism came not so much from Europe but from the United States. It was a closely targeted intervention, confined within the Caribbean almost entirely to the Greater Antilles and with little interest in the smaller islands or any of the colonies of the British, French, or Dutch. It often worked through informal empire rather than the possession of colonial territory and the United States sought to paint itself as a reluctant imperial power. In this period of high imperialism, in which European states scrambled for colonies around the globe, the United States was, indeed, a relatively minor player on the world stage, but a newly dominant power within the Caribbean.

The emergence of the United States as an imperial force in the Caribbean was no surprise. The spread of the nation across North America represented a colonial expansion as rapacious as any other of its type but seen by its founding citizens as their Manifest Destiny, the fulfilment of a god-given right to the land. This internal colonization preoccupied the United States until 1890. The extension of the imperial frontier across the seas seemed the obvious next step but this phase of expansion was not always accompanied by the active settlement of new lands by people from the old, especially tropical places, which retained a reputation as unhealthy environments. The islands of the Caribbean fell within the immediate circle of U.S. geopolitical interest, but making them American territories to be settled and prepared for full membership as states of the republic was rarely seen as the objective of imperial expansion.

Rather, this new imperialism built on the Monroe doctrine, enunciated in 1823 by James Monroe, fifth President of the United States, who declared that European states should not interfere in the politics of the American republics or seek further colonial possessions in the continent. The Europeans respected this notion, though perhaps more because they no longer had enthusiasm for Caribbean colonialism than that they lacked the capacity to challenge the United States. The British possessed the firepower but had no interest. Only Germany seemed to represent a threat in the early twentieth century but it was preoccupied elsewhere around the globe in places where its chances were better. Implicit in the Monroe doctrine was the view that the Western Hemisphere was the natural world-region of U.S. hegemony, and matched by the corollary that the United States should not seek to possess or control territory in the Old World.

Within the New World, the islands were attractive to new imperialists, just as they had been before, because of their relative smallness and their being surrounded by water. They made easy targets for gunboats. This vulnerability was both an advantage to U.S. imperial objectives and a source of anxiety. As well as wishing to protect and promote the economic interests of its own citizens, the United States sought also to prevent the islands of the Caribbean becoming indebted to other nations and potential targets for takeover by creditor states. Many of these international bankers were European and, increasingly, German, drawn to the region by the opportunities created by investment in infrastructure and refinancing public debt. Their governments – often driven by a newfound nationalism of their own – were equally capable of sending gunboats to protect the interests of their nationals. For these different reasons, the United States believed it had a stake in the stability of the region. It sought to ensure the public financial viability of the Caribbean territories, to make them safe places for investment, free of unrest and revolution, secure and peaceful. It was in the Caribbean region – the American Mediterranean – that the United States was most successful in establishing its hegemony.

The United States first showed imperial interest in the Caribbean islands in 1848 when it tried to buy Cuba from Spain. The offer was made again in 1854 but once more rejected; the United States tried to hatch a plan to take the island by force. These plans did not progress and the United States watched on as Cuba and Spain struggled to maintain their imperial connection. The first war of independence, the Ten Years War, stretched out from 1868 to 1878 but left Cuba a colony. It was only when the second Cuban war of independence broke out in 1895 that the interest of the United States was revived.

Led by the brilliant José Martí and his Cuban Revolutionary party, some Cubans fought this second war with the hope of achieving full independence. However, the rebels lost their leader early in the battle, in May 1895, when Martí was killed, a martyr to the cause of a free Cuba. Other Cubans fought simply for autonomy within the Spanish empire. Some advocated annexation to the United States. By the 1890s, the United States had heavy investments in Cuba, particularly in the sugar industry, and was anxious to protect its interests. When the U.S. warship *Maine* was blown up in Havana harbour in February 1898, the United States entered the war and, in April, called on Spain to relinquish its control of Cuba. In July, the United States had a naval victory at Santiago. The following month, Manila, in the Philippines, was captured and the islands of Hawaii transferred to the United States. By a treaty signed in December 1898, Spain ceded Cuba to the United States.

Rather than achieving independence, the Cubans found themselves under the heel of a new imperial power. How this relationship would be worked out remained to be seen. A free government was elected, though the franchise was limited, and Cuba got a president, congress, and flag. However, the new Cuban constitution of June 1901 made the island a virtual protectorate of the United States, through the so-called Platt Amendment (introduced by Senator Orville Platt), as a condition of the withdrawal of United States troops. The Platt Amendment entitled the United States to intervene in Cuba's internal affairs, including the economy, to negotiate international treaties, and establish a naval base at Guantanamo Bay.

Cuba's first president, Tomás Estrada Palma, was the political successor of Martí but did not share his bold dreams for Cuba and, indeed, sided with the annexationists. He did nothing to inhibit the rapid growth of U.S. investment and landownership, and the

Map 6.1. Cuba.

occupation continued until May 1902. Two years later, on the anniversary of Cuban independence, President Theodore Roosevelt announced a revised version of the Monroe doctrine, declaring that the United States had no ambitions to take territory but merely wished to see its neighbours living in states that were stable, prosperous, and orderly. Known as the Roosevelt Corollary, this new policy gave the United States the moral right to intervene in its own hemisphere wherever these conditions did not prevail. Having told the Germans and the British they had no right to interfere and in the absence of any accepted world authority, said Roosevelt, it was inescapable that the United States, however reluctant, had to take on the role of policeman in the Caribbean. It was a dramatic reinterpretation of regional policy and hegemony.

A Liberal revolt against the re-election of Estrada Palma led to a second United States intervention in Cuba, ordered by Roosevelt, that lasted from 1906 to 1909. Under this regime, a provisional government was set up to carry out reforms directed by a governor installed by the United States. Marines landed again in Cuba in June 1912 in response to violent demonstrations in Oriente (Map 6.1). This intervention was directed at the protection of U.S. property and investments, threatened by the armed rebellion of African–Cubans and their brutal repression by the Cuban government. At the root of the rebellion was discontent over persistent exclusion from public office on the basis of colour. When a political party, the Partido Independente de Color, was established to represent the black middle classes, it was quickly seen as a threat to Liberal hegemony and a law passed in 1911 to prohibit the formation of parties defined by ethnicity. In response, the Partido Independente de Color turned to armed rebellion and the conflict, centred in Oriente, left thousands of black Cubans dead.

U.S. Marines returned to Oriente and Camagüey in 1917, when the so-called February Revolution erupted at the height of the sugar harvest. This time, the objective of the United States was to support the government, rather than to replace it, chiefly in order to avoid a full-scale occupation. Munitions were supplied and targeted military assistance given to protect foreign interests from the insurgent bands, the United States taking responsibility under the Platt Amendment. The Marines stayed until 1922. The Platt Amendment was annulled by the United States in 1934, though, fatefully, it retained Guantanamo Bay.

The United States was not unwilling to tolerate full-blooded dictators and often they flourished in unholy alliance. What the United States hoped for in a leader in a place like Cuba or the Dominican Republic in this period was someone who could preserve power and ensure internal stability, while respecting property and interests. If such a leader happened to be a strongman who behaved as a dictator and extended his rule beyond its constitutional limits, he remained acceptable so long as he met the protective qualifications. There were already examples in place in Mexico and Venezuela.

On these grounds, the election of Gerardo Machado as President of Cuba in 1924 seemed a good outcome. His election, soon after the withdrawal of the Marines and in the midst of calls for reform, was greeted positively by the United States. From the point of view of Cuban nationalists, there was the advantage that the possibilities of intervention were much reduced under his regime. Although less than ideal in democratic political theory, Machado embraced the ideals of reform and regeneration while, at the same time, reassuring the North Americans that they had nothing to fear. United States investment continued apace. Machado himself had made a fortune from business and so represented the new class of nationalist entrepreneurs.

Working class Cubans became increasingly organized in the 1920s, led by tobacco workers (particularly cigar makers), stevedores, mechanics, and railroad workers, and hard times and trade losses led to greater militancy in this rapidly growing class. Although Machado encouraged local industrial development and diversification, he also made clear that he had no time for labour unrest and put down strikes with extreme force. Machado also began the surveillance of potential revolutionary groups. The Cuban Communist Party, founded in 1925, was immediately proscribed and its members persecuted. All of this was approved by the United States. However, the depression hit Cuba early, through the collapse of world sugar prices, long before the financial crisis on Wall Street. By 1927, unemployment marched across the island, filled as it was from coast to coast by sugar plantations that left little scope for the peasant to find a niche. Living standards plummeted and poverty stalked the land.

Faced by these harsh realities, Machado found means to amend the constitution and extend his regime, meeting no opposition from Washington and retaining Cuban support through his success in warding off intervention. Although the fundamental illegality and fraudulence of his position soon became obvious and, by 1929, he had been openly branded a dictator of the worst sort, Machado remained the best available option for the preservation of U.S. interests throughout the depression. He stamped on many small revolts. By 1933, the impact of the depression on Cuban trade had become so great that the United States began to lose its hold on the economy. Bankers feared default. People were starving. The political opposition called for a revolution to depose Machado, the workers threatened a general strike that would bring down the government, and the United States applied diplomatic levers, but Machado did not go quietly. Facing threats of U.S. intervention, the army stepped in to save the local bourgeois political classes. Pressured to resign, Machado left Cuba in August 1933, flying by night to the Bahamas with seven bags of gold.

A period of instability followed the departure of Machado, resolved only by the emergence of yet another strongman and incipient dictator, Rubén Fulgencio Batista Zaldívar. The son of a cane cutter, Batista had grown up in eastern Cuba in the shadow of

United Fruit, in close company with Jamaican immigrants. Escaping the cane fields, he joined the army in 1921 and rose through the ranks, to grasp the opportunity that came his way in the turbulence of 1933. Batista filled a vacuum created by the incoherence of more radical forces and by the failure of the traditional political parties with their roots in the middle classes to offer leadership. For a time, it seemed that genuine revolution might occur in Cuba in 1933, with the government openly attacking U.S. intervention and capital, while acting to dramatically improve the living conditions of the working classes. The opportunity was lost only when the army, led by Batista and his allies, moved to resolve the class conflict underlying the revolution. Stability was restored but the concept of revolution had become firmly embedded and persisted alongside the deep-seated notion that Cuba's future depended on the protection of foreign interests. A consequence was the abrogation of the Platt Amendment in 1934; it no longer seemed necessary, useful, or appropriate to Cuba's trajectory.

By 1936, Batista had emerged as Cuba's new strongman, using the army as a tool of government, seeking self-aggrandisement and ensuring the loyalty of the forces through bribery and corruption. Batista accumulated great personal wealth. He escaped assassination. Paradoxically perhaps, the Communist Party was legally recognized in 1938 and labour unions in 1940. Both became powerful and Cuba seemed to be moving towards a form of socialism. At first Batista pulled the strings of titular presidents, but when Cuba got a new constitution in 1940 he was elected president. By 1942 he was being compared with Trujillo, Latin America's most brutal dictator. However, when new elections were called in 1944, Batista, anxious to be seen as a genuine democrat and misreading the situation, stepped down and the election was won by the opposition. Batista had to wait to launch his resurrection.

The progress of government from intervention to dictatorship that marked the history of Cuba in the first half of the twentieth century provides a model for developments in the Dominican Republic, except that this time dictatorship came both before and after intervention. Unstable party government in the Dominican Republic in the 1870s was concluded by a free election in 1882 which saw General Ulises Heureaux installed as president. His regime did not diverge fundamentally from the patterns of government established by those who had gone before, notably Santana and Báez, but Heureaux emerged as a rigid absolutist, a true dictator. Although the constitution remained in place and elections were called periodically, he demolished the emerging system of political parties in order to ensure his dictatorial role. Terror, corruption, and the persistent Dominican fear of Haiti, together with foreign loans, kept him in power. Heureaux fostered the formation of a national bourgeoisie but was ruthless in exterminating his enemies. He spied on his friends. It was, however, a period of relative prosperity, making the Dominican Republic attractive to both foreign investors and Spanish immigrants. Assassinated in 1899, Heureaux was soon replaced by his killer, Ramón Cáceres, who provided an interval of relatively mild rule.

The Dominican Republic was deep in debt as a result of borrowing to build railroads and European lenders sought redress. The United States was reluctant to resolve the crisis either by annexing Santo Domingo or by making it a formal protectorate, but chose instead to take control of customs collections to make them free of corruption, in order to pay off the debt and stave off German intervention. This example of customs receivership operated relatively well down to 1910 and seemed to offer a model that might be used elsewhere. However, when Cáceres, in turn, was assassinated in 1911, disorder reigned once more. Continuing political unrest saw the United States occupy the Dominican Republic in 1916. At first the United States tried to rule through a provisional governor but, unable to find a compliant figurehead, quickly reverted to martial law. The United States remained in the Dominican Republic until 1924.

During the occupation, the U.S. Marines set up a constabulary force. The objective in the Dominican Republic was to depoliticize the military by disbanding the existing force, the Guardia Republicana, and setting up a new constabulary, the Guardia Nacional, which was trained and led, at least initially, by North Americans. The Guardia Nacional combined the previously separate army, navy, and frontier guard under a single commander. It was to enforce the law, protect the borders, and serve as an arm of military control, particularly against insurgents. The constabulary remained in place after the withdrawal of the United States in 1924. It was from the ranks of this force that the Dominican Republic's next dictator, Rafael Leónidas Trujillo Molina, emerged. Joining the Guardia Nacional in 1919, Trujillo eventually became its commander, ready to once more use the military as a political instrument. He had the advantage of having all the forces under his immediate command and the additional advantage that the occupation had reduced insurgent activity to a minimum and had disarmed the population. In these ways, Trujillo provides a striking example of the dictator who emerges from imperial intervention, equipped by the imperial power with skills and given ideal conditions in which to use those tools in ways unintended.

In 1930, following a series of failed governments, Trujillo engineered his election as president. The number of votes in his favour exceeded the number of voters. The techniques he used to remain in power were similar to those of Heureaux – intimidation, assassination, spy rings, and intelligence gathering – but he also knew the importance of his well-trained military forces and the value of keeping the United States on his side. He granted generous economic concessions and bribed politicians when it seemed useful, to ensure economic growth through U.S. investment. Trujillo and his family garnered immense property in plantations and factories.

The most brutal of Trujillo's atrocities was the premeditated massacre in 1937 of 20,000 Haitians, people who had crossed the border into the Dominican Republic and squatted on arable land or hoped to find employment on plantations. The border between the two states had been fixed in 1929 but renegotiated between Trujillo and the President of Haiti, Sténio Vincent, in 1936, when the line on the map was made more certain. The massacre brought criticism but was somehow smoothed over between Vincent and Trujillo and quickly became swallowed up in the appalling events of World War II. Some saw the massacre as evidence of a spreading fascism, one of a kind with the Italian assault on Ethiopia. However, although he aligned himself with fascism, Trujillo was no ideologue and when the United States was attacked at Pearl Harbour he readily declared war on the Axis forces. Trujillo ruled by decree, in a one-party state, with no more than a show of democracy. A ruthless dictator, he established a totalitarian state which remained functional for more than thirty years, until his assassination in 1961.

In Haiti, revolt and governmental instability led to the longest of all the U.S. occupations, lasting from 1915 until 1934. On top of the economic and political reasons for intervention were strategic issues coming out of World War I. The intervention was, however, greeted by vigorous resistance from peasant soldiers, led by Charlemagne Péralte, who was eventually killed in 1919. A broader based nationalist movement, uniting Haitians of different ethnic and ideological allegiances, emerged and began to call for U.S. withdrawal.

Of the twenty two presidents of Haiti between 1870 and 1945, not one succeeded in making himself a genuine dictator, emperor, or monarch. Only one lasted as long as ten years. Most depended on bribery and corruption and few departed office peacefully. The first forty years, from 1870 to 1911, represented a period of relative political stability and democratic republican government. There were ten presidents, most of them black men who, particularly in the 1880s and 1890s, faced opposition aligned along the old conflict of colour and class. This long period of stable government was followed by five years of chaos, with seven presidents holding office, six of them assassinated. It was this chaos that created the conditions that led to the U.S. occupation. The next thirty years – the twenty years of occupation 1915–1934, and the following ten to 1945 – were marked by a return to longer presidential terms, with five men holding office, all of them "mulatto".

The 1870s saw the emergence in Haiti of a variety of party politics. The Liberal Party was predominantly mulatto and the National Party, black. The black elite remained strongest in the rural regions, where they were landowners, and in Cap Haïtien; they depended on the peasants and the army for support. The mulatto elite, on the other hand, was centred in Port au Prince and engaged in commerce as well as land owning; they relied on the manipulation of the constitutional institutions for their power and abjured the populist ideology of the Liberals. Both parties declared their faith in a republican form of government, the Liberals claiming a desire to see the suffrage expanded and making the cabinet responsible to the legislature. There were also proposals to extend presidential terms from four to eight years and to set up the office of vice president in order to ensure greater continuity, but these had little practical effect. The closest any of the Haitian presidents came to dictatorship in this period was the longest serving, Lysius Louis-Félicité Salomon, who held office from 1879 to 1888. A francophile who ruled behind a constitutional front, Salomon advocated national unity, but when he tried to change the constitution to permit his re-election there were riots and he was forced to flee to France. After a brief struggle, a constituent assembly elected General F. M. Florvil Hyppolite, who, in turn, attempted to extend his rule but dropped dead in 1896 leading an expedition against his rivals.

Under the occupation, the government of Haiti was closely monitored by the U.S. high commissioner. One approach was to attempt to co-opt opponents of the occupation, to buy their accommodation and perhaps support. One such was President Sténio Vincent, who was successful in having his term extended, to stretch beyond the end of the occupation to the outbreak of World War II. Vincent was in power from 1930 to 1941. He favoured U.S. investment, banks, and trade, and vacillated in his negotiations with Trujillo over the massacre of 1937. However, when accused of behaving in a dictatorial manner and of having established a fascist regime, his hopes of a third term withered away. During World War II, Haiti drifted closer to the United States and the ground was prepared for a new revolution.

The intersection of intervention and dictatorship that characterized the political histories of Cuba, Haiti, and the Dominican Republic was not repeated elsewhere. Puerto Rico might have followed the same path as Cuba, but its fate was different. Puerto Rico had been made a province of Spain in 1869 but continued uneasiness in the island led to the grant of autonomy in 1897. When the United States invaded the island in July 1898, Spain quickly asked for terms and Puerto Rico was ceded to the United States along with Cuba. Puerto Rico became a U.S. territory in May 1900 under the Foraker Act that established civil government. The precise meaning of this new status remained to be worked out, however, and in December 1901 the U.S. Supreme Court declared that Puerto Ricans were not U.S. citizens. This ruling was overturned in 1917.

In contrast to the Caribbean republics and their dictators, Puerto Rico's dependent status imposed on it a different style of government. The civil government established in 1900 under the Foraker Act provided for a governor and an executive council or upper chamber, appointed by the U.S. President, and a popularly elected lower chamber, the House of Delegates. The Unionist Party of Puerto Rico, founded in 1904 and led by Luis Muñoz Rivera, dominated politics down to the 1930s and advocated greater self-government. Its advocacy led to the granting of a popularly elected Senate in 1917, the year Puerto Ricans gained U.S. citizenship. In 1922, a Nationalist party was founded, calling for a free and independent republic, but when it failed at the polls in 1932, it turned to armed struggle. Luis Muñoz Marín founded the Popular Democratic Party in 1938 and swept the election of 1944.

Imperial interventions and occupations commonly had their beginnings in the context of warfare. Not only did wars result in outright conquest, they also made it easier for states to behave in ways they could not so easily excuse in peace in the light of international scrutiny. For the United States, the Spanish–American war yielded Puerto Rico and, less completely, Cuba. World War I saw a greater number of events: the occupation of Haiti in 1915, the occupation of the Dominican Republic in 1916, the intervention in Cuba in 1917, and the purchase for US$ 25 million of the Danish Virgin Islands later that year. However, all four of these events occurred before the United States entered the war as a combatant. U.S. Marines landed at Santiago, Cuba, on 8 March 1917 and the takeover of the Virgin Islands occurred on the last day of that month. A week later, the United States declared war on Germany. Cuba did the same the following day. The occupations of Cuba, Haiti, and the Dominican Republic all extended well beyond the end of World War I in 1918, but none of them continued longer than 1934. The year before, 1933, U.S. President Franklin Delano Roosevelt had heralded a new policy in the Caribbean, one in which the big stick was to be put aside and the states were to live together as good neighbours. At the outbreak of World War II in 1939, there were no continuing occupations.

Purchase of the Danish Virgin Islands by the United States in 1917 was enthusiastically approved by the working people of the islands, believing it would bring many political and economic benefits. They hoped for universal suffrage, a fully elected government, the opening of occupations, and a living wage. However, the constitution drawn up following the purchase placed executive power in the hands of an appointed governor and the people of the islands were not made citizens of the United States until 1927. Down to 1931, the islands remained in the hands of the Navy Department but were then transferred to the Department of the Interior. Initially, less than 5 percent of the people got the vote in a franchise based on property qualifications, but from 1936, all literate adult citizens were given the right to elect members to the legislature. Political parties had difficulty establishing themselves in this climate and here was no independence movement equivalent to that in Puerto Rico.

The second world war, in contrast to the first, saw no large-scale occupations of Caribbean territory by the United States. Now, the hegemony of the United States in the Caribbean was firmly established and the islands faced relatively little threat from Germany. However, World War II did see the United States granted bases throughout the British West Indies, under the Anglo–American agreement of 1941, and control of these enclaves and airfields continued for some time after 1945. U.S. interests, as in the oilfields of Trinidad, contributed to this pattern as well as the immediate defence issues. Cooperation between the United States and Great Britain, under the agreement of 1941, led to the establishment the following year of an Anglo–American Caribbean Commission, set up to consider problems of mutual concern in the Caribbean. Initially, the Caribbean Commission was expected to monitor the flow of food supplies to the region and to ensure nutrition was sustained in the shadow of the newly founded Food and Agriculture Organization of the United Nations. The Caribbean Commission was also involved in facilitating the migration of workers to the United States, as part of the war effort. There followed a Caribbean Research Council, and the first West Indian Conference, held in Barbados in 1944, directed particularly at postwar planning and reconstruction.

Although several of the U.S. occupations of Caribbean territories may be seen as responses to revolts, similar revolts in Trinidad, St Lucia, and Jamaica were left to the British to resolve. None of the British colonies shifted allegiance within the period, though Trinidad and Tobago were joined by imperial fiat as a single colony in 1898, and Dominica was shuffled in 1940 from the Leeward Islands group to the Windward Islands.

Much the same applied to the colonies of the French and the Dutch. Martinique and Guadeloupe were assimilated to France in 1892, integrated into the system of government and tariff barriers. In 1922, the Netherlands Antilles became integral territories of the Kingdom of the Netherlands. Unlike the French system, however, the Dutch colonies were considered independent when it came to trade, and they used this to extract revenue by charging export duties on mineral ores, fertilizer, and salt.

Whereas the United States, as a new imperial power, experimented with a variety of ways of governing its protectorates and dependencies, the British attempted few innovations in colonial government between 1870 and 1945. The models they preferred had been worked out much earlier, though their application did vary significantly in the decades after 1870 and there was some tinkering with the details preliminary to the much more fundamental changes that were to occur soon after 1945.

The British colonies in the Caribbean fell into two contrasting types: crown colonies and partially self-governing colonies. These types had their origins in particular compromises made at the end of the eighteenth century, when new conquests were being accommodated to the empire, but their essentials proved resilient and maintained their validity under changed conditions. In both models, a governor and an Executive Council, appointed by the crown, comprised the executive arm of government. In the crown colonies, the legislative branch consisted of a Legislative Council made up of both official and unofficial members, most of them appointed in some way but, rarely, elected by popular (male) vote. In the colonies that had partial self-government, the elected representation was much larger but still limited, and the legislative branch typically consisted of two houses, a Legislative Assembly and an upper Legislative Council. Down to 1939, the qualifications for voting derived from gender and economic status, the latter generally set quite low but, reflecting the poverty of the time, allowing the franchise only to a privileged few.

The crown colony model was most widespread in the British islands in the late nineteenth century. Pure examples of the model, in which the governor ruled through a legislature with an official majority, were uncommon. Modified versions of crown colony government had legislatures in which nominated members, who were not officials, formed a majority. Even under the modified form, a governor had great political power because he could handpick the men he wanted and ignore the needs of the masses, while inhibiting the emergence of activist organizations. He had only to answer to the British government. Unlike his contemporary dictators, however, the governor of a British colony had limited opportunities for self-aggrandisement or making a fortune through bribery and corruption. His allies were the planter class but in these hard times they had little to offer beyond their loyalty and splendid dinners. The British governor depended on his salary and knew that his term was in the hands of his paymasters. Most of the British Caribbean colonies were, in any case, relatively insignificant during this long period and regarded as places from which to move up to greater things or, perhaps, unfortunate proof of failure. Only the occasional governor failed to fit the mould by showing enthusiasm for West Indian people and prospects.

The pure form of crown colony government was soon modified, by increasing the number of elected representatives allowed and so reducing the direct power of the governor. The only British sugar island to survive the entire period of colonialism without ever becoming a crown colony was Barbados, where the tight control on land and resources held by the white population almost from the beginning of settlement meant that a limited representative system was able to survive the threats seen elsewhere from a black bourgeoisie or a popular franchise. The British did attempt to introduce crown colony government to Barbados in 1876, in order to address the dire social conditions of the working people, by means of confederation with the Windward Islands. In 1876, there were only 1,664 registered voters in Barbados, from a population of 162,000. These voters elected twenty four members to twelve constituencies. The British attempt to change the system of government met with intense hostility from the oligarchy. A violent class war broke out but failed to become a revolution, held down by the planter militia. The British government finally abandoned its plan for confederation in 1884.

Depression, labour unrest, and unionization, as well as racial consciousness, the emergence of an educated black and coloured middle class, a growing awareness of anticolonial movements elsewhere in the empire, and the exposure to a wider world that came with migration and World War I all combined to contribute to a growing restlessness in the British colonies. They remained securely British and colonial in 1945, but major gains were made in moving towards democratic government and, less certainly, decolonization. Strikes and labour demonstrations began to become common immediately after 1918 but were much more common in the later stages of the depression of the 1930s. From the sugar fields of St Kitts in 1935 to the oilfields of Trinidad in 1937 and the wharves of Jamaica in 1938, workers demanded better wages and conditions.

The leaders of the labour unions that emerged from these continuing and widespread disturbances moved swiftly to use their power to mobilize political parties. Thus, Alexander Bustamante emerged as leader of the Jamaica Labour Party, which was closely allied with the Bustamante Industrial Trade Union, while the Barbados Labour Party led by Grantley Adams had its roots in the Barbados Workers' Union. The new union/party leaders also took advantage of the changes in government introduced by the British as a consequence of the enquiry – chaired by Lord Moyne and influenced by Fabians such as Lord Olivier – into the disturbances of the 1930s. They saw the necessity of social and political reform. The newborn political parties and the nascent two-party system soon appeared at the hustings, the first general election on the principle of universal adult suffrage occurring in Jamaica in 1944. The other colonies followed close behind and the parties that contested these first elections became dominant forces in the modern political scene.

Within the British West Indian colonies, there were moves towards increased integration of government functions, particularly in the eastern Caribbean. A West Indian Court of Appeal was established in 1920, made up of all the chief justices excepting Jamaica. Groups outside government, such as teachers, merchants, and labour unions, also made steps to establish regional agencies. Proposals for a more ambitious federation of the West Indian colonies were formulated within the context of planning for a postwar world, but remained muted until 1947.

A more significant example of regional–imperial integration in the period before 1945 occurred in the Caribbean territories of the Netherlands. In 1940, the territory of Curaçao – made up of the island of that name, together with Aruba and Bonaire in the southern Caribbean, and St Eustatius, Saba, and part of St Martin in the north – maintained a system of government along the lines of the crown colony model. The executive consisted of a governor and an advisory council, appointed by the crown. The legislative assembly had fifteen members, five appointed by the crown and the rest elected. Down to 1937, suffrage was restricted to males qualified by income or educational attainment. Fewer than 3 percent of the people had a vote.

The government of the French colonies of Martinique and Guadeloupe came to differ strongly from that in the British and Dutch from the time of assimilation in 1892. Under this arrangement, the French colonies were made part of metropolitan government and economic regulation. In 1940, Martinique and Guadeloupe were each represented in the French Parliament by one senator and two deputies. In the islands, government was then in the hands of a governor assisted by a privy council, comprising the executive branch, and a general council (with thirty six members elected by universal suffrage) that constituted the legislative branch. This solution to the colonial relationship represented a strong dose of inclusion and enfranchisement, along with an equally strong dose of cultural and economic submersion that brought the metropolitan agenda to the islands. The lines between democracy and the dictatorship of the imperial state were blurred, creating grounds for a continuing ambivalence.

The variety, and often contradictory tendencies, of government within the Caribbean represented shifts in the longstanding struggle between hegemony, possession, and dreams of independence. Between 1870 and 1945, the states that managed to achieve political independence and establish themselves as republics were most open to individualistic dictatorship. It was a great time to be a dictator. These were also the states most likely to be occupied by the new imperial power, the United States, when their internal government seemed to threaten the security of that power. On the other hand, the islands that remained firmly in the hands of European states remained free of this type of dictatorship but bound by the hegemony and cultural weight of their metropolitan masters. What was common throughout the Caribbean was the increased role of government in economic and social life, a tendency quite independent of political structure.

NEW MODELS OF GOVERNMENT GROWTH

In most parts of the Caribbean, whatever the structure of government, the role of the public sector expanded considerably after 1870. This growth had several aspects. In the first place, government expenditure increased markedly its share of total output. Secondly, there was an extension of government functions and public ownership of enterprises previously private. Thirdly, the sources of public finance were widened, particularly to include metropolitan grants and loans. More broadly and perhaps ironically, the period after 1870 – the high point of free trade – was influenced by economic thinking that led governments to take greater responsibility for economic and social development. It was also in this period that the concept of deficit-budgeting came to seem acceptable. Public debt grew to substantial proportions, as a consequence of borrowings and failures in the efficient collection of revenue through duties and taxation. Further, foreign borrowing meant foreign debt and the loss of local benefits.

Patterns of government investment in economic development and social welfare differed significantly and sometimes in unexpected ways. Perhaps surprisingly, the strongest involvement occurred in Cuba, Puerto Rico, and the Netherlands Antilles, where the public sector's share of gross domestic product approached 20 percent by 1940. Government investment in industrialization in Puerto Rico lifted this share as high as 30 percent by 1946. In Cuba, the U.S. intervention resulted in the imposition of sales taxes in the 1920s, though import duties were reduced in the 1930s for goods of U.S. origin. In Puerto Rico, unusually, income tax replaced excise duties as the major source of internal revenue as early as the 1940s. However, the island was heavily dependent on external, federal, sources of revenue.

The economy of the Dominican Republic remained weak throughout the period to World War I, but part of the trouble was the government's attempts to build railroads and other infrastructure through overseas borrowing. The customs collection system imposed by the United States from 1904 to 1910 resolved the problem only temporarily. Although the United States occupation of 1916 to 1924 was accompanied by road building and the improvement of communications, as well as schools and public health systems, much of this work was financed by private U.S. investors rather than the government, contributing further to a growing public foreign debt. Haiti depended more than any other place on customs duties for its revenue, about 90 percent as late as 1914. This was an important factor in the easy success of the United States in taking over public finance simply by occupying the customs posts, conveniently located in ports that could be threatened by gunboats.

In the colonies of the British and French, the imperial governments persisted in their support of the sugar industry – through indentured immigration and modernization – but also began to see the necessity of diversification and investment in essential infrastructure, especially communications. Down to World War I, most of the colonial governments raised too little revenue to be able to finance substantial public works and the economies were too weak to support continued borrowing. Beginning in the depression of the 1890s, the British government offered concessions to private investors willing to undertake public works but had more success when imperial grants or loans were made.

The idea that there should be a partnership between public and private enterprise, tapping metropolitan public funds, was novel and pointed the way forward. Down to the 1930s, however, it was the promotion of private enterprise that was thought most likely to enable economic development. Only in the late 1930s did the British government begin to recognize its financial responsibility to its colonial empire. The Colonial Development and Welfare Act of 1940 represented a more direct confrontation with the economic problems of the British West Indies but down to 1945 it was concerned, above all, with social welfare.

Although the scope of the public sector remained limited in the British sphere, it did expand considerably. In Jamaica, for example, the public sector doubled its share of the island's gross domestic product between 1870 and 1945, to reach about 12 percent as early as 1930. At the same time, the distribution of expenditure shifted from administration, justice, defence, and the church to education, health, public works, and social services. An increasing amount had to be allocated to paying off public debt, however – notably, the debt incurred in 1901 when the government purchased the privately owned railroad. The sources of revenue were not modernized but remained heavily dependent on customs duties, as before. Income tax was introduced in Jamaica in 1920 but down to 1945, contributed only about 10 percent of total tax revenue.

Similar patterns occurred elsewhere in the British West Indies, with slow growth in expenditure between 1870 and 1910 followed by a rapid spurt up to 1930. Indentured immigration remained an important item for Trinidad as late as 1910 but there also was a larger investment in land settlement than occurred in Jamaica in this period. Barbados, although not a crown colony, followed much the same trajectory, with heavy expenditure on education. The Barbados government also retained ownership of the island's railroad to the end of the 1930s, suggesting that colonial political status mattered relatively little in this development.

POPULATION AND LABOUR

The growth of government and its expanding role in economic development reflected changing attitudes to investment and regulation. It was equally a response to the rapid growth of population that occurred between 1870 and 1945 and the pressure this put on resources. Overpopulation was a new concept for the Caribbean but it went together with new ideas about the responsibility of governments and fears that economic tensions, represented for the first time in substantial unemployment, would spill over into political unrest. The period witnessed a fundamental demographic transition. From slow and even negative natural internal population growth and a heavy dependence on immigration, the Caribbean changed to become a region of rapid population increase and out-migration.

The total population of the Caribbean increased from 5 million in 1870 to 15 million by 1945. The rate of growth was not dramatically more than in the previous period, but the causes of growth were different and the numbers much larger. The people were much more densely packed and their pressure on the natural environment critically elevated. As before 1870, many of the smaller islands had already hit a temporary limit and stagnated or experienced decades in which they had absolute decreases – for example, Barbados between 1900 and 1920 or the Bahamas between 1911 and 1921 – largely due to emigration. Population growth continued to proceed most rapidly in the Greater Antilles, so that these islands increased their share of the total from 80 percent in 1870 to 87 percent by 1945. The most rapid growth of all occurred in the previously sparsely populated Dominican Republic, in which the population increased more than six times over the period.

Cuba, with 4.9 million, remained the most populous territory in 1945, followed by Haiti (3.1 million), Puerto Rico (2 million), the Dominican Republic (1.9 million), and Jamaica (1.3 million). Outside the Greater Antilles, the most phenomenal growth occurred in Trinidad and Tobago, where population increased five times between 1870 and 1945, to reach 558,000. These shifts in the geographical distribution of the population within the Caribbean went together with changes in allegiance and imperial connections. Over the period 1870 to 1945 the "Spanish" territories increased their share from 47 to 58 percent of the population, whereas the "French" (including Haiti) declined from 30 to 24 percent, and the "British" from 21 to 17 percent.

Population densities increased substantially, putting pressure on land resources and increasingly pushing people towards the towns and cities, and off the islands. In 1870, the only territories with densities greater than 100 persons per km^2 were small islands: Barbados (368), Martinique (144), St Kitts-Nevis (130), Antigua (125), Grenada (110), Danish Virgin Islands (110), and Montserrat (107). All of these were early-settled sugar colonies. They struggled even to double their densities by 1945. However, they were joined then by larger territories in the Greater Antilles, which grew more rapidly in spite of their size and inequalities in internal resources. Puerto Rico went from 79 persons per km^2 in 1870 to 225 in 1945; Jamaica from 46 to 115; and Haiti from 43 to 112. The Dominican Republic (moving from 6 in 1870 to 39 in 1945) and Cuba (13 to 44) also exhibited substantial increases in density of settlement but their second-phase sugar revolutions lacked the demographic impact of the first.

In some territories, the rapid growth of urban populations, particularly after World War I, reflected pressure on agricultural land created by the attainment of a state of saturation in the peasantry. In the early stages of the drift of population into the larger cities, people could be absorbed fairly easily. By the 1920s, however, new arrivals began to live in marginal settlements, in roughly constructed shelters on sites without amenities. In the Bahamas, the process of urban concentration in association with the development of the tourist industry based in Nassau saw New Providence grow twice as fast as the out islands between 1890 and 1945. In Kingston, Jamaica, and San Juan, Puerto Rico, governments first took action to clear slums in the 1930s.

The massive increase in Caribbean population between 1870 and 1945 was not so much a product of immigration as of substantial increases in fertility, reduced infant mortality, and improved health conditions. The decline in the infant mortality rate was particularly important, because it contributed to population growth without a necessary increase in fertility and because it indicated improved nutrition and hygiene. In many territories, the infant mortality rate was cut by half. Where the rate was heaviest, the fall was equally dramatic – for example, in Barbados, which had one of the highest birth rates in the region, where infant mortality fell from more than 400 per thousand in 1870 to 150 by 1945.

Improvements in public health, such as better sanitation in towns and the provision of piped water, together with public education regarding the importance of personal cleanliness, helped reduce the spread of diseases such as cholera, smallpox, and typhoid, and increased life expectancy. Campaigns against the mosquito reduced the prevalence of malaria and yellow fever. Thus, in spite of continuing poverty, the early twentieth century saw increases in life expectancy in at least some of the Caribbean islands as a direct consequence of these changes in public health and individual behaviour. In places occupied by the United States, improvement was promoted by the military governments, but relatively little was achieved outside the major cities.

Before 1930, the history of labour in the Caribbean was essentially one of shortage. Entrepreneurs and imperial governments went to extreme measures – through slavery, indenture, and truck systems – to ensure their individual control of people as potential workers, and invested heavily in free and forced migration. It had seemed to them necessary to bear the cost of having workers committed, by contract or compulsion, to give their labour to just one employer or one government. Only in the early twentieth century and particularly after 1930 did this balance turn around. The shift occurred first in a few densely populated places, such as Barbados, by the 1860s, but it was only after 1930 that unemployment emerged as a problem. Rather than looking for people to work and often forcing them to do so, governments were faced with the challenge of finding jobs for people who wanted work but could find none. This shift, which was to become increasingly intense, had its initial impact between 1930 and 1945, with major repercussions not only in the labour market but also in patterns of internal and external migration.

Women were particularly affected by the transition from labour shortage to surplus labour. Many occupations became more rigidly gendered. In agriculture, the harder tasks of plantation fieldwork increasingly became exclusively male. Domestic service, on the other hand, shifted towards women. In many places, domestic service peaked in the 1930s. These occupations were rarely regulated in the absence of strong unionization. By contrast, prostitution was first regulated in Puerto Rico in the 1890s and the Dominican Republic in 1917, through the creation of designated red light districts in major cities. Doing so helped build the image of the prostitute as a specialized category, and a threat to public health.

In some territories, immigration remained an important contributor to population growth – notably, European immigration to Puerto Rico and Cuba. Over the period 1870 to 1945, white people increased their share of the population of Puerto Rico from 55 to 75 percent and in Cuba, from 60 to 75 percent. Because these were the greatest gainers from immigration, the pattern widened the gulf between the "Spanish" and the other regions of the Caribbean, where people of African and Indian descent typically predominated.

The desire of the Dominican Republic to increase its white population and the equivalent desire of its creole population to identify as white or "Indian" (Taíno) developed in counterpoint with the growth of the black republic of Haiti and fears of renewed invasion or migration across the shared land border, culminating in the massacre of 1937. However, although the Dominican Republic actively promoted European immigration and some hundreds of Jewish refugees came in 1939, most of the schemes intended to promote settlement in government-sponsored agricultural colonies along the Haitian border or on unoccupied lands in the interior failed.

On the other hand, in the older colonies of the British, the white, mostly creole, populations shrank as a result of emigration and marriage outside the group. In Barbados, the proportion remained around 5 percent but in Jamaica and many other British colonies, the whites quickly dropped to less than 1 percent of the total, though retaining effective political and economic power through the possession of land and the control of government.

Indentured immigrants, almost all of them from India, continued to flow into the Caribbean down to the 1920s. More indentured Indians came to Trinidad after 1870 than before and in this later period, their labour not only saved the sugar industry but built the foundations of its continued prosperity by keeping costs relatively low. They also assisted the cocoa industry. Between 1870 and 1917, when the migration was stopped by the Indian government, some 103,000 Indians came to Trinidad. Although the system had many flaws, the opportunities offered were sufficient to encourage some people to migrate to the Caribbean for a second and even third indenture contract. Those who returned to the Caribbean generally did so with the expectation of starting a new life and accepting the conditions of a westernized colonial culture. Some had been so transformed by their first migration that they found it hard to settle again in India. In the 1870s, many indentured took the opportunity to accept land rather than seeking repatriation and in the following decades, purchases of crown land extended the scope of the Indian peasantry.

Jamaica received smaller contingents of indentured Indians and a few went to St Lucia, St Vincent, or Grenada as late as 1893.

Plate 6.1. East Indian plantation village, Trinidad, circa 1910. *Source:* "Vaquero", *Life and Adventure in the West Indies* (London: John Bale, Sons and Danielsson, Ltd., 1914), opp. 242.

Guadeloupe and Martinique stopped receiving Indians in 1885. Small numbers of Chinese workers continued to come to Cuba at the beginning of the 1870s but this migration dried up and by 1900 the island's Chinese population was less than 1 percent.

Movement within the Caribbean, from island to island, followed patterns firmly in place before 1870 but also opened up new pathways. In most cases, people moved from places where wages were low and opportunities for landholding limited to places where they could earn higher wages and there was a hope of owning land. Many thought their migrations would be temporary but ended up staying. People continued to move from the Leeward Islands to Trinidad, but began also to try their luck in the Dominican Republic's infant sugar industry, and in the U.S. Virgin Islands. Jamaicans started work on Cuban sugar estates in 1898 and, between 1902 and 1932, some 120,000 went there, many remaining permanently.

More important than these movements between the islands was migration to Panama, to work on building the Canal. In the 1880s, more than 80,000 Jamaicans left the island to work on this project as well as railroad building in Costa Rica. In the final construction of the Canal, under the United States, as many as 150,000 West Indians went to work on the project between 1904 and 1914. This migration, however, was largely limited to men from the British colonies, particularly Barbados and Jamaica, favoured because of their education in English. They suffered racism and segregation and discrimination and most were repatriated in the 1920s. The remittances sent home by these men contributed substantially to the economic welfare of their families and their islands.

Migration to the cities of the eastern seaboard of the United States also emerged as a new route, beginning in the 1870s, from Puerto Rico, Cuba, and other islands. Most significant for the originating population was the example of the U.S. Virgin Islands, which saw many people leave for the mainland after the Danish sale of 1917. By 1945, there were only about 25,000 people left in the U.S. Virgin Islands, down from 43,000 in 1835. Migrants to the United States also flowed from Jamaica and many other British and French islands, in smaller proportions, but this movement was quickly limited by restrictions imposed in 1924. The Great Depression saw a net flow back into the Caribbean, made up of both voluntary and involuntary return migrants.

EXPLOITING THE LAND

Agriculture remained the foundation of almost all of the Caribbean economies but the period from 1870 to 1945 was marked by conflicting trends in the pattern of production and land tenure. On one hand, the concentration of landownership reached its peak, particularly in the sugar industries of Cuba, Puerto Rico, and the British colonies. This concentration of ownership went together with a massive increase in the size of individual plantations. On the other hand, in many places, the peasant population reached a peak in this period, around 1930, after which very small holdings (those fewer than five acres) began to be amalgamated into larger, more viable units. Thus, in both the plantation and the peasant sectors, there was a long-term trend towards larger holdings. Further, in some cases, these two apparently opposed tendencies were able to coexist successfully, especially where the expansion of the peasant sector did not encroach on plantation land. Plantations could grow in size and be the property of fewer and fewer owners without necessarily engrossing a larger proportion of agricultural land.

The trend towards latifundia was well-established in Cuba before 1870 and depended only in part on U.S. interests and investments. The process continued virtually unhindered down to World War II. Sugar production increased massively once more, from 725,000 tons in 1870 to more than five million tons as early as 1925; it declined somewhat after that but was still around four million tons in 1945. Cuba was converted from an island in which landless free men once might have aspired to ownership to one in which this was no longer a realistic goal.

The fundamental cause of this transformation was the steam-powered sugar mill and railroad that made possible the *central*, mentioned in the previous chapter. The period from 1870 was characterized by massive growth in scale rather than technological change. Indeed, the period produced no significant innovations but fulfilled the potential of steam and steel. At first, the growth of the centrales had encouraged the subdivision of land on the plantation frontiers and the *colono* population came to occupy a large area of cane land. Around 1900, as the centrales began to reach full capacity, competition bid up the price the *colono* could ask for his cane, and the mills found it more profitable to purchase the land outright and include it in the plantation's own cane supply zone. This process occurred at the same time as the number of mills was reduced, from 1,000 in 1880 to just 180 by 1925, when the plantations occupied an average 30,000 acres each. The largest of the corporations, the Cuban American Sugar Company, alone owned 500,000 acres. This pattern changed little down to 1945 in spite of attempts to halt the concentration of wealth and in spite of the proscription of the latifundium in the Cuban constitution of 1940, which forbade holding more than 1,000 acres in a single property. The arrogance of capital meant the legislation was simply ignored. Much the same happened in Puerto Rico.

In the case of Puerto Rico, the development of latifundia began only after the island was ceded to the United States. In 1898, small farms of fewer than fifty acres remained common; about 90 percent of these farms were occupied by their owners. Landownership had grown to this extent largely because of the stagnation and decline of the sugar industry after 1870. Initially, it seemed this pattern would be respected, but from 1901, the establishment of free trade between Puerto Rico and the United States made the cultivation of sugar and tobacco highly profitable. Sugar production increased from a low 35,000 tons in 1899 to more than one million tons by 1933. This rapid growth was accompanied by the purchase and lease of large areas of land by U.S. corporations that ignored legislation intended to inhibit such development. By the 1930s, more than 80 percent of the cane land of Puerto Rico was farmed by plantations of more than 1,000 acres each, with the big four U.S. companies holding some 185,000 acres. In the process, many small farmers lost their land and absentee proprietorship once more became common. Efforts to turn this trend around were made as early as the 1920s, but the large-scale purchase or expropriation of land for redistribution to landless field workers begun in the 1940s had relatively little impact on the dominance of the corporations.

In the Dominican Republic, where sugar-making had had its sixteenth-century Caribbean origins, the long-moribund industry emerged in its modern form only after 1870, when it was promoted by Cuban immigrants. It grew to export 50,000 tons by 1898 and then, with strong U.S. investment and the land registration act of 1921, which promoted the expansion of large-scale plantations, increased production steadily to more than 500,000 tons by 1945. Although the Dominican Republic was not the leading producer, it did become the home of what was the world's largest plantation, La Romana, covering 60,000 acres and producing 125,000 tons in 1938. Individual farmers, squatters, and communal landholders were displaced by corporations, regardless of their tenure. During the U.S. occupation, Marines were deployed to protect the modern sugar plantations from guerrilla insurgency fuelled by the displacement of peasants, landless and desperate.

In Haiti, the state remained the largest land owner, but Salomon introduced a law in 1883 that opened up ownership of state land to peasants on the condition that they used the holdings to produce sugar, coffee, or cocoa. The constitution drawn up in 1918 following the U.S. occupation contained a vital element that allowed property rights to foreigners, something that had been denied since the revolution. Although the new law included the proviso that such foreigners should live on the land, it was used to facilitate the entry of U.S. sugar companies and modern technologies. By World War II, Haiti was producing about 50,000 tons of sugar, a quantity well below the colonial peaks of the 1780s. The impact on land tenure within Haiti was slight and the peasantry retained their primacy.

Outside the United States sphere of influence and investment, the sugar industries of the Caribbean performed erratically. Production was increasingly constricted to those regions where extensive level, fertile lands could be cultivated using modern tillage machinery, together with railroads or tramways and modernized steam-powered mills. The use of modern technologies reduced costs of production by 50 percent. The greatest successes occurred where these elements were combined with an indentured labour force, as in Trinidad, for example. There, sugar exports grew from 40,000 tons in 1870 to a peak of 154,000 tons in 1936. This growth in sugar occurred parallel to the expansion of peasant agriculture down to 1945, encouraged in part by the spread of cane-farming and crop-sharing systems between 1900 and 1930, and by the granting of land in lieu of return passages to India for the indentured beginning in 1870. By the end of the 1930s, cane farmers contributed almost half the cane crushed by Trinidad's mills. Government land-settlement schemes were commenced in the 1930s but these generally provided only one or two acres, just enough to cultivate ground provisions.

Following quite a different trajectory was Jamaica. Sugar production declined steadily from 1870 to a minimum in 1913, when fewer than 5,000 tons were exported, but then recovered to 178,000 tons by 1945. Production was then concentrated in a few select regions where extensive plains offered the preferred conditions for cultivation and massive new central mills had been built. These new plantations represented investment by British sugar refining companies, such as Tate and Lyle, and had a significant impact on local land tenure patterns. They helped stir up labour unrest with political repercussions. In Jamaica, in both the former sugar regions and in the extensive districts that had never grown sugar, the peasantry grew rapidly down to 1930, when it entered a period of saturation or stagnation. In 1870, there were about 50,000 holdings of less than fifty acres in Jamaica, the number growing to 185,000 in 1930, then falling to 155,000 in 1960. The first phase of this growth, down to 1895, resulted in part from government action to end squatting and establish legal title. After 1895, crown lands were made available and, from 1902, small settlers were given improved chances to purchase these lands using credit from agricultural loan banks.

Even in islands where the potential for modernization and large-scale operations was limited, planters were able to apply fertilizer, however sparingly, and cultivate improved cane varieties, even if the hoe continued to do more work than the plough. Cattle carts still often dominated transport on estates but ancient windmills and waterwheels were replaced with more efficient steam engines. The old estates remained at the core, with cane-farming marginal. Barbados, for example, lifted its production steadily from about 35,000 tons in 1870 to more than 100,000 by 1935. In Martinique, production declined from an early peak of 50,000 tons in 1875 down to a low of less than 20,000 in 1922, before climbing again to a new peak of 68,000 tons in 1938. Guadeloupe, where the larger number of indentured Indians had been taken, performed erratically, achieving an early maximum of 57,000 in 1882 that was not regained by 1945.

Elsewhere, sugar struggled to hold its former place in the island economies. St Croix continued to produce small crops down to 1945 but never came close to the peak achieved during slavery. Becoming a U.S. territory was not enough to induce investment. Other islands, such as St Kitts, Antigua, and St Lucia, barely managed to double their output over the period and became minor players. Central factories were established in Antigua in 1905 and St Kitts in 1910, but in many islands it was not profitable to replace antiquated technologies and the level lands were not extensive enough to justify the amalgamation of properties. Where the economies were more diversified and land relatively rugged, sugar as an export crop was completely abandoned. This occurred in Grenada by 1890, Dominica and Tobago by 1900, and Nevis, Montserrat, and St Vincent by 1920. In all of the Windward Islands, the abandonment of sugar enabled the peasantry to grow apace, well beyond 1945, thanks in part to the emergence of the banana as an export crop.

Although the banana and its close cousin the plantain had been important food crops in the Caribbean from the early sixteenth century, their fragility and perishability restricted use to domestic kitchens. The plantain was generally preferred, boiled or fried as a vegetable and baked as a sweet tart. The banana was eaten boiled when green or as a fruit when ripe. The export market that opened in North America in the late nineteenth century, however, was interested only in the banana as a ripe fruit. Getting it there in marketable condition depended on rapid and reliable steamship services. The availability of such technology, beginning in the 1860s, opened up new possibilities for a whole range of fragile tropical fruits, but the banana held centre stage. At first, the banana was an exotic luxury good and expensive, but from the 1880s it became much more affordable and exports increased dramatically, particularly from Jamaica but also Cuba and Santo Domingo. In the Caribbean, bananas had been regarded as a peasant crop, disdained by planters, but the decline of sugar made the fruit an attractive proposition and it began to be planted on a large scale.

The banana shippers, most of them from the United States, also began to see investment opportunities and bought up large areas for production. In this way, they developed a connected supply chain they controlled at every point. Large multinationals emerged, their reach stretching into Central America as well as the islands. The monster among these was the United Fruit Company, which took on an imperial shape. Direct shipment of bananas to the United Kingdom began in 1897 and there Elders and Fyffes became the dominant player, controlling production as well as trade, until absorbed by United Fruit in 1910. In Haiti, a banana export industry grew during the U.S. occupation, the Standard Fruit and Steamship Company being granted a twenty-five year contract in 1935 to develop the trade. Large plantations were consolidated by the company and, by 1939, Haiti was exporting more than one million bunches. It did not last, however, because the outbreak of war brought a rapid collapse. Haitian peasants pulled out their plantings and went back to doing what they had done before – growing food to feed themselves.

The combined growth of peasant and plantation agriculture placed pressure on the land and sea resources of the Caribbean

Plate 6.2. Loading bananas, Port Antonio, Jamaica, circa 1905. *Source: Picturesque Jamaica* (Kingston: A. Duperly and Sons, 1905), 50.

islands. Where the rainforest was cleared, erosion became common. With the cover gone, earthquakes, hurricanes, and storms generated frequent landslides and mudslides. Human activity contributed directly to making these hazards more common and more destructive. This was, however, largely understood as simply a matter of degree and beyond the power of human beings to control or moderate. The most spectacular environmental catastrophe of the period was the eruption of Mont Pelée in Martinique in 1902. Lava and ash poured down on the city of St Pierre at the foot of the volcano, destroying the town and killing its 30,000 inhabitants. Mount Soufrière in St Vincent erupted in the same year, causing up to 2,000 deaths.

By 1870, the rainforests of the Caribbean had little timber left to be exploited for building and furniture-making, and the islands became net importers of tropical hardwoods from mainland sources in Central and South America. Jamaica, Haiti, and the French colonies, however, remained major producers of dyewoods down to the 1920s, after which they began to face stiff competition from synthetic dyes. Logwood, the major dyewood, had a brief period of importance in the 1870s and 1880s when it benefited by the decline of sugar and could be harvested from trees that originally were planted as living fences that had run up in abandoned fields and pastures. In the 1890s, factories were set up to extract the dye, whereas formerly the logs had been exported for metropolitan processing.

In Haiti, the beginnings of ecological catastrophe appeared first in the early twentieth century, as the rapid growth of population put pressure on resources and the forest gave way to cleared slopes. During World War I, a short-lived boom in demand for logwood saw many large trees felled. A new assault on the forest occurred in World War II, when extensive areas were felled to make space for the planting of cryptostegia, a source of latex that helped ease the shortage of rubber. The creation of these new plantations put further pressure on food-producing lands.

Maritime industries produced little of importance to the island economies but did contribute to the long-term depletion of stocks and resources. Whaling flourished in the southern Windward Islands, particularly the Grenadines, between 1880 and 1920, when the fishery employed nearly thirty boats. Whale oil was exported to New England, while the meat was eaten by the islanders. The turtle industry, based in the Cayman Islands, continued steadily through the period to 1945. In the Bahamas, sponge fishing peaked around 1900, when the industry was the most productive in the world. It employed about one third of the labour force and involved up to 3,000 boats, most of them working under the inequitable truck system described in chapter 5. Sponges remained the major item of export from the Bahamas until 1938, when the industry was destroyed by a blight or fungus and natural sponges began to be displaced by artificial alternatives.

Mining, the extractive industry that Columbus had hoped would produce rivers of gold and silver, finally came into its own in the twentieth century with the development of the oil industry. Gold and silver continued to be mined in Cuba down to 1945 but only in small quantities and often as the byproduct of base metals such as copper, which remained at a fairly high level down to World War II. The quarrying of limestone, clay, and marble was important for local construction industries, but its impact was relatively slight in this period.

By far the most significant mineral fuel developed after 1870 was petroleum. Attempts were made in the late nineteenth century to mine crude oil in Cuba, Barbados, and Trinidad, but full-scale production did not begin in Trinidad until 1909 and Cuba in 1942. Asphalt, used both as a material in construction and as a fuel, mined from Trinidad's Pitch Lake and from sources in Cuba, remained important into the 1940s but was soon unable to compete with oil as a fuel. Oil production in Trinidad increased steadily to reach twenty million barrels in 1940. Importantly, and in strong contrast to the history of sugar in the Caribbean, Trinidad was a refiner rather than a simple exporter of crude. A major reason why the industry developed in this way was simply that Trinidad was an early comer and the potential remained unknown. The first true refinery in Trinidad was established in 1911 to supply the British navy. Down to 1920, the main products were kerosene (also known as paraffin, used for heating) and fuel oil (diesel being one type, used to power engines), which meant there was considerable waste and it was not worth shipping crude great distances to refine it. Only with the concentration on gasolene (also called petrol or benzine, used to fuel internal combustion engines) after 1920, and the growth of petrochemical industries after 1940, did refining become market oriented. Only then did it become profitable to ship crude oil in vast tankers over long distances.

Something different happened in the Dutch islands of Aruba and Curaçao. Although these islands had no reserves of their own, they were used to refine crude oil from the nearby oilfields of Venezuela. The reason for this unusual arrangement was that the refiners Royal-Dutch Shell and Standard Oil decided, in the context of World War I, that the islands offered a more secure defence against the disruption and destruction of infrastructure that might stem from political upheaval. Venezuela was then the major external supplier of the U.S. market.

Although economic growth through linkages to the oil industry or agriculture was limited, the period after 1870 did witness the emergence of a range of manufacturing enterprises. These enterprises typically were located in port towns, close to the biggest, most rapidly growing, concentrations of population. For Caribbean colonies, this was a new development and indicated the beginnings of a period of simple import-substitution as well as attempts to refine raw materials before shipping them abroad or to industrialize the products of craftspeople. The scale of change was not always dramatic, but it did suggest an alternative style of colonial economy. In 1870, for example, Barbados could boast nothing more than a factory making sulphur matches. By 1930, it had two biscuit factories, two ice factories, and other enterprises making cotton textiles, tobacco products, refined oil, and ceramics. The significance of bakeries, breweries, and ice factories was that, previously, ice, beer and commercial baked products were largely imported. Many of these products comprised a high proportion of water, so bottling plants often led the way. The larger the island, the more extensive the manufacturing sector. Cuba had a Coca-Cola factory as early as 1900.

The interruption of shipping during World War I also encouraged the development of local manufacturing businesses but, once again, this was moderated by market scale. In Cuba, national capital poured into manufacturing and light industry, following a great drop in imports from the United States. By the middle of the 1920s, national ownership of factories and businesses was common across the island in everything from food processing to cement and papermaking.

Electric power, first used to light the streets of major towns, also contributed to the development of the new manufacturing sector. Initially, electric power plants depended on imported coal or oil for their fuel, but hydroelectric power was harnessed in Jamaica and Puerto Rico by 1930. Electrification also stimulated the mechanization of tasks – for example, machines powered by electric motors to turn out cigarettes and cigars in volume. Thus, manufacturing became increasingly capital-intensive and the limited range of electric supply also helped concentrate enterprise in the major towns. Most of the traditional manufacturing industries, such as shoemaking, dressmaking, and tailoring, remained in the hands of craftspeople, many of them women. In Puerto Rico, for example, women employed in needlework and textile industries made up

Plate 6.3. Plymouth, Montserrat, circa 1910. *Source:* "Vaquero", *Life and Adventure in the West Indies* (London: John Bale, Sons and Danielsson, Ltd., 1914), opp. 190.

50 percent of the manufacturing labour force at the beginning of the 1930s.

The most substantial growth in the manufacturing sector occurred in Puerto Rico between 1930 and 1945. Although the pattern was similar to that seen elsewhere in the postwar period, in other territories with surplus supplies of labour and, often, superior natural resources, Puerto Rico had several special advantages derived from its relationship with the United States. Puerto Rico had direct entry to a large market and easy access to large capital resources, yet did not have to pay U.S. taxes. Initial growth in Puerto Rico was a response to unemployment pressures but as long as the Great Depression persisted, little concrete development occurred beyond an expansion of food processing and the hat-making and needlework industries. Under the New Deal, social overheads such as power resources and education were developed, but it was only with the establishment of the Puerto Rico Development Company in 1942 that new enterprises began to emerge. At first, local materials and local markets were emphasized in new factory-produced goods such as cement, glass, pulp and paper (recycling waste paper and bagasse from the sugar factories), ceramics, and shoes.

Banks became increasingly common in the major towns, many of them multinational, but they suffered the volatility of the times. Currencies came under siege. In Haiti, paper money had fallen to such a low rate against the U.S. dollar by 1870 that it had to be replaced with a new metallic currency. When the government of Haiti printed more notes than agreed with the banks, immediately before World War I, it helped create the conditions that led to the occupation. During the boom times known as the "dance of the millions" that followed World War I, numerous European and North American banks established themselves in Cuba and built up massive portfolios of loans. By the middle of 1921, as many as eighteen banks had crashed. The boom and bust at the end of the 1920s saw more banks rise and fall. At the grassroots level, banks were more successful in the long term. Savings banks increased their importance dramatically. For example, deposits in Jamaican banks increased from £150,000 in 1870 to £2,378,000 in 1945.

TRADE, TRANSPORT, TRAVEL

The period from 1870 to World War I was dominated by the concept of free trade, a policy promoted most aggressively by Great Britain, the industrial world's powerhouse and leading sea power, the trading nation with the most to gain. The effects on the Caribbean islands were mixed. Within the international division of labour, the role of the Caribbean was that of a supplier of raw materials and foodstuffs to the industrializing countries. When the British abolished import duties on all sugars in 1874, creating a system of pure free trade, the prices paid to Caribbean producers fell and continental European beet sugar, which was heavily subsidized, became popular with British refiners. Between 1870 and 1900, the high point of free trade, the British Caribbean islands lost their long-held hold on the British market and shifted exports to the United States. When the United States began to favour Cuba, granting a preferential tariff reduction from 1902, the British colonies turned to Canada. World sugar prices remained low down to 1914 but increased in the United States. Overall, competition became increasingly difficult for the more marginal Caribbean sugar producers, resulting in the abandonment of the crop in some islands, as noted earlier. The massive increase in sugar output coming from Cuba served to further reduce prices and make it difficult for marginal enterprises.

Trading patterns were disrupted by World War I and external trade ceased to grow as an element in the economies of the industrialized nations. Food and agricultural raw materials declined, whereas minerals and manufactures increased, so that the Caribbean became a less important element in the world economy. These changes, together with the Great Depression, led to new forms of protectionism. During World War I, continental beet sugar disappeared from the British and U.S. markets, creating boom conditions for the British islands and enabling a longer-term recovery in sugar. Prices were, however, low throughout most of the 1920s and 1930s, supported somewhat by imperial subsidies and quotas. The Caribbean became embroiled in international efforts to control and monitor agriculture and trade, though old ties to particular imperial states remained strong. An International Sugar Agreement signed in

1937 aimed to limit world production but achieved little increase in prices.

The U.S. occupations of Cuba, Puerto Rico, Haiti, and the Dominican Republic all had the reform of tariff and tax collection as a central objective. In the Dominican Republic, a new tariff introduced in 1920 reduced rates substantially overall and made many imports free of duty, but this was of benefit chiefly to U.S. traders, who provided more than 90 percent of the nation's imports, whereas the public revenue was further depleted by the reductions. Not only did the reduced tariff make it more difficult for local manufacturing industries to compete, it also inhibited domestic food production.

Down to 1939, British West Indian sugar, molasses, and rum paid duties on entry to the United States, but other goods – notably, bananas, cocoa, spices, sisal, and asphalt – entered free. After 1939, the United States placed the British West Indies under a most-favoured-nation treaty, meaning their goods paid import duties no heavier than those imposed on any other source. The preferential advantages granted by the British to their Caribbean colonies were balanced by imperial preference on imports – at rates from 25 to 50 percent – and from World War I this shifted trade away from the United States to Canada and the United Kingdom. This shift was most striking in the banana trade.

When the French colonies Martinique and Guadeloupe were assimilated in 1892, they enjoyed free trade with France and with other French colonies, but all legislation setting tariffs with other nations was enacted in the metropolis. The significant exception was that, down to 1928, colonial sugar, coffee, and cocoa entering France paid both import duties and consumption taxes; the import duty was removed in 1928 and France then deployed a system of quotas, as did the British. The outcome was that the assimilated colonies sent as much as 97 percent of their exports to France in the 1930s and received more than 60 percent of their imports from the metropolis. Something similar occurred in the case of Puerto Rico, where more than 90 percent of its imports and exports were traded with the United States. Thus, the separate metropolitan integration of the tariff systems of Puerto Rico and of Martinique and Guadeloupe meant that their prosperity was tied to those systems.

Where tariff barriers were low, as in the case of the French, there was little to gain by assimilation. On the other hand, high barriers gave Puerto Rico an advantage in the U.S. market but meant also that it was costly to obtain imports from alternative, cheaper sources.

Whereas Puerto Rico and the Virgin Islands benefited by becoming part of the U.S. tariff system, nominally independent Cuba was often in conflict with the United States. However, in spite of its different political relationship, 70 percent of Cuba's imports came from the United States in the 1930s and 80 percent of its exports went there. Even before its first intervention, the United States dominated Cuba's trade, taking 87 percent of the island's exports and supplying 38 percent of its imports as early as 1894.

To 1945, changes in the pattern of trade depended entirely on shipping. Aeroplanes carried only passengers and mail. In the period from 1870, the major change was the shift from sail to steam ship, and a less significant shift from coal to oil fuel. Ships became more reliable and significantly faster. Speed and reliability were essential to new trades in tropical products such as bananas. In addition to faster travel by sea, new modes of communication opened up. Cables were laid across the Atlantic. By 1945, almost one million telegrams were sent each year in Jamaica. Cuba had 75,000 telephones. Radios remained uncommon. In Haiti, a telegraph and a modern telephone system were set up in the 1920s, as well as a radio station, all of these seen as essential to carrying on international business.

On land, within the Caribbean, railroads connected many more places to sea ports. By 1945, Cuba had 5,000 kilometres of track. The motor truck penetrated further into interior districts, particularly in the 1930s, helping to build hierarchies of towns and villages with their markets, post offices, schools, and police stations. Cuba had 50,000 motor vehicles by 1929 but this proved an early peak. In Haiti, there were fewer than 3,000. Innovations in rail and road transport often made coastal shipping less efficient and it was no longer quicker to sail around an island in order to visit its ports. On land, travel by foot or riding a donkey or mule with baskets or carts loaded with produce destined for local markets remained the common mode for the poor and isolated.

A new kind of traveller emerged after 1870 – the tourist. Before 1870, the occasional voyager might make an expedition to the Caribbean and the occasional invalid might come to the islands for a health cure at one of the spas or in the cooler mountains. Most white Europeans and North Americans, however, avoided the tropics like the plague. Only with the control of disease and the mosquito, a byproduct of the new imperialism, and associated improvements in sanitation and hygiene, did these potential travellers begin to see the Caribbean islands as salubrious places – even a kind of paradise. This perception of the climate and healthiness of the Caribbean held a certain irony, in that this new image was fundamentally contradictory to that of earlier times. During slavery, when tourism was unheard of and the islands suffered heavy levels of mortality, European men flocked to the plantation colonies in hopes of making a fortune through the exploitation of land and people. Now, in the later nineteenth century, the region emerged as a great place to visit, but somewhere to which Europeans no longer wished to migrate.

Initially, tourist travel was all by sea and depended on existing shipping companies and schedules. Tourists competed with freight. However, the development of regular, scheduled shipping services and named lines was vital to the establishment of a better-regulated tourist industry and depended, in turn, on the reliability that steamships could offer, whether its main cargo be bananas or cruise ship passengers. Something similar happened with the early airlines, many of which depended on the carriage of high-value goods as well as travellers, but development was slow because the cost of air travel remained high down to 1945.

Many of the early hotels belonged to and were built by companies with primary interests in transport or commodities. For example, the Titchfield hotel in the banana-shipping town of Port Antonio, Jamaica, was built by the United Fruit Company. In some cases, the interdependence of hotels and transport worked in the opposite direction. Thus, the expansion of Henry M. Flagler's hotel chain from Florida into the Bahamas in the 1890s went together with a government requirement that he ensure frequent steamship sailings to and from Miami. In Trinidad, the Queen's Park Hotel in Port of Spain was owned by Pan American Airways. By the end of the

Plate 6.4. Hotel domestic servant, Martinique, circa 1910.
Source: "Vaquero", *Life and Adventure in the West Indies*
(London: John Bale, Sons and Danielsson, Ltd., 1914), opp. 147.

1930s, however, there had already emerged a model that was to prove influential – the standardization of the hotel so that it would seem a familiar piece of America, replicated in the manner of the Hilton chain, offering comfort wherever in the world it might happen to be located.

Tourist numbers remained small to most places down to the end of the nineteenth century. By 1938, however the West Indies together with Central America already accounted for about one fifth of all United States spending on tourism. Even apparently marginal places, such as the previously hostile Haiti, attracted tourists in the 1930s. President Vincent wished not only to promote an interest in Haitian folk culture but also considered trying to seduce wealthy Americans to gamble in hotel casinos. However, a lack of interest on the part of the major steamer lines meant little happened before 1945. Haiti could not compete with the allure of Cuba and its much more modern infrastructure and hotel industry. Puerto Rico and the Virgin Islands also developed resorts in the 1930s.

SOCIAL AND CULTURAL CHANGE

The period 1870 to 1945 saw the beginning of a significant shift in the distribution of wealth away from agriculture towards manufacturing and extractive enterprise. This change was accompanied by a shift away from the local plantocracy to foreign capitalists – increasingly operating through multinational corporations – who came to dominate in sugar and banana planting as well as mining and manufacturing. As noticed in the discussion of land tenure, the period 1870 to 1945 saw seemingly contradictory tendencies. The peasantry reached a peak around 1930 in Jamaica and Barbados, the same time that the concentration of landownership peaked in Cuba and Puerto Rico (where the peasantry had peaked about 1900). Foreign ownership of land and natural resources grew after 1900 in Cuba and Puerto Rico and, after 1930, elsewhere. State ownership was limited outside of Haiti.

These extremes in the distribution of wealth were paralleled by striking differences in the distribution of income and standards of living. In some places, such as Puerto Rico, the distribution of income became more unequal over the period as a result of population growth and the pressure on the peasantry, yet remained more equitable than in islands such as Barbados and Jamaica. Workers became increasingly dependent on wages but saw little improvement in their incomes down to 1940. The self-employed struggled. Differences in political status seemed to matter little. In Martinique and Guadeloupe, living conditions and wages on sugar plantations remained poor, in spite of the integration of the islands into the metropolitan economy and tariff regime. In Martinique, wealth remained in the hands of a small class of landowners and, when unemployment became acute, the opportunities for independent peasant cultivation were denied by this inequality.

In a few occupations, such as domestic service, wages were reduced absolutely after 1914 and remained low through the Great Depression. At the same time, the cost of living climbed steadily – slowly to 1914, then more rapidly. Changes in consumption patterns over the period included a growing dependence on imported processed and manufactured goods, with an impact on the local self-employed producing classes.

Differences in income and wealth carried over directly into systems of social structure based on colour and ethnicity. In some places, such the Bahamas, a rigid social structure based on a simple distinction between whites and the rest remained in place until World War II, in spite of the growth of a much more diverse middle class. This separation was reflected in residential segregation, sometimes at the level of an entire small out island but equally strongly within the town of Nassau. Elsewhere, although the differentiation was often much less stark, the correlations between wealth, colour, and class had a similar impact on the social landscape. In a few places, such as San Fernando in Trinidad, social and residential patterns also reflected differences rooted in caste, brought from India with the indentured migrants.

In Cuba, the prosperity of the 1920s unleashed forces that contributed to the development of a modified social order that included an entrepreneurial bourgeoisie separate from the increasingly corporate plantocracy. This new class had benefited by the closure of traditional trade networks during World War I and the opportunities created for import-substitution. By the middle of the 1920s, Cubans – more specifically, white male Cubans – outnumbered foreigners in industry and manufacturing. The national economic interests of these men fed into the making of a new political class, willing to advocate autonomy rather than pandering to foreign interests for political advancement.

The ethnic/racial heritages of political leaders sometimes were an issue – nowhere more so than in Haiti. The political parties, the Liberals and the Nationals, lined up as mulatto versus black, but it was the inadvertent consequence of the U.S. occupation that Haitians finally united under the label "black" and broadly accepted a *noiriste* ideology that contributed much to the intellectual development of the nation. In the 1920s and 1930s, the mulatto elite remained socially exclusive and economically advantaged, but the growth of a black professional class of doctors, teachers, and lawyers contributed directly to the creation of a cultural crisis. Similarly, in Cuba, the dictator Batista, who probably had Spanish, African, and Taíno ancestors, preferred to identify himself as simply "Cuban". His friends emphasized the Taíno side and his enemies, the African.

In the Dominican Republic, the U.S. occupation had good effects on the status of women but a less positive impact on race relations, encouraging an increasingly inflexible structure. The stability and economic growth that flourished under dictatorship enabled social mobility. Thus, Heureaux's lengthy regime enabled the emergence of a national bourgeoisie, with a strong role for elite women, whereas in Trujillo's early years, the growth of the economy and the bureaucracy enabled social mobility for people who lacked the trappings of the old aristocracy.

Creolization spilled over into westernization in cultural practice. Small contingents of new immigrants were typically absorbed by the larger culture but retained significant elements of individuality and identity. The indentured Indians, though a significant minority only in Trinidad and Guadeloupe, were sufficiently influential in those places to have an impact on many shared areas of life. They took on characteristics learned from the plantation regime, including a harsher view of personal relationships and an understanding of social hierarchy that had no respect for caste. They learned to drink alcohol, to eat fish and meat, to believe in Christ Jesus. Efforts to maintain their own Hindu and Muslim religious festivals, however, were opposed by the colonial governments, particularly in Trinidad in the 1880s, paralleling restrictions placed on the celebration of Carnival by Afro-Trinidadians, leading in both cases to riots and deaths. The Indians also had a significant impact on food habits and the smoking of ganja, even in places such as Jamaica, which had smaller minorities.

Creole faced strong competition in schoolrooms where European languages dominated as the medium of education. This became increasingly important after 1870, throughout the Caribbean, as access to education was improved and reading became more common. Literacy increased in many places. Native speakers of African languages became rare in the Caribbean populations. Spoken language had long established its creole base but schoolbooks, newspapers, and government had little time for it and even expressive literature was generally anxious about the use of creole. Education was a matter for European mother tongues.

Systems of free compulsory primary schooling became generally available in the British colonies, along with more limited access to secondary schooling. Many of these schools were run by the churches, but government financial support became increasingly substantial and in most of the British colonies, by 1945, the state had gained control of all levels of instruction. Literacy rates improved substantially. In the Bahamas, for example, the proportion of the population that was illiterate fell from 45 percent in 1890 to 22 percent by 1945. Education came to be seen as a means of social control, helping to create a society oriented to things British, but equally as a means of escaping the narrow confines of plantation culture and island life. The people invested in education wherever they could and governments did the same, though at differing levels. As early as 1930, education became the largest item of public expenditure in Barbados, long before this occurred in any other of the British West Indian colonies. An Imperial College of Tropical Agriculture established in Trinidad in 1911 was intended to serve all the colonies of the British in the region, as well as to conduct research through experiment stations.

The United States' occupations and annexations were typically accompanied by increased investment in education. Some ventures spread beyond the immediate area of American influence

Plate 6.5. Public library, Bridgetown, Barbados, circa 1890.
Source: Robert T. Hill, *Cuba and Porto Rico with the Other
Islands of the West Indies* (London: T. Fisher Unwin, 1898),
opp. 373.

and originated in private philanthropy. For example, the Rocke-
feller Foundation became deeply involved in education about public
health and hygiene and the Carnegie Corporation established public
libraries in many of the islands, included the British colonies.

In Haiti, in the 1880s, President Salomon opened up secondary
education, for the first time, to the children of blacks who were not
members of the elite. However, when the United States occupied
Haiti in 1915, as many as 97 percent of the population were illiterate. In the Dominican Republic in 1916, more than 90 percent of
the people were illiterate and fewer than 10 percent of school-age
children attended school even erratically. Outside the major cities
of Santo Domingo and Santiago, even primary schools were uncommon, so education was largely reserved to the wealthy city dwellers.
Although efforts had been made to improve the situation beginning
around 1900, success was limited. The military government moved
quickly to see primary schools built, particularly in the rural areas,
and to provide teaching. Methods of instruction were modified to

match those current in the United States, though without pushing the content of what was taught in that direction. At the same
time, the military government acted to absolutely reduce the provision of secondary education, confining the opportunities almost
entirely to Santo Domingo and Santiago. The financial problems of
the government, resulting from reductions in revenue in the early
1920s, brought growth to a halt across the system. Enrolments
declined and there was little improvement down to World War II.

In Cuba, Batista advocated a rural education program beginning
in 1935 and used the army to establish more than 1,000 new schools
across the island. These were not built by the army but were rather
the work of sergeant–teachers sent to locations where they had to
obtain land and labour, or existing buildings, to achieve the objective. Both children and adults attended, and the teaching timetable
was flexible to allow children to work on local farms and plantations in the busiest seasons. The emphasis was on reading and
writing but gradually shifted to vocational skills and agricultural
techniques. Improved hygiene and sanitation were also part of the
program. The schools became community centres, providing sites
for listening to radio broadcasts and watching movies. In addition
to Batista's interest in social control, the rural education program
served as a means of promoting the image of the army, the teacher
always dressed in military uniform.

Higher education remained uncommon. There were no universities in the British colonies, and students typically travelled to Britain
to take degrees. The long-established universities of the Spanish tradition did not prosper under U.S. military government. From the
late nineteenth century, the University of Santo Domingo had survived essentially as a professional school, including medicine, but
a faculty of arts and letters was restored in 1914 and, in 1916,
immediately before the occupation commenced, a second university
was established in Santiago. This was promptly closed by the military governor and the University of Santo Domingo reduced again
to a professional institute. Universities emerged as sites of political
protest. At the University of Havana, hopes of governmental reform
in 1923 led students to take control of buildings and demand autonomy for the university, the dismissal of incompetent teachers and
free higher education. A newly founded federation of university students from across Cuba, meeting in Havana, extended its demands

to the abrogation of the Platt Amendment and an end to United States interference in the island's internal affairs.

The nationalist fervour of the mid-1920s was associated in Cuba not only with student protest but also with a revived enthusiasm among writers and artists for the promotion of all things Cuban. Cuban nationalism also drew from broader cultural currents that swept through Latin America in this decade, drawing particularly on influences derived from revolutionary Mexico. Black nationalist writers from Haiti and the British and French West Indies emerged as a recognizable and influential group, especially within the international context of the Harlem Renaissance. Some of them were among the new migrant streams out of the Caribbean, to New York and Paris. Much of this writing of the 1920s and 1930s was born in and directed at foreign intervention and domination. It was paralleled by a growing understanding of a broader community of Afro-America and of belonging to an Atlantic diaspora. Francophone literatures coalesced in *négritude*, from the hands of Jean Price-Mars and Jacques Romain of Haiti, Aimé Césaire of Martinique, and Léon Damas of Guadeloupe, as well as Léopold Senghor of Senegal. Ironically, for Haiti in particular, this anticolonial literature took French as its language rather than creole and came to be associated with a conservative social ideology.

The role of North American images and voices in the development of Caribbean culture was nowhere more obvious than in the emergence of cinema. Movies were shown and made in the Caribbean beginning in the late 1890s, very soon after their invention. They proved popular with all classes. Early silent images typically portrayed the tropical world as exotic but even pictures of everyday life – showing black people loading bananas on to a steamship or making a straw basket – might be enough to find a market. Vodun, sorcery, sexual abandon, and barbarism proved more popular subjects for Hollywood in the talkies era of the 1930s. Products such as the horror movie *White Zombie* of 1932 and *The Emperor Jones* of 1933, starring Paul Robeson, drew complaint from Haitian and other Caribbean audiences (and also sometimes movie-goers in metropolitan cinemas). Stereotyping occurred in many other areas of visual and verbal representation – from newspaper advertisements to cultural anthropology – but it was the cinema that reached the largest audience and offered the starkest and most unpleasant images. The dominance of Hollywood meant also a dominance of the English language, with an American accent. In Haiti, cinemas employed creole translators.

In the Dominican Republic, the U.S. occupation irritated nationalistic cultural elements. The establishment of the *merengue* as the national dance of the Dominican Republic emerged during the occupation. Earlier, in the 1880s, the *meringue* had been identified as Cuban and was also increasingly popular in the Bahamas. In Trinidad, traditional dances such as the tambu bamboo, using natural materials to make music, remained popular but the more strident tones of metal began to emerge in the 1930s. In Haiti and many other places with French or Spanish influence, the kalenda survived strongly as a dance for pairs of partners, advancing and retreating on one another, making contact with the loins. With the similar chica of Cuba, the flirtatiousness of the kalenda offended the puritanical but had great popularity among creoles. These had their origins in Central Africa but drew also on European – particularly French – dance. The sport of stick-fighting blended easily into dance steps.

Dance and sport often overlapped before 1870. During slavery and the immediate post-slavery period, time was regularly found for music and dance but rarely for organized sport. Contests such as boat racing often had as much to do with working lives as with entertainment, and differed little from ploughing matches. Sailing contests emerged early – by the 1830s – in places like the Bahamas, where the sea was central to life, and early involved black people in regattas that included races for many classes of vessels, from sailboats to working rowboats. Only the leisured classes had time for extended and regular sport, such as hunting and horse racing. From the middle of the nineteenth century, a strong link was made between ideas of manliness and masculinity and the playing of sport. These ideas fed into concepts of the imperial, and, indeed, team sports were often modelled on struggles for territory or dominance, played according to sportsmanlike rules that might apply equally on the battlefield or frontier.

The particular team sports that were played tended to be closely associated with the traditions of the different imperial powers. Thus, down to 1945, games such as rugby football and polo were popular in the British colonies, but played mainly by local whites, civil servants, and army officers. Similarly, Martinique and Guadeloupe published five specialized sports magazines by the 1930s and broadcast much sports news by radio, particularly promoting cycling events such as a "tour de la Guadeloupe" along with football, boxing, and sailing. Individualistic sports, such as tennis and golf, largely remained in the hands of local whites and tourists, because of the substantial costs of playing these games. Poor people lacked the time and the equipment.

The game of cricket, which was common in North America until the late nineteenth century, when it was displaced by baseball, came to be identified as essentially British (even English) and colonial, but was embraced enthusiastically by all classes and colours of men from the abolition of slavery. Although whites long dominated, particularly in the captainship of teams, and although class played a role in the formation of clubs, skill became difficult to deny. Cricket was popular even in the Bahamas, on the margins of the American cultural frontier. The Nassau Cricket Club was founded in the 1870s, with its own ground. Cricket attracted spectators of all classes and colours. Versions of the game could be played on many different surfaces with the simplest of bats and balls taken from nature, and according to rules modified to suit the circumstances. The first overseas cricket tour from the West Indies, in 1886, went not to Britain but to the United States and Canada. In territories occupied by the United States there developed a taste for some of the sports played by the Marines. In particular, the popularity of baseball grew in the Dominican Republic and Cuba.

Cultural influences increasingly felt from North America through sport, cinema, literature, and education were matched by the spread of religious ideas. New versions of Christianity entered the Caribbean after 1870. Most of these arrived from the United States and were products of American revivalism, putting them in competition with the evangelical European churches. The Salvation Army, an English revival church, reached Jamaica in 1886, but was quickly joined by the Seventh Day Adventist church in 1894, and a Holiness Church of God in 1907. Pentecostal churches tested the waters in Cuba, the Bahamas, Barbados, and the Virgin Islands, but found the most fertile ground in Jamaica, where a Church of God was established in 1924. These enthusiastic branches of worship – characterized by the involvement of congregations and speaking in tongues – competed equally with the separate revivalist tradition in

Plate 6.6. Wedding party, Jamaica, circa 1900. *Source:* James Johnston, *Jamaica: The New Riviera* (London: Cassell and Company, 1903), p. 102.

the Caribbean, which had its roots in Africa and was accused by its critics of dabbling in magic. Local prophets emerged, promising miraculous translations.

These new churches displaced the mainstream Christian tradition but connected with the older religions derived from Africa. In Haiti, Vodun took on a new life in the 1930s as interest reemerged along with enthusiasm for other forms of folk culture. Vodun ceased to seem something to be ashamed of, as primitive or superstitious, and came to take its place among the pantheon of things Haitian in which pride could be shown. It quickly became also something to offer as a tourist attraction, as a commercial exchange, to be put on display rather than kept secret.

Africa was also the focus of the new religion Rastafarianism, which had its origins in Jamaica in the 1930s and remained largely confined to that island down to 1945. The central belief of

Rastafarians was that Haile Selassie, crowned emperor of Ethiopia in 1930, was the black messiah or reincarnated and immortal Christ. Although Rastafarians built no church, they followed the teachings of the Bible and identified with Zionism in its struggle against Babylonian captivity. Redemption, they believed, would come with their repatriation to Ethiopia, their spiritual home. This was a belief that connected directly with the ideas of Marcus Garvey, who established the Universal Negro Improvement Association (UNIA) in Jamaica in 1914 and was highly influential in linking racial consciousness across the diaspora with anticolonial ideology. Garvey, born in 1887, had been exposed to racism in Panama and quickly came to understand his experience in a broadly Atlantic framework that enabled his ideas to reach out across cultures and languages, following sea lanes that made his message global. He introduced the UNIA to New York in 1916. Whereas Rastafari looked steadfastly from their Caribbean captivity to salvation in Africa, Garvey had a larger understanding of his congregation, taking in the whole of the black "Negro" world in the Americas and the whole of Africa. Garvey fought actively to establish trade and migration to Africa but fell foul of imperial governments.

Equally important in the development of racial consciousness in the Caribbean was the experience of black soldiers who left the islands to fight alongside their imperial fellows in European battle fields in World War I. The enthusiasm they showed, to die in the cause of their metropolitan masters, was often rebuffed or denied, sowing the seeds of bitterness that contributed to anticolonial attitudes and racial consciousness. They became agitators, restless in their desire for political and social change, with personal experience of the metropolitan world and aware of a larger colonial world of injustice.

Garveyism spread rapidly into Haiti immediately after World War I. A Black Star Liner, part of the movement's commercial arm designed to bypass the existing major shippers and establish trade between Africa and the black diaspora, visited Port au Prince, where the Negro Factories Corporation was established by 1920. At first, Garveyism seemed to reinforce the nation's ancient divisions rooted in colour, the ideology being embraced enthusiastically by blacks but not by mulattoes. It remained more problematic in Haiti than in other parts of the colonial Caribbean but, to the extent Garveyism united rather than divided, its ideas worked in the same direction as the U.S. occupation – drawing the colours together in *noirisme*. To the British and U.S. governments, the UNIA's anticolonial message of race consciousness was dangerous and the movement was officially inhibited through surveillance, legal prosecution, and censorship. The UNIA played a somewhat different role in Cuba, where migrant Haitian and Jamaican workers often saw it as the only organization interested in their welfare.

The UNIA became global, providing the first port of call for black sailors around the world, a guiding beacon of identity and support for souls in distant lands. Voyagers and sojourners were especially grateful for such succour in this era, a time when the white settler states erected strict, exclusive barriers against red, yellow, and black people. In doing so, however, the UNIA and Garveyism lost their immediate Caribbean roots and tied the diaspora into a broader African blackness, an identity increasingly symbolized in the struggles of the black people of the United States, who faced lynching, segregation, and stigmatization on a scale unknown in the islands. The more localized travels of black and Hispanic Caribbean people similarly drew them into this American world, living along the eastern seaboard and working for the man in Panama. The experience was also brought into their own backyards, when employed to petroleum corporations in Trinidad or Curaçao or to sugar plantations in Cuba and Puerto Rico.

A new brand of imperialism had to be confronted, but, at the same time, becoming American in one way or another opened doors to new understandings of identity. The Caribbean person might eagerly become American – in speech, dress, and style – both in the United States and at home in the islands or, alternatively, remain stubbornly Cuban or Barbadian. Indeed, it was by coming in contact with this wider imperial world that people came to see more clearly the uniqueness of their own particular experiences, to think of themselves as Puerto Ricans or Hispanics or islanders. These were questions that had global currency but mattered most in the Caribbean person's ambivalent relationship with North America and the wider world.

7

The Caribbean Since 1945

At the end of World War II, most Caribbean islands remained in some sort of colonial or dependent relationship. Independent states were uncommon. The balance was quickly reversed, however, and the thirty years to 1975 brought independence to the majority. By 2010, there were thirteen independent nations in the Caribbean. Another eleven distinct polities made up of islands or island groups remained part of the territory of a country outside the region but these accounted for relatively few people. This rearrangement of allegiances marked a major transformation, the political and social significance of which are still being worked out. The process was complicated, not only because it occurred in the shadow of the Cuban Revolution of 1959 but also because the decline of formal imperialism and colonial status occurred in parallel with a great strengthening of long-term tendencies towards Americanization, internationalism, transnationalism, and globalization.

Caribbean people were caught up in this powerful process of change, both as individual actors moving relatively freely from place to place within the North Atlantic world and as the citizens of states that were almost always too small to be able to shape the world economy of material and cultural resources. They were contributors as well as receivers, particularly in the globalization of culture, but the new relationship that the islands now had with the wider world made the development of nationalism within the Caribbean more ambiguous and more ambivalent. Throughout almost the whole of the period, the Cuban Revolution provided a focal point or beacon that was difficult to ignore. For some it was a shining example of what might be possible, for others a terrible warning.

The revolution that began in Cuba on the first day of 1959, and continued half a century later, spanned the greater part of contemporary history. Its survival stood out as one of the great landmarks in the history of the Caribbean and, indeed, the modern world, alongside the survival of the state of Haiti. The revolution brought a genuine independence to Cuba and a genuine social reconstruction that favoured the popular classes, something achieved much less completely in any other Caribbean state. Although the revolution's viability was severely tested and although there were many reverses and paradoxes, it persisted and even thrived.

The immediate origins of the revolution may be found in the dictatorship of Fulgencio Batista. As mentioned in the previous chapter, Batista emerged as the strongman of Cuba in 1933 and was president from 1940 to 1944. He lost power in an election that year as a result of a tactical error, and was replaced by Ramón Grau San Martín as president. Batista faded into the background and the Auténticos – the Partido Revolucionario Cubano, formed in 1934 – won again in 1948. Rather than pursuing the idealistic goals of the 1930s, however, the Auténticos succumbed to the tempting fruits of office and fell to fighting over the spoils amongst themselves. Party politics descended to thuggery and gangsterism, graft and embezzlement, amidst the prosperity that came with the end of World War II and a new boom in sugar exports. The Communist Party lost ground but the Auténticos soon became disgraced and discredited. It was their broad moral and political failure that created Batista's chance.

When he moved against the Auténticos on 10 March 1952, Batista seized power quickly and easily by taking control of all means of communication – from the radio to the airport – and putting all banks and government offices in the hands of the army. There was only muted protest from the people, most of whom were glad to see the end of the corrupt Auténtico regime. None of the political parties had the backbone to oppose Batista. The United States had no complaint so long as its investments were not disturbed. Batista did, however, have to deal with outbreaks of internal rebellion from the earliest stages of his dictatorship. In July 1953, there was an attack on the Moncada barracks in Santiago de Cuba, led by Fidel Castro and his younger brother Raúl. The attack failed and the brothers were gaoled.

A sham election in 1954 returned Batista. He took every opportunity to extend his personal domain but from this point, armed resistance became almost inevitable. Clashes between students and the combined army and police occurred in 1955 and these were followed by an assault on the Matanzas barracks. In 1956, out of gaol, Fidel Castro orchestrated an uprising in Santiago, but it was quickly crushed. The few who managed to escape headed for the hills – the nearby Sierra Maestra in the southeastern corner of the island – where Castro raised a guerrilla army. Small initial victories in this isolated region, far from Havana, encouraged a deeper undercurrent of rural unrest and insurgency. Outlier contingents opened new fronts scattered across Cuba, two of them led by Raúl Castro and Ernesto Che Guevara.

Social and economic conditions deteriorated across the island in 1957 and 1958, and resistance to Batista's harsh regime began to surface in the cities as well as the countryside. The urban middle classes felt their advantages slipping away, while the rural masses faced unemployment and severe material hardship. The insurgency found disaffected allies within the armed forces. Threats of direct attacks on productive infrastructure, from railroads to sugar factories – designed to destabilize Batista – brought Cuba close to revolution and Batista close to desperation. By July 1958, Fidel Castro was recognized as the head of the resistance. Batista sent troops to the Sierra Maestra, backed up by aerial bombing of rebel refuges and naval bombardment of the coast, but without achieving victory. Many soldiers defected or simply gave up the fight. As the insurgents took more and more territory, the United States finally withdrew its material support of the dictatorship and Batista was forced to accept that he was done for. Although he pretended to remain confident of his ability to keep control of Cuba at the end of 1958, Batista chose to give up power on the last day of the year and, along with many of his officials and associates, fled the island.

Although Batista's dictatorship and the manner in which he was allowed or encouraged to run the island provided triggers for the revolution, its deeper roots drew on Cuban nationalism and the long-standing desire for genuine independence and social transformation. Batista's regime simply brought into sharp relief all of the forces opposed to change. When it collapsed, Castro's rebel army swept aside the old political parties with their reliance on the armed forces, making it possible for the Communist Party, banned by Batista, to reappear. These developments immediately turned the international spotlight on Cuba.

The United States was glad to see the back of Batista but quickly came to see the self-proclaimed revolutionary government as a threat to its many economic interests and, in the midst of the Cold War, a threat to regional stability. United States investments in Cuba were more valuable than in any other Latin American country with the exception of oil-rich Venezuela. Castro had not expressed strongly anti-American sentiments in the later phases of the guerrilla war or advocated expropriation of foreign-owned assets, and in the early months of 1959 even seemed to welcome new ventures. It soon became clear, however, that revolutionary change could not occur in Cuba if its economy was to be dominated by multinationals or draw capital from agencies such as the World Bank and the International Monetary Fund (IMF). The leaders of the revolution saw that changing the character of Cuban society must inevitably result in confrontation with the United States.

Castro, as prime minister, was firmly established as undisputed leader by the middle of 1959. Cuban exiles and expatriates returned to the island, enthusiastic to participate in the creation of a new society, and the first agrarian reform had popular support. At the same time, nervous members of the middle class left. Their fears were fuelled by the early nationalization of the Cuban Telephone Company, a branch of ITT, and the expropriation of sugar lands owned by U.S. companies early in 1960. By March 1960, the Central Intelligence Agency (CIA), had been authorized by the U.S. President to prepare Cuban exiles for a future invasion of Cuba. The revolutionary government had earlier, in the middle of 1959, begun to explore links with the Soviet Union and entered an economic agreement in early 1960. When Cuba commenced importing Soviet oil, the United States ordered the refineries – Esso, Texaco, and Shell – not to process it and they were expropriated. When, in July 1960, the United States stopped importing its sugar, Cuba retaliated by nationalizing all U.S. businesses and plantations, and, in September, U.S. banks. The United States then prohibited exports to Cuba, with the exception of food and medicines. In turn, Cuba confiscated all United States-owned retail and wholesale businesses. It was this tit-for-tat retaliation that led to the ultimate breakdown and cutting of diplomatic relations between the two countries in January 1961.

For the Cubans who remained in Cuba – thousands of urban middle class people left for Miami – the developments of 1960 were not simply an unfortunate failure in international relations. The consequences for the island and its people were momentous, creating the framework and constraints within which the revolution was required to work itself out and accelerating the process of change. Further, whereas the long loved and hated relationship with the United States was irretrievably broken, Cuba quickly embraced the Soviet Union and found there guarantees against U.S. invasion and intervention. An invasion of CIA-trained exiles at the Bay of Pigs in April 1961 proved a fiasco but helped to elicit Castro's clear affirmation of the radical nature of Cuba's socialist revolution and his identification of himself as a Marxist–Leninist.

Castro demonstrated his commitment to the defence of Cuba against U.S. intervention by allowing the installation of Soviet ballistic missiles in October 1962. The United States demanded their withdrawal and the world waited in fear of atomic warfare, the great dread of the Cold War. Without first consulting the Cubans, the Soviet Union agreed to dismantle its weapons in return for an understanding that the United States would not invade Cuba or seek to overthrow Castro's government. The process sowed the seeds of distrust. However, although this seemed a victory for the United States, in the longer term, the agreement ended its capacity to influence Cuban affairs and created space for Castro to pursue a more authoritarian style of government through strict party discipline and to advance the radical revolution. Cuba was firmly established as the first socialist state in the Americas, a thorn in the underbelly of its capitalist northern neighbour.

Cuba's neighbour to the south, Jamaica, had been independent just three months when the Soviets began dismantling their missiles. However, although decolonization had its birth in these dramatic first years of the Cuban revolution, none of the former British island colonies showed an immediate interest in taking the radical socialist path. This was to occur later, when the Cuban revolution had more securely established its credentials and conditions deteriorated in the newer states, but never with great success in the islands. Further afield on continental stages, however, Cuba did quite soon spread its influence with long-term consequences, in a way no other Caribbean state could afford or wished to attempt. It was a means of opposing U.S. hegemony wherever it occurred and of supporting anticolonial struggle, beginning with support for Algeria and Vietnam.

The first 25 years of the revolution brought many successes. Economic growth was sustained, even through the so-called energy crisis of the 1970s, which Cuba managed to avoid due to its dependence on Soviet oil. This enabled achievements in areas of central concern for the revolution – notably health and education – and the redistribution of wealth. Cuba also stood out for its altruistic international solidarity, sending medical and educational teams around the world, without always attaching political strings. Within Cuba, by the 1980s, government had settled into a centralized collectivist oligarchy, with a supreme leader who inevitably shared some of the characteristics of dictator and demagogue but delegated power all the way down to the labour unions. The Communist Party had grown strongly in membership and influence. Its Political Bureau contributed members to the Council of State and to the executive committee of the Council of Ministers. Over time, however, delegated authority became increasingly significant and factionalism declined. Mass organizations became institutionalized. Dissidents, those who fundamentally opposed the regime, were treated less harshly after the 1970s, though effectively excluded from participation in a government they, in any case, abhorred. The government, and its mission, had friends and foes all over the world.

Cuba's international contributions to medicine and health care were matched at home. The provision of free and universal health care was one of the great achievements of the Cuban revolution. Even in its most difficult times, Cuba increased the ratio of doctors to people and, by 2000, had one of the highest ratios in the world. An important consequence of these advantages was a reduction of infant mortality rates, from thirty-eight per thousand live births in 1960 to five in 2007. This was the lowest rate in the Caribbean; the highest was eighty-three, in Haiti. Cuban maternal mortality rates also improved dramatically. Although the embargo on trade imposed by the United States made some drugs scarce and limited the development of Cuba's biotechnology sector, Cubans came to be among the healthiest people in the Caribbean and, indeed, the world, with life expectancy of seventy-nine years for females and seventy-five years for males by 2003. Health care remained exclusively in the hands of the public sector. Cuba benefited by the emphasis placed on science in national development from the beginning of the revolution and from the island's early initiatives in biotechnology and genetic engineering, which commenced in the 1980s.

After three decades of achievements in economic equity at home and socialist internationalism abroad, Cuba entered a new phase of struggle in the 1990s, the so-called Special Period, in which it became increasingly isolated and unusual in its trajectory. Per capita income, which had remained relatively good down to 1985, when it was roughly equal to that in oil-rich Trinidad and Tobago, failed to grow thereafter. The collapse of the Soviet socialist bloc in 1991 and the apparent victory of the neoliberal democratic models of government left Cuba without allies. Expecting the revolution to implode, the United States upgraded its economic embargo to a blockade. Rather than relaxing the sanctions on trade and travel, the United States ratcheted up its pressure, demanding the restoration of assets to those who had owned them under Batista. Cut off from fuel and favourable trade agreements, the Cuban economy went into a tailspin and the standard of living suffered. Yet the government did not fall.

The challenge to survival thrown up in the Special Period created positive opportunities alongside the hardship. The inability to import fertilizers, pesticides, and other agricultural and industrial inputs was good for the natural environment and, indeed, matched objectives that had been advocated by conservationists around the world. The experience contrasted strongly with the input-intensive model of economic development that had dominated Cuba for most of the period of revolution, particularly in the sugar and tobacco industries. Fresh initiatives emerged with strong elements of sustainability – for example, the active promotion of urban agriculture in response to the intense scarcity of both imported and domestically produced food. Gardens flourished in the midst of the decaying fabric of Havana and other Cuban cities. Abandoned city lots were planted in food crops and fruit trees and chicken coops replaced the exotic flowers that formerly graced home gardens. By 1997, Havana alone had more than 25,000 formally registered agricultural plots designed to support the self-sufficiency of households.

People continued to flee the harsh economic conditions that forced them into leaky boats to seek the shores of the United States but the revolution remained. Further, despite its seeming isolation, Cuba remained a key player in world affairs. A United Nations (UN) resolution calling for an end to the embargo, first proposed in 1992, received strong support but was persistently opposed by the United States. Seeing the embargo as the greatest hindrance to their economic development, Cubans had to seek help elsewhere.

Cuba gained new life in 1999, when the socialist anti-American Hugo Chávez was elected leader of Venezuela and oil flowed again. The ideals of socialism, however battered, had new life breathed into them across Latin America. Closer to home, Cuba gained increased regard from its Caribbean neighbours, respecting its right to take an independent development path and coming to better appreciate the social and environmental advantages of alternatives to rampant capitalism, as well as the practical assistance given in education and social services. The economy began to grow again after about 2005, as trade with Venezuela increased, though hurricanes had disastrous impacts. Per capita income remained stagnant, however. By 2007, per capita income in Cuba was only half that in Trinidad and Tobago, its earlier equal, and Cubans fell behind citizens of the Dominican Republic.

From the earliest days of the revolution, Raúl Castro had been designated Fidel's successor. In spite of numerous assassination attempts and even more predictions of his imminent demise, Fidel lived long enough to be able to pass on the leadership to his younger brother in 2008. Although 187 countries voted in 2009 for the

UN resolution calling for an end to the U.S. embargo and those against were reduced to the United States, Israel, and Palau, the barrier remained firmly in place. The early euphoria and initial achievements had by then long gone, overtaken by the hardships of the persistent Special Period, but the revolution, along with the embargo, seemed immovable.

HAITI AND THE DOMINICAN REPUBLIC

When Rafael Trujillo was assassinated on 30 May 1961, there were hopes and fears that the Dominican Republic might follow the path of the Cuban revolution, which was then little more than a year old. Trujillo, the most notorious of all Latin America's totalitarian dictators, had dominated the Dominican Republic since the coup in which he took power in 1930. He extended his authority more comprehensively than any of his rivals, seizing control of the minds as well as the resources of the people. He and his relatives owned the radio broadcasters, the press, and the television station. Seeing himself as a paternal absolutist, he delighted in the title Generalissimo but also enjoyed being called Benefactor of the Fatherland or, alternatively, Father of the New Fatherland. He extended his wealth dramatically in the 1950s, buying up assets of all sorts, particularly land and manufacturing businesses. His companies made massive profits under the protection of government, often paying no taxes, while employing labour at the lowest wages or forcing convicts to work for them. The public sector and Trujillo's business enterprise became hard to tell apart. Large amounts were transferred to his private foreign bank accounts. When he was assassinated, Trujillo was one of the world's two or three most wealthy men.

In spite of the absolutism and the privatization of public profit central to the regime, the Dominican Republic's economy did experience a boom down to 1958. The population continued to grow rapidly and employment possibilities in towns were relatively good but the extent of the transition to a modernized capitalist economy was limited by the Trujillo family's monopolies and lack of conscience. Health and education suffered. The rural proletariat became impoverished.

Trujillo held power for more than thirty years, supported at almost every point by the United States. Although, at the election of 1952, he had his brother Héctor Trujillo made president and from 1960, Joaquín Balaguer, these men were Trujillo's puppets. He faced little real opposition internally, but an invasion attempted in 1959 by exiles, with support from Cuba, marked the beginning of widespread unrest and international condemnation of the regime. Trujillo responded by stepping up the terror, torture, and surveillance that had long underpinned his authority. With the example of the socialist revolution in Cuba confronting it, the U.S. government now became fearful of the consequences of propping up unsavoury dictatorships and actively encouraged his assassins.

In 1962, free elections in the Dominican Republic brought to the presidency Juan Bosch, who had been an exile in Cuba and Costa Rica during most of Trujillo's rule. Although his program was only broadly reformist, it was quickly labelled Communist. Much of the property privatized by Trujillo had already been returned to the state, but opposition to Bosch's rule emerged from the nightmares of industrialists who feared that the Dominican Republic was heading down a Cuban revolutionary path. In 1963, Bosch was overthrown by a military coup that handed power to the business elite. He then joined with Balaguer in opposition. When factions of all persuasions descended to civil war on the streets of Santo Domingo in 1965 and it appeared the forces in favour of Bosch were likely to prevail, the United States sent troops to quell the unrest and prevent the establishment of a new Communist state. These events occurred in the context of the U.S. escalation of the war in Vietnam. In order to prevent radical socialist revolution, the United States brought the Dominican army under its immediate control and ensured Balaguer's restoration to power. He maintained an anti-Communist trujillismo that denied civil rights down to 1974.

In the midst of this repression and with the benefit of U.S. investment and management, particularly through the Agency for International Development, the economy of the Dominican Republic achieved rapid growth after 1970. The transformation was so substantial that the radical opposition gradually fell away or was co-opted to the government's agrarian and educational reforms. This neutralization was so complete that by 1977 the Communist Party could be made legal. However, Balaguer's attempt to deny the outcome of the 1978 election saw him finally lose the support of the United States and he was replaced by Antonio Guzmán. Although elected on a reformist platform, Guzmán constructed a family-based oligarchy, concentrating the corruption that, however immense, had at least been broadly distributed under Balaguer. Having betrayed his party, Guzmán seemed on the way to adopting the example set by Trujillo. When the public debt grew to great proportions, the government resorted to printing money and fuelled runaway inflation. Guzmán's authority ebbed away and, in 1982, he shot himself in the head. On the edge of bankruptcy, the government entered bitter negotiations with the IMF and eventually devalued and dollarized.

In 1986, Balaguer, aged 80, became president for the fifth time. His party – the Social Christian Reformist Party – attempted to introduce spending cuts and austerity measures, but these were met by violence. He ruled until 1996. However, amendments made to the constitution of the Dominican Republic in 1994 prohibited presidents serving consecutive terms (their terms being limited to four years). These changes made long-running dictatorship less likely. The elections of 1996 brought to power another government committed to act against corruption and promote reform. Representing the Dominican Liberation Party, the new president was Leonel Antonio Fernández Reyna, and he was elected for another four-year term in 2004 and – freed by yet another amendment of the constitution – again in 2008.

A new Haitian constitution, approved by referendum in 1987, shared some of the same intentions as the amendments of 1994 in the Dominican Republic. The directly elected executive president was to be limited to a term of five years and allowed to stand for a second term only after an equal interval. As in the Dominican Republic, the hope was that dictators would find it harder to flourish in the increasingly barren soil of Haiti. In 1987, the country had barely regained consciousness following the dictatorship of François Duvalier (1957–1971) and his son Jean-Claude (1971–1986), a dictatorship longer lasting than that of Trujillo and lacking even the pretence of economic development and muted modernization.

Before the Duvaliers, Haiti had seen many presidents come and go, most of them remaining in office too short a period to get a firm grip on the levers of dictatorship. Élie Lescot (1941–1946) had taken advantage of the circumstances of war to attempt to avoid elections and extend his term, and commenced a rule of terror and repression of opinion, but was forced to resign when protests against his dictatorial ambitions became widespread. He fled to Canada. A provisional military government then held elections and the constitution was revised to permit only a single five-year presidential term. A new pattern of government-making emerged in which the army, rather than rural rebels, overthrew presidents, held provisional power for a period, then anointed a new leader, allowing the deposed president to beat a dignified retreat in an aeroplane.

In the manner of Batista in Cuba, the army chief, Paul Magloire, established himself as the acknowledged strongman of Haiti and, by 1950, he was elected president by popular vote. A new constitution limited the president's term to six years and ordered that under no circumstances was it to be extended. Consecutive terms were prohibited. The constitution also gave women aged 21 years and older the vote and guaranteed many freedoms. A series of relatively prosperous years enabled Magloire to commence development projects but he also took the opportunity to feather his own nest by dipping into the public revenue. The guarantees of freedom of the press and schooling were quickly forgotten and political opponents imprisoned without trial. Taking advantage of the atmosphere engendered by the fear of communism in the United States, Magloire reestablished the secret police and targeted dissidents of all persuasions. Magloire's dictatorship was short-lived, however, because when he attempted to override the constitution and hold power beyond the limits of his term, popular opinion turned against him and the business classes and many younger army officers combined to protest. In the last days of 1956, in the midst of a general strike and realizing that he no longer had the support of the United States, Magloire flew to Jamaica.

One of those who protested Magliore's clampdown on political meetings and broadcasts in 1956 was Dr François Duvalier, a medical doctor who had practised for twenty years before entering politics. The departure of Magloire was followed by months of chaos and more than one president and provisional government, until the election of Duvalier in 1957. He acted immediately to establish himself as an authoritarian ruler and, by making it clear that he would brook no criticism, forced many of his more influential opponents to leave the country. The Cuban revolution and the assassination of Trujillo played into his hands, making it possible for him to co-opt support for his regime from the United States and at the same time have less fear of invasion from the Dominican Republic or revolutionary Cuba. With the chances of attack from outside seemingly minimized, Duvalier deployed a civilian army of shadowy characters, the tontons macoutes – named for the character in folklore who carries away in his backpack children who have been naughty – to bring terror to the hearts of his domestic opponents. He broke the backs of the usual sources of opposition – students, shopkeepers, labour unions, and churchmen.

By 1964, Duvalier was sufficiently confident in the security of his regime to take the title of president-for-life. In spite of his tyranny and unconstitutional status, he remained able to attract investment and aid from the United States. The level of corruption became increasingly obvious, however, as the state neared insolvency. When he died in 1971 – known by then as Papa Doc, a title earned through his passion for Vodun – the presidency passed to his teenage son Jean-Claude by means of a constitutional amendment that permitted the nomination of a successor. Jean-Claude – later known as Baby Doc – eased the level of repression and took action on the economy. He managed to revive coffee, sugar, and tourism, and secured aid to improve roads and infrastructure. He was also able to greatly increase the amount of foreign aid given Haiti, particularly from the United States. At the same time, his personal wealth grew rapidly through embezzlement and corruption, fuelling a new level of conspicuous consumption. His excesses led eventually to broad-based demonstrations, including the northern port towns and the rural regions. Finally, the United States came to the view that Baby Doc was a liability. With the wealth he had creamed off already safely deposited in offshore bank vaults, he boarded his plane on 7 February 1986 to live in exile in France, though occasionally declaring an intention to return to Haiti.

The end of the thirty-year dictatorship of the Duvaliers encouraged many exiles to return to Haiti. In this fluid environment, new political parties emerged and trade unions were able to exist once more. A new constitution was agreed in 1987 and elections called but political violence led to their postponement and the suspension of the constitution. After a series of unsuccessful attempts to establish government firmly, Father Jean-Bertrand Aristide was elected president in 1990. He was, however, deposed by the army in less than a year and sent into exile in the United States. International pressure called for his reinstatement and, under the protection of U.S. troops, he resumed office in 1994, but was barred by the terms of the constitution from contesting the next election, when René Préval was elected. The U.S. troops withdrew and the Haitian army was disbanded. The 1990s proved a high point in the democratic government of Haiti and the nation was at the forefront of U.S. efforts to build a "community of democracies" in the Caribbean and Latin America. Aristide was anointed as Haiti's saviour.

Aristide won a new term in 2000 but this election was boycotted by most of the opposition and disparaged by international monitors. The United States and most international agencies froze aid to Haiti, hoping for a resolution of the political dispute and fresh elections. Aristide's inability to halt Haiti's continuing slide into poverty, let alone promote a vibrant democracy supported by economic development, made it almost impossible to control political unrest. Haiti was placed among the world's humanitarian disasters, suffering high levels of malnutrition and disease, and recognized as an environmental disaster as well. It was called a failed state. The police were unable to keep control and there were even calls for the restoration of the armed forces. Aristide refused to give way to his rivals and negotiations led by the Organisation of American States (OAS) and the Caribbean Community similarly failed to resolve the stalemate. Gangs and criminal groups, often connected with trade in guns and drugs, fought with political partisans. Demonstrators took to the streets.

When, in 2004, rebels took control of the northern region of Haiti, Aristide stood down on the understanding that a UN security force would be sent to restore order and back a government of national unity. Aristide boarded a plane chartered by the United

States but without a known destination. Finding himself in the Central African Republic, Aristide accused the United States of kidnapping him and supporting a coup. The Caribbean Community protested and refused to recognize the interim government. After two weeks in the Central African Republic, Aristide flew to Jamaica and spent two months there – upsetting the United States and the interim government of Haiti – before settling in South Africa. Following a tumultuous interval, in which armed rebels and paramilitary brigades interfered in the political process and the police proved ineffectual, Préval was elected again in 2006.

The strength of government in Haiti was sorely tested by the massive earthquake that struck the region around Port au Prince on 12 January 2010. More than 200,000 people died, large numbers were injured, and more than one million made homeless. It was a disaster not simply for Haiti and the Caribbean but one of the most destructive earthquakes of modern world history. The possibility of a strong earthquake was known to seismologists, with Port au Prince located close to a major faultline on the margins between the Caribbean and North American Plates. For the people, however, the risks had long faded from memory. There had been no major event since that of 1770, which had followed closely on the much larger earthquake of 1751. The lack of recent hazard experience together with the relatively poor state of infrastructure and architectural standards was a recipe for disaster. Similarly, the poor state of hospitals and security placed overwhelming demands on a weak government led by Préval. The consequence was an immediate need for external aid, to recover and rebuild, which quickly led to informal intervention by the United States and other regional nations. Cuban doctors were among the first to arrive. Many Haitians sought to leave the country but were not encouraged to do so either by their struggling Caribbean neighbours or by the more wealthy countries to the north. There were calls for annexation. Children were removed for adoption in other countries, sometimes with the approval of their parents, sometimes without. Fidel Castro and Hugo Chavez described U.S. actions as an occupation and called on the United Nations to assume a leading role. Once again, Haiti became a focus of world attention, at least temporarily, and, as always, problematically.

Although their paths of political development were quite different, Haiti shared with Cuba a strong strain of exceptionalism. Haiti's version had deep roots whereas Cuba's brand was forged in the Cold War but both developed in confrontation with a hostile imperial world and both were forced to choose between self-sufficiency and dependency. What Haiti shared with the Dominican Republic, apart from a land border – something unusual in the Caribbean – was its experience of dictatorship. Down to the 1980s, the dictators of Haiti and the Dominican Republic – Lescot, Magloire, the Duvaliers, Trujillo, and Balaguer – were typically replaced by other dictators or, temporarily, common varieties of chaos that led to tenuous versions of democratic government. Only the Duvaliers had worked out a succession plan and the beginnings of a dynasty, but the son never commanded the respect and loyalty enjoyed by the father, and managed to achieve no more than a corrupt and inefficient version of the original dictatorship.

DECOLONIZATION

Political developments outside the two largest islands generally lacked the high drama of the Cuban revolution and the dictatorships of Haiti and the Dominican Republic. On the other hand, it was in the smaller islands – with one quarter of the region's population – that the most fundamental changes occurred in sovereign status. Islands that had, for centuries, been colonies of European countries became masters of their own destinies with voices and votes at the table of international government.

It is perhaps ironic that the attainment of independence through decolonization occurred alongside the demographic explosion that forced people to seek their fortunes elsewhere, and that political freedom did little either to encourage creoles to stay put or to entice outsiders to come to settle. It is equally ironic that whereas the process of decolonization was relatively peaceful in the Caribbean, the newly independent states were then sometimes required to enter into violent struggles to defend the right to make choices that did not suit the agendas of the imperial world. To an extent, these seeming ironies stemmed from the fact that the notion of political freedom is typically fraught and ambiguous – as are most freedoms – and that independence, in itself, could not easily deliver a better life. But it also points to the essential ambivalence that inhabits Caribbean versions of nationalism and identity.

Decolonization was associated first and foremost with the British colonies in the Caribbean. In 1945, all of the Caribbean islands that had been made British possessions by 1815 were still colonies. Some had been colonies for more than 400 years, placing them amongst the longest-lasting examples of colonization in world history. Within forty years, however, almost all of the British colonies in the Caribbean were fully independent nations. The transformation occurred largely without violence but was part of a more general process of global decolonization that was, in other places, often marked by bloody battles and wars of national liberation. Some colonies were seen by imperialists as worth fighting over but the islands of the Caribbean were not among them. Of all the European countries that had taken land in the Caribbean, it was the British who seemed the most eager to rid themselves of the islands they had held so long.

Although the British decolonization occurred relatively free of violence and relatively smoothly, there was nothing inevitable about the way it occurred or about the final outcome. One alternative model proposed in the early 1950s recommended granting each of the territories the self-governing status of "Island City State", thinking back perhaps to the ancient Greeks, as did many modern colonial constructs. Limited federations already existed within the island groups of the Caribbean, and the British attempted federations also in East Africa and Malaysia. A West Indies Federation was formed in 1958 made up of eleven British territories but failed by 1961. It proved too difficult to achieve unity of purpose over such a scattered, discontinuous archipelago. In the long term, all that survived was the University of the West Indies and the West Indies cricket team, both of which preceded the Federation and were more inclusive. With this failure, it was clear that the smallest of the island colonies would struggle to survive as fully independent states and various styles of association were considered. Over time, however, the parameters guiding just how small a viable small state might be were pushed very hard.

The only two Caribbean island colonies of the British to escape any form of crown colony status, Barbados and the Bahamas, retained their legislative assemblies – the core of the old representative system – down to the eve of independence. Barbados introduced universal suffrage in 1951. Internal self-government with cabinet responsibility was granted in 1961 and full independence in 1966. The Bahamas achieved self-government in 1964 and full independence in 1973. In both Barbados and the Bahamas, white elites had long controlled government, and it was this control that had inhibited the imposition of crown colony status. The movement to independence, however, was led by black men – the labour leader Grantley Adams in Barbados and the people's advocate Lynden Pindling in the Bahamas – who carried the majority with them.

At independence, Barbados and the Bahamas continued to share the constitutional model of two-party democracies. In both states, the British sovereign remained its head, represented in the islands by a governor-general. The parliaments consisted of an elected House of Assembly and an appointed Senate, with five-year terms.

Although Jamaica's political history contrasted with that of Barbados, the island's progress to independence was little different, attaining internal self-government in 1959 and independence in 1962. Jamaica's constitution provided for a system of government matching that established in Barbados, except that the House of Assembly was called a House of Representatives.

Tensions were more obvious where islands were grouped politically, as in the Leeward Islands. Antigua and Barbuda (together with the uninhabited island of Redonda) were part of the Leeward Islands group from 1871 to 1956, joined the West Indies Federation from 1958 until 1962, became an Associated State of the United Kingdom in 1967, and gained independence in 1981 as Antigua–Barbuda. Barbuda, with a population of fewer than 2,000, was administered by an elected council. It did not seek separate independence. More volatile was the federation imposed on St Kitts, Nevis, and Anguilla. The people of Anguilla had objected to this association from the nineteenth century. When, in February 1967, the three-island colony was granted full internal self-government and association with the United Kingdom, the Anguillans, numbering about 10,000, refused to recognize the authority of the state.

Police from St Kitts were evicted. British security forces were sent to Anguilla and, from 1969, the island became effectively a dependency or "overseas territory" of the United Kingdom, though with increased autonomy from 1990. St Kitts–Nevis, the remnant state, was granted independence in 1983. Nevis, visible from St Kitts, was allowed its own assembly and premier, but the island also sent members to the unicameral legislature of St Kitts–Nevis. In 1998, a referendum seeking the secession of Nevis, with a population little more than 10,000, was unsuccessful.

The British Virgin Islands, once considered part of the Leeward Islands group, also became an overseas territory of the United Kingdom, under a system of ministerial government from 1967. Similarly, the Cayman Islands, administered by Jamaica until 1962, became a self-governing overseas territory of the United Kingdom in 1972, as did the Turks and Caicos Islands in 1973, and Montserrat in 1989.

In the Windward Islands, the British established a group known as the West Indies Associated States, granted internal self-government in 1967, with Britain responsible for security and foreign relations. Dominica left the group in 1978 to become an independent presidential republic, with a simplified parliament consisting of a House of Assembly, some of the members of which were nominated and the majority, elected. St Lucia became independent in 1979 but chose to retain the British sovereign as its head of state, represented by a governor-general, with an elected House of Assembly and an appointed Senate. St Vincent also gained independence in 1979, becoming known as St Vincent and the Grenadines, with a House of Assembly composed of elected members and appointed senators, and a governor-general.

In all of these former British colonies, government proceeded relatively smoothly, though with high levels of violence associated with some elections – notably the 1980 election in Jamaica when near to 1,000 people were killed – and accusations of fraud and misgovernment. Political dynasties were rare, though father and son, Norman and Michael Manley, were both prime ministers of Jamaica, with a gap of ten years; Tom Adams, second prime minister of Barbados, was the son of Grantley Adams, premier under self-government and prime minister of the Federation. There was a struggle between radical socialist and conservative political ideologies but this was generally played out within the context of democratic party contests. Some looked for models in Cuba, others to Britain and the United States, but the outcomes of elections were broadly accepted as representing the will of the people and, sometimes reluctantly, generally honoured. Things were less stable in the southern Caribbean.

Trinidad and Tobago had been federated, without any enthusiasm, at the end of the nineteenth century. Tobagonians, numbering more than 50,000 by 2000, frequently complained of the inequality of the relationship and threatened secession without doing much about it. The colony gained self-government in 1956 and independence in 1962, led by Dr Eric Williams, who served as prime minister until 1981. Trinidad and Tobago adopted a republican constitution in 1976, with a president as head of state and executive power in the hands of the prime minister. The legislature consisted of an elected House of Representatives and an appointed Senate.

The progress of government in Trinidad and Tobago was complicated by ethnic tensions that translated into party allegiances and was interrupted by two attempted coups. The first of these coups occurred in 1970, during the government of Williams, when soldiers mutinied and sought to align themselves with the Black Power ideologies that were sweeping North America, Puerto Rico, and Jamaica. The mutineers failed to attract popular support, however, and their rising was quickly suppressed by loyal troops and police. The second of Trinidad and Tobago's coups was more serious in intent and outcome. In July 1990, the Black Muslim group Jamaat al Muslimeen, led by Abu Bakr, stormed the parliament and took as hostages the prime minister, A. N. R. Robinson, and several members of his cabinet. The rebels also blew up the central police station in Port of Spain and took over the television station, following which there was widespread looting and burning of business places. Once again, loyal soldiers and police saved the government.

The only successful coup in the decolonized Caribbean occurred in Grenada in 1979, five years after the island became independent. Grenada's first prime minister, the messianic and authoritarian Eric Gairy, who had, himself, led a violent uprising of plantation workers in 1951, came to be reviled as eccentric and destructive of the island economy. Opposition rooted in Black Power ideas and sympathetic to the failed coup of 1970 in Trinidad and Tobago grew into the New Jewel Movement, which deposed Gairy. A socialist government – the Grenada People's Revolutionary Government – emerged and became closely aligned with Cuba and the Soviet Union. It ruled for more than four years but its leader, Maurice Bishop, was assassinated by an extreme Leninist faction. The army took charge in 1983 and the island was invaded by the United States, supported by regional soldiers and police, being formally requested to do so by a number of Caribbean states. The constitution of 1973 was restored. A governor-general once again represented the British sovereign and a two-party system participated in an appointed Senate and elected House of Representatives.

Although there were differences in the way decolonization was worked out in the British colonies, the connection with Britain and other former British colonies remained strong even among the republics. All of the British Caribbean colonies had joined the Commonwealth of Nations when established in its modern form in 1949, on India's becoming an independent republic. The British monarch was the accepted Head of the Commonwealth. All remained members after their independence, whether they became republics or remained titular monarchies, and none of them was ever suspended for failures of democracy. All came quickly to accept that parliamentary democracy, however flawed, possessed virtues that were worth clinging to. Even rebel leaders received relatively gentle treatment and, in some cases – that of Abu Bakr for example – were allowed to return to the political arena.

Regional varieties of association emerged among the British Caribbean colonies after independence. In 1968, the ten former participants in the Federation (together with Guyana) founded the Caribbean Free Trade Association. Less exclusive was the Caribbean Development Bank, established in 1969, which included in its membership not only the British Caribbean territories but also Colombia, Mexico, and Venezuela, and some countries outside the region – Canada, China, Germany, Italy, and the United Kingdom. The Organisation of Eastern Caribbean States, founded in 1981, was constituted of the British Leeward and Windward Islands, and excluded Barbados. Its mission was the promotion of co-operative approaches to the defence of their sovereignty and independence. More narrowly confined to monetary policy was the Eastern Caribbean Central Bank, established in 1983, but this was, again, made up exclusively of British-heritage territories.

When the Caribbean Community and Common Market (CARI-COM) was created from a looser free trade area in 1973, its membership initially was limited to Barbados, Jamaica, Trinidad and Tobago, and Guyana. These were joined over the next 25 years by other former British colonies, as well as Haiti and Suriname. Interest in including Cuba was unfulfilled. At first, the objectives of CARICOM were completely economic. Later, through a Conference of Heads of Government, it facilitated the establishment of a Caribbean Court of Justice, inaugurated in 2005. A CARICOM Single Market and Economy, first agreed to in 1989, was not launched until 2006 and developed tentatively towards common trade policies and a common external tariff, designed to facilitate the free movement of goods, services and capital, and (skilled) labour.

Chartered in 1948, the OAS sought to bring together all the states and territories of the hemisphere for the promotion of peace and security. It included all the Caribbean states, though Cuba was suspended in 1962 and readmitted only in 2009. In 2001, the OAS adopted a charter establishing democracy as a universal right and obligation of government. Cuba was also excluded from the Inter-American Development Bank, founded in 1959, the oldest regional development institution. These exclusions did not, however, extend to the United Nations, founded in 1945, in which all states have a part.

The most important step towards a more comprehensive regional association was the establishment in 1994 of the Association of Caribbean States (ACS), comprising 25 full member states, all of these being independent nations but including the rimland as well as the islands, stretching from Suriname through Central America to Mexico. Associate members were Aruba, France (representing Guadeloupe and Martinique), the Netherlands Antilles, and the Turks and Caicos Islands. Another eight non-independent territories were eligible to join. The objectives of the ACS were principally economic, directed at integration and co-operation, as in earlier forms of association, but also declared to be directed at sustainable development and the preservation of the environmental values of the Caribbean Sea. In 2009, the ACS agreed to make the "Greater Caribbean" the world's first sustainable tourism zone.

The tenuous position of the French and Netherlands territories within the ACS represented their ambiguous political status. Rather than following the British route to independence, the French and the Dutch sought to achieve decolonization by integration. The people of Guadeloupe or Martinique understood this process as achieving the full equality that had been part of French colonial policy under assimilation since the late nineteenth century and happily became departments of the French Republic in 1946. Even the poet Aimé Césaire, then a Communist, approved integration and represented Martinique in the metropolitan parliament. Each was administered by an elected general council, with a term of six years, but the islands also sent representatives to the National Assembly and Senate, in France. In the islands, the French government was represented by an appointed prefect. The internal administrative organization of the islands and their division into voting districts were theoretically identical to that of metropolitan departments, and entered a period of decentralization in the 1980s. This process led, in 2007, to the separation of St Martin, formerly a commune of Guadeloupe, to become an overseas collectivity. Independence from France was rarely considered a viable option.

The Netherlands Antilles, the most far-flung of all the imperial island groupings in the Caribbean, had a similarly ambiguous relationship to its metropole. Granted self-government in 1954, the islands became fully autonomous but integral to and constitutionally equal to the Kingdom of the Netherlands. Although they did not have representation in the parliament, they could send an official delegate to The Hague. The sovereign was represented by a governor who, together with a Council of Ministers, had executive power for internal affairs, but with responsibility to an elected unicameral legislature. The process of decolonization going on around them in the 1960s and 1970s did stimulate unrest and violent riots. Surinam, on the mainland, obtained full independence in 1975. Based on a referendum held in 1977, the southern island of Aruba was separated in 1986, with the declared intention of proceeding to full independence in ten years. However, the islanders had second thoughts and, by the 1990s, declared a desire to remain an autonomous part of the Kingdom. The other islands agreed at referenda between 2000 and 2005 to dissolve the federation of the Netherlands Antilles.

In 2000, St Maarten voted for outright autonomy. In 2004, Bonaire and Saba chose direct administration by the Netherlands government. In 2005, St Eustatius voted to remain part of a restructured Netherlands Antilles, while, in the same year, Curaçao favoured seceding from the Netherlands Antilles and becoming a territory of the Kingdom in its own right. These seemingly contradictory desires did not reflect differences between the northern and southern island groups but did suggest a general complaint about government from Curaçao rather than a dispute with The Hague.

As with the French departments, the dissatisfaction Netherlands Antilleans felt for their dependent relationship was outweighed by the many benefits of association. The islands might not have had their own currencies, flags, or postage stamps, but they did have the right to live in the metropolitan country and hold its citizenship, and to receive welfare and financial aid on an equal footing. Here was a case where the imperial power seemed more willing to surrender control and grant autonomy than the colonial people wished to embrace the possibility. For these small islands – the French as well as the Dutch – faced by uncertain economic futures, a lifeline to an apparently benign but prosperous European state came at last to seem an advantage. In a globalized postcolonial culture, transnational migrants could share pride in the language and culture of their former masters, and share the credit for its creation, seeing themselves as equals of a sort.

The political relationship of the United States with its outlying territories – Puerto Rico and the U.S. Virgin Islands – changed relatively little after 1945. Puerto Rico was proclaimed a commonwealth in 1952 and allowed to elect its governor, though the President of the United States remained chief of state. Puerto Ricans could not, however, vote in presidential elections and lacked voting representation in Congress. The island was governed by a House of Representatives and Senate, and allowed its own taxation system, but otherwise subject to the laws made by the federal government. Referenda in the 1990s showed few Puerto Ricans voting for independence and a strong but not decisive desire for statehood. Residents of the U.S. Virgin Islands similarly voted against greater autonomy, preferring the limited self-government provided in the 1954 act that granted a single elected chamber and an elected governor.

PEOPLE ON THE MOVE

The population of the Caribbean islands increased massively after 1945, growing from 15 to 42 million by 2010. Over the period, more than 400,000 were added to the population each year, compared with an average of less than 200,000 in the years between 1900 and 1945. The causes of this great growth in numbers after 1945 had little to do with the arrival of new migrants. The compelling desire felt by employers to bring workers into the Caribbean from other parts of the world was long dead. Rather, the islands became suppliers of labour to other places, the supply fed by the rapid increase in numbers and the growing pressure of overpopulation. Migration to places outside the region became common and played a major part in preventing the rate of population increase from being even larger.

Migration of all sorts underwent fundamental change, so much so that distinguishing between migrant and resident, sojourner and traveller, became increasingly difficult. People generally – not just the rich – became highly mobile. They shuttled back and forth, settling temporarily or permanently in foreign places, inhabiting worlds that were not their own. In many cases, creole Caribbean people became as numerous overseas as they were at home. For example, as early as the 1980s, roughly one half the population of Puerto Ricans lived outside the island. Thus, many of the region's migrants succeeded in keeping a foot in more than one camp, living truly transnational or translocal lives, with fractured global identities to match.

The high rates of population growth and migration experienced after 1945 did not disturb the long-term trend towards concentration in the Greater Antilles. Although the shift was less rapid than it had been in the first half of the twentieth century, by 2010, more than 90 percent of the region's people lived in the Greater Antilles, almost exactly the proportion of the Caribbean land area occupied by these islands (89 percent). This went together with an increased concentration in Spanish-speaking territories (60 percent of the population) and an equivalent decline in the English-speaking (down to 13 percent).

Driving this pattern of change was the increase of population in the Dominican Republic, where growth had been spectacular since 1870. Between 1945 and 2010, the population of the Dominican Republic multiplied five times, to reach ten million. Haiti increased less than three times, but also reached ten million. Together, the two states gave Hispaniola a population of twenty million, substantially more than its larger neighbour Cuba, where the population reached only eleven million in 2010. Puerto Rico and Jamaica both increased their populations at the same rate as Cuba, doubling between 1945 and 2010. Puerto Rico grew from two to four million, and Jamaica from 1.3 to 2.8 million. The only other state with a population of more than a million in 2010 was Trinidad and Tobago (1.3 million), followed by Guadeloupe (405,000) and Martinique (400,000).

There were some striking exceptions to the apparent relative decline of the territories outside the Greater Antilles. Some of these occurred in English-speaking islands that had previously been marginal to the plantation system. Growth in these exceptional places depended on a fresh assessment of resources and on changes in the global economy. Between 1945 and 2010, the population of the Cayman Islands increased from 7,000 to 55,000, growing seven times; the Bahamas grew five times to 343,000; and the Turks and Caicos grew four times, to 33,000. The U.S. Virgin Islands also quadrupled, to 110,000 in 2010, and, indeed, reversed the absolute decline experienced by the islands over the previous hundred years. Other small places, like St Kitts–Nevis, continued to stagnate. In Montserrat, the Soufriere Hills volcano erupted in 1995, for the first time known, covering the southern part of the island with lava and ash, including the capital town, Plymouth. Continuing activity required partial evacuation, down to 2010. The eruption of Mount Soufrière in St Vincent in 1979 had a lighter impact.

Although these shifts in absolute populations were important, what mattered more from the point of view of the people living in the islands was the density of settlement and the pressure on resources. Over the long term, small islands were typically associated with high population densities, partly because they were easier to fill up and partly because of their accessibility. Certainly, the islands of

Plate 7.1. Volcanic eruption, Soufriere Hills, Montserrat, 1997. Photo: Barry Voight.

the Caribbean had population densities substantially greater than anywhere else in the Americas. Within the Caribbean, however, the relationship between small size and high density was weaker after 1945 as some of the larger territories became as heavily peopled as the smaller ones, matching the growing concentration of the population in the Greater Antilles.

Barbados, notorious for its density since the sugar revolution of the seventeenth century, remained the most thickly populated island, with 440 persons per km^2 in 1945 and 675 in 2010. Closing the gap was the much larger island of Puerto Rico (225 in 1945, 456 in 2010). After these, the most densely populated places in 2010 were Martinique (364), the U.S. Virgin Islands (323), then Haiti (316) and St Vincent (314). The other territories of the Greater Antilles were less densely settled: Jamaica (245), the Dominican Republic (198), and Cuba (102). In spite of its rapid growth after 1945, the Bahamas remained the least densely peopled territory in 2010, with an average 29 per km^2, though with big differences between the many scattered islands.

The urban concentration of population continued apace after 1945 and even more strongly after the 1960s, as the countryside could no longer support the rapidly growing populations on fragmented plots. Only in rare cases, however, did the rural population become a minority. The largest of the cities were situated in the Greater Antilles, the islands with the largest overall populations. While some of the smaller islands had high urban:rural ratios, they were not large enough to support big cities. By 2000, there were twenty-seven cities with more than 100,000 people in the Caribbean islands, only one of them (Willemstad, Curaçao, with 125,000) located outside the Greater Antilles. Eleven of these large cities were in Cuba, five in the Dominican Republic, five in Puerto Rico, three in Haiti, and two in Jamaica. The less densely settled Cuba had a relatively large number of big cities, but most of them were at the lower end of the scale, spread across the extended length of the island. However, the two largest cities in the Dominican Republic together held almost five million, double the number in Cuba's two largest. The biggest of all was Santo Domingo with 3.5 million, followed by Havana (2.2 million) and Santiago de los Caballeros in the Dominican Republic (1.3 million), together with the Port-au-Prince urban agglomeration in Haiti (2 million). Together these large cities held 13.7 million people, about one third of the total population of the island Caribbean.

The growth to primacy of Santo Domingo reflected its importance as the administrative centre of the Dominican Republic's rapidly growing population and the concentration of the fast-developing manufacturing sector. Thousands of people left the countryside and the regional cities for the attractions of the metropolis. In 1980, only 46 percent of the population of the Dominican Republic lived in rural regions, compared with 70 percent in 1960 (and more than 80 percent before 1930). The improved health and sanitation of the city contrasted with the neglect of services in the countryside. The great migration to Santo Domingo, however, was soon followed, as elsewhere, by the sprouting of marginal settlements on the city fringe, accommodating the great reserves of poor people, poorly serviced, who were to supply cheap labour for decades to come. The rural population of Puerto Rico was equally reduced, with almost two thirds of the island's people living in urban areas by 1980 and relative depopulation particularly evident in the central mountain region.

The major driver of population growth after 1945 was increased fertility. At first, the consequent pressure on resources was relieved by emigration but, by the 1960s, programs of family limitation and birth control were introduced by governments, though sometimes opposed on ideological lines. The relationship between family organization and fertility was complex, but declining marriage rates and increased illegitimacy seem generally to have depressed birth rates, thus operating as an alternative mechanism of family limitation in spite of their lack of social respectability.

Mortality decline was also important, especially the reduction of infant mortality rates. By 2010, the improvement reflected medical advances as well as better living conditions and economic welfare. Malaria and yellow fever ceased to be major killers. Quarantine kept out cholera. Beginning in the 1980s, HIV-AIDS threatened new waves of epidemic but this became a reality only in the poorest countries such as Haiti, where 5 percent of the population was infected with HIV by 2005. People lived longer overall but the differences within the region remained striking. Haitians had the shortest lives, though improving from 45 years in the 1970s to 51 years at the beginning of the twenty-first century. The longest lived males then lived in Anguilla (77 years) and females in Martinique (82 years).

Public health services and hospitals improved their services significantly down to the 1970s but, with the exception of Cuba, where health care remained in the hands of the public sector, often then experienced hard times. Governments found their budgets short of revenue to maintain infrastructure. The rich increasingly travelled overseas for expensive specialized medical attention and the better-off occupied beds in private wings within public hospital grounds. Doctors and nurses became prominent among the emigrating hordes. Some of the doctors were replaced by practitioners from overseas and these became a visible part of the trickle of migrants into the Caribbean.

Migration into the Caribbean was relatively rare after 1945. The proportion of migrants living in the region declined steadily to 3 percent by 1990. Few of these were refugees. Foreigners were highly visible and numerous in some places but only on a temporary basis. This was a direct consequence of the development of tourism, with its often narrow zones of activity or hotel-strips, which concentrated these populations in small areas, often on a seasonal cycle. Even more transient was the flood of tourists released on shore from a cruise ship, funnelled into a tourist zone for just a few hours. Most tourists came from the developed countries of the North Atlantic. In the early stages of tourist development, from about 1945 to 1960, the tourists tended to be richer and they stayed for longer periods. Some bought or built "winter" houses. Visible exotics within this class included the writers Ernest Hemingway, who settled uneasily in Cuba, and Noel Coward and Ian Fleming in Jamaica. On the other hand, in order to hold on to the land for its people, the Bahamas, from independence in 1973, made a strict distinction between citizens and permanent residents which made it difficult for outsiders – even people born in the islands – to settle there.

Some Caribbean states actively attempted to entice European settlers. The most significant example was the Dominican Republic, which maintained its mission to become as European and white as possible, to distinguish itself from the blackness of Haiti and to thwart migration across the border from that densely settled, hard-pressed nation. Free land and passage were offered at various times and, in 1956, an attempt was made to promote immigration on a

Plate 7.2. Cruise ship, Jamaica, 2006. Photo: B. W. Higman.

large scale for colonization of farmlands, but this effort was made in the context of rapid population growth from natural increase that continued to boost the "mulatto" category. Some thousands came from Hungary and Japan but most lasted only a few years before moving on.

Although residence in the Dominican Republic was made easy and cheap for whites and indigenous American people, in the 1960s, there were only a few thousand Spanish-born people. Executive decisions were used to impose quotas on other (nonwhite) immigrants. The 20,000 Haitians who entered the country each year in the 1960s as sugar workers were never regarded as immigrants and their movements were closely monitored. Regardless, by the 1980s, about 200,000 Haitians were living in the Dominican Republic. Another 40,000 Haitians were in the Bahamas and a smaller contingent in Puerto Rico. People of the Leeward Islands similarly sought work in the Dominican Republic. At the same time, some 200,000 Dominicans lived in Puerto Rico.

Few migrants came to live in the Caribbean from any other part of the Americas. Small flows of non-European migrants came to the Caribbean for economic reasons but most of these were temporary residents. Asian, mostly Chinese, people were brought to work in economic free zones, from the 1980s, but they laboured under terms and conditions different and often inferior to those practiced by the host states. They lived separate lives for the period of their contract. Asians, mostly Chinese, Japanese, and Indian nationals, also came to the Caribbean to practice professions or trades, and sometimes used the islands as a staging-post for immigration into the United States.

These temporary residents joined the great outflow of people from the Caribbean. The strength of the desire to migrate varied from island to island but remained powerful throughout the period. The major contributors to this emigration ebbed and flowed but those who left chose as their destinations a limited number of North Atlantic countries, almost all of them former or continuing imperial powers. Those few Caribbean people who chose to migrate to Africa or India were generally thought eccentric. Rather than seeking to restore identities or return to long lost motherlands, migration choices were rooted in economics. The best opportunities were seen in North America and Western Europe – specifically, the United States, Canada, Spain, France, Britain, and the Netherlands. These places were attractive because they possessed a familiarity of language and culture and, more obviously, were relatively easily entered by their colonial subjects. With the exception of France, a nation that had long suffered depopulation and experienced substantial immigration between 1945 and 1970, there was heavy migration out of all these European countries in the postwar period. Thus, Caribbean people constituted a replacement population and, in some cases, the European governments, down to 1960, actively recruited workers from overseas.

The United States and Canada, known immigrant societies, actively recruited farm workers and domestic servants in the postwar era but the numbers were small. Migration to the United States increased dramatically after legislative reform in 1965 which opened the doors wider. From 1976, a limit of 20,000 was imposed on each country in the Americas, giving an advantage to citizens of the newly created sovereign states of the eastern Caribbean. The impact was great on the places with small populations, so that Dominica, Nevis, and St Lucia, for example, lost about 20 percent of their total populations in the 1970s. From a total Caribbean migration into the United States of 40,000 in the 1940s, the number increased to 120,000 in the 1950s, 520,000 in the 1960s, 760,000 in the 1970s, and 850,000 in the 1980s. Caribbean people increased their percentage of total U.S. immigration from 5 to 17 percent over the period. The changes in the rules also meant that the proportion of migrants from the English-speaking Caribbean increased, from 30 percent in the 1960s to 60 percent in the 1980s, with Jamaica the major source and women coming to outnumber men. Some of this movement represented a brain drain but from the 1990s, skilled and professional people became a smaller proportion of the movement and family reunion was emphasized. Canada received about 10,000 migrants per annum from the British Caribbean between 1962 and 1976.

Migration to Europe was less common than to North America but was marked by early peaks. Colonial British Caribbean people responded enthusiastically to the postwar recruitment drive, 150,000 going to the United Kingdom in the 1950s and 168,000 in the three years from 1960 to 1962. From the British West Indies, down to 1962, most people migrated to the United Kingdom. After 1962, the United States and Canada became the major destinations. By the middle of the 1980s, there were 80,000 French Antilleans living in metropolitan France and 200,000 from the Netherlands Antilles (and Suriname) in the Netherlands.

Of migrants to the United States, Cuba sent the largest numbers from the 1940s to the 1970s, but was displaced by both the Dominican Republic and Jamaica in the 1980s. Proportionally (and ignoring places with really small populations) Jamaica led the world as an exporter of people to the United States, sending 105 persons for every 10,000 of its population in 1981, followed in third place by the Dominican Republic (32), and, in seventh, Cuba (11). Jamaica was also a leading source of temporary farm workers to the United States.

Migration out of Puerto Rico peaked early, at about 40,000 each year from 1946 to 1960, when 615,000 Puerto Rican-born people lived in the United States. The number of migrants declined after 1960 but by 1980 more than two million U.S. residents had been born in Puerto Rico or were children of Puerto Rican immigrants, roughly the same number as the population of the island. The Puerto Ricans were the first to migrate in mass by plane, needing neither passport nor visa to enter the United States.

Cubans did not have these advantages but fled in large numbers to the United States following the revolution in 1959. At first, when emigration was unrestricted, they were mainly skilled and professional people, executives, managers, or clerical workers; ideological refugees or members of the Batista regime. Few of them were from rural Cuba, unskilled, or black. Between 1960 and 1962, some 200,000 people left the island, encouraged by the U.S. federal government, but the majority did not go far, many of them making temporary homes in Miami. The revolutionary government then established a more orderly system and monitored the occupational balance. Between 1965 and 1973, Cubans wishing to reunite with family were allowed to do so and more than 250,000 flew to Miami. Migration then became less common and more chaotic, culminating in the Mariel boatlift of 1980 when 125,000 fled to southern Florida.

Migration from the Dominican Republic began relatively late, as might be predicted from its slow population growth and search for immigrants. Emigration picked up after the assassination of Trujillo in 1961. In the next twenty years, 255,000 migrated legally to the United States, perhaps half of them living in New York City. Haitian emigration increased dramatically under the dictatorial regimes of the Duvaliers. By 1990, there were about 200,000 Haitian-born people living in the United States. Alternative destinations for Haitians were France, French-speaking African countries, and Mexico. In the late 1970s and early 1980s, large numbers of Haitians attempted to reach the Florida coast in small boats. This hazardous migration stopped only when the U.S. navy was permitted to patrol the waters off the north coast of Haiti, turning back the boats. The people were branded economic refugees, deserving of denial, whereas Cuba's refugees were termed political refugees, warranting a welcome.

ECONOMIC DEVELOPMENT

Throughout the Caribbean – whatever the system of government – the period after 1945 saw rapid growth in the role of the public sector and in development expenditure. Public works, communications, health, and education were everywhere major items but, increasingly, governments were faced by public debt charges. Public debt reached high levels as early as the 1960s. This was essentially a new feature of the economies, derived initially from the need to take loans for development projects but, more and more often, to make up for failures in revenue collection. A major reason behind this failure was the direction of expenditure towards infrastructure that was beneficial to private enterprise but did not generate commensurate returns because of the many concessions and tax holidays granted to investors. The growing public debt also became increasingly based on foreign borrowing, creating new varieties of dependency. National incomes drained overseas and multiplier benefits were lost to the Caribbean economies.

As well as overseas borrowing and private investment, capital flowed into the islands as development grants. This was particularly the case in the British West Indies, where, following 1945, the imperial government attempted to implement recommendations made by the Moyne Commission on the disturbances of the late 1930s. A Colonial Development and Welfare scheme was established by the British in 1945 which, although influenced by private enterprise through the old planter-based West India Committee, took a broad approach to the economic problems of the colonies. From about 1940, there was also a maturing opinion that the British government needed to shoulder its financial responsibilities for its colonial empire and, between 1946 and 1956, the West Indies received grants totalling £25 million. A similar scheme was worked out in 1946 for Guadeloupe and Martinique, when they became overseas departments of metropolitan France. The Netherlands Antilles, on the other hand, received less assistance after they were granted substantial political autonomy in 1949, but they were, in any case, relatively prosperous and less in need.

Government played a dominant role in Cuba after 1959, of course, with the introduction of the command economy, though the state had become significant as early as 1940. Perhaps surprisingly, the public sector was also substantial in Puerto Rico, where it accounted for 30 percent of gross domestic product in 1946 in consequence of its promotion of industrialization. It was also large in the Dominican Republic in the period following the assassination of Trujillo in 1961, when major enterprises – from sugar plantations to electric power companies – were nationalized on their confiscation from the dictator's estate. As in other Latin American dictatorships, the centralization of finance under Trujillo had promoted a directed and relatively rapid industrialization, something that happened in a much more ad hoc fashion elsewhere. Thus, at the end of the 1960s, the Dominican Republic had one of the largest state-enterprise sectors in the whole of Latin America.

United States enthusiasm for investment in economic development extended beyond its own possessions after 1945, leading to the establishment of the U.S. Agency for International Development in 1961. Such financing and dependence was tainted by its apparent neocolonialism. Even grants often seemed to end up in American pockets. Cuba, denied by the United States, turned to the Soviet Union, and, after 1991, to China.

The IMF became important for a number of governments and economies as early as the 1950s. The Dominican Republic, after decades of financial security, was forced to sign an agreement with the IMF in 1959, when Trujillo's personal transactions disturbed the balance. This was the first of many agreements for the Dominican Republic and, later, many other Caribbean states struggling to keep afloat – agreements that were always bound up with controls on trade and finance, as well as varieties of structural adjustment that changed the internal character of economies. Cuba's revolutionary government, however, made a conscious decision not to enter agreements with the IMF that would upset its independence of the capitalist world.

Many Caribbean governments could not afford the luxury of dismissing the IMF and, in the longer term, had little choice but to bend to the demands of structural adjustment and regular renegotiation. They were forced to do this both because their economies were typically too weak to generate adequate revenue and because several vibrant sectors operated outside the law and were beyond the reach of the tax collector. Further, the relatively prosperous period down to the early 1970s, when commodity prices were firm, was followed by increasingly unfavourable terms of trade. In Haiti, for example, good prices for coffee down to 1954 contributed to a relatively healthy public revenue and supported projects such as the Artibonite irrigation scheme and its dam. Thereafter, these sources dried up. In general, local revenue collection continued dependent on customs duties but shifted towards income tax, which was somewhat more equitable. It was notorious that U.S. corporations in Cuba evaded tax by undervaluing their assets, a fact Castro took advantage of when promulgating one of the first acts of his revolutionary government, the Agrarian Reform Law of June 1959.

Castro was also able to take advantage of a clause in the 1940 constitution that forbade the holding of more than 1,000 acres in a single property. Both foreign and Cuban-owned lands were included and exemptions allowed only to properties producing rice and cattle. Expropriation proceedings began with the 270,000 acres of the United Fruit Company, and a further two million acres owned by U.S. sugar companies were targeted after the sugar crop of 1960. Even before this, the redistribution of idle state land had begun. Some of the expropriated land was distributed to landless peasants but most was used to create co-operative sugar farms. By 1962, most of these had been converted into People's Farms, directed by the state rather than the co-operators. A second agrarian reform of 1963 eliminated individual ownership of units larger than 150 acres. Thus, the state became the major owner of land and the major farmer, with individual private ownership restricted to medium-sized holdings. This was a completely new development for Cuba, unlike many other Latin American countries where state ownership of land and the operation of productive enterprises was historically relatively common. The state also remained the major owner of land in Haiti.

By 1945, the Jamaican peasantry had already passed its peak. People were forced to leave the land for urban settlements or overseas, making way for a process of consolidation. Some of the consolidation was managed by government, through purchase and redistribution to the landless, but most of it was a response to market forces. Starting around 1955, government also began to acquire urban land for housing. The social distribution of landownership changed relatively little, however, with 45 percent of Jamaica's land held in units of more than 500 acres in 1968. Land settlement schemes continued in the 1960s but without much impact on the overall pattern.

Dramatic changes in land tenure occurred in some eastern Caribbean islands. In contrast to Jamaica, the peasantry continued to grow in Trinidad and the Windward Islands down to the 1970s. In Grenada, a program initiated by Eric Gairy gave land

Plate 7.3. St Kitts, from the sea, 1968. Photo: B. W. Higman.

to the landless between 1969 and 1979 through the distribution of abandoned and idle estate properties, and this was followed by the People's Revolutionary Government's policy of creating state farms and acquiring idle lands down to 1983. Small-scale agriculture prospered. Confiscated estate land was returned to owners in 1984 but much of this was then sold in sizeable lots to migrant Grenadians coming home to retire and used to build large, modern houses. Something similar happened in Barbados, where the peasantry as well as the plantation system declined. There, land became increasingly valuable and densely settled, not only by housing and retirement units – often owned by overseas nationals or returning residents – but also by hotels, golf courses, and vacation villas that put the squeeze on agriculture. An estate system persisted in St Kitts, where population stagnated, while, in Nevis, the latifundia disappeared completely when sugar production ceased in 1957 and the only large holdings were those acquired by government for pasture or housing.

Sugar continued to dominate the landscape into the 1960s. Only in a few small islands had it ceased to be the major export crop before 1945 – Grenada, Dominica, Tobago, St Vincent, and Montserrat, had all dropped out by 1920 – but decline set in after World War II in a larger number of territories, notably Puerto Rico (where production peaked around 1950) and the Leeward and Windward Islands (where bananas, plantains, avocadoes, and oranges prospered). Sugar was abandoned in St Kitts in 2005.

The locus of sugar production became highly concentrated within the Caribbean. After 1990, only Cuba, the Dominican Republic, and Jamaica found a place among the world's top twenty exporters. The survivors were the places with the best conditions of soil, climate, topography, and space. Parallel with the concentration of population, traditional export agriculture became increasingly associated with the Greater Antilles, whereas the eastern Caribbean pioneers of the sugar revolution were left behind and forced to find profitable economic alternatives. The exception in the Greater Antilles was Haiti, where agriculture remained more important than in almost any other Caribbean economy, accounting for 30 percent as late as 2000, but produced little sugar for export.

Cuba increased its dominance dramatically after the revolution and, by 1970, exported about seven million tons of sugar, more than twice as much as the rest of the Caribbean combined, though falling short of the fabled ten-million-ton crop campaign. Cuba was the world's largest exporter and maintained its high level of output and its first place down to 1994, pushed along by political imperatives. It then declined steeply as a consequence of cane disease and the loss of the Soviet market. It fell behind Brazil and then Australia. Exports dropped to 3.4 million tons in 2000 and 738,000 tons in 2007, when Cuba dropped to seventh place in the world, exporting less than Swaziland.

The second most important exporter was the Dominican Republic, the late-comer to the sugar industry, shipping 770,000 tons in 1970. As a result of the quota extracted from the United States by Balaguer, the Dominican Republic maintained a high level of production down to 1980, placing it fifth in the world, then declined to a low of 200,000 tons by 2000, little more than its rival Jamaica. The 1950s and early 1960s proved a boom period for Jamaica, exports reaching a long term peak of 500,000 tons but then declining rapidly in the 1970s and levelling off to an average 150,000 tons by 2007. Most cane was produced on broad-acre large plantations, but small-scale peasant cultivation persisted on the margins of the central mills. Sugar also prospered relatively well down to the 1960s in Trinidad, Barbados, Guadeloupe, and Martinique, then fell away. Barbados remained important in the world league as late as 1967 when it exported more than 200,000 tons but this was cut to less than 40,000 tons by 2007. Trinidad dropped out even earlier, exporting just 33,000 tons in that year.

In the Caribbean at large, sugar and rum ceased to be the most valuable legal agricultural exports, replaced in 2007 by cigars and other tobacco products. The primacy of tobacco was matched by its rank in both Cuba and the Dominican Republic. In Cuba, tobacco and sugar products were followed in 2007 by orange juice and honey and, in the Dominican Republic, by cocoa beans and bananas. In Jamaica, coffee, yams, and bananas followed sugar. In Haiti, the banana trade that had been built up during World War II quickly disappeared but coffee and sisal prospered down to the middle of the 1950s.

Bananas came to dominate the Windward Islands but the industry struggled when prices fell in the 1990s. Latin American countries such as Costa Rica and Ecuador were able to produce more cheaply than the islanders but the European Union protected the former colonies in the Caribbean (and Africa and the Pacific) by imposing differential tariffs. A long-running trade dispute – known as the "banana wars" – broke out in 1993 and continued to 2009, when the European Union finally agreed to cut its discriminatory import duties by 2016. In the Windward Islands, governments were, from the early 1990s, forced to subsidise farmers where diversification proved challenging. Europe agreed to provide aid to assist the islands in becoming more competitive, but the structural problems of scale and topography stood in the way, as before, as did the failure of multilateral international trade agreements intended to open access to alternative agricultural markets.

Less visible in the landscape and in the statistics of trade was the flourishing cultivation and export of marijuana. Under Batista, Cuba was a major cultivator and exporter and, with the connivance of the military, also a major transit point for the heroin trade.

Plate 7.4. Processing sisal, Haiti, circa 1955. *Source:* Fritz Henle and P. E. Knapp, *The Caribbean: A Journey with Pictures* (New York: The Studio Publications, with Thomas Y. Crowell Company, 1957), 95. Reproduced with the permission of HarperCollins.

From 1959, however, the revolution took a hard line against the production and trade in drugs, as well as closing down casinos and illegal nightlife run by the Mafiosi. The result was that other islands took up growing marijuana for export, in response to the great growth in demand in North America and Europe beginning in the 1960s. By 1985, marijuana exports from Jamaica, now the major grower, were worth $1 billion to $2 billion, contributing more foreign exchange than sugar, bauxite, and tourism combined. This was achieved in spite of the war on drugs, initiated by the U.S. Drug Enforcement Agency (DEA) in 1973, working together with national governments in eradicating growing crops and criminalizing possession and trade. These operations began in Jamaica but, by the 1990s, spread to other islands, including St Vincent, Trinidad, and Dominica.

Farmers responded to the destruction of their marijuana crops by planting in new, secluded niches in the bush, and local protests were sufficient to bring down governments. None of the islands became producers of cocaine but some Caribbean states, notably the Bahamas and the Turks and Caicos Islands, took advantage of their many scattered islands to become important transshippers in the Latin American drug trade. The Cuban government maintained its hard line, in unlikely cooperation with the DEA, once again leaving the door open for other islands. The travel and the circulation of islanders within the Atlantic realm provided opportunities for participation in the trade, the drugs concealed in cans with contrary labels or placed in condoms and swallowed.

In both Trinidad and Jamaica, considerable areas of land were taken up by mining industries. In the south of Trinidad, oil rigs and storage tanks dominated the landscape and, by 1960, oil and asphalt were more important than agriculture in the economy of Trinidad and Tobago. By 2000, agriculture accounted for less than 2 percent of the economy of Trinidad and Tobago, displaced by the oil and petrochemical industries. Refining, with its elaborate confusion of pipes and drums, generally took place close to the oil fields and became increasingly complex with the flourishing of the petrochemical industry after 1962, when incentive legislation was introduced. Trinidad came to produce more refined petroleum than crude oil, by importing crude from other places – notably Venezuela and the Middle East. The Netherlands Antilles, which had no crude oil resources and drew from Venezuela, also got into refining, but developed no great petrochemical industry. By the late 1960s, other nonproducers, such as Puerto Rico, Jamaica, and Barbados, established refineries. Puerto Rico entered fully into petrochemicals, fuelling the manufacturing sector. Production increased rapidly after about 1955, when global automotive demand took off. At the same time, employment in the industry declined in Trinidad as it became increasingly capital intensive. Cuba also produced oil in small quantities.

Beginning in 1952, bauxite/alumina companies were granted concessions to establish mines at scattered locations in Jamaica. The bauxite occurred naturally near the surface and the removal of the shallow overburden was followed by the much deeper excavation of the rich red bauxite. Roads and railroads, as well as cross-country moving belts, carried the ore to shipping points on both the north and south coasts, coating everything with a thin layer of red dust. Once an area was mined out, the scarred and broken landscape was re-vegetated and returned to pasture or housing. Alumina plants stuck out like sore thumbs and the red mud they produced as waste was channelled to dammed lakes.

Both oil and bauxite, more or less from the beginning, were the preserve of large corporations because of the massive infrastructural investment involved and the bulkiness of the commodities. There was never a place for the small prospector, as there was in precious metals and gemstones. European and North American companies competed for oil but bauxite was always dominated by North American firms. Bauxite had no value in the domestic economies of the Caribbean and the initiative for its mining came from companies already active in refining at their plants in North America. They sought to maximize their profits through vertical integration and therefore wanted control of the resource itself, paying only marginal fees to landowners and governments for temporary access. The model had been developed earlier, particularly in British Guiana and Surinam, which, by the 1930s, were the largest producers in the Americas. Aluminium became particularly important during World War II because the light weight metal was ideal for aeroplanes. This demand continued after 1945 as air travel became more popular and aluminium also came to be used in many household utensils and construction materials.

By 1956, Jamaica was the world's largest producer of bauxite. Haiti began mining in 1955 and the Dominican Republic in 1959. They were soon displaced by larger countries with larger deposits.

Alumina, the intermediate product between bauxite and aluminium, was first produced in Jamaica in 1953. However, although the process reduces weight by half, only about 20 percent of the bauxite mined was made into alumina in Jamaica. Much of this capacity was closed in 2009 in response to a global financial crisis that suppressed demand, with significant consequences for the island's economy.

Other mining included copper and lead in Cuba, with gold and silver strictly a byproduct after 1949; copper in Haiti after 1960; and nickel and gold in the Dominican Republic. In 1980, gold was, briefly, the most valuable export of the Dominican Republic. Clay was the basic material in the ceramics industry, with factories prospering in some places in the 1960s but not much beyond. Iron ore was sought in several islands but remained undeveloped.

Limestone mining or quarrying developed on a massive scale after 1945, mainly to meet the demand from local construction and the cement industries, but increasingly for export. Limestone quarries left highly visible scars in the landscape, the white quarry walls shining out from high hillsides framed by a background of green. In some places, whole hills were quarried to flatness. Cuba was the largest producer of limestone, using some of it in clarifying sugar.

Manufacturing had mixed fortunes after 1945. The traditional bulk users of water – the ice factories and breweries, for example – remained part of the landscape and prospered. Efforts to carry out systematic import-substitution programs generally struggled, however, in the face of cheap imports and trade agreements that prevented protectionist approaches.

The greatest success of manufacturing occurred in Puerto Rico, which derived special benefits from its relationship with the United States. From 1947, Puerto Rico combined these market advantages with tax exemptions to encourage private investment in manufacturing enterprise, moving on from the government-sponsored subsidiary model followed by the Puerto Rico Development Company from its establishment in 1942. As early as 1956, manufacturing contributed more to the economy than agriculture. At first, the emphasis was on small, labour-intensive factories operating as subsidiaries of U.S. companies but later it shifted to more capital-intensive activities, particularly petrochemicals. By the 1980s, pharmaceuticals and electronics products began to dominate.

Models somewhat similar to those followed in Puerto Rico were applied in the British colonies – for example, the Jamaica Industrial Development Corporation, set up in 1952. Broadly, however, these models failed to solve the problems of employment and productivity they had been designed to defeat. In the early days of the Cuban revolution, it was expected that industrialization would provide the engine of growth for the socialist economy and that sugar, with its capitalist plantation system, would fade away as a symbol of underdevelopment. This expectation was soon forgotten when the market conditions for sugar made it impossible to pay for the imported machinery and equipment required for centrally planned manufacturing industries. By 1963, Cuba was forced to accept a model of development in which sugar – sold to the Soviet Union at subsidized prices – would play a larger, not a smaller, role.

Import substitution also fuelled the growth of the manufacturing sector in the Dominican Republic under Trujillo and Balaguer, creating problems when oil prices rose in the 1970s. The sugar industry was neglected. Most of this industrial development was capital intensive and created few jobs. Further, even more than in most other Caribbean territories, almost all sectors of the economy of the Dominican Republic were heavily dominated by foreign multinationals, which took advantage of the offer of operating within tax-free zones. Gulf and Western, the leading U.S. company in the Dominican Republic down to 1985, when it sold up, employed more workers than any other multinational and was the largest private landowner.

Beginning in the 1970s, some territories pursued the windfalls that seemed to come easily from offshore financial services made possible by the deregulation of banking and the creation of new kinds of financial instruments. The Caribbean became an important site in this new system of international finance and, by the 1990s, at least fifteen jurisdictions, most of them smaller islands outside the mainstream of plantation economy, were known as offshore financial service centres or tax havens. Some of these, notably the Bahamas, the British Virgin Islands, and the Cayman Islands, were of the brass plate variety. Governments profited from the system by charging fees for the establishment of international business companies which had no concrete presence beyond a name on a wall or the door of a building. These fees were often small but added substantially to revenue because many of the so-called companies lasted only a few days before going into voluntary liquidation. However, when concern developed over the regulation of international banking, Grenada was accused of accommodating money-laundering operations and forced to tighten its regulation of offshore banking (as well as stopping the sale of passports to non-citizens). St Vincent was also accused of involvement in money-laundering but this was cleaned up by 2003.

The Cayman Islands, with few other resources to draw on, built a reputation as a tax haven backed by a traditional British sense of security but willing to do business without asking too many questions. Its banks received a large slice of the huge amounts of money transferred from the Dominican Republic when the Guzmán regime was coming to an end in 1982. By 2000, financial services constituted the largest sector of the economy, followed by tourism. Seventy thousand offshore companies were registered, as well as hundreds of banks. The system made Caymanians some of the best-off people in the Caribbean. However, the global financial crisis of 2007 undermined its viability and in 2009 the government had to obtain loans from the British even to pay public servants.

The growth of international finance after 1945 had significant implications for patterns of trade and payments. Before World War II, international trade was dominated by foodstuffs and agricultural raw materials. After 1945, minerals and the manufactured products of the industrialized countries greatly increased in importance, thus reducing the status of the Caribbean in the international economy. The prices of primary products deteriorated and the terms of trade turned against tropical agriculture. The international division of labour no longer worked to benefit the Caribbean. The strength of Caribbean territories in the international financial sector did something to redress the balance but innovations in transport technologies were equally influential.

The most important technological innovation in transport was the container ship, a concept unknown before 1956. Piling sealed metal boxes of standard size on a vessel finally made shipping cheap, but the technology also created major changes in the way goods were distributed geographically and in the scale and organization of ports. It fuelled the growth of the world economy and was a major factor in the development of a new balance of global trade that put paid to import-substitution manufacturing experiments in all but the largest of the Caribbean islands. These revolutionary changes occurred rapidly, concentrated in the 1960s and 1970s. One of the earliest large-scale operations was the Sea-Land company's development of container terminals in Puerto Rico in 1962, designed to take advantage of the rapidly growing trade between the island and the United States. Other islands followed quickly but only where they had the necessary scale.

The overall effect of containerization was to concentrate shipping into a relatively small number of transshipment ports, with carefully choreographed specialized machinery to handle the movements. Ships could be turned around in less than twenty-four hours, giving crews little time to enjoy the delights of the ports. Whereas the wharves of the Caribbean had previously been labour intensive and vital sites of working class protest with political implications, particularly in the 1930s, by the 1970s, the major ports employed fewer workers and were dominated by massive capital equipment. Often, new sites had to found to meet the needs of the technologies, moving shipping away from the old town centres. Growth in the size of oil tankers had similar effects.

Although these changes in shipping technology were not unique to the Caribbean, they had particular significance for the islands. Small-scale coasting vessels, lacking the capacity or need to carry complete containers, lost ground to the centralized ports and goods came increasingly to be moved across land by motor vehicles. Railroads similarly faced strong competition from road transport and flourished only where they had specialized functions, as in the transport of bauxite and other ores from mines to coastal shipping points. Many of the island railroads were closed down by 2000, carrying neither goods nor passengers. Small coastal towns lost their economic functions.

Where islands were small and densely distributed, as in the Bahamas and the Leewards, for example, many small companies began to offer local air services after 1945, using small aeroplanes to move people from island to island, competing with inter-island shipping. In the larger islands, after about 1980, heavy trucks hauling whole containers across the islands placed pressure on road networks that had been designed to carry much lighter traffic. Narrow, twisting, scenic roads were increasingly replaced with straightened and widened dual carriageways that cut through the small-scale diversity of island topography and created highway landscapes of concrete and metal.

These new systems facilitated the movement of imported goods to every corner of the islands, offering a bounty of competing articles at low cost. This seeming bounty was not equally distributed, however, because where the flow of containers was not in balance between imports and exports, shippers in the more heavily used direction had to carry the cost of returning empty containers, something they did not have to do with loose-cargo vessels. By 1998, almost three quarters of all containers sent northwards from the Caribbean to the United States were empty, thus making the cost of shipping southwards much higher and increasing the prices of food and other consumer goods imported into the islands. Once again, the advantage that the islands, and particularly the smaller islands, had possessed in earlier centuries in their easy accessibility was lost.

The increasing scale of the vehicles used in moving goods by sea and land was not matched in the movement of passengers. The big buses that predominated down to about 1970 typically decreased in size, enabling greater flexibility of routes and frequency of service. In some places, such as Trinidad, public taxis plying fixed routes provided even greater flexibility at low fares. Most importantly, the private motor car became common as the urban middle classes grew in wealth, after about 1960. The bicycle became the vehicle of the poor or a piece of equipment to be ridden in a gym. Motor cars poured into the islands, with only the occasional attempt at local manufacture or assembly. The great exception to this pattern was Cuba, where the embargo meant that the island gradually became a museum of 1950s auto culture, thus providing one of the best known images of the revolution as anachronism. Only when the Soviet Union began to supply vehicles in the 1970s did new stock arrive, much of it inferior to western design but, with careful curation, capable of long service.

Travel by air did not become a universal expectation until the 1970s, but when it did become relatively cheap, the opportunity to shuttle back and forth was embraced with enthusiasm. Early migrants leaving Puerto Rico or Cuba for the eastern seaboard of the United States in the 1950s had often taken planes, but the longer journey in the initial postwar wave of Caribbean migration to Europe was typically accomplished via a sea voyage. By the 1970s, however, tourists and Caribbean people were equally likely to travel by plane, close-packed in their cabins for a few hours, however contrasted their final destinations. Travel by boat across the Atlantic and through the Caribbean and the Panama Canal, on the other hand, became the experience of the leisured cruise passenger rather than that of the impecunious migrant on a banana boat.

The tourism boom that began in 1945 did not, at first, bring together the two streams of movement – the tourist and the migrant. The initial burst responded particularly to the prosperity and increased leisure enjoyed by North Americans, in the wake of the austerity of the Depression. Air travel, dominated by Pan American Airways, was more efficient than before the war but not immediately cheap. For North Americans, the Caribbean seemed close to home and a popular scene for the relatively sophisticated urban classes. Marketers began to target middle-income consumers rather than the rich who had previously been the biggest spenders. Cuba remained a favourite destination down to the revolution, because it seemed almost an extension of Florida, symbolized in the architecture of the hotels and late-model Buicks and Oldsmobiles that ferried tourists from beach to casino in preparation for a second life as revolutionary icons. The revolution opened opportunities for other islands to enter this lucrative market that depended on a replication of familiar models and a blurring of place with purpose.

Early postwar varieties of tourism sometimes followed a different path, placing the emphasis on the exotic and mysterious rather than the comfortable and familiar. In this market, Haiti possessed a perhaps unexpected advantage, offering liberal North Americans an antidote to materialism. Such "ethnic tourism" found an authentic alternative way of life, an elemental energy, in the rural peasantry of Haiti. Proud of their art and culture, Haitians obliged by exhibiting their best. However, although varieties of exotic and grassroots tourism persisted in the long run, and became popular with followers of alternative cultures – from the hippies of the 1960s to the faux dreadlocks of the 1990s – the numbers were necessarily small compared to the mass tourism that swamped much of the Caribbean island coastal zone.

Selling the Caribbean as a kind of paradise, a world of untouched natural beauty and a prime site for ecotourism, was often problematic. Whale watching and whaling provide a clear example of the potential for conflict. Thirty species of cetaceans – whales, porpoises, dolphins – swam in the Caribbean at the beginning of the twenty-first century. Watching these agile animals attracted 40,000 tourists to the region, in the seas from Puerto Rico to Grenada. Because most whale watchers disapproved of hunting, this branch of environmental tourism was fundamentally incompatible with the continuation of whaling. However, whaling did continue from bases in the Grenadines and St Lucia, the catch largely confined to pilot whales, dolphins, and porpoises. The International Whaling Commission had not then banned the taking of these smaller cetaceans, which remained relatively numerous in the southern Caribbean. Killer whales were also relatively ubiquitous. On the other hand, although classified as a vulnerable species, the hunting of humpback whales, which had been ended in 1926 due to drastic population decline, was proposed for reopening after 2000 from Grenada. Further, it was well known that some of the smaller island states of the Caribbean joined forces to vote in international forums for the continuation of whaling globally, enticed by inducements to sell their souls.

By the 1970s, package deals brought plane loads of tourists looking for hedonistic bargains. This brand of tourism provided employment for many, though at low wages, both as hotel workers and builders. In the Dominican Republic, for example, tourist arrivals tripled during the 1970s, to reach half a million annually. By the 1990s, some Caribbean destinations were known as sites of sex tourism, for men and women. These included not only the Dominican Republic, St Martin, and Jamaica, but also Cuba. The initial intention of the Cuban revolution was to eradicate prostitution but it survived to flourish when tourism was revived as a matter of necessity in the Special Period. Tourism was, however, disturbed by the threat of HIV-AIDS, particularly in Haiti, where arrivals fell drastically in the early 1980s, when the country was declared a high-risk destination.

Some forms of tourism flourished without any significant contact with local populations. All-inclusive hotel complexes placed tourists in walled and gated compounds, with their own stretch of beach, and meeting almost all of the visitor's needs within their narrow confines. There was no incentive to consume outside the hotel, to spend on things already paid for. Such enclaves had little economic impact on the local regions in which they existed except for employment. Even less connected with local people was the cruise ship industry, in which passengers might spend a few hours on shore but retreated at dusk to the security of their cabins and consumed on board the lavish spreads that made up part of the cost of their ticket. The bigger the ship, the less likely it was to call at a minor port. Launched in 2009, the world's largest cruise liner, Oasis of the Seas, was so big that few ports could accept it and a special docking station was built for it at Labadee in Haiti. This cruise ship was a world unto itself, carrying 5,400 passengers and 2,300 crew, big enough to intimidate a small island.

The aeroplanes that carried tourists and Caribbean travellers also played an important role in the development of modern means of communication. From about 1960 they took over the movement of the post, enabling people to keep in much closer touch. To receive a reply to an air letter took only about two weeks. Telegrams also crossed the seas in large numbers until they went into steep decline in the 1970s, after which the telephone began to become affordable. By the 1990s, communication by phone became the norm, with rates substantially lowered. It also made communication in creole possible, something the writing process inhibited, however literate the author. Thus, enthusiasm for the telephone and the authentic voice applied both to communication overseas and internally, and the trend was extended significantly when mobile phones became relatively cheap and common among the rural people of the Caribbean islands. For the middle classes, electronic communication through the internet paralleled the use of the telephone, but it remained beyond the reach of the poor.

Radio prospered throughout the period, often broadcasting overseas content by rediffusion down to the 1970s. Television reached the Caribbean in 1960 and it, too, broadcast a good deal of foreign content, particularly from the United States, but increasingly became capable of live transmission from distant places of breaking news and sporting events. By the late 1970s, satellite dishes began sprouting from Caribbean rooftops, connecting the world to the poor and the isolated. Newspapers came and went but the longest established generally managed to survive into the twenty-first century, despite periods of censorship and propaganda.

EQUALITY AND INEQUALITY

Although the Caribbean continued to be marked by poverty, the distribution of wealth and income did become somewhat more equal after 1945. Per capita incomes increased, something they had rarely done in the first half of the twentieth century. The organization of labour by unions helped as more people became dependent on wages but their influence and power declined from the 1980s in the face of capitalist agendas and the imposition by international financial agencies of so-called structural adjustment schemes. Large differences between social classes and among territories remained but the great weight of population in Cuba ensured the overall regional tendency was progressive. By 1985, the distribution of income in Cuba was roughly as equitable as it was in the Scandinavian countries, generally regarded as the world's most equal societies in this period. Before 1959, the poorest 40 percent got only 7 percent of total income in Cuba but this had increased to 26 percent by 1985. Cuba became a truly egalitarian society by almost every standard. The harsh economic impact of the Special Period badly damaged this achievement, however, and by 1999 the share had dropped to 13 percent and continued to deteriorate, a trend particularly affecting the unemployed and the service classes.

Unions remained strong in Cuba into the twenty-first century, whereas in most other places, they declined and new forms of performance-based human resource management systems were used to increase labour productivity in situations of demographic pressure and exposure to a wider world of work. From the 1960s, able-bodied Cubans were guaranteed work but expected to labour for moral rather than mercenary, monetary rewards. Workers received the same pay regardless of differences in individual productivity and learned not to expect anything additional when they worked overtime. The seasonal character of employment was eliminated but productivity did not respond well to moral incentives and so-called volunteers were deployed to the cane fields, along with soldiers; the taking off of the sugar crop became a military campaign in the years leading to the marvellous harvest of 1970. By 2000, only in Cuba did workers continue to have relative security of employment, as well as a real power to influence policies and priorities at a local level and to collectively manage the surplus they produced. It was in the arena of labour that Cuba remained most committed to socialist principles and opposed to neoliberal policies.

The dictators of Haiti and the Dominican Republic accumulated vast wealth for themselves and their cronies in the postwar boom, and Trujillo's fortune was, indeed, large enough to affect the overall pattern of inequality. The long-term effects were not uniform, however. By the 1980s, at the end of the Duvaliers dictatorship, Haiti was the poorest country in the western hemisphere and its position was in decline both relatively and absolutely. The people of the Dominican Republic did somewhat better under Balaguer. The prosperity of the 1970s was narrowly distributed, with new categories of rich added to the old rich, who got richer. At the same time, government edict froze the wages of the numerous state bureaucrats and high rates of unemployment, together with the suppression of labour unions, kept the wages of most workers depressed in the midst of galloping inflation that pushed up prices.

Dependency sometimes seemed to offer the best possibilities for equality in the distribution of wealth and income after 1945. Thus, the people of Martinique and Guadeloupe benefited by their status as departments of France, achieving parity with metropolitan France in minimum wage levels and social welfare payments. The thirty-five hour week was also implemented simultaneously in the islands and the metropole. By 2000, per capita income in Martinique was second only to the Bahamas, though still little more than half as much as in the metropole. The downside of this equality was that, with high unemployment and limited agricultural alternatives, the islands seemed headed towards welfare dependency.

The correlation between colour/ethnicity and income persisted throughout the period, though in many places it became confused by class and education. Thus, although the Cuban revolution directed benefits particularly to the poor, and the black population gained by the transformation, longstanding gaps in relative standards of living and health persisted. Blacks were strong supporters of the revolution and less likely to become exiles, at least down to 1980, yet few found their way into the upper ranks of government and party. In Haiti, the black middle classes became politically predominant and François Duvalier's regime was self-consciously *noiriste*, though it also commenced the political incorporation of merchant families of Middle Eastern origin. His son Jean-Claude lost support among the black majority by marrying a mulatto, in 1980, symbolizing the abandonment of the regime's original ideology of anti-mulatto racialism. Elsewhere, Black Power ideologies were influential but did not leave a lasting mark on the structure of society or politics.

Women's liberation and feminist movements were similarly popular and influential but limited in their lasting impact on gender roles and behaviour. The Cuban revolution had mixed outcomes for women. The chances were increased that they would marry and divorce. In the early stages of the revolution, women were encouraged to join the labour force but, by the 1980s, some government policies were directed at capping their participation and reserving occupations for men. Women did increasingly pursue education and professional careers but even here, their numbers – in medicine, for example – were limited. Few found their way into politics and the upper ranks of the Communist Party. Women had little more success in Haiti though from the 1990s they occasionally had the role of prime minister. Elsewhere in the Caribbean, women became more visible in political leadership. Women served as prime ministers in the Netherlands Antilles in the 1980s and 90s. Eugenia Charles, elected prime minister of Dominica in 1980, held office until 1995. Jamaica's first woman prime minister, Portia Simpson-Miller, was appointed in 2006 but failed at the ballot box. In 2010,

Kamla Persad-Bissessar was elected prime minister of Trinidad and Tobago.

Efforts to reduce inequalities rooted in ethnicity and gender were often tackled through formal education. For most of the period after 1945, colonial and independent governments devoted a good deal of effort to driving down levels of illiteracy. Notably, the Cuban revolution mobilized literacy brigades in its early days, reducing illiteracy from 23 to 4 percent in the great campaign of 1961. In Haiti, illiteracy remained as high as 80 percent in the 1970s. By 2002, illiteracy in Haiti had been reduced to 48 percent but remained high compared with Puerto Rico (6 percent) and Cuba (3 percent). In Cuba, enrolments in primary and secondary schools were also increased from the beginning of the revolution, but this upsurge was matched by adult education programs offered in factories and offices, farms, and night schools. By 1985, some 38 percent of Cubans had completed secondary schooling, compared to fewer than 5 percent before the revolution. Puerto Rico also boasted high levels of enrolment in schools and institutions of higher learning.

Beyond the simple fight against illiteracy, there was a broad effort to make curricula more relevant to the Caribbean region and the experience of the school pupils. New textbooks were written and local examinations boards set up. At the same time, there remained a determination to ensure education was at a high standard and this often meant the continuation of external assessment systems. As before 1945, the languages of instruction were typically those of the former colonial masters. Teaching in creole was generally frowned on, though it was the common language of schoolyard and street.

In Cuba, the proportion with higher education increased from fewer than 2 percent in 1950 to 15 percent by 2007, when enrolments were equal to those in most economically advanced countries. Although a significant number of University of Havana professors left Cuba soon after the revolution of 1959, enrolments increased. Only in the Special Period of economic difficulty did enrolments begin to lag and this was quickly rectified by means of a crash program directed at making higher education universal by combining study with work and creating multiple university branches to provide easy access.

Universities were established for the first time in the British Caribbean. In 1948, a University College of the West Indies was set up as a federal institution, with a single campus in Jamaica, attached to the University of London. Campuses were added in Trinidad in 1960 (building on the Imperial College of Tropical Agriculture) and in Barbados in 1963. The University of the West Indies became independent in 1965, responsible for its own curricula and granting its own degrees. By the 1980s, additional universities were established, some of them by government and others by churches and offshore operators. Most of the new institutions had roots in the United States and many students left the islands for colleges in North America. Some of these students got scholarships on the basis of grades obtained on U.S. tests – the Scholastic Aptitude Test or SAT becoming very popular – but the better-off routinely sent their sons and daughters to institutions overseas.

Sending students overseas for their education had an effect similar to that of going overseas for medical care. It meant that the middle classes and the rich could afford services superior to those that could be offered by most Caribbean governments and that local hospitals and clinics were starved of funds. For the poor, it meant access to inferior services. Something similar happened to law and order. The war on drugs, imposed on the Caribbean from outside the region, contributed massively to prison populations and preoccupied criminal justice systems. It also helped corrupt the police. One response was the creation of independent, commercial security firms, paid by individuals and enterprises to protect their particular properties, with the consequence that the poor were forced to put up with inferior and underfunded public services.

Capital punishment became uncommon, though generally remaining part of the law. Prisons filled up. Even in Cuba, prison populations tended to overrepresent the black and poor people who found themselves most vulnerable to the law and to patterns of policing. Faced by ruthless gangs, police and private security operations sometimes carried out their own executions. Although generally less violent than most of Africa and South America, the Caribbean region contained pockets of terror. In Jamaica, the murder rate increased rapidly from the late 1950s to reach 50 per 100,000 by the beginning of the twenty-first century, regularly placing it among the top three or four nations globally. These trends all pointed to continuing problems of inequality and social inclusion. Further, the development of networks of migration and movement facilitated new patterns that might see a gunman on the streets of Kingston one day and the Bronx the next.

Although murder typically was domestic or associated with gang violence, it was sometimes directed against minorities such as homosexuals, who experienced continuing intolerance. Homophobia was pervasive into the 1960s and homosexual acts commonly were punishable by imprisonment. In Cuba, the first decade of the revolution saw extensive incarceration under harsh conditions, but by the end of the 1970s, legal prohibitions had been removed. Gay and lesbian rights movements emerged by the 1980s and Haiti and Puerto Rico followed the more liberal model of Cuba. Homosexuality remained a crime in many places, however – particularly the former British colonies. Violence against individuals was often accompanied by explicit disgust in popular culture, the more extreme examples occurring in Jamaica.

FOOD, CLOTHING, SHELTER

For the poor, the malnourished, and the homeless, the necessities of life were daily preoccupations. Even for the better off, decisions about what to eat and what to wear had an important place in the construction of personalities and images of the self. Elements of material culture, to some degree, were shared but at the same time they were used to distinguish individuals along the lines of wealth, culture, and ideology and to exhibit varied experiences of nationalism and transnational migration. National identity most commonly was associated with food culture, whereas the portability of clothing made it ideal as a means of representing individuality. The house was the least mobile of the basic elements of material culture but through its scale and fabric, and its very location, it served as an indicator of wealth and style displayed in the context of a larger landscape.

Food came to be understood as a marker of identity in the period after 1945 in ways it had rarely been understood in earlier times. Thus, for those Caribbean people who joined the diaspora, it was the food of their home islands that they missed most and did their best to replicate in strange surroundings. Housing was not easily transportable or easily accommodated to environments north of Florida, though the interior spatial order of houses was often derived from Caribbean models and characterized by an intense use of colour and pattern that served as a nostalgic evocation of accommodation left behind. Clothing similarly confronted the impracticalities of contrasting climates. By contrast, even the most perishable food items could be transported in airline baggage. Markets developed in North America and Europe where, thanks to the container ship and the aeroplane, Caribbean food items, fresh and processed, could be purchased. These technologies made possible the satisfaction of tastes that could not easily be met before 1945. It was the importance of food as an indicator of identity in the diasporic world, in interaction with creole nationalism and creole taste within the Caribbean itself, that pushed its consumption to the fore.

Ironically perhaps, although Caribbean food played this important role in the period after 1945, consumption patterns within the Caribbean itself were affected by a growing dependence on imported food brought to the islands in the same homogeneous containers that shipped exotic foods to the rest of the world. The transition was driven in large part by international trade and aid agreements that privileged the free movement of goods and the reduction of protective duties, but it also reflected subsidies granted by metropolitan countries to their own producers. For example, imported food became increasingly common in the Dominican Republic in the 1960s, where local agricultural production proved unequal to the challenge of the lower prices that resulted from cheap financing through the U.S. Credit Corporation. Most importantly, the revolution in world transport and trade shifted food preferences and consumption patterns in the Caribbean, creating altered tastes that did not match the remembered delights that the migrants left behind. Some of these trends were already well established before the war but it was in the period after 1945 that the quantitative changes became substantial. Grains increased their role dramatically at the expense of starches derived from tubers and fruits. The biggest winners were rice, wheat, and corn.

Rice was grown in small amounts in Caribbean fields but its cultivation declined and in many islands it was abandoned by the 1980s
in the face of cheap imports. Rice displaced yam, taro, cassava, plantain, and banana. The triumph of wheat was even greater since it
could not be grown successfully within the region but always had to
be imported, most of it coming from North American fields. Before
1945, most wheat reached the Caribbean as flour or baked products but after the war, flour mills became common in the islands
and the wheat largely arrived as grain. This was a small gain for
local economies but, as in the case of rice, the consumption of
bread and pastry products increased dramatically at the expense of
yam and taro, plantain and banana. Although corn was indigenous
to the Americas and grown successfully in the islands, the cheap-
ness of North American corn made it difficult for the local product
to compete and, from about 1980, demand was so great that the
islands became heavily dependent on imports. Corn competed with
the local starches but the great increase in its use was indirect, most
of it fed to chickens and feedlot cattle and pigs, raised for their
meat.

Rice, wheat, and corn were the leaders in the triumph of imported
food items but they were joined by many others. Perishable foods,
previously unsuited to transportation, could now be frozen fresh or
shipped chilled in refrigerated containers. Fish and meat, formerly
imported only after pickling, drying, or canning, became common
in supermarket freezers. Local cattle farmers lost ground and the
dairy industry came under siege. The fishing industry was encouraged and fishers used extreme means – such a dynamiting – to
increase their catches, but still found it difficult to contribute more
than 50 percent of the islands' fish consumption. These activities
contributed to the declining health of the coral reefs surrounding
the islands. By the 1990s, the local production of even the most
common perishable vegetable crops was forced into decline, in the
face of cheap imports of potatoes, onions, cabbages, carrots, let-
tuces, and tomatoes. Even in the countryside, roadside sellers came
to include among their offerings imported fruits and vegetables, as
well as imported kitchen utensils, mixed up indistinguishably with
the products of surrounding food, forest, and clay pit.

Some of the smaller islands, particularly those of the eastern Caribbean, had depended on imported food for centuries. The shift was most dramatic in the Greater Antilles, where, in earlier periods, the islands had been able to successfully exploit their diverse resource bases to produce most of their own food, even when dominated by sugar and the plantation. Efforts to reverse this trend and make the islands self-sufficient, generally associated with socialist political tendencies, were only partly and temporarily successful.

In Jamaica, for example, Michael Manley's democratic socialist government of the 1970s established Food Farms and later governments similarly attempted to stimulate food production for local consumption. It was a losing battle. Even the revolution in Cuba, so successful with health provision, failed to make the island self-sufficient in food. Not only did food production fail to increase along with population growth, it declined dramatically, and the island depended on imports and was often reduced to rationing. In part, the failure resulted from the revolution's early agrarian reforms, which swept up local food production along with the enthusiasm to transform the plantation–export sector. At its climax in 1968, state ownership and management were extended to restaurants and bars, and even street food vendors, creating queues for ice creams at regulated kiosks. Even after the decline of sugar production in Cuba around 2000, food for domestic consumption remained in short supply, hit by the closing off of fertilizer and other inputs from the former socialist states. State farms and co-operatives suffered systemic planning and management problems. After 1985, there was decline in crops such as rice and potatoes, though partly balanced by growth in plantains and beans. Milk, eggs, poultry, and beef all declined, with only pork showing a steady increase in output over the first fifty years of the revolution. The urban agriculture of the Special Period made a difference but not enough to change the bigger picture.

Although poverty-stricken Haiti was, of necessity, relatively self-sufficient in food, it too was dragged into financial aid schemes and encouraged to open its doors to trade in ways that often threatened its food security. Following the end of Duvalierism in 1986, imported rice was brought in, often as contraband, lowering the price below the local farmers' break-even point. By 2008, Haiti had emerged as a global hot-spot where shortages created riots, particularly over imported cereals such as rice. The consequence was widespread malnutrition. Dependence on charcoal for cooking fuel hastened deforestation. The denudation of Haiti's hillslopes, the forest cut to extend the area of cultivable land, had catastrophic effects. Rainstorms and hurricanes washed away the soil and silted streams. People died in mudslides. Although killing many more people, the earthquake of 2010 had a lesser impact on the long-term productivity of the land. The relocation of population from Port au Prince to the countryside in response to the earthquake did, however, increase pressure on rural resources and exaggerated the need for food aid.

Elsewhere in the Caribbean, the impact was less catastrophic but often along lines parallel to the experience of Haiti. Across the border, the Dominican Republic was more prosperous but saw a similar advance of the agricultural frontier into forested areas in response to population pressure and increased demand on food production systems. Deforestation followed the expansion of hillslope farming into mountainous regions, for both crops and livestock, leading rapidly to soil erosion and slippage. The only alternatives appeared to be either a continued degradation or a halt to deforestation and increased reliance on external sources for food supplies. From the 1960s, the Dominican Republic had followed an unusual state food policy, establishing a nationwide system of silos, storage facilities, trucks to collect and distribute food, stores and markets, school breakfasts, and low-price restaurants. This system was designed to bestow political patronage by subsidizing basic commodities, distributing food baskets at Christmas, and caring for those affected by flood and hurricane. In the 1990s, when the economy had to be bailed out, the IMF recommended ending this state food system, but it survived into the twenty-first century and, indeed, government handouts of food played a role in the competition for votes at the presidential election of 2008. By then, the system seemed an anachronism but it played a significant role not only in the political democratization of the Dominican Republic but also in the defence of the forest against agricultural advance.

In contrast, Puerto Rico's forest recovered from a low point in the 1940s, when it was just 10 percent of the landscape, to 40 percent at the beginning of the twenty-first century. This achievement, however, was accomplished only through a shift from agriculture to manufacturing industry, together with internal migration from rural to urban areas. It was the consequence of Puerto Rico's openness to economic globalization. The rapid recovery of the forest was also a product of secondary succession, which means that abandoned agricultural lands quickly returned to forest maturity, with strong local biodiversity yet also a legacy of exotic plants and a broad-scale homogenization of species, in everything from trees to earthworms, that was inherited from the former plantation systems. The other side of the coin was that the resurgence of the forest meant an acceptance of Puerto Rico as a restructured postagricultural economy that could not aspire to self-sufficiency in food supply.

This bleak picture of increasing dependence on imported food products sits uncomfortably beside the exotic image of Caribbean food portrayed in cookbooks and tourism promotions. It also seems to conflict with the image Caribbean people themselves held of their food. However, it meshes well enough with the broader forces of globalization that worked to flatten markets and standardize preferences, and introduced to the islands fast food chains such as McDonald's and Kentucky Fried Chicken, which competed with local versions of street food. These multinational chains did not prosper everywhere, however, and the strength of the local brand was sufficient to enable "Puerto Rican food", for example, to retain a unique identity that was not merely a nostalgic notion but reflected what people actually ate. Jamaicans came to refer to ackee-and-saltfish as their national dish, though the ackee was a naturalized fruit introduced from West Africa and the saltfish imported from the North Atlantic. As early as the middle of the nineteenth century, Cubans had developed a national cuisine and "creole food" became a central symbol of national identity. Food took on revolutionary significance after 1959. The embargo, which cut off supplies of canned peaches and processed cheese previously imported from the United States, brought to the fore the cooking of the rural poor and emphasized the central role of roots, tubers, and plantains in that tradition, so distinguishing Cuban food from the high cuisine inherited from Spain. In the midst of shortages, the peasant's farm represented a bountiful resource, a self-sufficient garden paradise.

Shelter, the second of the basic elements of material culture, similarly reflected elements of globalization mixed with unique local architectural traditions. Perhaps the strongest characteristic of Caribbean houses, especially after 1945, was their unwillingness to conform to a particular style. The house served as an element in the individual's desire to achieve respect through the image it projected, to be added to the person's handsome personal appearance and dress, and, if it could be afforded, a shiny car. Alongside this diversity, however, creole vernacular architectures could be found in Puerto Rico and other islands and also a common fabric and plan in much of the modern middle class bungaloid design that came from developers in this period.

The great migration of people from rural regions to the larger cities of the Caribbean after 1945 placed immense pressure on the existing housing stock. Poor people, uncertain of their tenure and hoping to move on quickly to greener pastures, built shanty towns from whatever materials they could lay their hands on. Lengths of lumber, bricks, and sheets of galvanized iron were combined with metal cut from oil drums and even cardboard to construct shelters surrounded by palisades of wooden stakes or the more traditional living fence of cactus or prickle bush. Unplanned laneways wound their way through these settlements, many of which had only minimal access to running water and sanitation and electric power. Governments continued efforts begun in the 1930s to improve the quality of housing in these places and, in the 1960s and 1970s, sometimes cleared the land and built tower blocks of apartments, but the marginal quality of these settlements remained a problem and the breeding ground of crime as well as cultural creativity.

The houses of the shanty towns contrasted starkly with those of the middle class suburbs that spread across large stretches of land on the fringes of the cities after 1945. Whereas the structures of the poor offered little protection from hurricane and earthquake, the new middle class houses were commonly built of reinforced concrete and concrete blocks, often with flat roofs and metal louvre blades rather than glass windows. Although not uniquely Caribbean, this style responded to specific local hazards and expectations, and made use of local resources to a large extent – particularly the cement that was a leader in manufacturing sector growth. Bricks and timber became uncommon. The model was found throughout the Caribbean, built by developers as single units on small or large blocks of land, but fatefully relatively uncommon in Haiti where few could afford such solid construction and where there was no fresh memory of the devastation that powerful earthquakes might deliver. Elsewhere, by the 1970s, reduced versions became more common as the market for working class housing opened up, and these were joined by townhouse and apartment developments of varying scale. Traditional vernacular housing based on appropriate technology, such as the chattel house of Barbados, began to be replaced by expensive, immobile cast-concrete houses, promoted by government from the 1980s. Indigenous diversity was overtaken by homogeneity and inorganic building materials.

Perhaps surprisingly, housing proved one of the less successful areas of the Cuban revolution. Effort in construction was directed primarily at schools, hospitals, and military installations, so the physical stock of residential units remained poor and deteriorated. As in many other places with rapid demographic growth, many people were poorly housed.

Whether the product of capitalist or socialist construction, the people of the Caribbean displayed considerable inventiveness in the ways in which they modified the basic structures they received from developers and government building schemes. As soon as money could be found, houses were extended up and out. Also, the rise in crime that paralleled the growth of the middle classes and the building of their suburbs quickly had householders renovating to achieve a more defensive style of architecture. The most ubiquitous of these developments was the burglar bar, a mesh of welded iron rods designed to permanently enclose a window, surround a veranda or duplicate a door. Perimeter fences, topped by barbed wire or broken bottles, rose higher and higher. In some houses, internal padlocked barriers were added. The delights of sitting on an open veranda were lessened. By the 1990s, gated communities emerged to solve this problem, surrounding like-minded people within a secure outer barrier and closely monitoring entry.

In spite of the fear that prompted burglar bars and other protective barriers, the design of such security features became the subject of creativity and stylishness. In this way, the fantasy landscapes of the all-inclusive hotels (the prototypical gated communities) was brought home and expressed in wrought metal shaped into the pattern of a spiderweb or a flower, while decorative blocks adorned balconies, concrete pillars mimicked Doric columns, and cast concrete lions topped entrance gates. Those with capital – often earned overseas, legally or illegally – were able to go the whole hog, building mini-castles reminiscent of the planter's great house. Such dwellings were scattered widely across the landscape, not concentrated in urban areas. Playfulness and public performance existed in domestic architecture just as they came to be applied in the treatment of the body and its clothing.

To begin with the head, the straightening of hair, using hot combs and chemicals, became more common among black Caribbean women after 1945 as the middle class expanded and exposure to Afro-American culture increased through travel and the media. In the late 1960s and early 1970s, however, Black Power and other protest movements brought new fashions, notably the Afro hairstyle and headwraps. Caribbean men were less likely to straighten their hair but did adopt the Afro. Hats were replaced by caps, some of them knitted from wool, and designed specifically to accommodate voluminous dreadlocks.

The most striking example of a truly Caribbean contribution to hairstyling was the dreadlocks, with its roots in the beginnings of Rastafarianism in Jamaica in the 1930s. The hair was allowed to grow long and lanky and encouraged to form locks, which might hang loosely down the back or be covered by a cap. In the 1950s and 1960s, the hair and its covering sometimes ascended vertically, with the ends of the locks protruding. In this period, locks were worn mainly by men. A distinction developed between those Rastafarians who had beards and those who did not. The spread of Rastafarianism into the middle classes, beginning in the later 1960s, was often marked by the adoption of dreadlocks and beard. These fashions spread from Jamaica into many other islands along with associated practices and ideologies.

Clothing with an "African" flavour such as the kaftan or mu-mu for women became popular at the same time as the adoption of the Afro hairstyle, particularly among the middle classes, and men of all colours might be seen in dashiki and safari suits in the early 1970s rather than collar-and-tie and jacket. This style was less obviously African, however, and had parallels in the casual clothing of Castro and his revolutionary followers in Cuba, where the formal dress of dictatorship was replaced by a more egalitarian costume that bespoke its suitability to the tropics, in opposition to the straight-jackets of temperate fashion imposed from above. Outside Cuba, however, these styles survived only briefly – for example, during the revolution in Grenada and the period of democratic social-ism in Jamaica. Sandals were often part of the uniform, empha-sizing the casual attitude but also connecting with the footwear of the poor, who, down to the 1960s, sometimes fashioned them from the rubber of discarded car tyres if they could not afford leather.

By the 1980s, Caribbean clothing styles had become more eclec-tic. The leaders of fashion were then found in the arenas of music and dance. They remained radical but confronted established ideas of social respectability rather than political conservatism. Elements were widely borrowed and rearranged – the foreign with the local – in jarring combinations of colour and glitz that flaunted skin and bling. Women returned to straightening their hair, but also coloured it or covered it with wigs of flowing straight hair of every hue. Whereas straight hair had previously often been regarded as "good hair", its status was now more ambiguous. At the same time, prod-ucts designed to lighten the colour of the skin became popular. The appeal to an African look had receded in populist culture, surviving only amongst political ideologues and traditionalist Rastafarians.

Everywhere, throughout the period, poor people remained con-servative in dress. The poorest scrambled together what they could and the slightly better off put on simple, practical shirts, pants, skirts, and blouses. The poor as well as the better off dressed respectably when going to church, putting on their best and behav-ing with decorum. Both traditional Revival churchwomen as well as their Pentecostal sisters maintained a uniform white dress, indicative of purity. Such behaviour and attire persisted strongly to the end of the twentieth century.

Touristic visions of the Caribbean – Bermuda shorts, Hawaiian shirts, and broad-brimmed straw hats – rarely matched the attire of any class of creole. What was observed but not broadly copied was the model provided by stage performers, a model decidedly not directed at respectability. It drew on the mocking tradition of role reversals found particularly in Carnival but brought the style into everyday life. Shared concepts of appropriate dress broke down, so that mourners at a funeral might sport purple wigs and bared bellies alongside cousins in three-piece suits.

The conflict between emerging self-confident populist social attitudes and older ideologies of respectability that bubbled up towards the end of the twentieth century was closely connected with broader issues of language and education. For generations, aspiring Caribbean people had sought to find their way out of adversity by taking advantage of a good education, if they could get it, and behaving in a courteous and respectable manner. These worthy values could be traced to the teaching of Christian missionaries in the nineteenth century but had their secular manifestation in public schooling through the advocacy of ethical responsibility and polite behaviour. Unsurprisingly, the education given to Caribbean colonials was strongly oriented to knowledge that had its base in the western tradition. This approach was not abandoned with independence, though the content of education was given a much stronger Caribbean foundation, and was followed equally in the republics. Only in Haiti did a strong intellectual and literary tradition develop that cut across this Western European tradition, though new religions, such as Rastafarianism, did more to fundamentally challenge the essential authority of knowledge.

Respectability and a fear of disorder, including political and economic instability, also connected with a dread of drug culture. The smoke haze of marijuana, enveloping a self-conscious rejection of hard work and sobriety as the appropriate paths to a worthy status, represented a threat that needed to be controlled or eliminated. The great push to control drug use globally after 1945 was driven by forces external to the Caribbean and was often opposed by those who preferred to maintain the tolerant attitude that had been shown to marijuana and alcohol since the nineteenth century, but the initiative appealed to the many who had grown up to diligence and denial. Calls for the legalization of marijuana came initially from Rastafarians, on the grounds of religious freedom and by analogy with the doctrine of transubstantiation, but they were joined by mainstream voices, including medical and legal professionals.

CREOLIZATION VERSUS GLOBALIZATION

The modern history of the Caribbean was dominated by a struggle between, on the one hand, the homogenizing and integrating forces of global economies and world systems, and, on the other, the creative products of creolization that sprang from the grounded experience of the islands. This struggle was well underway by the seventeenth century but received added stimuli in the late nineteenth century from Americanization and technological change. Tendencies towards globalization strengthened after World War II but simultaneously took on aspects of creolization, creating a much more interactive pattern that brought the Caribbean back to the centre of the world.

At the same time, Caribbean people became increasingly willing to think of themselves as indigenous, not simply in the sense that their ancestors had been born in the islands but because they were, in fact, descendants of pre-Columbian aboriginal inhabitants. Documentary proof of such descent was typically impossible to find but memory could be privileged and, indeed, scientific genetic testing established that indigenous DNA was shared by many Caribbean people, though in smaller proportions than the African and European lineages. This revived or new-found indigenous consciousness was personalized rather than seen as a component of national identity, making it merely one element in a larger array of ancestral roots. It was portable. A similar development was the acceptance of Latino or Hispanic as a label for people from the Spanish-speaking Caribbean, used to identify a panethnicity that transcended nationality and could be diffused by migrants. Typically, the value of such markers was learned in transnational locations outside the Caribbean and brought back through return migration.

Migration inevitably stretched the bonds of family, especially when a parent or partner went ahead to find the way overseas, leaving children with grandparents. Throughout the Caribbean, women continued to head households, particularly among the poor, for whom formal marriage had little to offer. Only the middle classes, with property to transfer, worried much about legal ties. In the Dominican Republic, for example, in 1990, only about 20 percent of cohabiting partners were legally married. Whatever their formal family relationships, remittances became essential to the welfare of many of those left behind. This was particularly true for Haiti. Equally important was capital brought back by returning residents. These people, often absent from their home islands for thirty or more years, also came with accumulated cultural baggage that both made it difficult for them to fit in and gave them a status as citizens of the world. Apart from anything else, they no longer were young. Some of them spoke differently, too.

Globalization and its precursor Americanization privileged the English language. The Caribbean was, by no means, immune to this growing hegemony, in spite of the fact, already noticed, that the "English-speaking" territories accounted for a declining percentage of the population, reduced to just 13 percent by 2010. Even within these territories, English increased its status at the expense of creole. In St Lucia, for example, the French-based Kwéyòl gave way to English, as young people looked to North America for a better life, travelled, and watched television. There, the process was centred in the capital town and port, Castries, but spread through the rural communities, elevating English as the medium of daily discourse. In response, cultural nationalists encouraged the active use of Kwéyòl in radio broadcasts and festivals, but failed to convince governments (or parents) that it should be used in schools. In Haiti, the official language remained French though it came naturally only to a minority, whereas everyone was fluent in the creole. By the late 1970s, there were efforts to make creole an equal official language and it was eventually recognized in the constitution of 1987. As in St Lucia, efforts to use it as the language of instruction in schools met opposition.

A different struggle occurred in Puerto Rico where, down to 1948, the island's governors had insisted on English but thereafter all public schools were required to instruct in Spanish, with English taught as a compulsory second language into the first years of university. However, some private schools chose to teach in English and, by the 1970s, there were also a significant number of students – reverse migrants born in the United States – whose first language was English and who needed special tuition. Whereas people came generally to see English as an important element of education, nationalist attitudes politicized the issue by arguing that learning English degraded Puerto Rican identity.

Language determined how people referred to their island identities and allegiances but, most often, when living in the islands, the name of the state was the preferred choice. These names, almost all of them transformed in the period of European colonization, had, by the twentieth century, become familiar and natural. Decolonization in the Caribbean was not followed by wholesale renaming, at any level, in strong contrast to the experience of many other countries around the world. This was true not only for the names of the states and islands, but generally also true for towns and cities, streets and lanes, institutions and individuals.

The literature of the period was often political but also, at the high end, the product of exile and expatriation. The Haitian novelist Jacques Stéphen Alexis, who contributed to the growth of magical realism and thus undermined the contentions of *negritude*, was executed when he sailed from Cuba to Haiti in 1961 hoping to lead a revolt against François Duvalier (himself an ethnologist). Similarly, the poet René Depestre criticized the regime from exile in Cuba and came to contend that *negritude* could be blamed for providing the ideological underpinnings of Duvalierism. Other exiles, notably those from the British Caribbean, were not always explicitly political in their fiction writing. These writers tended, most often – particularly early in the period of decolonization – to choose to live in the old imperial metropolis. Some settled there permanently.

The postwar period saw the building of large air-conditioned cinemas throughout the Caribbean, though open-air theatres remained popular to the end of the twentieth century. Drive-ins were, as elsewhere, a passing fad, matched by soda fountains and other American indulgences of the 1950s and 1960s. Inevitably, most of the films projected were foreign but a few were set in Caribbean landscapes. Hollywood produced a number of island romances, some of them, such as *Island in the Sun* (1956), tackling topics such as interracial sex in problematic paradigms that must have appeared extraordinary to most Caribbean cinema-goers. Films made in India were popular in plantation regions with large Indian communities, decades before Bollywood reached the world.

The teaching of art and drama was often associated with the development of national training schools, particularly in the decolonized empires. Outside these formal institutions, a distinctive style of landscape painting emerged to satisfy a demand from tourists, and these works were often displayed in craft markets amongst carvings, straw hats, and seed beads. An alternative style emerged early among Rastafarians, particularly in painting and carving. In public galleries, works in the Rastafarian style were hung along with paintings coming out of the art schools, the latter applying a variety of modern techniques to local subjects or modernist abstraction. On the streets, graffiti was mixed with sometimes extensive murals and images of local heroes. These types of high and low art jostled for attention and sometimes for purchasers. By the 1980s, tourist markets were also stocked with carvings that offended the respectable – men with large erect penises proudly on display.

The bubbling conflict between high and low culture was, perhaps, most fully expressed in dance, reflecting the way in which the movement of the body had offered a vital mode of resistance since the eighteenth century. The allusions of quadrille, calypso, and rock and roll were left behind by the 1990s and replaced with a raw sexuality that was often condemned as obscene. In this way, the dance of the yard and the street was blended with performances previously confined to clubs, and brought to the public arena. This development may be understood as a fashion but it emerged from longer-term tendencies and had deep roots in the history of the island cultures.

Although the islands were open to outside influences through radio, television, and cinema, they successfully blended foreign styles with local music and dance, and contributed in a major way to the creation of hybrid varieties that went around the world. In Trinidad, the steelband emerged from World War II as a working class instrument, created by recycling oil drums and tuning them to produce a full scale. They appeared first on VE Day in 1945, then entered Carnival and developed into orchestras that performed internationally. More important on the world stage was the Jamaican musician and singer Bob Marley, who emerged around 1968. His music came to symbolize the situation of the poor and the oppressed around the world, and contributed to the global reach of dreadlocks and the music-dance genre reggae. Reggae had its roots in earlier Jamaican styles of the 1950s and 1960s, notably ska and rock-steady, and drew on rhythm and blues, but it was an authentic music and Marley, a unique voice.

Other sounds created in the Caribbean after 1945 seemed more ephemeral, though the calypso of Trinidad also had wide influence through the splendour of Carnival, and the Cuban big bands of the 1950s had visibility. In the 1990s, the Buena Vista Social Club provided a musical example of the Cuban revolution as museum culture. Older forms of street dance and display, such as Junkanu, declined in some islands whereas Carnival prospered. Thus, there was evidence of regional interaction as well as a vibrant nationalism found in, for example, the Ballet Folklorico of Cuba and the National Dance Company of Barbados. These companies made much of their authentic creole character yet represented the high end of dance culture in the islands, a studied style that contrasted with the forms favoured by populist performers.

Like music and dance, sport became increasingly public and national in its performance. Poor people continued to play games that required minimal or improvised equipment and surfaces, but the rapid growth of the middle class, together with exposure to international standards, pushed sport into specialized arenas and raised the bar of expectations. The development of school and university infrastructures contributed substantially to the stock of playing fields and the coaching of teams. Sports that, before 1945, had been played only by men were increasingly taken up by women. Class and colour remained influential in various ways down to the 1960s – for example, participation in the more expensive sports such as polo, tennis and yachting, and in selection for roles of captaincy and management in team sports – but raw ability tended to win out after decolonization.

Unlike music and dance, the Caribbean was not an innovator in sport. No new sports were invented in the region after 1945, and the same was broadly true worldwide. Popularity waxed and waned but the overall pattern had been set long before and rules that governed games were rarely tampered with. As in the period before 1945, certain sports continued to be regarded as indicators of identity and generally confined to territories with a particular imperial tradition. For example, cricket remained a sport played by men and, to a lesser extent, women from the British connection. It also had an active role in drawing together the territories within the Caribbean, with a West Indian team selected from across the region sent abroad to play against other nations, such as England, Australia, New Zealand, India, Pakistan, Sri Lanka, and South Africa (with an interval during the period of protest against apartheid). The newly independent states also played against one another as national teams but the inclusive West Indies cricket team remained intact after the collapse of the Federation.

The territories that did not play cricket often played baseball but this was most common in the Dominican Republic, Puerto Rico, and Cuba. Baseball remained popular after 1959 in spite of its American associations, but Cuba then emerged as a leading nation in a wide range of sports, from athletics to volleyball. Interest in cricket waned in the Bahamas, on the fringes of British cultural influence, after about 1970, but some players moved on to the United States to join the ranks of the baseballers. Basketball, with its roots traceable to the ball game of the Taínos, also became popular. Baseball and basketball were particularly attractive because scholarships could be won that took aspirants to U.S. colleges. In some territories, basketball was joined by netball, a version played only by women. Few Caribbean states identified with a specific sport, though the Bahamas did, in 1993, formally declare sloop sailing its national sport.

Most popular of all games in the Caribbean was soccer, which became known in this period as "the world game", with a World Cup series attracting more attention than the Olympic Games. Soccer had the advantage that it required only a round ball and a relatively flat playing surface. In territories where other varieties of football survived after 1945, soccer quickly moved to dominance. No Caribbean team won the World Cup, but qualifying was, in itself, cause for celebration. A united Caribbean team might seem to have better chances, but the federal model offered by West Indies cricket was not followed in any other sport. Caribbean people gained greater international visibility in individual performances, notably some branches of athletics, starting with the Olympic Games of 1948. By the beginning of the twenty-first century, the sprints – the short running races – came to be dominated by Caribbean men and women, who outran even their better-off North American cousins.

Spectators became much more numerous and geographically scattered, particularly as a consequence of television. This widening of the audience for sport enabled a more active nationalism that meshed with the diasporas of the period beginning in 1945. Thus, players of Caribbean birth or descent became increasingly visible and identifiable as members of national European and North American teams in basketball, baseball, and soccer, for example. This was matched by a broader internationalization of sport in which players were increasingly recruited to professional teams, signing contracts for sums that far exceeded anything they were able to earn as local Caribbean players. This gap sometimes created conflict between players and Caribbean national team managers, when players held out for rewards competitive with international standards. The commercial motive and the enhanced audiences offered through television occasionally encouraged new versions of games, as in abbreviated cricket matches played over a day or half-day rather than four or five days, which demanded the patience of the true believer.

In Haiti, the constitution of 1950 recognized all religions and cults but allowed special privileges to the Roman Catholic church, as established in the nineteenth century. Papa Doc Duvalier was more hostile to the church and took Vodun as his personal cult. He expelled a series of prelates and, in 1961, was excommunicated. Duvalier's campaign to be made president-for-life in 1964 was rooted in religious symbolism, and he had himself painted as God's chosen one. As part of his contest with the Roman Catholic church, Duvalier welcomed Protestant groups, particularly the purportedly apolitical evangelical varieties. By 1966, however, Duvalier had made peace with the church and the Vatican accepted an indigenous ecclesiastical hierarchy. The constitution of 1987 rescinded legislation against Vodun.

In the Dominican Republic, where more than 95 percent professed Roman Catholicism, the church traditionally sought protection by making alliances with the rich and powerful. For many years, it failed to speak out against the atrocities of Trujillo. It finally found its voice in time to protest the mass arrests of 1960 but became as divided as the rest of the country during the civil war of the later 1960s. Its influence became eroded, as indicated, for example, by programs introduced by Balaguer to promote family planning through state agencies and to liberalize the divorce laws. As in Haiti, Protestant missions made inroads.

American Pentecostalism in its various branches extended its reach rapidly after 1945. In Jamaica, for example, older enthusiastic churches such as the Baptists declined steeply after 1945, displaced by even greater growth in adherence to the Church of God, Seventh Day Adventist, and Pentecostal versions of Christianity. By the 1980s, the Church of God claimed the largest congregation, about 20 percent of the Jamaican population. A more difficult entry faced the Church of the Latter Day Saints, who, until the 1980s, doubted the capacity of black people to enter the kingdom of heaven. Churches of many varieties were spread densely across Jamaica, though more than 20 percent of the people declared no religious affiliation.

The ungodly were represented most boldly by Cuba. Even before the revolution, Cubans were recognized as the least religious people of Latin America. Syncretic religions – notably Santería – rooted in African cosmologies persisted and Protestant churches had made inroads beginning in the later twentieth century, but the Catholic church retained its privileged position. In the first decade after 1959, all forms of religion were placed under scrutiny but only those institutions that proved themselves obstacles to social reconstruction were sanctioned. By the mid-1970s, Afro-Cuban religions had been accepted officially as elements of national culture. What Castro looked for was sincere practical Christianity rather than a sudden interest in social issues that had not previously concerned the church. Even without harsh treatment, acknowledged membership of the Catholic church dropped dramatically, from 90 percent in 1960 to just 39 percent in 1983. Practicing Christians became less than 2 percent of the population. In order to halt this seeming collapse in faith and in the context of contemporary liberation theology movements, the church entered dialogue with the revolutionary government, and a Christian–Marxist compromise was reached by the end of the twentieth century. A Marxist did not need to be an atheist but an active Christian or Jew could not hold membership of the Communist Party and open evangelization was restricted. Jehovah's Witnesses and Seventh Day Adventists were watched closely as fundamentally counterrevolutionary. Reconciliation was symbolized in the visit of Pope Paul II to Cuba in 1998.

Outsiders and exiles, and people born and living in the islands, sometimes called the Caribbean a paradise. Others thought it a living hell, a place in which they had been put against their will and in which they struggled for bread. The uprooted sometimes saw paradise elsewhere on earth – in Ethiopia, perhaps – but found themselves in Babylonian captivity. The distribution of material things was far from equitable and many lived in poverty. Faith in a theological heaven brought comfort.

Except for Haitians, by the beginning of the twenty-first century, most Caribbean people could expect to live long earthly lives. In 2007, calculations derived from the UN Human Development Index showed that only one country in the world had achieved "sustainable development", combining an acceptable carbon footprint with decent levels of life expectancy, per capita gross domestic product, and adult literacy. This was Cuba. Most countries of the world, including the other Caribbean states, had either low levels of human development or made high demands on global resources through consumption. It was an earthly achievement of sorts, a creole Caribbean achievement, but not one owned even by all Caribbean people.

8

Canoe, Caravel, Container Ship

Set in the sea, off the beaten track of early migration routes, the islands of the Caribbean waited long for the beginning of their human history. When people did eventually come to inhabit the islands, almost all arrived in boats carefully crafted to cross the water. Even when it became possible to fly, few of those who travelled in planes became residents and, indeed, the plane was used much more often as a machine in which to escape. Three sea-crossing technologies – canoe, caravel, and container ship – serve as symbols of the main periods of Caribbean history. The last – the container ship – defines a short period, the past fifty years. The caravel stands for a period ten times as long, the 500 years from 1492. The canoe accounts for another multiple of ten, the previous 5,000 years or more. Each of these vessels carried with them whole cultures, representing an increasingly global cargo.

For thousands of years, people paddled canoes to move from one island to the next, to circumnavigate islands, and to get to and from the American mainland. They knew no other way. It was virtually impossible for them to develop connections with a world wider than the archipelago and its continental hinterlands. This did not limit the possibility of building a population and a civilization but the effect was to tie the island cultures to those known from the mainland and these continental foundations were essential to developing an indigenous response to the natural environment of the islands.

Particularly during the Ceramic Age (2500 BP to AD 1492), the islands served as an effective chain, closely integrated into a connected system of communication and exchange, loosely shackled to the mainland. The Lesser Antilles, in particular, became a kind of superhighway along which people, goods, and ideas travelled rapidly in both directions, moving through a marine landscape that permitted few diversions or possibilities of unwanted adventure. This diminished the perception of insularity as an enforced isolation, whereas the relative speed of movement across water – compared with the progress of burdened walkers on land – enabled continuous interaction and creative stimulus. The canoe kept the people close to their origins and close to shore.

The caravel, with a crew no more numerous than the paddlers of a large canoe, used the wind to carry it across wide oceans, speedily and without need of fuel. It was the vessel of choice for early modern European imperialism. Without the caravel, the voyages of Columbus could not have happened the way they did. It was the caravel and its cousins that brought to the islands the people, plants, animals, and technologies that completely transformed their cultural economy. These ships remained small for centuries but there were many of them and it was necessary only to bring small samples – in the manner of Noah's ark – to initiate the growth of substantial populations. Just a few oranges and a few pigs were enough to change the landscape, and to do so rapidly. The speed of the caravel enabled it to circle the globe, bringing things to the Caribbean islands from almost everywhere. The result was a creolized landscape and environment, made up of all these elements but constructed into something truly unique and naturalized. Imported elements were part of the picture, but the essence of the Caribbean world was created in the islands themselves.

European imperialism, carried in the caravel, contrasted strongly with the pattern of colonization followed by the first peoples of the Caribbean. The European states picked out what they could in competition with their rivals, like shooting from a distance at a line of targets. This was a process that nurtured a greater insularity, with people in neighbouring islands speaking distinct languages and living under different systems of law and government. Slavery could persist on one island while it had been abolished on its neighbour, and the metropolitan link might remain firm on one while its neighbours had political independence. Allegiances and communication came to follow imperial links, associated with the intelligibility of languages, so that "the English-speaking Caribbean" seemed to make sense even after political independence.

Only after World War II did the fundamentals of this pattern of shipping and exchange undergo a thorough revolution, with the invention of the container ship and its counterparts, the tanker and the jumbo jet. The container ship was a key symbol and tool of globalization. It made it cheap to transport finished manufactured goods, as well as food and other perishables, all around the world. Local production and local tastes came under great pressure as a result. The islands found it increasingly difficult to compete. Food systems were overturned, with imported wheat, rice, and corn displacing the roots and fruits on which they had so long depended. The competition was comprehensive. Small states, particularly islands, typically lack a diversity of resources and therefore are dependent on world markets for much of what their inhabitants wish to consume, the products of the modern world economy.

The outcome of this recent history, still being worked out, is a relocation of the Caribbean in the world and a rethinking of what it is to be an islander and a Caribbean person. These changes occurred in parallel with the achievement of independent sovereign status by most of the region's territories, in addition to the Cuban revolution, and mass migration to North America and Europe. The movement of people became disconnected from shipping. By the end of the twentieth century, only refugees got into boats hoping to emigrate. The vast majority of migrants and transient residents then travelled almost exclusively by plane, their journeys characterized by movement through a series of "non-places" – the linear conduits created by airport and airplane. Becoming part of a globalized world had both benefits and hazards. In this complex system, the container ship stood as symbol of standardization and homogeneity. Stacked high with metal boxes, of standard shape and size, the container gave no clue to its contents. Opened, the container might disgorge a cornucopia of goodies or prove to be Pandora's box.

Although the small nation-state had much about which to be proud in its new-found sovereignty, it might equally find itself overwhelmed by the cargo unloaded from the container ship and vulnerable to the whims of markets and global agreements that suited other, larger, more powerful states that could wipe out the competitiveness of a carefully cultivated crop or service overnight. Microstates were even more vulnerable under these conditions and, indeed, as elsewhere around the globe, truly small islands often found it a struggle to stave off depopulation. Those islands that were flat as well as small took the brunt of hurricanes and storms, which increased in frequency and intensity as a result of the global pattern of climate change that created a warmer, wetter region.

On the other hand, globally, there is no straightforward correlation between the size of states and their relative prosperity. This is equally true of the Caribbean itself, with the largest of the region's states by no means the most prosperous. Smallness has advantages for transformation, whether physical or cultural. Small states can prosper so long as they are effectively integrated into the world economy. They tend to benefit by international free trade and suffer under protectionism. But the cost of government is inevitably disproportionate and it is this that makes integration and even annexation appear attractive in times of stress.

The merging of islands into a single unitary state continued to hold attractions for Caribbean politicians but, apart from any geopolitical difficulty, the extended history of separatism and colonial political conflict and competition that infected the Caribbean made such a model an improbable possibility. The colonial experience of the Caribbean contrasted strongly, for example, with that of the Indonesian archipelago, where a single European nation, the Netherlands, had effectively created Indonesia as a political unit by annexing scattered islands and states into the Dutch East Indies. It is an interesting question to ask what might have occurred if the Caribbean had had a similar colonial history. It was not an impossibility. What might have been the outcome if Spain had maintained interest and hegemony throughout the islands?

These three periods of Caribbean history, symbolized by maritime technologies, applied to all of the islands, whatever their size or location, but the impact was not everywhere the same. In the first period – canoe – people spread throughout the islands to eventually colonize all of them and form dense populations, but the most complex societies developed in the larger of the islands, the Greater Antilles. The second age, that of the caravel, demonstrated the insidious way in which small samples of animals and plants could reproduce to destroy existing cultivations and promote the deadly spread of disease. The demographic catastrophe that followed was greatest in the same large islands, the Greater Antilles, but the caravel and its allies proved ideal in shifting the population and economic focal point to the smaller islands of the eastern Caribbean. This was a product of the sugar revolution, which brought millions of enslaved people across the Atlantic from Africa. In the middle of the eighteenth century, the Greater Antilles accounted for merely 40 percent of the total Caribbean population, and they regained their 90 percent dominance (lost around 1520) only in the age of the container ship, the age of mass migration out of the islands.

It may appear a paradox that islands as beautiful, as paradisiacal, as those of the Caribbean were in the very long term not particularly attractive as places in which to live. Problems of accessibility initially situated the islands beyond the human horizon and, in consequence, the first people to enter the Caribbean came late in the course of human history. The second wave of colonization and migration, in the turbulent wake of Columbus, included a very large proportion of people who did not want to be there and came to the islands as forced migrants. Those who made vast profits from the exploitation of the labour of these unwilling migrants, the planters and merchants, often, themselves, demonstrated no great desire to live in the islands. Many of them became absentees. Further, when the inflow of forced migration came to an end, the next movement was often an emigration out of the Caribbean rather than a willing inflow. By the middle of the twentieth century, this outflow of people had become a flood, a diaspora.

Throughout history, almost all of the people who migrated to the Caribbean islands, whether willingly or unwillingly, had their origins in continental places – the Americas, Africa, Europe, and Asia. Before they came to the islands, with the exception of the British, all of these immigrants knew only places with vast terrestrial hinterlands. They had to learn to think of themselves as islanders. Those who eventually left the islands in the modern diaspora typically made a similar choice, in reverse, by migrating to continental states, though rarely to the places from whence their ancestors had come. At the same time, the people who stayed had no feeling of inferiority from the fact of their islander status. Indeed, especially in the larger places where the sea is often hidden from sight and there is no intervisibility to other islands, the people rarely referred to themselves as islanders. From the earliest times, the people who came to live in the islands of the Caribbean remained connected – psychologically and spiritually, if not always physically – to their continental roots. Similarly, those who fled the islands in the wake of revolution, decolonization, and ecological disaster retained their identities and their loyalties. They, as well as the people who chose never to leave, thought of their islands, large or small, as worlds in themselves – not so much microcosms as continents in their own way for those who inhabited them.

SUGGESTIONS FOR FURTHER READING

The history of the Caribbean has been a fertile field for writers since the sixteenth century, with a specialized literature in many related disciplines developing strongly over the past fifty years, in the leading languages of the region. An extensive list appears in B. W. Higman (ed), *General History of the Caribbean, Volume VI: Methodology and Historiography of the Caribbean* (Paris: UNESCO Publishing/London: Macmillan, 1999). Works included in the present selection are confined to books in English, all of them first published since 1980. The readings are organized to match the periods studied in the chapters of this book. Some works do not fit this chronology neatly, but each of them is listed in only one place, located in its dominant period. A number of general works provide guides to longer periods and broader subjects.

GENERAL WORKS

Hilary McD. Beckles, *A History of Barbados from Amerindian Settlement to Nation-State* (Cambridge: Cambridge University Press, 1990)

Bridget Brereton, *A History of Modern Trinidad 1783–1962* (Kingston: Heinemann, 1981)

Alan Cambeira, *Quisqueya la Bella: The Dominican Republic in Historical and Cultural Perspective* (Armonk, NY: M. E. Sharpe, 1997)

Michael Craton and Gail Saunders, *Islanders in the Stream: A History of the Bahamian People* (Athens, GA: University of Georgia Press, 1992 [volume 1], 1998 [volume 2])

L. Antonio Curet, Shannon Lee Dawdy, and Gabino La Rosa Corzo (eds), *Dialogues in Cuban Archaeology* (Tuscaloosa: University of Alabama Press, 2005)

James L. Dietz, *Economic History of Puerto Rico: Institutional Change and Capitalist Development* (Princeton, NJ: Princeton University Press, 1986)

P. C. Emmer, *The Dutch Slave Trade, 1500–1850* (New York: Berghahn Books, 2006)

Reinaldo Funes Monzote, *From Rainforest to Cane Field in Cuba: An Environmental History since 1492* (Chapel Hill: University of North Carolina Press, 2008)

J. H. Galloway, *The Sugar Cane Industry: An Historical Geography from Its Origins to 1914* (Cambridge: Cambridge University Press, 1989)

Malena Kuss (ed), *Music in Latin America and the Caribbean: An Encyclopedic History* (Austin: University of Texas Press, 2004–2007)

J. R. McNeill, *Mosquito Empires: Ecology and War in the Greater Caribbean, 1620–1914* (Cambridge: Cambridge University Press, 2010)

Sidney W. Mintz, *Sweetness and Power: The Place of Sugar in Modern History* (New York: Viking, 1985)

Arturo Morales Carrión, *Puerto Rico: A Political and Cultural History* (New York: W.W. Norton and Co., 1983)

Karen Fay O'Loughlin and James F. Lander, *Caribbean Tsunamis: A 500-Year History from 1498–1998* (Dordrecht: Kluwer Academic Publishers, 2003)

Louis A. Pérez, Jr., *Cuba: Between Reform and Revolution* (New York: Oxford University Press, 1988)

Bonham C. Richardson, *The Caribbean in the Wider World, 1492–1992: A Regional Geography* (Cambridge: Cambridge University Press, 1992)

David Watts, *The West Indies: Patterns of Development, Culture and Environmental Change since 1492* (Cambridge: Cambridge University Press, 1987)

Charles A. Woods and Florence E. Sergile (eds), *Biogeography of the West Indies: Patterns and Perspectives* (Boca Raton, LA: CRC Press, 2001, second edition)

Before 1492

P. Allsworth-Jones, *Pre-Columbian Jamaica* (Tuscaloosa: University of Alabama Press, 2008)

Lesley-Gail Atkinson (ed), *The Earliest Inhabitants: The Dynamics of the Jamaican Taíno* (Mona, Jamaica: University of the West Indies Press, 2006)

L. Antonio Curet, *Caribbean Paleodemography: Population, Culture History, and Sociopolitical Processes in Ancient Puerto Rico* (Tuscaloosa: University of Alabama Press, 2005)

André Delpuech and Corinne L. Hofman (eds), *Late Ceramic Age Societies in the Eastern Caribbean* (Oxford: Archaeopress, 2004)

William F. Keegan, *The People Who Discovered Columbus: The Prehistory of the Bahamas* (Gainesville: University Press of Florida, 1992)

William F. Keegan, *Taíno Indian Myth and Practice: The Arrival of the Stranger King* (Gainesville: University Press of Florida, 2007)

Ramón Dacal Moure and Manuel Rivero de la Calle, *Art and Archaeology of Pre-Columbian Cuba* (Pittsburgh, PA: University of Pittsburgh Press, 1996)

Lee A. Newsom and Elizabeth S. Wing, *On Land and Sea: Native American Uses of Biological Resources in the West Indies* (Tuscaloosa: University of Alabama Press, 2004)

Basil A. Reid, *Myths and Realities of Caribbean History* (Tuscaloosa: University of Alabama Press, 2009)

Irving Rouse, *The Tainos: Rise and Decline of the People Who Greeted Columbus* (New Haven, CT: Yale University Press, 1992)

Peter E. Siegel (ed), *Ancient Borinquen: Archaeology and Ethnohistory of Native Puerto Rico* (Tuscaloosa: University of Alabama Press, 2005)

Antonio M. Stevens-Arroyo, *Cave of the Jagua: The Mythological World of the Taínos* (Albuquerque: University of New Mexico Press, 1988)

Jalil Sued-Badillo (ed), *General History of the Caribbean, Volume I: Autochthonous Societies* (Paris: UNESCO Publishing/London: Macmillan, 2003)

Thomas M. Whitmore and B.L. Turner II, *Cultivated Landscapes of Middle America on the Eve of Conquest* (Oxford: Oxford University Press, 2001)

Samuel M. Wilson, *The Archaeology of the Caribbean* (Cambridge: Cambridge University Press, 2007)

Samuel M. Wilson, *Hispaniola: Caribbean Chiefdoms in the Age of Columbus* (Tuscaloosa: University of Alabama Press, 1990)

Samuel M. Wilson (ed), *The Indigenous People of the Caribbean* (Gainesville: University Press of Florida, 1997)

1492–1630

David Abulafia, *The Discovery of Mankind: Atlantic Encounters in the Age of Columbus* (New Haven, CT: Yale University Press, 2008)

Kenneth R. Andrews, *Trade, Plunder and Settlement: Maritime Enterprise and the Genesis of the British Empire, 1480–1630* (Cambridge: Cambridge University Press, 1984)

Kathleen Deagan and José María Cruxent, *Columbus's Outpost among the Taínos: Spain and America at La Isabela, 1493–1498* (New Haven, CT: Yale University Press, 2002)

Pieter C. Emmer (ed), *General History of the Caribbean, Volume II: The Caribbean in the Long Sixteenth Century* (Paris: UNESCO Publishing/London: Macmillan, 1999)

Felipe Fernández-Armesto, *1492: The Year Our World Began* (London: Bloomsbury, 2010)

Alejandro de la Fuente, *Havana and the Atlantic in the Sixteenth Century* (Chapel Hill: University of North Carolina Press, 2008)

Peter Hulme, *Colonial Encounters: Europe and the Native Caribbean, 1492–1797* (London: Methuen, 1986)

Francisco Morales Padrón, *Spanish Jamaica* (Kingston: Ian Randle Publishers, 2003)

William D. Phillips, Jr., and Carla Rahn Phillips, *The Worlds of Christopher Columbus* (Cambridge: Cambridge University Press, 1992)

Nicolás Wey Gómez, *The Tropics of Empire: Why Columbus Sailed South to the Indies* (Cambridge, MA: MIT Press, 2008)

1630–1770

Philip P. Boucher, *France and the American Tropics to 1700: Tropics of Discontent?* (Baltimore, MD: Johns Hopkins University Press, 2008)

Trevor Burnard, *Mastery, Tyranny, and Desire: Thomas Thistlewood and His Slaves in the Anglo-Jamaican World* (Chapel Hill: University of North Carolina Press, 2004)

Barbara Bush, *Slave Women in Caribbean Society, 1650–1832* (Bloomington: Indiana University Press, 1989)

Doris Garraway, *The Libertine Colony: Creolization in the Early French Caribbean* (Durham, NC: Duke University Press, 2005)

David Barry Gaspar, *Bondmen and Rebels: A Study of Master–Slave Relations in Antigua* (Baltimore, MD: Johns Hopkins University Press, 1985)

Errol Hill, *The Jamaican Stage 1655–1900: Profile of a Colonial Theatre* (Amherst: University of Massachusetts Press, 1992)

Karen Ordahl Kupperman, *Providence Island, 1630–1641: The Other Puritan Colony* (Cambridge: Cambridge University Press, 1993)

Jon Latimer, *Buccaneers of the Caribbean: How Piracy Forged an Empire* (Cambridge, MA: Harvard University Press, 2009)

Bernard Moitt, *Women and Slavery in the French Antilles, 1635–1848* (Bloomington: Indiana University Press, 2001)

Matthew Mulcahy, *Hurricanes and Society in the British Greater Caribbean, 1624–1783* (Baltimore, MD: Johns Hopkins University Press, 2006)

Robert L. Paquette and Stanley L. Engerman (eds), *The Lesser Antilles in the Age of European Expansion* (Gainesville: University Press of Florida, 1996)

Stuart B. Schwartz (ed), *Tropical Babylons: Sugar and the Making of the Atlantic World, 1450–1680* (Chapel Hill: University of North Carolina Press, 2004)

Richard B. Sheridan, *Doctors and Slaves: A Medical and Demographic History of Slavery in the British West Indies, 1680–1834* (Cambridge: Cambridge University Press, 1985)

S. D. Smith, *Slavery, Family and Gentry Capitalism in the British Atlantic: The World of the Lascelles, 1648–1834* (Cambridge: Cambridge University Press, 2006)

Karol K. Weaver, *Medical Revolutionaries: The Enslaved Healers of Eighteenth-Century Saint Domingue* (Urbana: University of Illinois Press, 2006)

1770–1870

Laird W. Bergad, *Coffee and the Growth of Agrarian Capitalism in Nineteenth-Century Puerto Rico* (Princeton, NJ: Princeton University Press, 1983)

Steeve O. Buckridge, *The Language of Dress: Resistance and Accommodation in Jamaica, 1760–1890* (Mona, Jamaica: University of the West Indies Press, 2004)

Jorge Luis Chinea, *Race and Labor in the Hispanic Caribbean: The West Indian Immigrant Worker Experience in Puerto Rico, 1800–1850* (Gainesville: University Press of Florida, 2005)

Edward L. Cox, *Free Coloreds in the Slave Societies of St Kitts and Grenada, 1763–1833* (Knoxville: University of Tennessee Press, 1984)

Laurent Dubois, *A Colony of Citizens: Revolution and Slave Emancipation in the French Caribbean, 1787–1804* (Chapel Hill, NC: Omohundro Institute of Early American History and Culture, 2004)

Laurent Dubois, *Avengers of the New World: The Story of the Haitian Revolution* (Cambridge, MA: Harvard University Press, 2004)

Carolyn E. Fick, *The Making of Haiti: The Saint Domingue Revolution from Below* (Knoxville: University of Tennessee Press, 1990)

Luis A. Figueroa, *Sugar, Slavery, and Freedom in Nineteenth-Century Puerto Rico* (Chapel Hill: University of North Carolina Press, 2005)

John D. Garrigus, *Before Haiti: Race and Citizenship in French Saint-Domingue* (New York: Palgrave Macmillan, 2006)

David Patrick Geggus, *Slavery, War, and Revolution: The British Occupation of St Domingue, 1793–1798* (New York: Oxford University Press, 1981)

Neville A. T. Hall, *Slave Society in the Danish West Indies: St Thomas, St John and St Croix* (Mona, Jamaica: University of the West Indies Press, 1992)

Gad J. Heuman, *"The Killing Time": The Morant Bay Rebellion in Jamaica* (London: Macmillan, 1994)

B. W. Higman, *Slave Populations of the British Caribbean, 1807–1834* (Baltimore, MD: Johns Hopkins University Press, 1984)

Howard Johnson, *The Bahamas from Slavery to Servitude, 1783–1933* (Gainesville: University Presses of Florida, 1996)

Franklin W. Knight (ed), *General History of the Caribbean, Volume III: The Slave Societies of the Caribbean* (Paris: UNESCO Publishing/London: Macmillan, 1997)

Allan J. Kuethe, *Cuba, 1753–1815: Crown, Military, and Society* (Knoxville: University of Tennessee Press, 1986)

Gelien Matthews, *Caribbean Slave Revolts and the British Abolitionist Movement* (Baton Rouge: Louisiana State University Press, 2006)

James E. McClellan III, *Colonialism and Science: Saint Domingue in the Old Regime* (Baltimore, MD: Johns Hopkins University Press, 1992)

Robert L. Paquette, *Sugar Is Made with Blood: The Conspiracy of "La Escalera" and the Conflict Between Empires Over Slavery in Cuba* (Middletown, CT: Wesleyan University Press, 1988)

Diana Paton, *No Bond But the Law: Punishment, Race, and Gender in Jamaican State Formation, 1780–1870* (Durham, NC: Duke University Press, 2004)

Félix V. Matos Rodríguez, *Women and Urban Change in San Juan, Puerto Rico, 1820–1868* (Gainesville: University Press of Florida, 1999)

Francisco A. Scarano, *Sugar and Slavery in Puerto Rico: The Plantation Economy of Ponce, 1800–1850* (Madison: University of Wisconsin Press, 1984)

Verene A. Shepherd, *Livestock, Sugar and Slavery: Contested Terrain in Colonial Jamaica* (Kingston: Ian Randle Publishers, 2009)

Verene A. Shepherd (ed), *Slavery Without Sugar: Diversity in Caribbean Economy and Society since the 17th Century* (Gainesville: University Press of Florida, 2002)

Arthur L. Stinchcombe, *Sugar Island Slavery in the Age of Enlightenment: The Political Economy of the Caribbean World* (Princeton, NJ: Princeton University Press, 1995)

Alvin O. Thompson, *Flight to Freedom: African Runaways and Maroons in the Americas* (Mona, Jamaica: University of the West Indies Press, 2006)

1870–1945

César J. Ayala, *American Sugar Kingdom: The Plantation Economy of the Spanish Caribbean 1898–1934* (Chapel Hill: University of North Carolina Press, 1999)

Fitzroy André Baptiste, *War, Cooperation, and Conflict: The European Possessions in the Caribbean, 1939–1945* (New York: Greenwood Press, 1988)

Patrick Bryan, *The Jamaican People, 1880–1902: Race, Class and Social Control* (London: Macmillan Caribbean, 1991)

Carl Campbell, *The Young Colonials: A Social History of Education in Trinidad and Tobago, 1834–1939* (Kingston: The Press, University of the West Indies, 1996)

J. Michael Dash, *Literature and Ideology in Haiti, 1915–1961* (London: Macmillan, 1981)

Alan Dye, *Cuban Sugar in the Age of Mass Production: Technology and the Economics of the Sugar Central, 1899–1929* (Stanford, CA: Stanford University Press, 1998)

Ada Ferrer, *Insurgent Cuba: Race, Nation, and Revolution, 1868–1898* (Chapel Hill: University of North Carolina Press, 1999)

David Healy, *Drive to Hegemony: The United States in the Caribbean, 1898–1917* (Madison: University of Wisconsin Press, 1988)

H. Hoetink, *The Dominican People 1850–1900: Notes for a Historical Sociology* (Baltimore, MD: Johns Hopkins University Press, 1982)

Thomas C. Holt, *The Problem of Freedom: Race, Labor, and Politics in Jamaica and Britain, 1832–1938* (Baltimore, MD: Johns Hopkins University Press, 1992)

Teresita Martínez-Vergne, *Capitalism in Colonial Puerto Rico: Central San Vicente in the Late Nineteenth Century* (Gainesville: University Press of Florida, 1992)

Brian L. Moore and Michele A. Johnson, *Neither Led nor Driven: Contesting British Cultural Imperialism in Jamaica, 1865–1920* (Kingston: University of the West Indies Press, 2004)

Manuel Moreno Fraginals, Frank Moya Pons, and Stanley L. Engerman (eds), *Between Slavery and Free Labor: The Spanish-Speaking Caribbean in the Nineteenth Century* (Baltimore, MD: Johns Hopkins University Press, 1985)

Louis A. Pérez, Jr., *Cuba Between Empires, 1878–1902* (Pittsburgh, PA: University of Pittsburgh Press, 1983)

Louis A. Pérez, Jr., *Cuba Under the Platt Amendment, 1902–1934* (Pittsburgh, PA: University of Pittsburgh Press, 1986)

Brenda Gayle Plummer, *Haiti and the Great Powers, 1902–1915* (Baton Rouge: Louisiana State University Press, 1988)

Bonham C. Richardson, *Caribbean Migrants: Environment and Human Survival on St Kitts and Nevis* (Knoxville: University of Tennessee Press, 1983)

Eric Paul Roorda, *The Dictator Next Door: The Good Neighbor Policy and the Trujillo Regime in the Dominican Republic, 1930–1945* (Durham, NC: Duke University Press, 1998)

Rebecca J. Scott, *Slave Emancipation in Cuba: The Transition to Free Labor, 1860–1899* (Princeton, NJ: Princeton University Press, 1985)

Verene A. Shepherd, *Transients to Settlers: The Experience of Indians in Jamaica 1845–1950* (Leeds: Peepal Tree Books, 1994)

Matthew J. Smith, *Red and Black in Haiti: Radicalism, Conflict, and Political Change, 1934–1957* (Chapel Hill: University of North Carolina Press, 2009)

Michel-Rolph Trouillot, *Peasants and Capital: Dominica in the World Economy* (Baltimore, MD: Johns Hopkins University Press, 1988)

Oscar Zanetti and Alejandro García, *Sugar and Railroads: A Cuban History, 1837–1959* (Chapel Hill: University of North Carolina Press, 1998)

After 1945

Robert Aldrich and John Connell, *The Last Colonies* (Cambridge: Cambridge University Press, 1998)

José Alvarez, *Cuba's Agricultural Sector* (Gainesville: University Press of Florida, 2004)

Charles D. Ameringer, *The Cuban Democratic Experience: The Auténtico Years, 1944–1952* (Gainesville: University Press of Florida, 2000)

Frank Argote-Freyre, *Fulgencio Batista: From Revolutionary to Strongman* (New Brunswick, NJ: Rutgers University Press, 2006)

Hilary McD. Beckles and Brian Stoddart (eds), *Liberation Cricket: West Indies Cricket Culture* (Kingston: Ian Randle Publishers, 1995)

Antonio Benítez-Rojo, *The Repeating Island: The Caribbean and the Postmodern Perspective* (Durham, NC: Duke University Press, 1992)

Bridget Brereton (ed), *General History of the Caribbean, Volume V: The Caribbean in the Twentieth Century* (Paris: UNESCO Publishing/London: Macmillan, 2004)

Carl Campbell, *Endless Education: Main Currents in the Education System of Modern Trinidad and Tobago, 1939–1986* (Kingston: The Press, University of the West Indies, 1997)

Barry Chevannes, *Rastafari: Roots and Ideology* (New York: Syracuse University Press, 1995)

Barry Chevannes (ed), *Rastafari and Other African-Caribbean Worldviews* (London: Macmillan, 1998)

Peter Clegg, *The Caribbean Banana Trade: From Colonialism to Globalization* (New York: Palgrave Macmillan, 2002)

Sergio Díaz-Briquets and Jorge Pérez-López, *Conquering Nature: The Environmental Legacy of Socialism in Cuba* (Pittsburgh, PA: University of Pittsburgh Press, 2000)

Samuel Farber, *The Origins of the Cuban Revolution Reconsidered* (Chapel Hill: University of North Carolina Press, 2006)

Obika Gray, *Demeaned but Empowered: The Social Power of the Urban Poor in Jamaica* (Kingston: University of the West Indies Press, 2004)

Jorge Heine (ed), *A Revolution Aborted: The Lessons of Grenada* (Pittsburgh, PA: University of Pittsburgh Press, 1990)

Kamala Kempadoo (ed), *Sun, Sex, and Gold: Tourism and Sex Work in the Caribbean* (Lanham, MD: Rowman and Littlefield Publishers, Inc., 1999)

John M. Kirk, *Between God and the Party: Religion and Politics in Revolutionary Cuba* (Tampa: University of South Florida Press, 1989)

Alan M. Klein, *Sugarball: The American Game, the Dominican Dream* (New Haven, CT: Yale University Press, 1991)

Hal Klepak, *Cuba's Military 1990–2005: Revolutionary Soldiers during Counter-Revolutionary Times* (New York: Palgrave Macmillan, 2005)

Franklin W. Knight and Teresita Martínez-Vergne (eds), *Contemporary Caribbean Cultures and Societies in a Global Context* (Mona, Jamaica: University of the West Indies Press, 2005)

Franklin W. Knight and Colin A. Palmer (eds), *The Modern Caribbean* (Chapel Hill: University of North Carolina Press, 1989)

Christian Krohn-Hansen, *Political Authoritarianism in the Dominican Republic* (New York: Palgrave Macmillan, 2009)

Kathleen E. A. Monteith, *Depression to Decolonization: Barclays Bank (DCO) in the West Indies, 1926–1962* (Kingston: University of the West Indies Press, 2008)

Jason C. Parker, *Brother's Keeper: The United States, Race, and Empire in the British Caribbean, 1937–1962* (Oxford: Oxford University Press, 2008)

Louis A. Pérez Jr., *On Becoming Cuban: Identity, Nationality, and Culture* (Chapel Hill: University of North Carolina Press, 1999)

Brenda Gayle Plummer, *Haiti and the United States: The Psychological Moment* (Athens: University of Georgia Press, 1992)

Alejandro Portes, Carlos Dore-Cabral and Patricia Landolt (eds), *The Urban Caribbean: Transition to the New Global Economy* (Baltimore, MD: Johns Hopkins University Press, 1997)

Robert B. Potter, David Barker, Dennis Conway and Thomas Klak, *The Contemporary Caribbean* (Harlow, UK: Pearson Education Ltd., 2004)

Ernesto Sagás, *Race and Politics in the Dominican Republic* (Gainesville: University Press of Florida, 2000)

Lars Schoultz, *That Infernal Little Cuban Republic: The United States and the Cuban Revolution* (Chapel Hill: University of North Carolina Press, 2009)

Michel-Rolph Trouillot, *Haiti: State Against Nation: The Origins and Legacy of Duvalierism* (New York: Monthly Review Press, 1990)

Kevin A. Yelvington (ed), *Trinidad Ethnicity* (London: Macmillan, 1993)

INDEX

Abandonment: of crops, 102, 163–8, 227, 229, 234, 288–9, 309, 312; of islands, 29, 47, 49–50, 61, 83

Abolition: of slavery, 100, 132, 141, 153–69, 172–3, 176–7, 181–9, 192, 195, 247; of slave trade, 154–62, 188, 191

Absenteeism, 96, 105, 120, 136–7, 147, 169, 224, 331

Adams: Grantley, 212, 268–9; Tom, 269

Africa: 3, 67, 185, 196, 249–50; Central, 147, 246, 265; and China, 57; cultures of, 76, 84, 132–3, 139, 174, 180, 242, 316; disease in, 76, 133; East, 267; and Europe, 68, 78, 80, 91, 93, 100, 121; migration from, 3–4, 10, 52, 54, 67, 77–80, 84, 124, 131–2, 139, 154, 159, 162, 331; migration to, 135, 249, 282, 284; religion in, 186–7, 248, 325; South, 265, 323; trade with, 62, 68, 80, 91, 121, 124, 179, 249, 290; West, 28, 51, 79–80, 179, 312

Africanization, 160

Africans, 74, 77–90, 115, 123, 130, 134, 142, 147, 154, 163, 183, 219, 318

Agrarian reform, 254, 287, 310

Agriculture: 174, 222, 230, 234, 239, 289, 292–6, 312; diversified, 98, 102, 106, 129; education for, 242, 244; incipient, 10; intensification of, 28, 39; and labour, 83, 166, 219, 304; origins of, 10, 16, 22, 27, 51; peasant, 122, 165, 218, 225–7, 288; plantation, 99–100, 105–6, 122, 165, 219, 223, 227, 288; and population, 39, 92, 109, 162, 164; rainfed, 37; spread of, 38–9, 52, 73, 83, 100, 220, 311; systems of, 20, 32, 39, 71, 88, 92, 122, 131; and trade, 234, 257, 289–90, 308; urban, 258, 310

Agüeybaná, 43

Aid, 194, 263–5, 274, 290, 308, 310–1

Air travel, 236–7, 284, 293, 297, 299–301, 308, 327, 329

Alexis, Jacques Stéphen, 320

Aluminium, 293–4

Amazon, 24, 29

Amelioration, 188

American Revolution, 141, 144–5, 162, 187, 196

Amerindians, 25, 54, 61, 68–9, 81, 86–9, 93, 95, 99, 112, 123, 130, 142; see also Taínos, Kalingo

Anacaona, 43, 73

Anegada, 5, 32

Anglo-American Caribbean Commission, 209

Anguilla, 112, 173, 268–9, 280

Animism, 54

Annexation, 150, 191, 195, 199, 204, 242, 265, 330

Other Books in the Series (continued from page iii)

A Concise History of Hungary
MIKLÓS MOLNÁR, TRANSLATED BY ANNA MAGYAR

A Concise History of Modern India, 2nd Edition
BARBARA D. METCALF AND THOMAS R. METCALF

A Concise History of Italy
CHRISTOPHER DUGGAN

A Concise History of Mexico, 2nd Edition
BRIAN R. HAMNETT

A Concise History of New Zealand
PHILIPPA MEIN SMITH

A Concise History of Poland, 2nd Edition
JERZY LUKOWSKI AND HUBERT ZAWADZKI

A Concise History of Portugal, 2nd Edition
DAVID BIRMINGHAM

A Concise History of South Africa, 2nd Edition
ROBERT ROSS

A Concise History of Spain
WILLIAM D. PHILLIPS JR. AND CARLA RAHN PHILLIPS

A Concise History of Sweden
NEIL KENT

A Concise History of Wales
GERAINT H. JENKINS